Genesis
Volume II

Genesis

Volume II

Translated by William Heynen

G. Ch. Aalders

ZONDERVAN PUBLISHING HOUSE
OF THE ZONDERVAN CORPORATION
GRAND RAPIDS, MICHIGAN 49506

PAIDEIA
P.O. Box 1450
St. Catharines
Ont. CANADA L2R 7 JB

THE BIBLE STUDENT'S COMMENTARY
Originally published in Dutch under the title KORTE VERKLARING DER HEILIGE SCHRIFT

Copyright © 1981 by The Zondervan Corporation
Grand Rapids, Michigan

Library of Congress Cataloging in Publication Data

Aalders, G. Charles (Gerhard Charles), 1880–
     The Book of Genesis.

     (The Bible student's commentary)
     Translation of: Het boek Genesis.
     1. Bible.   O.T. Genesis—Commentaries.   I.   Title.
II.   Series: Korte verklaring der Heilige Schrift,
met nieuwe vertaling.   English.
BS1235.3.A213   222'.11077   81-4677
Zondervan: ISBN 0-310-43968-X   AACR2
Paideia: ISBN 0-88815-102-0

The translation used in THE BIBLE STUDENT'S COMMENTARY is the *Holy Bible, New International Version.* Copyright © 1978 by New York International Bible Society.

Designed and Edited by Edward Viening

Printed in the United States of America

Genesis
Commentary

8. The Announcement of the Coming Birth of Isaac Repeated (18:1–15)

This section, as well as the rest of chapter 18 and all of chapter 19, is usually ascribed to source "J." The announcement of the coming birth of Sarah's son is then treated as a parallel to Genesis 17:15–21, which is ascribed to "P." More careful reading of these passages, however, makes it clear that we are dealing with two distinct announcements. The former announcement was primarily addressed to Abraham. In our present passage the message came specifically to Sarah. Although it is presented as a revelation to Abraham, it becomes clear that Sarah also heard the message (v. 10). In verse 14 it seems that Sarah was actually present for that part of the communication and in verse 15 she was addressed personally. When this is compared with 17:21, we can conclude that these two revelations came shortly after each other. This also is textually acceptable.

There was something unique about this "appearance" of the Lord. Verse 1 speaks of an appearance of the Lord, but verse 2 speaks of "three men." Verse 9 uses the plural, "they asked him," but in verse 10 we return to the singular. Then in verse 13 we are told that the speaker was "the LORD." These circumstances have led some scholars to insist that we are dealing with a narrative that was drawn from two different sources. In the one narrative it was only the Lord who appeared to Abraham. In the other, three angels (or two) were also present, but this is an unjustified fragmentation of the text.

Other scholars have tried to explain the peculiarities of this passage by suggesting that this is a monotheistic reworking of what had originally been a polytheistic legend. According to this interpretation, the original narrative involved three gods. An appeal is made to Greek mythology, which has a story about three gods who visited an old man who extended wonderful hospitality to them. As a reward for his kindness to the gods he was told to make a wish. Since the old man was childless he "wished" for a child. This wish was granted. These scholars claim that this ancient saga was reworked by the redactor of Scripture and applied to Abraham. The plural "gods" had to be changed to the singular "God" in order to fit Abraham's concept of deity.

This rather fanciful presentation needs a reply. First of all, we must observe the basic rule of interpretation that a few points of similarity can never become the basis for establishing the identity of two distinct passages or narratives. The desire for a child, even on the part of elderly people, is a natural phenomenon. It can be expected that this would become a part of many different legends and stories. More importantly, it should be observed that, although there are a few similarities, there are also some critical differences between these two accounts. Probably the most telling difference is the way the child came into the world. In the Greek saga this is so far removed from the account of the birth of Isaac that it makes the comparison of the two rather odious. While Isaac is born via the natural process of childbirth, even though it was a miraculous conception, the Greek myth presents a preposterous happening. It seems that the three gods injected their sperm into the hide of a steer and then buried this in the ground. And from this, then, a child came forth. Does this really need a reply?

It should be observed that the change from the plural to the singular when referring to the visitor(s) is by no means consistent in the biblical narrative. In verse 3 Abraham used the singular. In verses 4 and 5 he used the plural. In verse 9 he used the plural and in the very next verse, 10, he returned to the singular. It certainly is unthinkable that a redactor, who allegedly reworked an existing legend he found somewhere in order to make it conform to his monotheistic concepts, would have been so utterly careless. No person in his right mind would have turned out such a contradictory account. This fact, in itself, places the whole claim that this is a borrowed narrative which was reworked in the category of the ridiculous.

Our only conclusion, then, is that the unity of this passage, as it is given in the text, must be maintained. The peculiarities that appear in the text will be treated in the course of our interpretation.

18:1 *The LORD appeared to Abraham near the great trees of Mamre while he was sitting at the entrance to his tent in the heat of the day.*

Again Abraham received an "appearance" or theophany of the Lord. We refer to our treatment of the nature of such an appearance under 12:7.

Regarding this particular appearance we are given certain details. It was the hottest time of the day, and Abraham, who still lived by the Oaks of Mamre, was sitting in the shade at the entrance to his tent.

18:2 *Abraham looked up and saw three men standing nearby. When he saw them, he hurried from the entrance of his tent to meet them and bowed low to the ground.*

When Abraham looked up he suddenly saw three men standing before him. It is obvious that we must understand the presence of these three men as being "the appearance" of the Lord that is mentioned in verse 1. In verse 9 we are told that they asked Abraham about Sarah's whereabouts. When he told them where she was, we read in verse 10 that "the LORD" continued the conversation. We hear the Lord speaking also in verse 13. Some ancient exegetes have suggested that this was a manifestation of the Trinity. This however is not possible, since 19:1 informs us that two of the "men" were angels. Even so, they were also called men. (See also 18:16; 19:10, 12, 16.) A comparison of all these passages strongly suggests that what we have here is a manifestation of God, appearing in human form, accompanied by two angels, also in human form. God appearing in human form is, of course, no more than a symbol of His presence, similar to His earlier appearance as a flaming oven in 15:17. The Eternal Spirit does not have a material, limited human form.

When Abraham saw the three men he did not immediately recognize this as a manifestation of the presence of God. He became aware of this only gradually. At first he saw the three men only as travelers who happened to pass by and who at this time of the day were in need of rest and refreshment. Therefore he offered them his hospitality. His bowing low to the ground was no more than a proper Eastern mode of greeting distinguished visitors. Later we find Abraham greeting the Hittites in the same way (Gen. 23:7, 12). So also Jacob greeted Esau (Gen. 33:3ff.), Joseph welcomed his father (Gen. 48:12), Solomon greeted his mother (1 Kings 2:19), and the sons of the prophets greeted Elisha (2 Kings 2:15).

18:3 *He said, "If I have found favor in your eyes, my lord, do not pass your servant by.*

It is striking that Abraham addressed the three men, whom he assumed to be strangers, in the singular, "my lord. . . ." Some have concluded from this use of the singular that Abraham immediately recognized one of the men as God Himself. The rabbinical scholars have therefore included this concept of deity in the vocalization they have placed on this term. But it is inconceivable that Abraham would immediately have offered a meal to his guest if he had been aware that he was speaking to God Himself.

Also, the expression, "If I have found favor in your eyes," cannot be used to support the theory that Abraham knew he was speaking to God. This same expression is used when men speak to men. (In this connection see Gen. 30:27; 32:5; 33:8, 10, 15; 34:11; 47:25, 29; Ruth 2:13; 1 Sam. 27:5; Esth. 5:8; 7:3.) The expression is no more than a polite form of address and a respectful way of extending an invitation. The fact that Abraham used the singular in addressing his visitors strongly suggests that one of the three obviously was the most important and distinguished of the group. Thus, although the invitation included all three visitors, it was addressed to the apparent leader of the group.

18:4, 5 *Let a little water be brought, and then you may all wash your feet and rest under this tree. Let me get you something to eat, so you can be refreshed and then go on your way—now that you have come to your servant."*

"Very well," they answered, "do as you say."

It is therefore natural that Abraham continued his gracious offer of hospitality by using the plural. He called for water so that his guests might wash their feet. This was most urgent for Eastern travelers who walked along the hot dusty paths wearing only sandals on their feet. Abraham further invited them to stop and rest in the shade of the tree. The term implies that they were invited to recline or lie down. This reclining position was customary at that time when people gathered to eat and drink. Some have quibbled about the mention of only one tree when other references indicate that there were a number of trees (see v. 1). But it would be wholly natural for Abraham to invite his visitors to rest under the specific tree under which or near which his tent was located. Finally, Abraham also offered them something to eat so that they could be refreshed and then go on their way again. Abraham pressed his invitation by gently urging them to accept his hospitality since they had come this way in their travels.

Abraham's hospitality was accepted in one brief statement, "Do as you say." So the significant meeting was under way.

18:6–8 *So Abraham hurried into the tent to Sarah. "Quick," he said, "get three seahs of fine flour and knead it and bake some bread."*

Then he ran to the herd and selected a choice, tender calf and gave it to a servant, who hurried to prepare it. He then brought some curds and milk and the calf that had been prepared, and set these before them. While they ate, he stood near them under a tree.

Abraham promptly busied himself in making the necessary preparations for the proper reception of his guests. Here we see the patriarch in all the glory of Eastern hospitality. He had invited the strangers who stopped by to have "a little food," but now he prepared a sumptuous meal for them. Sarah was put to work baking a large batch of the kind of bread that was eaten at that time. This bread resembled our pancakes since it consisted of flat cakes which were made of fine flour and then baked on hot stones. One of the servants was dispatched to slaughter a tender calf which Abraham himself had selected from his herd. To this was added curds and milk. The curds were a thick by-product of milk which even today forms a favorite drink in Syria and Arabia. While the guests ate, Abraham stood nearby, under the oak tree, as a gracious host ready to serve their every need or wish. The entire scene as it is pictured here is a vivid reminder of the way a Bedouin sheik would entertain honored guests even today.

Jewish commentators have traditionally held that the eating on the part of the three visitors was only apparent and that they did not actually partake of the food. This is also the interpretation offered by some modern Roman Catholic scholars. But this is in no way supported by the text. To be sure, it is difficult to conceive of spiritual beings eating physical food. We cannot forget, however, that we are dealing here with beings who had assumed human forms that were outwardly real. This is further emphasized by the fact that they ate this food. This would also suggest that the two angels did not appear in their usual spiritual form but were present in actual human form. Undoubtedly we are presented with facts here that are beyond our comprehension. It is totally beyond our understanding that God Himself should appear with two of His holy angels in such realistic human form that they actually ate human food. But this is precisely what God tells us in His word and we can accept this in the faith that "nothing is impossible with God." This lends to these "appearances" of God to Abraham a quality of the miraculous and the divine that makes them all the more impressive to the believing heart.

18:9 *"Where is your wife Sarah?" they asked him.*
"There, in the tent," he said.

After they had eaten, the guests inquired of Abraham, "Where is your wife, Sarah?" This question already revealed that these were not ordinary travelers who just happened to pass by. They not only knew Sarah's name, but they obviously had come to bring a message especially intended for Sarah. The use of the plural here does not indicate that all three of the men spoke at the same time but rather that one of them served as a spokesman for the group.

18:10 *Then the Lord said, "I will surely return to you about this time next year, and Sarah your wife will have a son."*
Now Sarah was listening at the entrance to the tent, which was behind him.

When Abraham told them that Sarah was in the tent, the spokesman continued by announcing that He would return in a year and that at that time Sarah would have a son. This announcement revealed an even more wonderful knowledge on the part of the spokesman than the question of verse 9 had manifested. He obviously knew about Sarah's childless condition. Thereupon he made the same announcement that Abraham had previously received from God Himself (Gen. 17:19–21). This caused the scales to fall from Abraham's eyes. This was the Lord Himself! God had again appeared to him, now in the form of a stranger to whom the patriarch had shown hospitality.

The expression "in one year" is a very interesting one. It actually says, "When the times comes again," thus indicating the same time of the year one year in the future.

Some have argued that there is something lacking in the Book of Genesis at this point. They insist that to make the narrative complete the three "forms" should have returned to Abraham one year later. But this is without basis. God actually returned to Abraham one year later in the miracle of the birth of Isaac.

The incredible promise that was made had not gone unheard by Sarah, who was standing within hearing range in the shelter of the tent. This information is added in order to explain how Sarah could have thought that her presence was unknown to the speaker.

18:11, 12 *Abraham and Sarah were already old and well advanced in years, and Sarah was past the age of childbearing. So Sarah laughed to herself as she thought, "After I am worn out and my master is old, will I now have this pleasure?"*

As had been the case with Abraham when he first received the promise of the birth of a son (Gen. 17:17), so now also Sarah found this announcement too much to believe. So she laughed inwardly. It seemed impossible to her. The word "old" or "aged" that is used here is a very strong word. It indicates something that is worn out by age. Thus the announcement that she in her aged condition would bear a child was wholly unthinkable to her.

18:13, 14 *Then the Lord said to Abraham, "Why did Sarah laugh and say, 'Will I really have a child, now that I am old?' Is anything too hard for the Lord? I will return to you at the appointed time next year and Sarah will have a son."*

Now the full majesty of the divine answer was revealed. "The Lord said to Abraham." The cloak of concealment was thrown off. "Why did Sarah laugh? . . Is anything too hard for the Lord?" The all-knowing God knew Sarah's inner thoughts. He knew that Sarah had laughed inwardly. He knew that she considered this all to be wholly impossible. So the announcement was repeated with new emphasis as a direct promise from God. Sarah would indeed have a son at this same time the following year.

18:15 *Sarah was afraid, so she lied and said, "I did not laugh."*
But he said, "Yes, you did laugh."

At this Sarah became afraid. She had expressed a lack of faith in God, so she resorted to a lie and denied that she had laughed. The words that had been spoken were addressed to Abraham but Sarah felt they were intended for her and she was overcome with a sense of being trapped in her unbelief. This foolish and sinful reaction on her part was then also rebuked when the Lord said, "Yes, you did laugh."

The inspired writer brings the matter of "laughter" into the foreground once again (see Gen. 17:19 and 21:6) in order to focus on the name that was to be given to this promised child, namely, Isaac, which means "he laughs" or "laughter."

9. *Abraham's Intercession for Sodom* (18:16–33)

Many scholars have ascribed this section, for the most part, to a secondary source of much later date. This material was supposedly interpolated into "J." Only verses 16, 20–22a, and 33b are considered to be actual "J" material. This section, it is argued, serves only to tie 18:1–15 to the later narrative of Lot and Sodom in chapter 19. This material is described, however, as a monotheistic reworking of an original polytheistic saga. We have discussed this approach to the biblical text under 18:1–15, and what we said there would apply here also.

The grounds that are given for assigning the rest of this passage to a later secondary source, aside from some untenable assertions about word usage, are the following:

1) According to verse 17, the Lord already knew what He would do and in verse 23 it is obvious that Sodom's destruction had already been de-

cided. Abraham sought to prevent this destruction by his intercession, but in verse 21 it is implied that God did not know how bad conditions really were in Sodom.

2) In verse 19 the Lord spoke of Himself in the third person.

3) It is argued that there is a conflict between verse 22a, which says that the three men went to Sodom, and verse 22b, which indicates that the Lord stayed with Abraham. So also there is conflict between verses 22b and 33a, which indicate that the Lord had not yet gone to Sodom, and verse 21, where the Lord claims to know what conditions were in Sodom.

4) God's promise to Abraham in verse 19 included a conditional statement, to "direct his children and his household after him to keep the way of the LORD. . .," while, the critics claim, the former promises to Abraham were unconditional.

5) Supposedly, the concept of God here was far different from that expressed in Genesis 18:1–15. In the one passage God ate bread and meat, while in the other He was "the Judge of all the earth."

6) The intercession in behalf of Sodom that is ascribed to Abraham was, supposedly, completely out of harmony with the spirit of ancient Israel.

In responding to these claims of the critics, we will deal with the first three in the course of our commentary following. With respect to the fourth claim, namely, that in the oldest manuscripts the promises are always unconditional, we would reply that this interpretation is defensible only if one first accepts the theory of the splitting of sources. A case in question would be Genesis 17. There the promise is definitely conditional, but the critics assign this section to a very late source. This is, of course, a matter of trying to prove their own assumptions on the basis of their own assumptions.

But even if the theory of divided sources is accepted, the case with respect to this claim is by no means clear. Certainly in 12:1 the call to "leave your land and your people" is conditional for the promises given in verses 2 and 3. Without Abraham's faith-obedience these promises would not have been realized. So too in Genesis 15:6, which the critics assign to the early source "J," Abraham's faith is made conditional for the covenant blessing.

The fifth claim of the critics is that there is a difference in the concept of God between 18:1–15 and 18:16–33. It should be noted, however, that the concept expressed in verse 14, "Is anything too hard for the LORD?" is essentially the same as the one expressed in verses 25 and 27. To be sure, the three men ate and drank and acted as normal human beings, but this is no more than an indication that God is able to manifest Himself in the true form of a human being. This is no more than an outward manifestation of

God's power and is not a revelation of God's actual being. Now, there may be those who insist that God does not have such powers. But this is certainly a very arbitrary insistence, since this passage speaks so strongly about the unlimited, almighty power of God. Furthermore, to insist that God is not capable of manifesting Himself in human form calls into question the entire revelation of God both in Scripture and in Jesus Christ.

With respect to the sixth and final claim of the critics, namely, that Abraham's attitude was not in harmony with the spirit of ancient Israel, this is really irrelevant. The real question would be whether this was in harmony with the spirit of Abraham as this is revealed in the rest of his life. When we call to mind Abraham's noble attitude toward his nephew Lot (Gen. 13:9), and his great generosity toward the king of Sodom (Gen. 14:21–24), his attitude in this instance is wholly consistent. Moreover, even if it could be established that Abraham showed a different spirit here than he did at some other times in his life, this would prove nothing. All people have their better moments and also their times of weakness. Abraham was no exception to this. This great hero of faith repeatedly demonstrated his magnanimous spirit, but he also had his weak moments, as in the scene in Egypt when he lied to save his own skin. Certainly this cannot be used as a basis for the claim that we are dealing with two sources. All that is indicated here is that Abraham was a normal human being with weaknesses and strengths.

18:16 *When the men got up to leave, they looked down toward Sodom, and Abraham walked along with them to see them on their way.*

As a sequel to the events recorded in 18:1–15, the inspired writer portrays another scene in which Abraham communicated with the three "men" who had suddenly appeared to him under the oak tree. Abraham extended to them the usual courtesy offered to distinguished guests in his day; he accompanied them on their way as they left his camp. By this time Abraham realized that his guests were more than ordinary travelers and that God Himself had appeared to him. This gave him all the more reason to offer every proper courtesy to these honored guests.

18:17–21 *Then the LORD said, "Shall I hide from Abraham what I am about to do? Abraham will surely become a great and powerful nation, and all nations on earth will be blessed through him. For I have chosen him, so that he will direct his children and his household after him to keep the way of the LORD by doing what is right and just, so that the LORD will bring about for Abraham what he has promised him."*

9

Genesis 18:17–21

Then the LORD said, "The outcry against Sodom and Gomorrah is so great and their sin so grievous that I will go down and see if what they have done is as bad as the outcry that has reached me. If not, I will know."

Just how far Abraham accompanied them on their journey is not mentioned in the text. There is a tradition that the place where this recorded interview took place was Capherbanuche, which lies northeast of Hebron. This is situated at approximately the highest point in the hills of Judea and from this vantage point there is a view of the Dead Sea, if one looks through a cut in the mountains. We have no textual evidence to support this exact location, however. Even so, at a certain point along the trail God turned to Abraham to inform him about what was to happen.

Before the announcement of what was to take place was made, the Lord offered His reason for sharing this information with the patriarch. He mentioned that Abraham stood in a special relationship to Him and He did so in terms previously recorded in 12:2–3. As an added motive for His communication with Abraham the Lord mentioned that the patriarch was to direct his descendants to walk in the ways of the Lord and do what was right. Here the specific stipulation is made that this righteous life on the part of Abraham's descendants was to be a condition for the fulfillment of the promise that God had made to them. The intent of this becomes obvious from what follows. The judgment of the Lord upon the wickedness of the cities of the plain was to serve as a warning to Abraham's descendants.

When the Lord said, "I have known Abraham," we must see this as a knowledge similar to that expressed in Jeremiah 1:5 and Amos 3:2. It involves a distinction—a setting apart. Thus our translators have rendered it, "I have chosen him."

It may seem strange that the Lord spoke of Himself in the third person as He discussed His decision with Abraham, but this is not unusual. We find similar usage in Genesis 9:6, 16; Isaiah 40:1–2; Jeremiah 2:2–3; 25:5–6.

The announcement God made to Abraham dealt with the wickedness of Sodom and Gomorrah and the coming judgment that would fall on these cities. Although the coming destruction of these cities was not specifically mentioned, God's emphasis on the greatness of the wickedness of these cities implied that judgment had to come. The Lord mentioned the "outcry" of the wickedness of these cities, and this reminds us of the expression in Genesis 4:10. The wickedness actually cried out for God's wrath and judgment.

When we are told that the Lord planned to go down into the valley in order to determine whether the wickedness was actually as bad as He had heard, we are, of course, dealing with an anthropomorphism (see Gen.

10

11:5). Certainly the Lord knew what was going on in these cities, but just as a judge in a trial first conducts an investigation, so God would make His final determination that the wickedness was so utterly bad that judgment could no longer be delayed. Thus there is no conflict between this statement and what we are told in verses 17 and 23. There are some interpreters who want to omit "Gomorrah" in verse 20 because only Sodom is mentioned in verses 16, 22, and 26. There is no reason for doing this.

18:22 *The men turned away and went toward Sodom, but Abraham remained standing before the LORD.*

After this communication, two of the "men" moved on toward Sodom, while the Lord continued His conversation with Abraham. Some claim that there is a conflict here between the first and second parts of the verse. They insist that "the men" must refer to all three of Abraham's companions. The context as a whole clearly indicates, however, that God Himself, in His human manifestation, did not go on to Sodom. He sent His two servants to accomplish the task described in verse 21.

18:23–32 *Then Abraham approached him and said: "Will you sweep away the righteous with the wicked? What if there are fifty righteous people in the city? Will you really sweep it away and not spare the place for the sake of the fifty righteous people in it? Far be it from you to do such a thing—to kill the righteous with the wicked, treating the righteous and the wicked alike. Far be it from you! Will not the Judge of all the earth do right?"*

The LORD said, "If I find fifty righteous people in the city of Sodom, I will spare the whole place for their sake."

Then Abraham spoke up again: "Now that I have been so bold as to speak to the Lord, though I am nothing but dust and ashes, what if the number of the righteous is five less than fifty? Will you destroy the whole city because of five people?"

"If I find forty-five there," he said, "I will not destroy it."

Once again he spoke to him, "What if only forty are found there?"

He said, "For the sake of forty, I will not do it."

Then he said, "May the Lord not be angry, but let me speak. What if only thirty can be found there?"

He answered, "I will not do it if I find thirty there."

Abraham said, "Now that I have been so bold as to speak to the Lord, what if only twenty can be found there?"

He said, "For the sake of twenty, I will not destroy it."

Then he said, "May the Lord not be angry, but let me speak just once more. What if only ten can be found there?"

He answered, "For the sake of ten, I will not destroy it."

This passage presents Abraham's moving intercession for Sodom. He was obviously fully aware that a terrible judgment was about to fall on the cities of the plain. His concern was not only for his nephew Lot and any other righteous people who had not conformed to the gross wickedness of these cities; he was concerned also for those wicked people who were about to be subjected to God's righteous wrath and judgment. So he pleaded for their deliverance.

Abraham based his appeal on the righteousness of God. Certainly God would not destroy the righteous along with the wicked. Surely the Judge of all the earth would deal justly and spare the city for the sake of the righteous people who still lived there.

Abraham began his intercession by mentioning a possible number of fifty righteous people. But even if five should be lacking of that number, would the lack of five cause the city to be destroyed? Since he was aware of the boldness of his appeal because he was no more than dust and ashes in the presence of the most high God, Abraham proceeded with cautious insistence. Gradually he reduced the number of possible righteous people in the city to forty, to thirty, to twenty, and finally to ten. In each instance the Lord agreed. We have before us a clear-cut example of the principle of solidarity and the principle of representation or substitution in God's dealings with mankind. These concepts, of course, reach their highest expression in Jesus Christ—the one righteous Person who brings deliverance to countless sinners.

18:33 *When the LORD had finished speaking with Abraham, he left, and Abraham returned home.*

After this moving exchange, the Lord left Abraham. We are not told where He went or how He took His departure. Obviously, this theophany had come to an end. Thereupon Abraham returned to his home under the oaks of Mamre.

10. *The Destruction of Sodom and the Deliverance of Lot* (19:1–29)

Those who divide the sources usually treat this passage much like 18:1–15, and they generally ascribe this section to "J." However, many claim that this passage also is a mixture of two sources or a monotheistic revision of what originally was a polytheistic saga. In reply to this position we refer the reader to the arguments presented under 18:1–15. We add only a few comments regarding the specific characteristics of this passage which supposedly suggest two different sources.

According to the one source, the critics hold, the passage seeks to establish the punishment that God brings on Lot for his selfishness. He is punished by the loss of all his earthly possessions in the destruction of Sodom. The other source, it is claimed, emphasizes the fact that this is an example of God's righteousness and mercy. Another evidence of two sources, allegedly, is that in the one case only Lot and his two daughters are delivered, while in the other presentation Lot, his wife, and his sons and daughters are rescued. This latter claim will be answered when we treat the verses in question.

With respect to the former claim of the critics we would reply that there is no evidence in the passage for two distinct sources. The view that Lot was punished by the loss of all his possessions isn't even mentioned. But even if these two points of view were clearly presented they would not be in conflict with each other. God's righteous judgment of Sodom could at the same time have been punishment for Lot's avarice. Also, God's mercy shown in delivering Lot indicates only that God would not destroy Lot along with his wicked fellow-townsmen.

The critics also claim that the words in verse 23, "By the time Lot reached Zoar," must be a later insertion. They argue that since verse 16 says that they "led them safely out of the city," the request of Lot comes too late in the passage. They point out that verse 15 states that dawn was just breaking while verse 23 says that "the sun had risen over the land." Moreover, they insist that Lot's request was much too lengthy for someone who was hastily fleeing from imminent destruction. These arguments are quite unconvincing. First of all, there is no reason to hold that what follows in verse 16 comes too late to fit into the scene. Once Lot had been taken out of the city there certainly was ample time and opportunity for this brief exchange to have taken place. Furthermore, Lot's request in verses 18–20 certainly is not a lengthy speech. The whole exchange could have taken place in less than a minute, and this is not inconsistent with the haste of their departure. In fact, Lot's request arose precisely out of the urgency of the whole situation since he feared that they would not be able to reach the hills in time. The order is very logical. During this brief time after Lot had been dragged out of the city, and it was agreed that he could flee to nearby Zoar rather than to the more distant hills, the sun had risen above the horizon.

It is also argued that the incident concerning Lot's wife, as well as the mention of his wife in verses 15 and 16, was a later insertion from another, secondary source. This too, it is claimed, comes too late in the passage (coming after v. 23), but this argument can hardly be taken seriously. There is no reason why the sacred writer could not include the sad story of the disobedience of Lot's wife and her sudden death at the close of the entire incident.

13

Finally, it should be noted that the critics usually ascribe the last verse of this section, verse 29, to "P." The only basis for this is that the name used for God is "Elohim." We refer you to what we have said about this basis for dividing sources in our Introduction. It seems hard to believe that if "P" included a narrative about this whole event, only this limited reference was included in the passage. Certainly the redactor would have drawn on more of that material in putting together this dramatic narrative.

19:1–3 *The two angels arrived at Sodom in the evening, and Lot was sitting in the gateway of the city. When he saw them, he got up to meet them and bowed down with his face to the ground. "My lords," he said, "please turn aside to your servant's house. You can wash your feet and spend the night and then go on your way early in the morning."*

"No," they answered, "we will spend the night in the square."

But he insisted so strongly that they did go with him and entered his house. He prepared a meal for them, baking bread without yeast, and they ate.

According to 18:22, two of the three "men" went on to Sodom. Here they are called the "two angels." This confirms what we observed under 28:2, that this was an appearance of God accompanied by two angels. These two angels now arrived in Sodom to fulfill the task that had been assigned to them (18:22).

They arrived in the city toward evening. Lot was seated in the city square, which was an open area near the gate where much of the public life of the city was carried on. In Eastern cities of that era, this was where the market was held (2 Kings 7:1; Neh. 13:19). This was where matters of justice were tried (Deut. 21:19; 22:15; 25:7; Josh. 20:4; Ruth 4:1ff.; Ps. 127:5; Prov. 22:22; Amos 5:15). This was the area where David presented himself to the people (2 Sam. 19:8). This was the place where the subjects of the day were discussed (Ps. 69:12; Prov. 31:31). And this was where public announcements were made (Prov. 1:21; 8:3).

When the strangers arrived at the gate of the city, Lot immediately stepped forward to offer them hospitality. In this connection we should consider what we mentioned in our treatment of 18:2–5. As in the case with Abraham, Lot's gesture of hospitality was in no way an indication that he recognized the visitors for who they really were. The visitors first refused Lot's invitation and decided to spend the night in the square. This would not have been unusual. Judges 19:15 suggests that travelers who were not given hospitality customarily would camp in the city square, but Lot was very insistent and finally the visitors accepted his invitation.

The fact that the angels ate human food has been discussed under 18:8. In this instance specific mention is made of "unleavened bread." This was the same kind of bread Israel later ate with the Passover lamb (Exod. 12:8; etc.). In this case it probably was dictated by the lateness of the hour, which did not permit the preparation of bread baked with yeast. In the same way the unleavened bread that Israel used for the Passover celebration was to symbolize the haste of their departure from Egypt (Exod. 12:33–34).

19:4, 5 *Before they had gone to bed, all the men from every part of the city of Sodom—both young and old—surrounded the house. They called to Lot, "Where are the men who came to you tonight? Bring them out to us so that we can have sex with them."*

It now became clear that the wickedness of Sodom had reached the worst extremes (cf. 18:21). News of the arrival of the strangers quickly spread through the city, and soon a crowd of the citizens of Sodom gathered around Lot's home with the obvious intent of sexually abusing these visitors for the fulfillment of their homosexual lusts. The word used here is the same word Paul uses in Romans 1:27 to describe deplorable homosexual acts. Mention is made of the fact that this involved all the men of the city, young as well as old. It certainly gives a clear indication of the depth of immorality to which these cities had sunk and in turn sets the stage for the justness of the coming judgment.

19:6–8 *Lot went outside to meet them and shut the door behind him and said, "No, my friends. Don't do this wicked thing. Look, I have two daughters who have never slept with a man. Let me bring them out to you, and you can do what you like with them. But don't do anything to these men, for they have come under the protection of my roof."*

Lot, however, tried to prevent his fellow citizens from carrying out their evil purposes. He went out into the street, closing the door behind him to prevent them from pushing their way into his house. He pleaded with them in a friendly manner, urging them not to abuse the hospitality he had extended to these strangers. He went so far as to offer these lecherous men his two virgin daughters for their sexual pleasure. In order to protect the strangers he had taken into his home, he was willing to sacrifice the honor and purity of his own daughters.

It is extremely difficult for us to understand, much less justify, Lot's offer to the men of Sodom. In the light of Scripture as a whole, this can only be seen as a serious moral lapse on Lot's part. In order to be fair in our judgment of Lot, however, we must bear in mind the fact that he was in an extremely difficult and even dangerous situation. He knew how dissolute and uncontrollable the Sodomites were. (Cf. 2 Peter 2:7–8.) He therefore tried to prevent the more serious evil by proposing a lesser evil. His reasoning seems to have been that it would be better that they satisfy their uncontrollable sexual cravings through natural acts than by grossly unnatural excess. To be sure, this evidenced a serious moral weakness on Lot's part. Even so, it must be seen as the product of sheer desperation. It was in a spirit of complete hopelessness that Lot made his offer in order to protect those to whom he had extended his hospitality. We read, ''Don't do anything to these men, for they have come under the protection of my roof.''

19:9–11 *''Get out of our way,'' they replied. And they said, ''This fellow came here as an alien, and now he wants to play the judge! We'll treat you worse than them.'' They kept bringing pressure on Lot and moved forward to break down the door.*

But the men inside reached out and pulled Lot back into the house and shut the door. Then they struck the men who were at the door of the house, young and old, with blindness so that they could not find the door.

The Sodomites, however, would not be dissuaded. Angrily they shouted at Lot to get out of their way. They accused him of being an interloper who was trying to dictate to them. They threatened him with worse treatment than they had planned for his visitors. They obviously planned to carry out their threats as they moved forward and tried to break down the door.

At the height of the crisis, the angels suddenly intervened. They pulled Lot into the house and closed the door. Thereupon they effectively quelled the mob outside the door by striking them all, young and old, with ''blindness.''

The term ''blindness'' requires some definition. The word is used in only one other instance in the Scripture, in 2 Kings 6:18. Obviously it was not a matter of total blindness. It was, rather, a matter of confused vision that came on them by a supernatural intervention. It is evident from 2 Kings 6:19–20 that the Syrian troops who were sent to take Elisha prisoner could still see but their vision was confused. They did not recognize the prophet, and when he served as their guide they found themselves in the middle of Samaria without knowing where they were. Only when their ''eyes were opened'' by another supernatural intervention did they realize where they were. The same condition seems to have been brought upon the Sodomites by the angels. Their vision was confused so that they could not find the door to Lot's house. As a result of this ''miracle'' they left the scene and Lot and his guests regained their peace and security.

19:12, 13 *The two men said to Lot, ''Do you have anyone else here—sons-in-law, sons or daughters, or anyone else in the city who belongs to you? Get them out of* *here, because we are going to destroy this place. The outcry to the L*ORD *against its people is so great that he has sent us to destroy it.''*

The time had come to inform Lot of the purpose of their visit. The angels now presented themselves as messengers from God to carry out the destruction of the city because of its great wickedness. Their specific mission to Lot was to warn him of the impending doom and to rescue him and his family before the judgment would fall.

Mention is made of Lot's sons-in-law and sons and daughters. It is interesting that Lot's wife is not mentioned. This can be explained, however, by the inclusion of Lot's sons-in-law, thus clearly implying that his entire family was included, not excluding his wife.

The fact that the angels mentioned ''sons'' as well as ''daughters'' has caused some scholars to insist that this material came from two distinct sources. If we consider the nature of verse 12, however, there is no conflict with verses 15 and 16. The angels referred to his family in a broad inclusive way without designating precisely who were included in that family. The question whether Lot actually had sons cannot be answered with certainty, and it certainly cannot be determined on the basis of verse 12. In that verse the angels simply inquired as to the makeup of Lot's family. Moreover verses 15 and 16 do not indicate that he did not have sons. If he had sons, they no longer lived in the parental home. Verse 15 would suggest that he did not have sons, since Lot went to his sons-in-law and warned them of the coming doom. If he had had sons, he certainly would have warned them also, but the passage does not say that he did not do so. Actually, the question is of no great importance.

19:14 *So Lot went out and spoke to his sons-in-law, who were pledged to marry his daughters. He said, ''Hurry and get out of this place, because the L*ORD *is about to destroy the city!'' But his sons-in-law thought he was joking.*

We are further told how Lot, now fully convinced of the seriousness of the situation, brought the warning to his sons-in-law. Obviously these men had not yet married Lot's daughters but were engaged to them. Some, however, insist that this must be translated ''were married to'' and then conclude that Lot had more daughters besides the two who still lived under his roof. Most interpreters, however, hold to the former reading. In either case, the young men did not believe Lot but passed it off as a joke.

19:15, 16 *With the coming of dawn, the angels urged Lot, saying, ''Hurry! Take your wife and your two daughters who are here, or you will be swept away when the city is punished.''*

When he hesitated, the men grasped his hand and the hands of his wife and of his two daughters and led them safely out of the city, for the LORD was merciful to them.

As soon as daylight dawned the angels urged Lot to make haste in his flight from the city. Lot, his wife, and his two daughters had to leave the city immediately or they would be destroyed with the rest of the citizens of wicked Sodom. Lot, however, hesitated, not because he did not believe the message of the angels, but because it was difficult for him to leave everything he had accumulated. So the angels took them by their hands and led them to safety outside the city.

19:17–22 *As soon as they had brought them out, one of them said, "Flee for your lives! Don't look back, and don't stop anywhere in the plain! Flee to the mountains or you will be swept away!"*

But Lot said to them, "No, my lords, please! Your servant has found favor in your eyes, and you have shown great kindness to me in sparing my life. But I can't flee to the mountains; this disaster will overtake me, and I'll die. Look, here is a town near enough to run to, and it is small. Let me flee to it—it is very small, isn't it? Then my life will be spared."

He said to him, "Very well, I will grant this request too; I will not overthrow the town you speak of. But flee there quickly, because I cannot do anything until you reach it." (That is why the town was called Zoar.)

As soon as they were outside the city walls, they were further urged not to remain in the immediate area but to flee to the hills in order to escape the conflagration that was about to fall. By this time Lot was so terrified that he feared he might not be able to reach the hills, which were some distance away, in time to escape death. So he pleaded for yet another favor as he asked permission to escape to the smallest of the five cities of the plain (see Gen. 14:2). He based his plea on the fact that it was a small, unimportant town and could offer a refuge at closer range if it would be spared from the destruction that was about to descend on Sodom and Gomorrah. His request was granted, but once again it was stressed that haste was imperative if he and his family were to be saved.

Of some significance here is the fact that the messengers, who up to now have been described as two, using the plural, suddenly are referred to in the singular. It seems that the conversation was carried on by Lot and only one of the angels.

At the close of verse 22 we are told, "That is why the town was called Zoar." Previously the place had been known as Bela. The name Zoar is based on the same word Lot used to describe it and means "small" or "insignificant." It must have been situated on the southeastern end of what

oday is known as the Dead Sea, slightly beyond the area that was wiped
)ut by the conflagration that struck the other cities.

9:23–25 *By the time Lot reached Zoar, the sun had risen over the land. Then the
ᴏʀᴅ rained down burning sulfur on Sodom and Gomorrah—from the Lᴏʀᴅ out of the
ʰeavens. Thus he overthrew those cities and the entire plain, including all those
iving in the cities—and also the vegetation in the land.*

By the time Lot reached Zoar the sun had risen well above the horizon
ɪnd was shining brightly upon the earth. Then, suddenly and unexpectedly
cf. Luke 17:28–29), the judgment announced by the angels fell. A rain of
ɪulfur and fire fell out of the sky and destroyed everything. The Hebrew
ɪtructure probably indicates "burning sulfur" as our translators have also
ʳendered it.

How are we to understand that this burning sulfur rained from the
ʰeavens? Does this imply that it did not have its origin from the earth? Or
ɴust we think of this as a product of nature and powers of nature that the
ᴧord used for His purposes? When we consider other destructive forces
ʰat were unleashed upon the earth such as the plagues in Egypt, the fiery
ɪerpents in the wilderness, the hailstones that struck the Canaanites at Beth
Horon, and also the judgments that are predicted for the last days (cf.
2 Peter 3:10), the latter interpretation would be acceptable. It would not be
ɪoo difficult to understand that this rain of burning sulfur was possible when
ᴧve remember that this plain had vast deposits of asphalt (tar pits, Gen.
4:10). This product, which is produced by oxidation of oil deposits in the
ɪarth, could easily have developed enormous pressures of flammable gas-
ɪes under the earth's crust. Then an earthquake or some other upheaval in
ʰe earth's crust could have suddenly released these gasses with immeasur-
ɪble force so that they drove huge deposits of sulfur, which abounds in the
ɪrea, high into the air. This mass of gas and sulfur could have exploded
nto fire, either by lightning or by natural combustion, and then could have
ɔeen dumped on the earth in the form of burning sulfur at extremely high
ɪemperatures.

It goes without saying that this in no way removes the miraculous ele-
ɴent from the event. It was only by the almighty power of God that this
ɪatastrophic upheaval in nature took place precisely at this place and at this
ɪime. God thus used these natural powers and products to carry out His
udgment on the cities of the plain.

If we accept this interpretation we can also conceive of the further
ɪevelopment in that area. The Dead Sea was already present at that time
ʹsee 14:3). When vast amounts of the combustible materials in the plain, to

19

the south of the Dead Sea as it then was, were consumed by this conflagration, this resulted in a considerable area sinking down in relative sea level and eventually being inundated by the spreading waters of the Dead Sea That this is what occurred is suggested by the discovery that the Dead Sea as it is today, actually consists of two basins. The northern basin has an average depth of about 98 feet while the southern basin has an average depth of only about 13 feet. This southern basin would then be the area where the cities of Sodom and Gomorrah were situated. There are a few scholars who believe that these cities were located on the northern shores of the Dead Sea, but the vast majority of Middle East scholars accept the position of their location in the southern area.

We must add one word about the expression "overthrew" which literally means "turned upside down," in verses 25 and 29. This term is used repeatedly in the Old Testament when reference is made to the destruction of Sodom and Gomorrah (Deut. 29:23; Isa. 13:19; Jer. 49:18; 50:40; Amos 4:11). The word that is used, however, does not indicate anything specific regarding the nature of the destruction that was carried out. It simply means "destroyed" or "devastated," and then implies that the destruction was so total, it was as though the object was turned upside down. That this is the intent of the word is confirmed by its use in 2 Samuel 10:3 and Isaiah 13:19, where it describes the destruction of a city as carried out by the invasion of enemy troops.

When verse 24 declares that "the LORD rained down burning sulfur . . . from the LORD out of the heavens," some have tried to make a distinction between the Lord who was on the earth and the Lord who was in heaven. There is no justification for such a distinction. The passage makes it clear that the judgment that was carried out on the earth was effected by angels (see vv. 1 and 15). The Lord who rained down burning sulfur is the same as the Lord in heaven. It should be noted that this form of reference to God, not using the pronoun but repeating the name of God, is quite common in the Old Testament. Genesis 1:27 says, "So God created man in his own image, in the image of God (not his image) he created him." Thus also in Genesis 5:1, "When God created man, he made him in the likeness of God," not "in his likeness." In Genesis 9:16 God says, "Whenever the rainbow appears in the clouds, I will see it and remember the everlasting covenant between God (not me) and all living creatures. . . ." In the same way we read in our present passage that the Lord rained down burning sulfur from "The LORD in heaven" rather than "from himself." The point that is emphasized by this expression is that the destruction of Sodom and Gomorrah was not the result of some happenstance of nature or some human carelessness, but was the result of a direct act of God. God Himself punished the gross wickedness of the inhabitants of these cities by sending the rain of fire on them and destroying them.

When it is stated that "the entire plain" was destroyed, this does not imply that nothing remained of the entire "plain of the Jordan." There are later references to this area which indicate that there still was such a district in southern Palestine (1 Kings 7:46; 2 Chron. 4:17). Obviously, that portion of the plain of the Jordan on which these cities were located was the most fertile part of the whole area. And this was the area that was wiped out by the conflagration God brought on these cities.

19:26 *But Lot's wife looked back and she became a pillar of salt.*

Lot's wife, however, perished on the way to Zoar. She disobeyed the specific command of the angel (v. 17) and looked back as they were fleeing from Sodom. Just what her motive was is not recorded. She may have had doubts regarding the carrying out of the threatened punishment and decided to see for herself. She may have felt such a sense of loss with respect to all their belongings that she wanted to catch just one more longing look at it all. In any case, she disobeyed and the punishment for that disobedience was that "she became a pillar of salt." This does not mean that while she was in a standing position she suddenly changed into a pillar of salt. It should be noted that the word "changed" does not appear here. What probably is intended is that she was suddenly struck dead and that her body, lying along the road, gradually was covered with a layer of salt. This is not uncommon in that area. Objects that are left exposed to the elements gradually become encrusted with salt. A number of such columns of salt have been discovered in this area, and there was a tradition that one of these actually was the body of Lot's wife. Tourists were told that one specific column was the salt-covered body of Lot's wife. However, that particular column later disappeared and then another one was so designated. There is obviously no substantiation for these claims.

19:27–29 *Early the next morning Abraham got up and returned to the place where he had stood before the LORD. He looked down toward Sodom and Gomorrah, toward all the land of the plain, and he saw dense smoke rising from the land, like smoke from a furnace.*

So when God destroyed the cities of the plain, he remembered Abraham, and he brought Lot out of the catastrophe that overthrew the cities where Lot had lived.

Early the next morning Abraham made his way to the vantage point from which he had made his plea to God to spare the cities. He may have wondered whether there had been ten righteous people in the cities so that they could be spared, but then he saw the cloud of dense smoke rising in the distance from the area where the cities had stood. Even so, his interces sion had not been in vain. There may not have been enough righteous people to forestall God's judgment, but God did spare righteous Lot from the fiery devastation that wiped out the cities of the plain.

11. *Lot and His Daughters* (19:30–38)

This brief narrative, just as the rest of chapters 18 and 19, is ascribed to "J" by those who divide the sources. Some have argued that it was a later insertion which was motivated by the hatred of the Israelites for the Moab ites and the Ammonites. The territory east of the Jordan remained battleground through the centuries. This would have been one way in which the Jews could express their deep disdain for the peoples who occupied this area. Some have even suggested that this was a saga that came from Moabite or Ammonite sources. A parallel is sought in Greek mythology where we have the tale about Myrrha who got her father drunk and then bore a son by him, the mighty Adonis.

Such presentations do not require much discussion. They flow from a view of Scripture that is in sharp contrast to our concept of the Word of God. We accept this narrative as part of the inspired revelation of God and as such to be true to fact.

19:30 *Lot and his two daughters left Zoar and settled in the mountains, for he was afraid to stay in Zoar. He and his two daughters lived in a cave.*

By way of introduction to the narrative we are told that Lot decided not to stay in Zoar. Although this town served as a refuge for him when he escaped from Sodom, he felt uneasy there. This was one of the cities of the plain and the possibility that it could still fall under the destructive judg ment of God alarmed him. So he moved to the hills, just as the angel had originally commanded him to do (19:17). There he took up his residence in a cave, far removed from the rest of the people of the area. Some have argued that within this passage there is a repetition of the same information and therefore it must be ascribed to two sources. Hebrew style, however, not averse to a certain amount of repetition. It is, in fact, a common figure of Hebrew speech. So here we are first told that Lot left the city and went to the hills. Then we are given the specific detail that he went to the hills and lived in a cave.

19:31–35 *One day the older daughter said to the younger, "Our father is old, and there is no man around here to lie with us, as is the custom all over the earth. Let*

---

get our father to drink wine and then lie with him and preserve our family line through our father."

That night they got their father to drink wine, and the older daughter went in and lay with him. He was not aware of it when she lay down or when she got up.

The next day the older daughter said to the younger, "Last night I lay with my father. Let's get him to drink wine again tonight, and you go in and lie with him so we can preserve our family line through our father." So they got their father to drink wine that night also, and the younger daughter went and lay with him. Again he was not aware of it when she lay down or when she got up.

Lot's two daughters, who had stayed with their father, feared that in this isolated location they would find no male companionship and consequently would remain childless. They therefore devised a plan whereby they would get their father drunk and then have sex with him while he was in a drunken stupor. In this way they hoped to produce children to carry on the family.

There is no need to dwell on the immorality of this whole sordid procedure. Lot's daughters were guilty not only of dishonoring their father, but also of the sin of incest. Moreover, Lot himself showed little moral strength when he permitted his daughters to entice him into such excessive drinking of wine.

19:36–38 *So both of Lot's daughters became pregnant by their father. The older daughter had a son, and she named him Moab; he is the father of the Moabites of today. The younger daughter also had a son, and she named him Ben-Ammi; he is the father of the Ammonites of today.*

The plan of Lot's daughters was effective and both of them became pregnant by their father and gave birth to sons. The oldest daughter named her son "Moab," and he became the father of the Moabites. The younger daughter named her son "Ben-Ammi," and he became the tribal progenitor of the Ammonites.

Attempts have been made to relate the meaning of these names to this narrative. Moab has been interpreted as meaning "of the father." Ben-Ammi can mean "son of my people," but it has also been translated "son of a relative" and even "son of my father." It would be difficult to establish that this was actually the intent of the giving of these names. There is no such formula in the text, as there is, for instance, in Genesis 4:1; 5:29; or 10:25. The Septuagint has added such a formula in this passage also, but there is no basis for this in the original text. It is possible that the narrator suggested this connection by the repeated use of the term "of the father" (vv. 32, 34), and the use of "by their father" (v. 36). But there is no textual proof for this suggestion.

12. *Abraham in Gerar* (20:1–18)

Those who divide the sources see this chapter as the first independent section representing the "E" source. Previous to this only a few isolated verses in chapter 15 had been ascribed to this source. It is claimed that chapter 20 is a doublet of 12:10–20, just as chapters 17 and 15 allegedly cover the same material. Since 12:10–20 was ascribed to "J," our present passage would normally have been ascribed to "P." These scholars, however, advance a number of arguments for ascribing this material to a third source and this is designated as "E." Their arguments run as follows:

1) Although the name "Elohim" is consistently used here to designate God, and this is characteristic of "P," the verb that is used with this name in verse 13 is plural and this never occurs in "P." This is certainly a weak argument. The use of the plural with Elohim when the name refers to the living God is so sporadic that it is impossible to draw any firm conclusions from this usage. The form occurs only in two other references in Genesis (31:53 and 35:7). In the first of these instances it is possible that an actual plural is intended since the God of Abraham and the God of Nahor may be different gods (See my, *De Goddelijke Openbaring,* p. 67.) We would also refer our readers to our interpretation of 31:35.

It should also be pointed out, in connection with this argument, that the name "Jahweh" appears in verse 18 of this section. But, as could be expected, the critics simply ascribe this verse to a redactor. Actually, the name "Elohim" is completely understandable in this chapter because we are dealing with a revelation of God as "the Almighty One" to Abimelech, who was a pagan.

2) It is argued that "E" uses a different word for "slave woman" than is normally used in "J." It should be noted, however, that although this Elohistic word for slave woman is used in verse 17, the usual Jahwistic words for slave men and slave women are used in verse 14. The critics neatly circumvent this bit of textual evidence by describing this statement in verse 14 as a "gloss" borrowed from 12:16. This procedure certainly cannot be accepted as objective scholarship.

3) It is argued that this is the only place where Abraham is called a "prophet" (v. 7). But this offers no evidence for ascribing the entire passage to another source.

4) It is claimed that placing Abraham in Gerar at this time is in conflict with 13:18; 14:13; and 18:1, which indicate that he was living near Hebron. In reply we would point out that it is certainly possible that Abraham had moved. In 21:33–34 and 22:19 it is evident that Abraham was not living near Hebron. The critics avoid this evidence by claiming that 22:19

also must have come from "E," and that 21:33 was misplaced, while 21:34 was a later interpolation, but this kind of avoiding of evidence does not alter the fact that in Genesis 20 Abraham was no longer living at Hebron. It wasn't until many years later that we again find him near Hebron (see 23:2 and compare 23:1 with 17:17; 21:5).

5) It is argued that, although the name Elohim is used here and this is supposed to be characteristic of "P," the unadorned and schematic style which characterizes "P" is missing here. This then becomes one of the main grounds for ascribing this material to a third source. We have discussed this procedure in our Introduction to the Book of Genesis and there is no need to add to that in this connection.

None of these arguments carries much weight, in our judgment. The real issue is whether this chapter forms a duplication of 12:10–20, as is claimed, and thus represents another tradition that is introduced into the Genesis text at this point. It should be noted that in both instances the patriarch introduces his wife as his sister, with the result that the ruler of the country he is visiting picks her up for his harem. In both instances God intervenes; Sarah is liberated and returned to her husband.

But when we look more closely at these two narratives there is a great deal of difference between them. In chapter 12 the patriarch was in Egypt and it was the pharaoh who appropriated Abraham's wife for his harem. In our present chapter Abraham was in Gerar and Sarah was taken by Abimelech, king of Gerar. There is also a difference in the way God intervened. In Egypt the pharaoh had to determine, by his own investigation, what was causing the plague that had struck his household. In Gerar the king received a special revelation in a dream that informed him of the cause of his affliction. In the Egypt account, moreover, we are not told what the nature of the affliction was. Here at Gerar we are specifically told that God closed the wombs of all of Abimelech's wives and concubines.

A third difference that should be noted is that the pharaoh expelled Abraham out of the land of Egypt because of his deceit, while Abimelech allowed him to remain in his territory. Moreover, the pharaoh gave Abraham gifts before he discovered the truth about Sarah while Abimelech presented him with gifts after the offense came to light in an obvious attempt to offset the offense he had unknowingly committed. A small detail that can also be observed is that the pharaoh was told about the physical attractiveness of Sarah by his servants while nothing of the kind is mentioned in the Gerar incident. On the other hand, Abimelech made a direct inquiry of Abraham regarding his reasons for giving such a false impression and Abraham frankly answered him. No such inquiry is mentioned in the Egypt account. Finally, in the case of Abimelech we are specifically told that he had not had physical intercourse with Sarah and that, in fact, God had prevented this from occurring. But there is no basis for making the same conclusion in the case of Sarah's stay in the pharaoh's harem. We read that Abimelech informed his servants about the crisis that had befallen them. Further, mention is made of Abraham's prayer in behalf of Abimelech's affliction and this led to the removal of the curse. Neither of these factors is mentioned in chapter 12.

When we take careful note of the similarities and the differences between the two accounts it would be possible to conclude that we are dealing with one incident that is told from two radically different perspectives. But, with equal validity, we can also conclude that we are dealing with two distinct events. The latter possibility is strengthened, moreover, when we note in verse 13 that Abraham's conduct in this whole matter was motivated by his fear for his safety when they encountered situations such as this. It could be expected that he would be inclined to use the same technique each time he faced such a threat in the course of his travels. This is further confirmed by the fact that later Isaac used the same ruse to protect himself. We realize that the critics have interpreted the incident of Isaac in 26:7 as yet a third version of one and the same event. But this is taking far too much liberty with the sacred text, and stretches credibility beyond all limits. If we start from the assumption, which we of course must do, that we are dealing with three authentic records of three distinct events, it is clear that the patriarchs were dealing with a real threat to their own safety in their nomadic lifestyle in ancient times. This was, then, one of the ways in which they tried to adapt to the perils of their way of life as they moved about among peoples and tribes who were hostile to them and who were unscrupulous in the way they treated strangers and visitors.

There is still another textual difficulty as well as a very practical objection we must contend with. This is the problem of Sarah's advanced age at this time. How could a woman of her age be so physically attractive to another man? Moreover, a comparison with closely related passages would strongly suggest that she was pregnant at the time. Certainly this latter fact would preclude the possibility of Abimelech's actions in her regard. This difficulty must be honestly faced.

Even assuming that people lived to be far older at that time, it has been pointed out that Sarah is described in 18:12 as "worn out," like an item of clothing. What ruler would desire such an aged woman for his harem? For most scholars this argument is conclusive and dictates the position that this incident could not have happened at this point in Abraham's life. This, then, leads these scholars to ascribe chapter 20 to another source which describes the same incident that we have already seen in chapter 12. At that time Sarah was still young and attractive. A few scholars, such as the Roman Catholic Heinisch, are of the opinion that we are dealing with a separate incident but that it took place at a much earlier time in Abraham's life. The only reason it is inserted here, they claim, is because the next chapter deals with Abimelech (see 21:22ff.).

In reply to all of these assertions we would declare once again that we accept the historicity of the entire Genesis narrative as it is presented in the text. We believe that Sarah experienced a physical miracle that enabled her to bear a child at an extremely advanced age. This miracle of physical rejuvenation could well have caused Sarah also to retain or, if need be, to regain her physical attractiveness to such an extent that she would draw the attention of Abimelech. The arguments given above assume, moreover, that the interest in women on the part of such ancient monarchs was the same as is popularly conceived today. This need not be true at all.

With respect to Sarah's condition of pregnancy, it should be pointed out that there is nothing in the text that necessitates the conclusion that this was already obvious. The message Abraham had received was that Sarah would have a son one year later (Gen. 18). There certainly would have been enough time for Abraham to go to Gerar and for Sarah to be taken into Abimelech's harem before she was so obviously pregnant that it would be recognized by even a casual glance.

Dr. Ridderbos, in his *Abraham, de Vriend Gods,* points out that not all Genesis narratives are in precise chronological order. There is, for example, the instance of Genesis 11:32 as compared with Genesis 12:4. But in the light of all the considerations mentioned above, we see no reason for insisting that Genesis 20 is not in its proper chronological position.

20:1 *Now Abraham moved on from there into the region of the Negev and lived between Kadesh and Shur. For a while he stayed in Gerar.*

The narrative begins with the announcement that Abraham broke camp at the oaks of Mamre, near Hebron (Gen. 13:18; 14:13; 18:1), and moved to the southland—the Negev (see 13:1). No reason was given for this move, as was done for the move mentioned in 12:10. It need not surprise us that Abraham decided to move after staying in one location for some 20 years (cf. Gen. 13 and 18).

There had been some changes in the peoples among whom Abraham lived in the area of Hebron. Earlier we read about Amorites such as Mamre, Eshcol, and Aner, who were allies to Abraham. But in chapter 23 we learn that the Hittites had moved into the area. Scholars formerly insisted that this was impossible. More recent discoveries, however, have revealed that by the time of Abraham the Hittites had already made deep inroads into southern Canaan. It would be understandable that, if such an invasion by the Hittites took place in the area of Hebron, Abraham would have decided to move to find a place that was more secure for his tribal household. Although this is conjecture, it is not without considerable historical basis.

Two places are mentioned in connection with Abraham's move, Kadesh and Shur. Kadesh, also known as Kadesh Barnea, lies at the southern border of Canaan, at the very edge of the Negev. Shur, also mentioned in 16:7, must be located close to the borders of Egypt. It was between these two places that Abraham now established his base of operations, and the territory in which he settled was known as Gerar. This probably was located on what today is known as Wadi Jeror, which is some four hours west-southwest of Kadesh. Some claim that Gerar was much farther north, near Gaza, but this would in no way conform to the designation "between Kadesh and Shur." Otherwise we would have to assume that Abraham first moved to some location between Kadesh and Shur and then later again moved northward to Gerar. But this is in no way suggested in the text.

20:2 *And there Abraham said of his wife Sarah, "She is my sister." Then Abimelech king of Gerar sent for Sarah and took her.*

In Gerar Abraham had a very unpleasant experience, similar to what had happened in Egypt some years earlier. He declared that the beautiful Sarah was his sister, and as a result Abimelech, the king of Gerar, claimed her for his harem. This was in keeping with the custom of that day, for a ruler could claim any unmarried woman, even if she was a temporary visitor in his land, for his harem. Understandably, this situation posed a serious threat to the fulfillment of God's promise that Abraham was to have a son by Sarah (Gen. 17:19–21; 18:10–14).

20:3–7 *But God came to Abimelech in a dream one night and said to him, "You are as good as dead because of the woman you have taken; she is a married woman."*

Now Abimelech had not gone near her, so he said, "Lord, will you destroy an innocent nation? Did he not say to me, 'She is my sister,' and didn't she also say, 'He is my brother'? I have done this with a clear conscience and clean hands."

Then God said to him in the dream, "Yes, I know you did this with a clear conscience, and so I have kept you from sinning against me. That is why I did not let you touch her. Now return the man's wife, for he is a prophet, and he will pray for you and you will live. But if you do not return her, you may be sure that you and all yours will die."

But the Lord watches over His people. Human weakness and moral lapses would not nullify God's purposes. During the night Abimelech had a dream in which God revealed to him that the woman he had acquired for his harem was already married. In that case the king and his family were threatened with death if the woman was not promptly returned to her husband.

Abimelech naturally defended himself by declaring that both Abraham and Sarah had told him that they were brother and sister. God thereupon assured him that He was aware of the situation and it was for that reason that He had warned Abimelech in time to prevent a serious sin.

It is striking that Abraham is here referred to as a prophet. This is the first time that the word "prophet" appears in Scripture. (For a detailed interpretation of this word see my book: *Profeten des Ouden Verbonds,* pp. 5–11.) The function of the prophet is here related to Abraham's prayer, and this probably indicates that prophets stood in a special relationship with God. We are reminded of what we are told about Abraham's relationship to God in 12:3, where he is called "the friend of God."

Abimelech is assured that if he returned Sarah to Abraham, the patriarch would intercede for him. God would hear Abraham's prayer and Abimelech would be spared from punishment.

20:8, 9 *Early the next morning Abimelech summoned all his officials, and when he told them all that had happened, they were very much afraid. Then Abimelech called Abraham in and said, "What have you done to us? How have I wronged you that you have brought such great guilt upon me and my kingdom? You have done things to me that should not be done."*

As soon as it was morning, Abimelech called his officials together and briefed them on the situation. They too were frightened by what had happened. Thereupon, Abimelech called Abraham in and rebuked him for his deception. He charged Abraham with being responsible for bringing serious guilt on the king and his officials. Even though they had done it unknowingly and unintentionally, they had, in principle, committed adultery. That the act of adultery had not actually been consummated was certainly not due to Abraham's actions. The king literally accused Abraham of doing things to him which should never be done.

20:10–13 *And Abimelech asked Abraham, "What was your reason for doing this?"*
Abraham replied, "I said to myself, 'There is surely no fear of God in this place, and they will kill me because of my wife.' Besides, she really is my sister, the daughter of my father though not of my mother; and she became my wife. And when

God had me wander from my father's household, I said to her, 'This is how you can show your love to me: Everywhere we go, say of me, "He is my brother."'"

Abimelech confronted Abraham with a direct question when he asked the patriarch why he had done this thing. Abraham admitted that he had been motivated by fear. This fear had moreover been inspired by the conviction that there was no fear of God in Gerar. He further told Abimelech that Sarah actually was his sister, since they had the same father with different mothers. He also indicated that this ruse had not been planned with only Gerar in mind. This had been a prearranged safety precaution, planned by Abraham and Sarah, to protect him from violence or death wherever they traveled together.

We need not comment about the moral implications of Abraham's actions in this situation. We have already discussed those in our treatment of Genesis 12:11–13. We should comment, however, on the fact that Abraham's guilt in this case was far greater than it was in the incident in Egypt. At that time he had been clearly informed about the serious consequences of this reprehensible maneuver. Obviously he had refused to heed the lesson that God had tried to teach him at that time. He had not learned to trust in the Lord for protection rather than to rely on his own ill-conceived schemes. How weak and small Abraham appears here! It became evident, even more clearly than in the former incident (12:1–20), that Abraham's courage and strength of faith were in no sense of his own merit or of his own virtue. They were totally the fruit of God's grace and faithfulness.

20:14, 15 *Then Abimelech brought sheep and cattle and male and female slaves and gave them to Abraham, and he returned Sarah his wife to him. And Abimelech said, "My land is before you; live wherever you like."*

After the stern rebuke Abimelech dished out to Abraham, the king gave the patriarch a generous gift consisting of sheep, cattle, and male and female slaves. This was obviously an attempt on the part of the king to make reparation for the offense he had given. He also returned Sarah to Abraham. Then, in a very generous gesture, he assured Abraham that he need not be afraid but that he could set up his camp anywhere he chose within Abimelech's domain.

20:16 *To Sarah he said, "I am giving your brother a thousand shekels of silver. This is to cover the offense against you before all who are with you; you are completely vindicated."*

A special gift was given to Abraham in behalf of Sarah. It is interesting that in this connection the king referred to Abraham, probably ironically, as Sarah's brother. The special gift consisted of 1000 shekels of silver. These "shekels" must not be considered to be coins as we think of them today. They refer rather to a measure of weight; thus the gift probably consisted of some 25 pounds of silver pieces. Just what the value of that much silver was in present-day value cannot be determined, but it certainly was a considerable sum and a very impressive gift.

Some interpreters hold that this was not a separate gift but that it was the calculated value of the sheep, cattle, and slaves that Abimelech had given to Abraham. There is no basis for this claim in the text, however. Abimelech told Sarah that in the eyes of all who were with her, this gift would cover the offense of what had happened. The intent seems to have been that this gift would give Sarah an answer to anyone who might mock or degrade her for what had taken place. The gift represented an admission on the part of Abimelech that what had happened was entirely his fault, although we know that Sarah was certainly not without blame herself. The reading of this statement is not altogether clear, but the translation we have before us is the most satisfactory in the light of the text.

20:17, 18 *Then Abraham prayed to God, and God healed Abimelech, his wife and his slave girls so they could have children again, for the LORD had closed up every womb in Abimelech's household because of Abraham's wife Sarah.*

Thereupon Abraham prayed to God for Abimelech and his people and the punishment that God had already brought upon them was removed. From this it becomes clear that God had not only threatened Abimelech with death (vv. 3, 7), but the affliction that God was to bring upon them had already taken effect. It is at this point that we are told exactly what that affliction consisted of. God had closed the wombs of all the women in the household of Abimelech, including his entire harem and his slave women, who obviously also served as concubines for the king. That this affliction included the reproductive powers not only of the women but also of the men is clear from the statement that "God healed Abimelech. . . ." The fact that God had made Abimelech temporarily sterile was a miraculous protection for Sarah. Thus it was also God's protection for the promised child that Sarah was to produce.

Some critics have charged that the inspired writer bent over backwards to try to whitewash Abraham in this whole despicable maneuver. This charge is not justified, however. A careful reading of the story reveals that Abraham was in no way justified or exonerated for what he had done. He

31

was, rather, roundly rebuked for his action and there was not one word of defense offered in his behalf. Any evaluation of the moral implications of Abraham's actions must take into account the teachings of the entire Scripture. When seen in this light there can be no question that Abraham's actions must be branded as downright sinful.

The fact that God intervened in behalf of Abraham and Sarah cannot be interpreted as an implied sanction on God's part of what they had done. God's intervention must be seen, first of all, as an expression of His determination to fulfill the covenant promise He had made to Abraham and Sarah. Furthermore, when God helps or blesses someone, this does not imply that He approves of what that person is doing or has done. He often delivers gross sinners out of danger in order to give them time to repent. And He certainly also delivers His faithful children from difficult situations they have brought upon themselves by their own sinful actions.

13. *The Birth of Isaac* (21:1–7)

These few verses are fertile soil for those who are intent on dividing the sources of the Genesis record. They claim to find three distinct sources in this brief passage.

The actual division of the material among these sources differs widely, however. The most common theory is that 1a, 2a, 6b, and 7 must be ascribed to "J"; 6b to "E"; 1b, 2b–5 to "P." This division, however, immediately flounders on the appearance of the name "Jahweh" in 1b. This can easily be resolved by simply declaring that the original must have used the name "Elohim" at this point.

Other scholars, although agreeing in general with the basic division of their fellow critics, insist that 6a belongs to "J," and 6b to "E." Still others insist that all of 6 must be ascribed to "E" and 7 to "J." Some scholars would place 1b, 2a, 6b, and 7 with "J," and then assign 1a and 6 to "E" and 2b–5 to "P." The only point on which there is general agreement among this school of interpreters is that 2b–5 must go to "P." The reasons given for this are that there is a chronological detail given in verse 5 and 2b–4 is related to 17:12 and 19–21, which is usually ascribed to "P."

There is no need to respond to all of this playing with the text of Scripture. The wide differences among the scholars who belong to this school again raise a serious question about the validity of this method of interpretation.

21:1, 2 *Now the Lord was gracious to Sarah as he had said, and the Lord did for Sarah what he had promised. Sarah became pregnant and bore a son to Abraham in his old age, at the very time God had promised him.*

As we have already seen in 17:15–21 and 18:10–14, the Lord had promised that Sarah would have a son. The very time when the child would be born had even been announced. It was to occur after the passing of one year. We now have the description of the fulfillment of that promise. We are told that Sarah conceived and bore Abraham a son, precisely at the time that the Lord had announced. Literally the text says that the Lord "visited" Sarah. The word used here commonly means "to seek" something that is lost, or "to visit" someone. It is frequently used to indicate an act of God with respect to a specific person. This may be an act of punishment (visitation) as in Isaiah 24:21; Jeremiah 9:25; Hosea 12:2. It may also indicate an act of grace or favor as in Genesis 50:24; Ruth 1:6; 1 Samuel 2:21. Our translators have chosen this latter meaning and rendered the word "was gracious to."

21:3–5 *Abraham gave the name Isaac to the son Sarah bore him. When his son Isaac was eight days old, Abraham circumcised him, as God commanded him. Abraham was a hundred years old when his son Isaac was born to him.*

In keeping with God's command in 17:19, Abraham named his son "Isaac." When he was eight days old he circumcised him as a sign of the covenant. At this time Abraham was exactly 100 years old (cf. 17:1). Thus, that for which Abraham had waited in faith for so many years finally was realized.

21:6, 7 *Sarah said, "God has brought me laughter, and everyone who hears about this will laugh with me." And she added, "Who would have said to Abraham that Sarah would nurse children? Yet I have borne him a son in his old age."*

Sarah expressed her happy amazement at the miracle of God's provision in a brief statement of praise to God. Her statement was related to the name "Isaac" (Hebrew *yishāq*) which means to "laugh" or "he laughs." She sang, "God has brought me laughter." The miraculous way in which God had fulfilled His promise brought her joy and happiness. Some have tried to read this as though Sarah implies that she fears that people will laugh at her, an old lady having a baby, in a mocking way. This is supposedly found in the statement in 6b and 7, but there is no substantial basis for this interpretation. The entire statement expressed her grateful joy in God's favor.

14. *Isaac and Ishmael (21:8–21)*

This passage is generally ascribed to "E" by those who divide the sources. The reasons given for this are the use of the name "Elohim" for

God, and the use of the so-called Elohistic word for "slave woman."

With respect to this latter argument, we should recall that in chapter 20, which is also ascribed to "E," both this supposed Elohistic word and the Jahwistic word for "slave woman" appear. When we examine these words a bit closer, it becomes apparent that the two words may refer to different levels of slavery. In 20:14 the Jahwistic word refers to slave women in general, but in 20:17 the Elohistic word designates slave women who were specifically used as Abimelech's concubines. It is possible, therefore, that the word that is used here to designate Hagar indicates that she was Abraham's secondary wife, as distinguished from the rest of Abraham's slave women. In this connection we should compare the use of the word in Judges 9:18 and 8:31 where it designates Gideon's secondary wife.

The main point of the critics, however, is that this passage forms a duplication of Genesis 16. It cannot be denied that there are some similarities between the two narratives. Both deal with Hagar, Abraham's Egyptian secondary wife. Both relate to an experience she had in the desert. In both instances the angel of the Lord appeared with a message of deliverance for her.

But there are also major differences between these two accounts. In the first instance she fled from Abraham's camp, while in the second event she was sent away. In the first instance she was told to return. In the present passage there is no mention of this. In the first experience Ishmael had not yet been born, but this narrative centers on Ishmael. Her motives for leaving Abraham's household are radically different in the two accounts. Taken as a whole, the differences between the two accounts are so substantial, even without mentioning minor details, that this cannot reasonably be considered to be a doublet of the former narrative. We are obviously dealing with two distinct events that are separated by a number of years.

21:8 *The child grew and was weaned, and on the day Isaac was weaned Abraham held a great feast.*

In accordance with Eastern custom, Abraham prepared a feast on the occasion of Isaac's weaning. In that culture children were weaned at a considerably older age than is customary today. Children were nursed by their mothers until they were at least three years old (see 1 Sam. 1:22–24).

21:9 *But Sarah saw that the son whom Hagar the Egyptian had borne to Abraham was mocking,*

On the occasion of this feast Sarah noticed that Ishmael was mocking his young half brother. Some interpreters read this as "playing with" and then give it a rather innocent quality. They insist, then, that Sarah's disturbance was caused by what she feared for the future, rather than by what she saw at that time. She considered what would happen when these two little boys would become grown men. They would have to share Abraham's inheritance and this is what Sarah wanted to avoid by any possible means.

This interpretation loses sight of the fact that Ishmael was a young man of about 17 by this time. He was born when Abraham was 86 years old and thus was 14 years older than Isaac. To picture these two boys as playing together like little children does not accord with the facts. We realize that those who divide the sources can get around this factor of the time span by ascribing different passages to different sources at will. But even their best efforts cannot erase the fact that there was a considerable space of time between Abraham's taking of Hagar as his secondary wife and the birth of Isaac. The reason that is given (16:2) for Abraham's marriage relationship with Hagar was Sarah's barrenness, while the matter of her old age does not enter the narrative until 17:17 and 18:11–12.

In reply, it has been argued that there are factors in the narrative of Hagar's experience in the desert that suggest that Ishmael was still a small child. This, however, results from a misunderstanding of certain expressions in the text. This will be brought out in the course of our commentary below.

Besides all this, the word which some have translated "playing" definitely means "to mock." It is a strengthened form of the word that means to laugh at someone or something. The same word was used in 19:4 to describe the reaction of Lot's sons-in-law when they were told about the coming destruction of Sodom. The word is also used by Potiphar's wife (Gen. 39:14, 17) when she accused Joseph of "making sport" of her. In Exodus 32:6 the same basic word is used of the Israelites when they worshiped the golden calf. There the translators have rendered it "revelry." In Judges 16:25 the Philistines brought the blind Samson out and made him "perform" for their entertainment. Just what this was is hard to determine, but it obviously was not innocent child's play. In all of these cases the word has an unfavorable connotation and there is an aura of mockery and taunting that is associated with it. The only place where it has a more favorable connotation is in Genesis 26:8 where we read that Isaac "caressed" his wife. There it seems to imply some kind of courting gesture. In the light of all this, the use of the word here, describing Ishmael's "sport" with little Isaac, strongly suggests some kind of mockery or jesting.

Some have even suggested that whatever Ishmael did in his mocking sport was of pagan origin and involved something that was very improper for the people of God. It is even possible that he made fun of the promises of God with respect to Isaac, thereby expressing his disdain for these sacred promises. In that case we would have the conflict between ''flesh'' and ''spirit'' of which Paul speaks in Galatians 4:29. This mockery of Isaac by Ishmael would then be a veiled preview of the persecution of the church by the hostile world, of the seed of the covenant by those who stood outside of that covenant.

21:10 *And she said to Abraham, ''Get rid of that slave woman and her son, for that slave woman's son will never share in the inheritance with my son Isaac.''*

Sarah was so upset by what she saw that she went to Abraham and demanded that he expel the slave woman and her son from their household. The reason she gave was that the son of the slave woman should not share in the inheritance of her son. This was not just a matter of petty jealousy on Sarah's part, as some have claimed it was. Sarah recognized the difference between the seed of the promise and the child of the flesh. The latter was not to share in the inheritance. To be sure, there may have been some motherly prejudice on Sarah's part and this could be expected, but even so, the primary motivation voiced involved the covenant promise that had been given to Abraham and Sarah. No doubt this is also why God instructed Abraham to yield to Sarah's wish.

21:11 *The matter distressed Abraham greatly because it concerned his son.*

Abraham, however, was not immediately ready to grant Sarah's demand. Although he may have been well aware of the distinction that had to be made between these two sons with respect to the covenant promises, Ishmael was also his son. Abraham was reluctant to resort to the drastic measures Sarah proposed.

21:12, 13 *But God said to him, ''Do not be so distressed about the boy and your maidservant. Listen to whatever Sarah tells you, because it is through Isaac that your offspring will be reckoned. I will make the son of the maidservant into a nation also, because he is your offspring.''*

But God intervened and instructed Abraham to go along with Sarah's proposal. The reason given by God was that Abraham's offspring would continue through Isaac. That was to be the seed of promise and it was only upon those descendants that the covenant blessings would be bestowed.

Abraham knew this, of course, because God had specifically directed His promise through Isaac (Gen. 17:21). Now Abraham was once again reminded of this. Therefore, Ishmael had to be expelled. Abraham's inheritance had to be exclusively for Isaac. Ishmael had demonstrated a spirit of disdain for God's promises and he and his mother had to be removed from the circle of Abraham's family. God does, however, repeat the promise He had given earlier that Ishmael also would become a great nation. This probably offered some comfort to Abraham as he proceeded with the painful task of sending Hagar and Ishmael out of his household.

21:14 *Early the next morning Abraham took some food and a skin of water and gave them to Hagar. He set them on her shoulders and then sent her off with the boy. She went on her way and wandered in the desert of Beersheba.*

Early the next morning Abraham prepared provisions for Hagar and her son. In accordance with custom, he provided her with bread and water, placed them on her shoulder, and then sent Ishmael and her away.

Several interpreters have insisted that the child also was placed on Hagar's shoulder. This would imply that he was still a mere infant who could be carried by his mother. This is then related to verse 15 where we read that she placed the child under a bush. Having reached the conclusion that Ishmael was still a very small child, the critics then proceed to declare that this is in conflict with 16:16 and 21:5 where it is implied that Ishmael was at least 14 years old by this time. This, in turn, allegedly offers proof for multiple sources for the text.

In reply to this we should observe that the object "the boy" follows the verb "gave" and not the verb "lay" or "set." There is no textual basis for the translation of the Septuagint and the Peshitta which read "and he laid the boy on her shoulder." If this were indeed the original reading, there would be no way in which we could explain how the Hebrew text we have today could have been changed to read as it does. The reference to verse 15 will be dealt with when we discuss that verse.

When Hagar left Abraham's household, she wandered about for a while in the wilderness of Beersheba, and this location has caused some confusion. According to 20:1, Abraham was tentatively living in Gerar between Kadesh and Shur. Consequently, when we read that Hagar was wandering around in the desert far to the north of this location, it is obvious that she did not head for Egypt as she had done when she fled from Sarah on a previous occasion (see 16:7). Some interpreters have insisted that Abraham must have been living near Hebron at this time and then Hagar's location near Beersheba would be on the way to Egypt, but there is no basis for this in the text. In 21:31–33 we find Abraham not in Hebron but in the area of Beersheba. Thus it is not clear exactly what route Hagar took when she left Abraham's household.

21:15, 16 *When the water in the skin was gone, she put the boy under one of the bushes. Then she went off and sat down nearby, about a bowshot away, for she thought, "I cannot watch the boy die." And as she sat there nearby, she began to sob.*

Before long the limited supply of water that Hagar had been able to carry with her was exhausted. As a result, Ishmael began to faint from lack of water. The fact that he began to grow faint before his mother did has caused some of the critics to insist that he must have been a small child rather than a robust 17-year-old young man. In reply it has been pointed out that Hagar was a slave woman and was accustomed to long hours of hard work in the desert heat. As such she was more able to cope with the rigors of the desert than her son was. It is also possible that the young man had not yet learned how to conserve his energy in the way that his mother had learned through years of exposure to desert conditions. Add to this the fact that mothers are often given a special supply of strength and energy when the welfare of their children is at stake in a time of crisis.

When Ishmael could go no further, his mother tried to make him as comfortable as possible in the shade of a desert bush. When we are told that she "put the boy there," this does not imply that she had carried him up to this point. Rather, when he began to stumble and falter she supported him and helped him reach the most comfortable place she could find for him in the cruel desert heat. Then she withdrew a short distance so she would not have to witness the agony of her son dying of thirst. She did not go far away, only the distance of a bow shot. Thus she would be near enough to offer help to her son if there was anything she could do for him. There she sat down and cried bitter tears of misery.

21:17–19 *God heard the boy crying, and the angel of God called to Hagar from heaven and said to her, "What is the matter, Hagar? Do not be afraid; God has heard the boy crying as he lies there. Lift the boy up and take him by the hand, for I will make him into a great nation."*

Then God opened her eyes and she saw a well of water. So she went and filled the skin with water and gave the boy a drink.

As is common in such cases, Ishmael also cried out in his agony, and we are told that God heard the cry of the young man. Suddenly the angel of God called to Hagar. Regarding the term "the angel of God" see our interpretation of 16:7. The voice of the angel encouraged her with a "Do not be afraid." He assured her of God's care for her and for her son. She was to go to her son, take him by the hand, and help him to his feet. Ishmael was not going to die out here in the desert, for God was going to make a great nation of his descendants. It should be noted that the angel said, "I will make him into a great nation," thus indicating, as was the case in chapter 16, that this angel was identified with God Himself.

At this point God miraculously opened Hagar's eyes and a well of water came into view. Hagar quickly filled her waterskin and gave Ishmael a drink. We are convinced that the well of water was there all the time, but that Hagar had failed to see it because of her depression and grief. It should be remembered that such water supplies were often hidden in the desert. Only those who knew of their location could avail themselves of this water. So it would not have been unusual that Hagar had at first failed to discover this water. The miracle, then, was that God enabled her to see the water supply just at the point of utter desperation.

21:20, 21 *God was with the boy as he grew up. He lived in the desert and became an archer. While he was living in the Desert of Paran, his mother got a wife for him from Egypt.*

The story closes with the note that God continued to bless Ishmael. He grew fast and became a powerfully built man. He lived in the desert, became a skilled outdoorsman and an excellent archer. His mother, who was a native of Egypt, saw to it that the young man got an Egyptian wife. The location where Ishmael settled was called the Desert of Paran, which lay between the Gulf of Aqaba and the Gulf of Suez (cf. 14:6). This was to the south of Kadesh Barnea. Thus Hagar and her son must have traveled to the south after their miraculous deliverance in the Wilderness of Beersheba.

15. *The Alliance Between Abraham and Abimelech* (21:22-34)

Those who divide the sources ascribe this passage to both "J" and "E." The name "Elohim" is used in verses 22 and 23, while in verse 33 the name "Jahweh" is used. It is charged that the making of an agreement is mentioned twice, in 27 and 32, and that the continuity of verses 24-27 is broken by verses 25 and 26. Consequently these scholars ascribe 22-24, 27, and 31 to "E." The rest of the passage is ascribed to "J," except verse 34, which they consider to be a redactor's interpolation.

Other scholars ascribe the entire passage to "E." The name "Jahweh" in verse 33 is then considered to be an insertion by the redactor. They correctly insist that there is no evidence here for two distinct sources. The irregularities that have been pointed out are completely consistent with the Hebrew style of narration.

We do want to point out that the use of the name "Elohim" in verses 22 and 23 has an obvious explanation. The name is used by Abimelech, who was a pagan, and it cannot be used as evidence for a specific source. Therefore some scholars, with equal validity, ascribe the whole passage to "J." Once again, the two-source theory with respect to a passage such as this is unconvincing and arbitrary.

The one factor which bears some weight in ascribing this passage to "E" is that it reintroduces Abimelech, who was first introduced in chapter 20, and that chapter is also ascribed to "E." However, when the basis for this ascription of chapter 20 is disproved, there remains no basis for so assigning this passage either.

21:22, 23 *At that time Abimelech and Phicol the commander of his forces said to Abraham, "God is with you in everything you do. Now swear to me here before God that you will not deal falsely with me or my children or my descendants. Show to me and the country where you are living as an alien the same kindness I have shown to you."*

Abimelech, the king of Gerar (see 20:2), and Phicol, the commander of his armies, visited Abraham and proposed that they enter into an alliance. This proposal recognized Abraham, who up to that time had been a nomadic visitor in Abimelech's realm, as a ruler of equal station with the king. Approaching him as an equal, Abimelech proposed that Abraham and he should form an alliance. He had observed the wonderful way in which Abraham's God had blessed everything the patriarch did. The agreement was to apply not only to the two leaders themselves, but also to their descendants. The king reminded Abraham that he had been treated kindly as a stranger in their midst and now he pleaded for the same kind of consideration on Abraham's part. The king wanted to seal this agreement immediately, at this first meeting.

21:24–26 *Abraham said, "I swear it."*
Then Abraham complained to Abimelech about a well of water that Abimelech's servants had seized. But Abimelech said, "I don't know who has done this. You did not tell me, and I heard about it only today."

Abraham expressed his willingness to enter into such an agreement, but he felt constrained to mention one small complaint he had about his treatment at the hands of some of Abimelech's servants. It seemed that

Abimelech's servants had seized a well from Abraham. In desert country the availability of water is vitally important. Abimelech quickly assured Abraham that this had been done without his knowledge. The question "Why didn't you tell me?" was undoubtedly addressed to Abraham. A few scholars have suggested that the question was addressed to the commander of the army, Phicol, but this is not convincing. Although it is not specifically stated, the implication seems to be that Abimelech agreed to return the well to Abraham immediately.

21:27–30 *So Abraham brought sheep and cattle and gave them to Abimelech, and the two men made a treaty. Abraham set apart seven ewe lambs from the flock, and Abimelech asked Abraham, "What is the meaning of these seven ewe lambs you have set apart by themselves?"*

He replied, "Accept these seven lambs from my hand as a witness that I dug this well."

After removing this minor area of difficulty, Abraham and Abimelech proceeded to formally seal their alliance. Abraham brought sheep and cattle and gave them to Abimelech. Exegetes are generally agreed that this must be considered as a gift of friendship. In this way the agreement they had reached was memorialized. I am convinced, however, that these animals were intended to be used for a ceremony of making a covenant, similar to the event recorded in 15:9–17. It should be noted that the word that is used here for "making" a covenant is the same word used in 15:18, which literally means "to cut." If it was intended merely as a gift, Abimelech certainly would have brought a gift also. The ceremony took place in Abraham's territory and therefore he provided the animals that were required for the ceremony of sealing the alliance into which they had entered. This we are told in verse 27.

Thereupon, in verses 28–30, we are told about seven ewe lambs that Abraham "set apart by themselves." When Abimelech inquired about these animals, Abraham told him that these were a gift that was to guarantee Abraham's sole right to the well discussed in verses 25 and 26. This was like earnest money that secured the change of ownership of a piece of property. This, then, followed the formal ceremony of the making of the covenant or alliance.

21:31 *So that place was called Beersheba, because the two men swore an oath there.*

In this verse we are told about the name of the well. It was called "Beersheba." The inspired writer tells us that it meant "well of the oath,"

41

in honor of the event that took place there at this time. This would imply that when this name was used earlier (21:14) it was used in anticipation of what this area would later be called.

With respect to the meaning of the term there is probably some play on words here. The Hebrew word *šebá* includes the root letters of the word that means "to swear." But the word also means "seven," which would call to mind the seven ewe lambs that Abraham set apart on this occasion. It has been suggested that the number seven had some symbolic significance with respect to the swearing of an oath. This relationship became so strong that the words could actually be substituted for each other and one could speak of "sevening an oath." Naturally such play on words offers real difficulties when translating such expressions into modern languages in which the relationships that are implied are meaningless.

21:32 *After the treaty had been made at Beersheba, Abimelech and Phicol the commander of his forces returned to the land of the Philistines.*

This verse concludes this incident and then sees Abimelech and Phicol returning to the land of the Philistines. Although Beersheba was not a part of the land of the Philistines, it must have been near the border of that territory. Witness to this would be the well that had been under dispute.

The matter of interest here, however, is that up to this point Abimelech had been presented as king of Gerar. Now, suddenly his territory is designated as the land of the Philistines. Many interpreters, then, insist that this must be an error in the text which was taken from some other source or which was slipped into the text by the redactor. It is argued that the Philistines did not migrate to this coastal area of southern Palestine until about 1200 B.C., which was centuries after the time of Abraham. Thus, it is claimed, the reference must be seen as an error.

In reply we would like to observe that there is no reason to question the presence of the Philistines in this area at the time of Abraham. To be sure, both in the record of Scripture and in Egyptian sources there is mention of intense activity on the part of the Philistines in this area during the time of Samson and Saul. But this does not mean that they could not have been in this area long before that time. What probably happened was that the Philistines were present in the coastal area to the south of Canaan toward Egypt at the time of this narrative. Then, about the year 1200 B.C., there were sizeable migrations of these people from elsewhere. In this connection see our interpretation of Genesis 10:14 and our conclusion to chapter 10. There is also a mention of the presence of the Philistines in that area in Genesis 26. Moreover, in Exodus 13:17, in the time of Moses, it appears that the Philistines were already well established in the area between Egypt and Canaan. The shortest route from Egypt to Canaan would have passed directly through the land of the Philistines, but to avoid conflict with these people, God led Israel around this territory. Now these records can be branded as unhistorical, but there is no basis for doing so.

Although there is no substantial basis for rejecting the fact that Abimelech was king of the Philistines, it should be noted that at this time the Philistines were situated a bit farther to the south. In this connection we should note what was said about the location of Gerar in 20:1. Later the Philistines moved northward into the coastal area of Canaan and that is where they were centered during the time of Samson and Saul. This would then place Abimelech's realm on the extreme northeastern borders of the territory that was occupied by the Philistines at that time.

21:33 *Abraham planted a tamarisk tree in Beersheba, and there he called upon the name of the LORD, the Eternal God.*

We are told that Abraham planted a tamarisk tree at the location where the treaty with Abimelech had been sealed. This tree had the quality of becoming very old. As such it served as a suitable memorial for the event that had transpired there.

We also read that Abraham "called upon the name of the LORD." This means that he engaged in public worship (see 12:8; 13:4). Some have claimed that Abraham established a "holy place" here which was to become a center of religious life. It is further claimed that the tamarisk tree was considered to be a holy tree and became an object of worship. There is no basis for these claims in the text, however. It just so happens that the two events —the planting of this tree and the public worship service—took place at this location at about the same time. Both are related to the alliance made with Abimelech. The tree was no more than a memorial of that event. The worship of God invoked God's blessing and favor on the action that had been taken.

21:34 *And Abraham stayed in the land of the Philistines for a long time.*

This narrative concludes with mention of Abraham's extended stay in the land of the Philistines. A question has been raised whether this long period refers to the time before the making of the alliance with Abimelech or after that event. Linguistically either could be possible. To apply this to the time after the meeting with Abimelech would not be in conflict with verse 33, as some have claimed. It is not stated that Abraham settled at

Beersheba, which is just outside the territory of the Philistines. What probably happened was that after the events of this passage Abraham again moved into the territory of Abimelech, which was the land of the Philistines. If he was situated in the northern part of Abimelech's domain, he would not have been far from Beersheba. Thus there is no real conflict between these two locations. At any rate, we are told that Abraham stayed there for a considerable period of time.

16. *Abraham's Faith Put to the Test* (22:1–19)

The moving story that is told in this passage has been of great significance for the life of faith of God's people throughout the centuries.

Those who divide the sources of the Genesis account have universally ascribed this portion to "E." The following grounds have been adduced for this designation:

1) The use of the name "Elohim" for God.

2) The fact that the divine revelation comes during the night. This is supposedly suggested by verses 2 and 3.

3) The way conversation is introduced in verses 1, 7, and 11. The person is addressed by name and then responds with, "Here I am."

4) The expression in verse 1, "After these things," or, as our translators have rendered it, "Some time later."

All of these expressions are supposedly characteristic of "E," but the last three mentioned have very little substance. With respect to the second reason, there is nothing in the text that says that the revelation came to Abraham during the night. The fact that verse 3 tells us that he rose early in the morning certainly does not establish the fact that the message had come to him during the preceding night. Obviously the reason for rising early was that they had a long journey before them on that day.

Turning to the matter of the way conversation was introduced in verses 1, 7, and 11, this offers little support for ascribing this passage to "E" since these expressions have not appeared in any of the passages that have been ascribed to "E" thus far. The expression translated "after these things," in verse 1, also appears in 15:1, and that is considered to be an "E" passage. However, the expression is not literally the same in both passages and thus it offers little support for ascribing the entire passage to a separate source.

This leaves us with the first and probably the most important ground in the argument of the critics. It is striking, however, that in this passage the name "Jahweh" appears just as often as the name "Elohim." Both names appear five times. It is true that two of the Jahweh references refer to "the angel of the Lord" but this is of no consequence. The critics try to avoid this refutation of their position by suggesting that the Jahwistic redactor changed what originally was an Elohistic passage. Or, they argue, the passage is a combination of a Jahwistic and Elohistic reading of the same narrative. If either of these processes was followed, however, one name would have been used consistently throughout. The fact that this passage uses both names once again establishes, as we pointed out in our Introduction, that the use of different names for God does not substantiate the theory of multiple sources.

22:1, 2 *Some time later God tested Abraham. He said to him, "Abraham!"*
"Here I am," he replied.
Then God said, "Take your son, your only son Isaac, whom you love, and go to the region of Moriah. Sacrifice him there as a burnt offering on one of the mountains I will tell you about."

We are immediately told that what is recorded here is an event in which God tested Abraham. The word is sometimes used of an exchange between two persons. First Kings 10:1 tells us how the queen of Sheba came "to test" Solomon. She wanted to determine whether Solomon's wisdom was really as great as had been reported to her. So she asked him questions and plied him with riddles. The term is also used in connection with God's dealings with people (see Exod. 16:4; Deut. 8:2, 16; 13:3; 2 Chron. 32:31). In each case the person was tested with respect to his faith in God and his consistent walk in the ways of the Lord.

There is still a third use of the term in which man tests God. This flows from a sinful attitude of doubt on man's part. Man, then, wants to determine whether God's power is adequate, and this has the effect of "tempting" God. Examples of this are in Exodus 17:2, 7; Numbers 14:22; Isaiah 7:12.

The test God placed before Abraham was a staggering one. God came to him with the astounding demand that he offer his son Isaac as a sacrifice to Him. This demand was spelled out literally. He was to offer his son as a burnt offering. It was to be done on a specific mountain that God would designate. Abraham was to slay his son with his own hands and offer him as a burnt offering to the Lord, and the seriousness of the demand is emphasized by the reference to Isaac as "your son, your only son Isaac, whom you love."

Mention of Isaac as Abraham's "only son" does not deny the reality of his other son, Ishmael. But Isaac was the son of promise and as such he was the only one in whom those promises could be realized. In other words, God asked Abraham to destroy the last and only hope he had for the fulfillment of God's covenant promises, for which he had waited so long.

Abraham is told to go to the land of Moriah to a mountain that God would show him. Many believe that the name ''Moriah'' must be related to what we are told in verse 14. ''Moriah'' is then interpreted as ''the mountain of the Lord's appearance.'' We will treat this more fully when we discuss verse 14.

At this point we want to express our reservation to giving this meaning to the name of the place before the event in question. After all, Abraham had to know where he was supposed to go, so the name ''Moriah'' must have had definite significance for him. God's instruction told him precisely where he had to go. Thus the expression in verse 14 cannot possibly be related to the name of the place as it is given here.

Others choose to follow the Syriac Peshitta which uses the name ''the land of the Amorites,'' instead of ''the land of Moriah.'' But this is most unlikely since the present Hebrew text is supported by every ancient manuscript.

There still is the question where this land of Moriah was located. It cannot be identified with Mount Moriah in Jerusalem on which the temple of Solomon was built (2 Chron. 3:1). That is definitely described as a specific mountain and in our present passage we are dealing with a district or a land. The writer of Chronicles, moreover, gives considerable detail about Mount Moriah, such as that it was the threshing floor of the Jebusite, Ornan. It would be unthinkable that, if this was the location at which Abraham made his historic declaration of faith, this would not have been mentioned by the Chronicler. It does seem obvious that the land of Moriah lay in a northerly direction from where Abraham was living at the time. Since the journey required three days, it could very well have been in the area of Hebron.

The fact that the place where the sacrifice was to be brought was some distance away was significant from the viewpoint of the test Abraham was to face. Abraham could not just fulfill God's command by a quick, spur of the moment decision. He had to sweat it out for at least three days, and this was a time of severe trial and testing for the patriarch. It would have been so easy for him to turn back or to take another route. The very nature of the test was that he would be obedient to God's demand in every detail after due consideration and considerable effort.

22:3 *Early the next morning Abraham got up and saddled his donkey. He took with him two of his servants and his son Isaac. When he had cut enough wood for the burnt offering, he set out for the place God had told him about.*

Because of the distance to be traveled, Abraham started early in the morning. The necessary preparations are mentioned, including the cutting of enough wood for the sacrifice. The hills of Palestine were, for the most part, without trees; thus the wood needed for a sacrifice had to be carried with them. Besides his son Isaac, who as yet knew nothing of what was to happen, Abraham took two of his servants along.

22:4, 5 *On the third day Abraham looked up and saw the place in the distance. He said to his servants, ''Stay here with the donkey while I and the boy go over there. We will worship and then we will come back to you.''*

On the third day the small traveling party approached the area to which God had directed Abraham. At that point Abraham left the two servants and the donkey that had been used as a pack animal. Abraham obviously wanted to be alone with his son when he carried out the terrible sacrifice God asked of him. The servants probably did not know the purpose of the journey. Abraham informed them that he and his son were going a short distance further to perform an act of worship and then would return. He apparently did not dare to tell them he would be returning alone. We can assume that, now that they had arrived in the designated area, the specific mountain on which the sacrifice was to be made was pointed out to Abraham. Just how he was informed of this we are not told.

22:6 *Abraham took the wood for the burnt offering and placed it on his son Isaac, and he himself carried the fire and the knife. As the two of them went on together,*

Abraham now placed the wood, which presumably had been carried by the donkey up to this point, on the shoulder of his son. This would confirm the fact that Isaac was no longer a small child. So father and son proceeded up the mountain together. What a conflict must have raged in Abraham's soul as he trudged up that mountain!

22:7, 8 *Isaac spoke up and said to his father Abraham, ''Father?''*

''Yes, my son?'' Abraham replied.

''The fire and wood are here,'' Isaac said, ''but where is the lamb for the burnt offering?''

Abraham answered, ''God himself will provide the lamb for the burnt offering, my son.'' And the two of them went on together.

After they had walked along in silence for a while, Isaac asked the understandable question, ''Where is the animal for the sacrifice?'' The question must have cut right through Abraham's heart, but it was the issue he had to face. Even now he could have turned back, but he had to bring his sacrifice in the full consciousness of his own decision to do so. He was obviously prepared for this, but he still did not feel free to tell his son that he was to be the sacrifice. Thus he gave an answer that was somewhat evasive but at the same time was the truth: ''God himself will provide the lamb for the burnt offering.'' The Hebrew literally reads, ''God sees before Him the lamb for the sacrifice.'' That this choice of God was Isaac himself, Abraham does not reveal at this time. This would become evident in due time.

The answer seemed to satisfy Isaac; they went forward together. The narrative is dramatically told, and we can almost visualize the two moving quietly up the slopes, step by step. We can feel the agony that must have gripped Abraham with each upward step.

22:9, 10 *When they reached the place God had told him about, Abraham built an altar there and arranged the wood on it. He bound his son Isaac and laid him on the altar, on top of the wood. Then he reached out his hand and took the knife to slay his son.*

The inspired writer provides considerable detail about their activity after they reached the top of the mountain. First they built an altar. Then the wood was carefully laid on it. And then came the fateful moment when Abraham had to tell his son that he was to be the sacrificial lamb. Isaac apparently offered no resistance as his father bound him and lifted him up on the altar. Then Abraham seized the knife and prepared to butcher his own, beloved son. The full drama of the scene must be carefully considered.

22:11, 12 *But the angel of the LORD called out to him from heaven, ''Abraham! Abraham!''*

''Here I am,'' he replied.

''Do not lay a hand on the boy,'' he said. ''Do not do anything to him. Now I know that you fear God, because you have not withheld from me your son, your only son.''

This was as far as Abraham had to go. God did not desire the death of Isaac. His only concern was Abraham's attitude and commitment. Human sacrifice was certainly not pleasing to God, and it is consistently presented as something offensive to Him (see Deut. 12:31; 18:10; 2 Kings 16:3; 17:17; 21:6; 2 Chron. 28:3; Jer. 7:31; 19:5; Ezek. 16:20–21). To conclude from this test of Abraham that the sacrifice of children was a common practice in Israel is completely indefensible. This was a pagan practice which, tragically, was found in Israel later, but it always was in clear violation of God's law.

At the decisive moment when Abraham lifted his arm with the knife in his hand and was about to slay Isaac, the voice of the angel of the Lord sounded from heaven like a clarion call. Abraham was commanded not to harm his son. We discussed the nature of "the angel of the LORD" under 16:7, and as was the case in 16:10 and 21:18, the angel spoke as though he were God Himself. "Now I know that you fear God, because you have not withheld from me your son, your only son." That this message comes from the "angel of the LORD" is the more striking since the original command to offer Isaac clearly had come as a message from God Himself. Obviously the angel of the Lord was the same spokesman who had addressed Abraham in verses 1 and 2.

The phrase "now I know" raises the question whether God did not know previously what Abraham's attitude was. In reply we must say that God certainly knew the strength and the measure of Abraham's faith. That faith had been worked within Abraham's heart by God Himself and God knew its true qualities. The expression "now I know" must then be seen as a human way of speaking which illustrates the fact that Abraham had withstood the test and had demonstrated that his faith was so total that he would have sacrificed his beloved son, the son of promise.

Was then this test of Abraham's faith necessary? It certainly was not necessary for God since He knew very well what the quality of Abraham's faith was. But for Abraham it was intended to reassure him of the complete effectiveness of his faith in God. It also serves to bring home to all readers of Scripture that, by the grace of God, those who truly trust in the Lord can face any trial and any test without fear.

22:13 *Abraham looked up and there in a thicket he saw a ram caught by its horns. He went over and took the ram and sacrificed it as a burnt offering instead of his son.*

As Abraham recovered from the trauma of the experience through which he had just passed, he saw a movement in the bushes that had not attracted his attention before. He saw a ram caught in the heavy undergrowth that covered the top of this mountain. He immediately realized that this was God's provision for an animal to be sacrificed in place of his son. Thus the altar had not been built in vain and the other preparations were not wasted, for a sacrifice was offered to the Lord. It was not Abraham's son but it was a sacrifice which God Himself had provided there on the lonely mountaintop.

22:14 *So Abraham called that place "The LORD will provide." And to this day it is said, "On the mountain of the LORD it will be provided."*

Abraham now realized the full meaning of his own statement as they were climbing the mountain. "The LORD will provide a lamb for the sacrifice." God actually provided the sacrifice He demanded. He, who had put Abraham to the test by demanding that he sacrifice his son, had already provided the sacrificial animal for this sacrifice, even though Abraham was not aware of it at the time. Now it all became clear to him. He could in full trust leave everything in God's hand and be completely obedient to His demands. God saw! God provided! God's divine provision took care of everything. Therefore Abraham named the place "The LORD will provide."

The last part of this verse includes a comment that has caused much difficulty for translators and expositors. The problem stems from the vocalization that is given to the inspired text. As a consequence of this vocalization the verb is in a passive form, rather than active. Our translators have rendered it, "On the mountain of the LORD it will be provided." Others have translated it, "On the mountain the Lord was seen." The rendering of our translators and of many others as well presents the difficulty of giving that mountain the name "the mountain of the LORD." This probably would make sense to Abraham on the strength of his experience on this mountain, but there is nothing in the narrative of Scripture prior to this that would give any reason for so designating this particular mountain. Furthermore, when we read, "it will be provided," we naturally ask, "What will be provided?"

The other translation that is very common is, "On the mountain God is seen" or "God appears." This presents even greater difficulties. The account says nothing about an appearance of God. The voice that stopped Abraham came from heaven. Thus this would establish no connection with the event that took place there.

All difficulty with this statement disappears, however, if we change the vocalization of the verb from a passive to an active mood. Then we read, "On the mountain the LORD provides." In our Introduction to this commentary we discussed this matter of the vocalization in the received text of the Hebrew Old Testament. In this case the active and passive forms of this verb use exactly the same letters. It should be remembered that the vocalization points were not part of the original Hebrew text. They were added much later by the Masoretic scholars. Thus, in this verse a change in those vocalization marks is wholly justified. Therefore, the name of the mountain "the LORD provides" fits the entire narrative. It also became the continued description of this mountain, "On the mountain the LORD provides." This became a proverb among the people of Israel. Just as Abraham experienced that the Lord provided when he reached the top of the mountain, so all of

God's people can be assured that when they reach the summit of their faith and their commitment, the Lord will always provide.

Returning once again to the name "Moriah," those who establish a relationship between that name and this verse (14) do so on the strength of the translation, "On the mountain the LORD is seen." But when we reject that translation, as we have done, this connection disappears. Furthermore, there is some serious question about the meaning of the name "Moriah" as "the place of the LORD's appearance." It is more probable that this name was an old name, used long before the event in our present passage occurred, the meaning of which is uncertain.

22:15–18 *The angel of the LORD called to Abraham from heaven a second time and said, "I swear by myself, declares the LORD, that because you have done this and have not withheld your son, your only son, I will surely bless you and make your descendants as numerous as the stars in the sky and as the sand on the seashore. Your descendants will take possession of the cities of their enemies, and through your offspring all nations on earth will be blessed, because you have obeyed me."*

After Abraham sacrificed the ram, the voice of the angel of the Lord came to him again. As a reward for his faithfulness, demonstrated in his willingness to sacrifice his son, Abraham is reassured of the promises he had previously been given. This assurance is now given with an oath. The Lord swears by Himself. We have similar expressions in Isaiah 45:23; Jeremiah 22:5; 49:13. An oath consists of calling the almighty God to witness. When God swears an oath by Himself, He declares that there is no one above Him upon whom He can call as a witness to the truth of what He declares (Heb. 6:13). There is none other who can guarantee the veracity of a statement He has made on the basis of the immutability of His own being.

What God now declares to Abraham with an oath is that He will abundantly bless him (Gen. 12:2), will give him a multitude of descendants (Gen. 17:2), as numerous as the stars of the heavens (Gen. 15:5), the sand of the seashore (Gen. 13:16; "like the dust of the earth"). In his seed all nations of the earth would be blessed (Gen. 12:3). To these promises now was added, "Your descendants will take possession of the cities of their enemies." This probably refers to the occupation of the Promised Land (Gen. 15:7).

22:19 *Then Abraham returned to his servants, and they set off together for Beersheba. And Abraham stayed in Beersheba.*

Abraham and Isaac now returned to the servants waiting at the foot of the mountain, and they all traveled to Beersheba, where Abraham stayed. At the close of chapter 21 we observed that Abraham had settled in the general area of Beersheba. Whether we must now think of him moving into Beersheba itself is not altogether clear. It is possible that the name Beersheba refers to the general area rather than to the city only.

It has been asserted that this powerful narrative is no more than an ancient saga. Attempts have been made to find the origin of this story outside the experience of the people of God. It has been pointed out that in Phoenician mythology there is a myth about a god named El who sacrificed his son Jedoed to his father Oeranos in a time of great crisis. A special altar was built for this burnt offering. An attempt has been made to relate the name Jedoed to the Hebrew word *yāhîd,* which means "only," as used in verses 2, 12, and 16. But even if the Phoenician word and the Hebrew word were identical, which they are not, this would form no basis for ascribing the entire narrative to Phoenician mythology. The differences between the two stories are enormous. The same is true when our passage is compared with a story taken from Greek mythology. There the king, Agamemnon, wanted to bring his daughter Iphigenia as a sacrifice in order to change the direction of the wind which was keeping the fleet from sailing for Troy. Then the goddess Artemis rescued the girl by means of a doe.

All such attempts to identify this narrative with heathen mythology must be categorically rejected. We are dealing with biblical history and we must accept that history as it is given in Scripture. Some have tried to present this as a deep-seated spiritual struggle which went on inside of Abraham. Following the practices of the heathen peoples who lived about him, he then allegedly prepared to sacrifice his son in order to find peace with God. This interpretation would imply that the whole idea originated with Abraham himself. Later, supposedly, he had some second thoughts about his plan and decided that God probably would not approve of child sacrifice.

Such presentations may have an appeal for those who start from the assumption that all religion evolved from lower to higher forms. But they are in complete conflict with the entire revelation of Scripture in which true religion is the product of special divine revelation. As it stands, the event fits well into the biblical account of God's dealings with Abraham. It also complements the entire history of redemption as it is unfolded in the Bible as a whole.

17. *The Descendants of Nahor* (22:20–24)

22:20–24 *Some time later Abraham was told, "Milcah is also a mother; she has borne sons to your brother Nahor: Uz the firstborn, Buz his brother, Kemuel (the* *father of Aram), Kesed, Hazo, Pildash, Jidlaph and Bethuel." Bethuel became the father of Rebekah. Milcah bore these eight sons to Abraham's brother Nahor. His concubine, whose name was Reumah, also had sons: Tebah, Gaham, Tahash and Maacah.*

It is remarkable that this brief genealogy of Nahor is generally ascribed to "J" by those who divide the sources. In view of the opening statement, which our translators have rendered "Some time later" (see 15:1 and 22:1), it would be expected that they would assign this to "E." Or perhaps, since it includes a genealogy, it could be ascribed to "P" which supposedly is evident in chapter 23. What, then, are the reasons for designating this material "J"?

Besides a few expressions that are allegedly characteristic of "J," there are two factors which supposedly point to "J" as the source for this passage:

1) The family line from which Uz and Aram descended is different here than it was in Genesis 10:22-23 and that passage is generally assigned to "P." 2) The names of the sons of Nahor which are given here would seem to place these people in the desert areas of Syria and northern Arabia. This, however, conflicts with the usual presentation, ascribed to "P" and "E," which places the family of Nahor in Haran in Mesopotamia.

With respect to "1," above, it is true that according to Genesis 10:23 Uz is presented as a descendant of Aram, while here his name is given as one of the sons of Nahor. In our interpretation of 10:23, we pointed out that there probably were two different men who carried that name. It is even possible that the Uz mentioned here was still another person, in distinction from either of those mentioned before. It can also be granted that in 10:22 Aram is mentioned as a son of Shem, while here he is introduced as the son of Kemuel. Here, again, it is questionable whether these refer to the same person. There may well have been two people with the same name. Furthermore, in Genesis 10:22 we are undoubtedly dealing with names of tribes or family groups—the Syrians and the Arameans—rather than names of individual persons. This is probably not the case in our present passage.

It has been pointed out that some of the names here also appear as names of tribal groups or districts. This does not mean, however, that these specific names designate such ethnic groups. The text strongly suggests that Abraham is informed about the sons of his brother Nahor and that these names are personal names. This is certainly the case with the last named son, Bethuel, since in verse 23 specific mention is made of his daughter Rebekah.

Although it can be argued that Aram is here presented as a tribal head and that Kemuel must therefore be seen as the father of the Syrians, this conclusion is by no means necessary. The name Aram could well be a personal name here, even as it is in another Old Testament passage, 1 Chronicles 7:34. There it appears as the name of one of Jacob's descendants through his son Asher.

In view of all of these considerations there really is no conflict between the names given here and those given in Genesis 10.

With respect to argument ''2'' above, it can readily be assumed that some of the descendants of Nahor left Mesopotamia and relocated in the areas of Syria and northern Arabia. We are dealing with nomadic people, and such an assumption would be wholly reasonable.

There are some critics who hold that Nahor was not a historical figure at all. They argue that since Nahor had twelve sons, and four of these were born to his concubine, this is a parallel to Jacob's twelve sons, four of whom were also born to slave women. This supposedly is evidence that the record of Nahor's children is no more than a pious fiction that was created to support the tradition of the twelve tribes of Nahor. It should be pointed out, however, that the text does not speak of tribes, but of persons. Actually we have a choice here of accepting the veracity of Scripture or accepting some ingenious theories of critical scholars. For those who accept the Bible as trustworthy that choice is altogether clear and, incidentally, altogether reasonable.

With respect to the contents of these verses we offer only a few comments.

The report that is brought to Abraham about the family of his brother Nahor continues only through verse 22. The information in verses 23 and 24 was obviously added by the inspired writer. It is even possible that the names given in 21 and 22 were not part of the message Abraham received but were added later by the narrator. The message given to Abraham could well have been of a general nature, since in chapter 24 the grandchildren of Nahor are introduced as adults. Although there was some communication between the various nations already at this early date, it is possible that Abraham had heard nothing about his family for many years.

The name of ''Milcah'' was already mentioned in 11:29, and she was the daughter of Haran who had married her uncle Nahor.

Regarding the specific names that are given we point out the following. The name ''Uz'' appears already in 10:23 (see our commentary on that verse). ''Buz'' is mentioned in Jeremiah 25:23. There, according to the context, we should think of this name as indicating an Arabian tribe. ''Elihu'' is mentioned in Job 32:2 and is described as a ''Buzite.'' We have already discussed the name "Aram." "Kesed" has been identified by some scholars as being the same as "Kasdim." He would then not be related to the Chaldeans, but to a tribe that lived in another area, near the mountains of Hauran. "Hazo" has been identified with "Hazu," a land that is mentioned in some of the Tablets and is also located in the area of Hauran.

Bethuel receives considerable attention in chapters 24 and 25. He was the father of Rebekah who became the wife of Isaac. It is probably for that reason that Rebekah is mentioned here rather than her brother Laban.

The "concubine" who is mentioned here must have been a household slave woman similar to Hagar. Her son "Tebah" can probably be identified with "Tibhath" in 1 Chronicles 18:8, which was a town that belonged to Hadadezer, king of Zoba in Syria. In the parallel passage in 2 Samuel 8:8, the name is given as "Betah," but this is probably a copy error for "Tebah," thus referring to the same name. Whether we can relate "Tahash" with "Tachshi" in the Amarna Tablets is doubtful. "Maacah" appears also in 2 Samuel 10:6, 8, and in 1 Chronicles 19:6–7, as the name of a district in Syria. It also appears in 1 Kings 2:39 as the personal name of a Philistine king, and in 1 Chronicles 27:16 as the name of an Israelite.

18. *The Death and Burial of Sarah* (23:1–20)

The critics universally ascribe this chapter to "P." This is rather striking since the primary basis for dividing the sources, the names used for God, does not enter here. God's name does not even appear in this chapter. It is also interesting that some of the other factors that supposedly are characteristic of "P," such as an affinity for genealogical material and a certain looseness of style, are difficult to find here as well. The few evidences that do allegedly point to "P" are so inconsequential that this chapter actually calls the whole theory of divided sources into serious question.

23:1, 2 *Sarah lived to be a hundred and twenty-seven years old. She died at Kiriath Arba (that is, Hebron) in the land of Canaan, and Abraham went to mourn for Sarah and to weep over her.*

When Sarah was 127 years old, thus some 36 or 37 years after the birth of Isaac (see Gen. 17:1, 17; 21:5), God called her to Himself. At that time Abraham and Sarah were living near Hebron, which was still known by its ancient name of Kiriath Arba. Thus we can conclude that, after the events recorded in the preceding chapters, the patriarch again moved northward. He had spent some time in Philistine territory (20:1; 21:31–34; 22:19), now he had moved back into the territory that can more properly be described as the land of Canaan. The text specifically mentions that Sarah died in the land of Canaan.

Earlier Abraham had lived in this same area. The name Kiriath Arba (Josh. 14:15; 15:13; 21:11) means "City of Arba," and Arba was one of the Anakim, the giants who were found in this area. Many interpreters, however, disagree and interpret it as "the city of four." They then explain this as a city divided into four sections, or lying at the crossroads of four roads, or even serving four gods. The wide difference in the interpretations does not recommend this theory. Moreover there is no evidence to support any of these readings.

After Sarah's death, Abraham observed the customary time of mourning as it was practiced in the Eastern culture of his day.

23:3, 4 *Then Abraham rose from beside his dead wife and spoke to the Hittites. He said, "I am an alien and a stranger among you. Sell me some property for a burial site here so I can bury my dead."*

Since early interment was imperative in that climate, the burial often took place on the day of death. Thus Abraham had some hasty preparations to make in order to provide a suitable place of burial for his wife. He immediately approached the people who occupied the area in which he was camped and offered to buy a burial plot. These people are here called the Hittites.

In an earlier scene (20:1), we made mention of the fact that the Amorites lived in this area. In that connection we discussed the objection that some have raised to placing the Hittites in southern Canaan. We now repeat what we pointed out before, that obviously some advance groups of Hittites had already migrated into this area by this time.

It should be noted that Abraham approached the children of Heth with all due courtesy. In the presence of those who occupied that territory he presented himself as a stranger who, although living among them, claimed no rights of citizenship or ownership. He therefore acknowledged that acquiring a burial plot was not a right but a favor.

23:5, 6 *The Hittites replied to Abraham, "Sir, listen to us. You are a mighty prince among us. Bury your dead in the choicest of our tombs. None of us will refuse you his tomb for burying your dead."*

The Hittites responded with equal graciousness. They began by insisting that, although Abraham was a stranger in their midst, they acknowledged him as a prince of God. They probably had observed that God bestowed a special favor upon Abraham. They therefore assured him of their fullest cooperation and offered him the choice of their burial plots.

23:7–9 *Then Abraham rose and bowed down before the people of the land, the Hittites. He said to them, "If you are willing to let me bury my dead, then listen to me and intercede with Ephron son of Zohar on my behalf so he will sell me the cave of Machpelah, which belongs to him and is in the end of his field. Ask him to sell it to me for the full price as a burial site among you."*

In order that the Hittites as a group would not object if he made an offer to one of their number for a specific plot of ground, Abraham then proceeded to make a concrete request. Thus far, in accordance with Eastern custom, the deliberations had been carried on with all parties seated. This allowed ample time for all the proper courtesies to be observed. At this point, however, Abraham stood up and bowed formally in acknowledgment of their graciousness. He then proceeded to propose the purchase of a specific plot that was owned by one of their number. The site he singled out was the Cave of Machpelah, which was at the edge of a field owned by Ephron, the son of Zohar. It is interesting to note that Abraham does not approach Ephron personally. He rather asks the Hittites as a group, since they have offered him a burial plot, to arrange for the transfer of Ephron's cave to his ownership. Although this was, in part, a matter of Eastern protocol, it also constituted an attempt on Abraham's part to avoid any possible misunderstanding with the Hittites as a whole. Abraham made it clear that he was interested in purchasing a plot that would serve as his own burial ground, rather than accepting the courtesy of using one of the burial grounds of the Hittites. He therefore offered to pay the full price required to obtain ownership of such a burial ground.

23:10, 11 *Ephron the Hittite was sitting among his people and he replied to Abraham in the hearing of all the Hittites who had come to the gate of his city. "No, my lord," he said. "Listen to me; I give you the field, and I give you the cave that is in it. I give it to you in the presence of my people. Bury your dead."*

Now Ephron spoke up. He obviously had heard Abraham's request. In keeping with Eastern custom, he first insisted that he would not sell the cave to Abraham but that he would present to Abraham as a gift the cave and the field on which it was located. This was, of course, a wholly insincere offer, but all the formalities of Eastern custom had to be duly observed. The scene for this exchange was undoubtedly in the public marketplace or the city square. All the dignitaries of the city were gathered for this solemn occasion. The fact that Ephron mentioned the field on which the cave was located, as well as the cave itself, immediately implied that if Abraham was to purchase the cave he would be obligated to buy the whole parcel of ground in order to acquire the cave he wanted.

23:12, 13 *Again Abraham bowed down before the people of the land and he said to Ephron in their hearing, "Listen to me, if you will. I will pay the price of the field. Accept it from me so I can bury my dead there."*

Abraham made it clear that he had no objection to this. He again bowed formally, in acknowledgment of the offer, and he accepted Ephron's proposition. Only, as had been expected, he insisted on paying the full price for the field in order that he would have full rights to bury his dead there.

The phrase that our translators have rendered "if you will" is actually an incomplete statement. It indicates the utmost courtesy and formality that went into this exchange. What the phrase actually says is, "If you truly are willing to sell this plot of ground and the cave. . . ."

23:14, 15 *Ephron answered Abraham, "Listen to me, my lord; the land is worth four hundred shekels of silver, but what is that between me and you? Bury your dead."*

Thereupon Ephron stated his price. He did not do this directly but he spoke effusively about the insignificance of the value of this property for two such wealthy and prominent men. There certainly would be no need for them to quibble about the price. It should be noted, however, that the price that Ephron quoted, veiled in all his flowery speech, was exorbitantly high. Although we do not know the exact size of the field, when the price is compared with land values that have been discovered in Babylonian records, it is completely obvious that this sly Hittite took gross advantage of Abraham's situation and quoted a price that was unconscionably high. Although we do not know the exact weight and value of a shekel of silver at that time, 400 shekels constituted a great deal of money, even by present-day standards. The buying power of that much money would have been enormous in the time of Abraham.

23:16–18 *Abraham agreed to Ephron's terms and weighed out for him the price he had named in the hearing of the Hittites: four hundred shekels of silver, according to the weight current among the merchants.*

So Ephron's field in Machpelah near Mamre–both the field and the cave in it, and all the trees within the borders of the field–was deeded to Abraham as his property in the presence of all the Hittites who had come to the gate of the city.

Ephron probably anticipated that Abraham would do some bargaining about the price, in keeping with the custom of the day. But Abraham immediately accepted the figure Ephron quoted. As a wealthy and powerful sheep and cattle rancher, Abraham maintained his dignity and counted out the 400 shekels of silver in the presence of the Hittite leaders. No price was too great for a proper burial place for his beloved Sarah. The silver probably was in the form of silver bars that had to be weighed. The expression, "according to the weight current among the merchants," indicates that the whole transaction was carried out in strict conformity to the practices that were common in the business world of that day.

The transfer of the property from Ephron to Abraham was also effected with all due ceremony in the presence of witnesses. Thus Abraham became the legal owner of the field and the cave of Machpelah.

23:19 *Afterward Abraham buried his wife Sarah in the cave in the field of Machpelah near Mamre (which is at Hebron) in the land of Canaan.*

Abraham proceeded to bury his wife Sarah in the cave he had purchased. We are told that the site was near Mamre, and then we are given the added information "which is at Hebron." Remember that 13:18 clearly indicates that Mamre and Hebron were not the same. The "oaks of Mamre" received their name from the head of one of the native Amorite tribes that occupied that area (Gen. 14:13–24). Obviously it kept this name even after the Hittites took over the area. Thus the reference to Hebron must indicate that it was located in the general area of Hebron.

We are told, further, that this was in "the land of Canaan." This is most significant because, even though Abraham spent much of his life outside the Promised Land, in the end he was able to bury Sarah in the land that God had promised as the inheritance of Abraham and his descendants.

23:20 *So the field and the cave in it were deeded to Abraham by the Hittites as a burial site.*

The event is concluded with a reiteration of the acquiring of ownership of the field and the cave as a burial plot. This is obviously where the inspired narrator wanted to place the emphasis.

The promises of God, which were so extensive and so inclusive, also with respect to material blessings and possessions, must be accepted in faith. Abraham experienced little of the actual fulfillment of those promises. All he possessed of the land of Canaan was a small burial plot. This is significant in the light of the entire revelation of Scripture regarding

Abraham's faith in God. Hebrews 11:14–16 reminds us that the patriarchs were "longing for a fatherland." The only piece of ground that Abraham possessed, in fulfillment of God's promise, was a grave, and this spoke of the end of life here on earth. From this he had to learn not to set his heart on earthly possessions but to look for the heavenly inheritance (Heb. 11:16) for "God had prepared a city for them." *

19. *A Bride for Isaac* (24:1–67)

Formerly those who divide the sources ascribed this chapter to "J." Their main reason for doing so was the frequent use of the name "Jahweh" for God. We will not discuss this again at this time because we have referred to this repeatedly in the Introduction and in previous sections of this commentary.

More recently, however, scholars have questioned the unity of this chapter. They have allegedly found contradictions and repetitions that point to more than one source for this material. A few have suggested that there was a dual tradition which was brought together in one source, namely "J." Mostly, however, the scholars have ascribed the material to both "J" and "E."

Although there are a number of minor, inconsequential inaccuracies that have allegedly been found, the main points of conflict and repetition that have been adduced are the following:

1) In verse 7 Abraham expresses the confidence that the Lord would prosper the journey of his servant. But in verse 8 he seems to allow the possibility that it might prove to be a failure.

2) Rebekah's ancestry is recorded twice—in verse 15 and again in verse 24.

3) It is charged that Rebekah is given the bridal dowry on two different occasions, first in verse 22 and then in verse 53.

4) According to verse 52, Rebekah's family had no comment regarding the request of Abraham's servant. But in verse 51 it appears that they gave their definite approval.

5) According to verses 50b and 51 it seems that the family made the decision for Rebekah. But in verses 57 and 58 they asked her to make her own decision.

6) According to verse 61 Rebekah took a number of servants with her. But in verse 59 it is suggested that only her nurse accompanied her.

---

*There is some difficulty with this passage when it is compared with Acts 7:16. There Stephen gives what appears to be a different account of the purchase of this grave site. This will be discussed when we treat Genesis 49:29–32.

None of these allegations carries much weight. Most of them evidence a certain effusiveness of style in ancient Eastern narration rather than indicate conflicts or contradictions. To judge such a narrative on the basis of modern Western modes of expression is an evidence of ignorance rather than of genuine scholarship. Whatever difficulties there actually are in the text will be treated when we discuss the verses in question. Only let us declare here that there is no substantial basis for questioning the unity of this chapter when it is read with a degree of objectivity.

24:1–9 *Abraham was now old and well advanced in years, and the LORD had blessed him in every way. He said to the chief servant in his household, the one in charge of all that he had, "Put your hand under my thigh. I want you to swear by the LORD, the God of heaven and the God of earth, that you will not get a wife for my son from the daughters of the Canaanites, among whom I am living, but will go to my country and my own relatives and get a wife for my son Isaac."*

The servant asked him, "What if the woman is unwilling to come back with me to this land? Shall I then take your son back to the country you came from?"

"Make sure that you do not take my son back there," Abraham said. "The LORD, the God of heaven, who brought me out of my father's household and my native land and who spoke to me and promised me on oath, saying, 'To your offspring I will give this land'–he will send his angel before you so that you can get a wife for my son from there. If the woman is unwilling to come back with you, then you will be released from this oath of mine. Only do not take my son back there." So the servant put his hand under the thigh of his master Abraham and swore an oath to him concerning this matter.

After the death of Sarah, Abraham called his oldest and most trusted servant to assign him to a very special mission. It is generally accepted that this servant was Eliezer (see 15:2). Having been reminded that his own days were also running out, Abraham now charged his servant with the responsibility of seeking a wife for Isaac from his own family. Abraham was sensitive to the gross idolatry that characterized the religious life of the people who surrounded him in the land of Canaan. Therefore he felt it was imperative that Isaac should not marry into such religious depravity (see 15:16). A marriage with one of the daughters of the land would have violated the purity of the elect race. Abraham therefore earnestly impressed on his servant that under no circumstances was Isaac to marry one of the Canaanite women. He must travel to Abraham's former homeland and there he must choose a wife from Abraham's own kinfolk. Although the pure worship of God had been compromised there also (see Gen. 31:19, 30; 35:2; Josh. 24:2, 14–15, etc.), when compared with the depravity of the Canaanites, it had maintained far greater faithfulness to the true God.

The old servant was placed under oath to insure that he would fulfill his charge with great care. The way in which this oath was taken was unique. The act of placing the hand under the thigh has caused a great deal of discussion among Bible scholars. Some Jewish scholars, as well as some modern exegetes, are convinced that this is no more than a discreet way of referring to the male penis. The Jews seek to relate this in a symbolic way to circumcision. Modern scholars generally try to relate it to the powers of reproduction. The oath would then involve the descendants of the parties involved who were, as it were, called to witness and to maintain the sacredness of what was sworn to in the oath. It is obvious that we are dealing with an ancient custom. The exact nature of the action has long since become a historical unknown. It is hardly justified, then, to draw any firm conclusions from a practice about which we know little or nothing. Similar ceremonies have been discovered among some Arabian tribes and even among some of the native people of Australia. The one point we want to make in this connection is that there is no basis for ascribing the practice of phallicism to Abraham on the basis of this method of taking an oath. This practice was later found among the Greeks but there is no evidence for its presence in Abraham's day.

Abraham's servant foresaw a possible difficulty in his master's plan. What if the girl, if indeed he found a suitable wife for Isaac, would not be willing to accompany him on the long journey back to Canaan? Was he then to take Isaac back to the land of Abraham's kinfolk? Abraham reassured his servant by expressing the faith that God would grant him success in his mission. At the same time he emphatically stipulated that under no condition was Isaac to be taken to the land of his forefathers. Isaac must remain in the Land of Promise. If, by chance, the woman refused to return with him, then the servant would be freed from the demands of his oath. But, and this is repeated, Isaac was not to be taken back there. This apparently satisfied the old servant, and so the oath was consummated.

24:10–14 *Then the servant took ten of his master's camels and left, taking with him all kinds of good things from his master. He set out for Aram Naharaim and made his way to the town of Nahor. He had the camels kneel down near the well outside the town; it was toward evening, the time the women go out to draw water.*

Then he prayed, "O LORD, God of my master Abraham, give me success today, and show kindness to my master Abraham. See, I am standing beside this spring, and the daughters of the townspeople are coming out to draw water. May it be that when I say to a girl, 'Please let down your jar that I may have a drink,' and she says, 'Drink, and I'll water your camels too'—let her be the one you have chosen for your servant Isaac. By this I will know that you have shown kindness to my master."

Thereupon Abraham's trusted servant departed to accomplish his serious and delicate mission. His master was a very wealthy man, so he carried with him many costly gifts for the bride-to-be and her family. The servant traveled in an impressive caravan with ten camels. These beasts of burden not only carried the supplies for the journey and the gifts, but also were to serve to carry the new bride and her retinue back to the land of Canaan. We are told that the destination for his journey was Mesopotamia which in Hebrew is *Aram Naharaim,* where the city of Nahor was situated. There is considerable disagreement among scholars regarding the meaning of that name Aram-Naharaim, and the precise boundaries of this territory. The city of Nahor undoubtedly must be understood to have been Haran (see 27:43; 28:10; 29:4).

We are given no details about the journey itself, which must have required considerable time. We are immediately brought to the point of arrival at their destination. There was a well outside the city and it was there that Abraham's servant made his camels kneel as they prepared to set up camp for the night. It was the time of day when the women of the city usually came to the well to draw water. This offered an excellent opportunity to catch a glimpse of the young women of the city who might possibly qualify as a bride for Abraham's son. But how was the man to know which girl to approach?

The old servant was a very pious man. He paused to pray to the God of Abraham, who was also his God, and he asked God to give him success on his mission and, in that way, to show favor to his master, Abraham. He also asked God to give him a sign in order that he might be able to identify the girl whom the Lord had chosen for Isaac. He would ask one of the girls for a drink from the well. If this girl then replied, "Drink, and I'll water your camels too" this would constitute a sign from God that this was the girl of God's choice. The sign that the servant included in his prayer was not wholly meaningless in itself. Watering camels was no small task since these animals are known to consume vast quantities of water after a day traveling across the desert. Any young woman who would volunteer such a demanding service would be demonstrating a spirit of genuine friendliness and willingness to serve.

24:15–21 *Before he had finished praying, Rebekah came out with her jar on her shoulder. She was the daughter of Bethuel son of Milcah, who was the wife of Abraham's brother Nahor. The girl was very beautiful, a virgin; no man had ever lain with her. She went down to the spring, filled her jar and came up again.*

The servant hurried to meet her and said, "Please give me a little water from your jar."

"Drink, my lord," she said, and quickly lowered the jar to her hands and gave him a drink.

After she had given him a drink, she said, "I'll draw water for your camels too, until they have finished drinking." So she quickly emptied her jar into the trough, ran back to the well to draw more water, and drew enough for all his camels. Without saying a word, the man watched her closely to learn whether or not the LORD had made his journey successful.

The prayer was answered in a most wonderful way. Even while the servant was praying, Rebekah, the daughter of Bethuel and a granddaughter of Abraham's brother Nahor and his wife Milcah, arrived at the scene. The sacred writer immediately identifies this girl even though Abraham's servant did not learn who she was until later. We are also told that she was very beautiful and that she was still an unmarried virgin.

When Rebekah went down to the spring, filled her pitcher with water and returned, Abraham's servant quickly approached her and made his request for a drink of water. She responded graciously, offered him a drink, and then made the critical offer to draw water for his camels also. Filling the trough from which the camels drank required several trips to the spring. The old servant remained silent, observing the girl carefully. Could it be that the Lord had prospered his journey so promptly and so remarkably?

24:22–27 *When the camels had finished drinking, the man took out a gold nose ring weighing a beka and two gold bracelets weighing ten shekels. Then he asked, "Whose daughter are you? Please tell me, is there room in your father's house for us to spend the night?"*

She answered him, "I am the daughter of Bethuel, the son that Milcah bore to Nahor." And she added, "We have plenty of straw and fodder, as well as room for you to spend the night."

Then the man bowed down and worshiped the LORD, saying, "Praise be to the LORD, the God of my master Abraham, who has not abandoned his kindness and faithfulness to my master. As for me, the LORD has led me on the journey to the house of my master's relatives."

When the animals had finally finished drinking, the man approached the girl and offered her a few costly gifts, a golden nose ring and a pair of golden bracelets. The exact value of these gifts is difficult to determine, but they were undoubtedly very costly. It should be noted that these were not bridal gifts since the man did not know at this time that this was the right girl or that she would accompany him. He probably hoped that this would be the case but at this time he was just beginning his inquiry. Thus, these gifts must be seen as an expression of appreciation and a way of introducing himself with a view to the request he was to make later.

He first asked who she was and whether there would be lodging available at her father's house for him and his retinue. She introduced herself and also assured the man they had ample lodging for him to spend the night and plenty of provisions for his camels. The old servant now realized that the Lord had blessed his mission with success and he fell on his knees to give thanks to God.

24:28–33 *The girl ran and told her mother's household about these things. Now Rebekah had a brother named Laban, and he hurried out to the man at the spring. As soon as he had seen the nose ring, and the bracelets on his sister's arms, and had heard Rebekah tell what the man said to her, he went out to the man and found him standing by the camels near the spring. "Come, you who are blessed by the* Lord," *he said. "Why are you standing out here? I have prepared the house and a place for the camels."*

So the man went to the house, and the camels were unloaded. Straw and fodder were brought for the camels, and water for him and his men to wash their feet. Then food was set before him, but he said, "I will not eat until I have told you what I have to say."

"Then tell us," Laban said.

Rebekah hurried home to tell her family about her experience at the well. The point of interest here is that the text says she told "her mother's household," rather than "her father's household" as would be expected. This has given rise to various assumptions.

Some have tried to interpret this as indicating that this family was a matriarchy. But this is in conflict with the rest of the narrative which presents Laban, Rebekah's brother, as the spokesman for the family. Some have assumed that Bethuel had passed away. This, however, conflicts with verse 50 where Bethuel enters into the discussion. Some have resorted to removing or changing the name of Bethuel in verse 50 to avoid this difficulty, but that is a purely arbitrary alteration of the text.

How must we then explain that the text says she went to "her mother's household"? Some have suggested that it was customary for the women to dwell in separate living quarters. This would conflict, however, with the presence of Laban (v. 30), who actively participated in the entire discussion. Others hold that the girl naturally ran to her mother to show her the beautiful gifts she had received and to tell her about her exciting experience at the well, and for this reason the parental home is referred to as "her mother's house."

We propose another explanation that maintains the integrity of the text.

In Hebrew it is possible to read this word as "grandmother" rather than "mother." An example of this usage is found in 1 Kings 15:2 when compared with 1 Kings 15:10. In our narrative the name of Rebekah's mother is nowhere mentioned. But the name of her grandmother, Milcah, is mentioned repeatedly (vv. 15, 24, 47). It is possible then that Nahor, Milcah's husband, had passed away and that the family continued to live in the ancestral house that now had become Milcah's household. Even though Bethuel and his family lived there, it was still considered to be the house of Rebekah's grandmother. This explanation resolves all difficulty with this statement as it appears in the text.

When Rebekah's brother, Laban, heard her story and saw the gifts his sister had received, he hurried out to the spring to find this man and to invite him into the house. With a single stroke of the pen the author reveals the character of this man Laban, which was somewhat less than noble. His hospitality was largely motivated by the gifts Rebekah had displayed. Even so, he did extend elaborate hospitality with a stable and provender for the camels, water for the feet of the travelers (see 18:4), and a sumptuous evening meal.

Abraham's servant, however, was determined to state the purpose of his mission before he sat down to eat. Laban, moreover, invited him to tell them what he had to say.

24:34–49 *So he said, "I am Abraham's servant. The Lord has blessed my master abundantly, and he has become wealthy. He has given him sheep and cattle, silver and gold, menservants and maidservants, and camels and donkeys. My master's wife Sarah has borne him a son in her old age, and he has given him everything he owns. And my master made me swear an oath, and said, 'You must not get a wife for my son from the daughters of the Canaanites, in whose land I live, but go to my father's family and to my own clan, and get a wife for my son.'*

"Then I asked my master, 'What if the woman will not come back with me?'

"He replied, 'The Lord, before whom I have walked, will send his angel with you and make your journey a success, so that you can get a wife for my son from my own clan and from my father's family. Then, when you go to my clan, you will be released from my oath even if they refuse to give her to you—you will be released from my oath.'

"When I came to the spring today, I said, "O Lord, God of my master Abraham, if you will, please grant success to the journey on which I have come. See, I am standing beside this spring; if a maiden comes out to draw water and I say to her, "Please let me drink a little water from your jar," and if she says to me, "Drink, and I'll draw water for your camels too," let her be the one the Lord has chosen for my master's son.'

"Before I finished praying in my heart, Rebekah came out, with her jar on her

shoulder. She went down to the spring and drew water, and I said to her, 'Please give me a drink.'

"She quickly lowered her jar from her shoulder and said, 'Drink, and I'll water your camels too.' So I drank, and she watered the camels also.

"I asked her, 'Whose daughter are you?'

"She said, 'The daughter of Bethuel son of Nahor, whom Milcah bore to him.'

*"Then I put the ring in her nose and the bracelets on her arms, and I bowed down and worshiped the L*ORD*. I praised the L*ORD*, the God of my master Abraham, who had led me on the right road to get the granddaughter of my master's brother for his son. Now if you will show kindness and faithfulness to my master, tell me; and if not, tell me, so I may know which way to turn."*

The man began by introducing himself. He proceeded to tell his hosts about the blessing of the Lord on Abraham and the great wealth he had acquired. Then he told them about the remarkable birth of Isaac, who was to inherit all of Abraham's wealth. This was an obvious tactical move, which would support his later request for a bride for Isaac. He continued by recounting the oath Abraham had required of him regarding the choice of a wife for Isaac, his prayer for divine guidance at the spring, and the providential meeting with Rebekah. He told them about his gratitude to God for having been led to Rebekah. Then he made his request to Rebekah's family to allow her to accompany him in order to become his master's son's wife. He waited for their response in order that he might know how he was to proceed from this point on.

24:50, 51 *Laban and Bethuel answered, "This is from the L*ORD*; we can say nothing to you one way or the other. Here is Rebekah; take her and go, and let her become the wife of your master's son, as the L*ORD *has directed."*

The response was made by Laban and by Bethuel, who, now that a decision had to be made, also entered into the conversation. They were impressed with the way the Lord had directed in this whole matter. Therefore, there was nothing for them to do but to concur in what had obviously been a work of the Lord. Rebekah was to be at the disposal of Abraham's servant. She was free to be the wife of his master's son.

As we mentioned earlier, some scholars are convinced that the name of Bethuel should not appear here. They either replace his name with that of Rebekah's mother, whose name is not given, or choose to read it, "Laban and his family." But this is an arbitrary altering of the text.

It is striking also that Laban's name is mentioned first, before the name of his father. This can be explained by the custom of that day. In families where there was more than one wife and thus the possibility of half brothers and half sisters, the full brother of a younger sister assumed a certain responsibility for the supervision of his sister. Thus, in this case the decision was made by her full brother and her father. How she felt about the whole matter herself did not seem to enter into the decision. The statement in verses 5 and 8, ''What if the woman is not willing to come back with me?'' must probably be understood as ''What if her family is not willing to let her go?'' This is also the reading that is given to this statement in verse 41.

24:52–58 *When Abraham's servant heard what they said, he bowed down to the ground before the LORD. Then the servant brought out gold and silver jewelry and articles of clothing and gave them to Rebekah; he also gave costly gifts to her brother and to her mother. Then he and the men who were with him ate and drank and spent the night there.*

When they got up the next morning, he said, "Send me on my way to my master."

But her brother and her mother replied, "Let the girl remain with us ten days or so; then you may go."

But he said to them, "Do not detain me, now that the LORD has granted success to my journey. Send me on my way so I may go to my master."

Then they said, "Let's call the girl and ask her about it." So they called Rebekah and asked her, "Will you go with this man?"

"I will go," she said.

The favorable response on the part of Rebekah's family again brought the old servant to his knees in thanksgiving to God. He then hastened to present the bridal gifts which consisted of gold and silver jewelry and fine garments. In addition to the gifts for Rebekah, he also gave gifts to her brother and to her mother (grandmother—see under v. 28). These gifts have sometimes been interpreted as being the so-called ''mohar'' or purchase price that was to be paid to the bride's family, although this is by no means certain in this case.

Thereupon the meal was served and all retired for the night. In the morning the old servant was eager to be on his way. The brother and the mother (grandmother) urged him to let the girl stay with them for a period of some ten days before her departure. The servant, however, would not hear of such a delay. Now that the Lord had signally blessed his mission, he was eager to return to his master as soon as possible to report on the success the Lord had granted. They agreed to let the girl decide. (Note, she was not to decide whether or not she was to go, but only whether she would leave immediately or after some delay.) Rebekah decided to leave as soon as the preparations for the journey could be completed.

24:59–61 *So they sent their sister Rebekah on her way, along with her nurse and Abraham's servant and his men. And they blessed Rebekah and said to her,*
"Our sister, may you increase to thousands upon thousands; may your offspring possess the gates of their enemies."
Then Rebekah and her maids got ready and mounted their camels and went back with the man. So the servant took Rebekah and left.

Thus Rebekah's family sent her on her way with their blessing. The nurse, who had cared for her from the time of her infanthood, accompanied her as her personal attendant. This was customary among the wealthy and elite of that day and is still practiced in some Arabian countries. Her family expressed their good wishes for great fruitfulness—thousands and thousands of descendants. The term which describes her descendants as possessing "the gates of their enemies" we have already discussed under 22:17. Undoubtedly Rebekah was also given a number of slaves to attend her. The camels were loaded and the caravan, led by Abraham's trusted servant, was on its way to the Promised Land.

24:62–67 *Now Isaac had come from Beer Lahai Roi, for he was living in the Negev. He went out to the field one evening to meditate, and as he looked up, he saw camels approaching. Rebekah also looked up and saw Isaac. She got down from her camel and asked the servant, "Who is that man in the field coming to meet us?"*
"He is my master," the servant answered. So she took her veil and covered herself.
Then the servant told Isaac all he had done. Isaac brought her into the tent of his mother Sarah, and he married Rebekah. So she became his wife, and he loved her; and Isaac was comforted after his mother's death.

With respect to the return journey, as was the case with the outward journey, no details are given about the trip itself. The inspired writer moved immediately to an account of the first meeting between the bride and groom. It was toward evening and Isaac was walking in the field. He found himself in the Southland (the Negev) near the well of Lahai Roi, which was to the west of Kadesh. Our translators tell us that this was the area where Isaac was living at the time (see 16:14 and 13:1). When we recall that Abraham lived in the area of Hebron when Sarah died, it is possible that Abraham had moved his camp farther south. Although the Negev did stretch from the hill country near Hebron down to the area of Kadesh, the fact that we now find Isaac in the southern part of the Negev strongly suggests such a move. Some have suggested that Isaac had taken a journey to the south by himself and was at some distance from the family residence, but this is unlikely. The caravan came from the north. If Abraham's residence was still near Hebron, they would have reached this before they came to the area of Lahai Roi. Abraham's servant would certainly have headed directly toward his master's home. We are therefore convinced that at this time Abraham was no longer living near Hebron but had moved to the south to the area of Kadesh. That the biblical text makes no mention of such a move need not strike us as strange. We have similar instances in 22:19 and 23:2 (see our commentary on these verses).

A few scholars have tried to make a case for the possibility that Abraham had died while his servant was on this journey. This, however, cannot be correct. After Abraham's servant had accomplished his difficult mission for his master, he would certainly want to report to his master about the wonderful success that God had granted on his journey. If at that point the servant had discovered that his master had died while he was away, some mention would certainly be made of the crushing disappointment this would have been to this devoted servant. Besides this, Genesis 25:7 tells us that Abraham lived to be 175 years old. We are also told that Isaac was 40 years old when he married Rebekah (25:20). Since Isaac was born when Abraham was 100 years old (21:5), it is obvious that the patriarch lived for another 35 years after the events recorded in our present narrative. It is acknowledged that some scholars try to negate these figures by ascribing them to a different source. This, however, does not change the fact that they are clearly spelled out in the biblical text.

Isaac had gone out to the field "to meditate," as our translators have rendered it, while others use the term "to pray." This is the only place where this word appears in Scripture. I also give my preference to the meaning "to meditate." Isaac probably was restless as he awaited the return of his father's servant, so he spent some time by himself quietly contemplating what the future might hold for him.

Suddenly he saw the caravan approaching in the distance. At about the same time Rebekah caught sight of the lonely wanderer out in the field. She probably had been told that they were nearing the end of their journey. She may even have surmised that the man walking in the field was her husband-to-be. She quickly dismounted the camel she had been riding, for it would have been wholly improper for her to meet this man while she was in a more elevated position than he was. At her inquiry the old servant confirmed that this man was indeed his master's son. In keeping with the custom of the day, Rebekah quickly placed a veil over her face since the man was not to see the face of his bride until after they were married (see our discussion under 29:25).

The servant now gave Isaac a complete report of his trip, after which

Isaac and Rebekah were married. We read significantly that he loved her. Isaac then brought his new bride into the tent of his mother, for this also was an Eastern custom and was part of the consummation of a marriage.

The statement regarding Isaac being comforted after his mother's death has caused considerable discussion. It has been objected that Sarah had been dead for some three or four years by this time, so Isaac certainly was no longer in mourning for her. (Cf. 23:1 and 25:20.) Some have concluded that the text is in error here. They hold that this should read "his father" and then insist that Abraham had died shortly before this scene (see above). But there is no justification for such a change of the text. It is understandable that there had been a degree of emptiness in Isaac's life ever since the death of his mother. Now that emptiness was filled by having his lovely new bride occupy his mother's tent and fulfill his needs for companionship.

The fact that Abraham is not mentioned in the closing part of this narrative need not surprise us. The sacred writer places all emphasis on the young bridal couple. From the nature of the entire account, however, we can safely conclude that Abraham was fully informed of all that had transpired and that he received the lovely Rebekah into his family circle with joy and loving approval.

20. *Abraham's Marriage to Keturah* (25:1–11)

In the past, those who divide the sources of the Genesis text have ascribed verses 1–6 to each of the three alleged sources. In later years some scholars have even ascribed this section to a fourth source. There really is no purpose served by considering all the various arguments that have been used to defend each of these conflicting opinions.

That verses 2–4 have some of the characteristics of the Table of Nations presented in Genesis 10 is obvious. We find names that indicate tribes and nations rather than individual persons. Thus we have references to the Asshurites, the Letushites, and the Leummites. We also read about the "sons of" Midian and of Sheba and Dedan, which actually were nations. This, of course, does not imply that the names in verse 2 cannot also be considered to be personal names. We note, for instance, "she bore him," which refers to one specific child. We found similar instances in Genesis 10. Even so, these individual persons could very well have become heads of families or tribes that carried the same name. One example of this would be "Midian," whose descendants were known as the Midianites.

Verses 7–10 are generally ascribed to "P," and the grounds for this designation are very unconvincing. One factor that is mentioned is the careful recording of Abraham's exact age. Another argument stresses the expansive style of the narrative. These bases for dividing the sources have been discussed repeatedly and there is no need for further refutation at this point.

Finally, verse 11 calls forth various conflicting opinions. Usually the verse is divided into two sections. The first part of the verse is then ascribed to "P" or "E." The second part, "Isaac, who then lived near Beer Lahai Roi," is given to "J." But those who support this division of the text have been able to offer little substantiation for their claims.

25:1–4 *Abraham took another wife, whose name was Keturah. She bore him Zimran, Jokshan, Medan, Midian, Ishbak and Shuah. Jokshan was the father of Sheba and Dedan; the descendants of Dedan were the Asshurites, the Letushites and the Leummites. The sons of Midian were Ephah, Epher, Hanoch, Abida and Eldaah. All these were descendants of Keturah.*

At the beginning of chapter 24 we are given the impression that Abraham considered his life to be approaching the end. It was not as though he was on his deathbed, as some expositors insist, but the impression is given that he considered the end of his life to be rapidly approaching. Now, in chapter 25, we are surprised to read that the old patriarch entered into another marriage and produced no less than six sons by that union.

One resolution of this difficulty would be to accept the possibility that his marriage to Keturah took place before he sent his servant to Haran. We have noted earlier that the Genesis record is not always chronologically arranged. For example, the death of Terah is recorded in 11:32, but it did not occur until 60 years after Abraham left Haran (see Gen. 12:4). Efforts have been made to prove that Abraham married Keturah before the events recorded in chapter 24, not only, but even before the death of Sarah. The grounds adduced for this conclusion are as follows:

1) Keturah is called a concubine. This implies that she took her place alongside Abraham's wife as a secondary wife or mistress.

2) The fact that Abraham sent Keturah's sons away, giving them gifts in lieu of an inheritance, suggests that they were grown men. This would have been, at best, improbable, if all of these sons were born after the events of chapter 24.

We consider this second argument to have little substance. With respect to the first claim, we would reply that the fact that Keturah was a concubine does not necessarily imply that Sarah was still living. It is possible that after the death of Sarah Abraham took one or more of his slave women to fulfill his need for companionship and love.

The main argument raised against the late date of Abraham's marriage to Keturah is that it would have taken a miracle of God for a man of Abraham's great age to produce a family of six sons. In defense it has been contended that if God could enable Abraham to produce a son when he was 100 years old, He certainly could have enabled him to produce six healthy sons by a young slave girl at the age of 150. Although we admit that it is possible that this relationship with Keturah took place considerably earlier, this is by no means a necessary conclusion.

The apparent conflict with the beginning of chapter 24 disappears when we recognize that Abraham had no way of knowing that he was to live another 35 years after the death of Sarah. Thus, when Sarah died, he considered that it was time to provide for Isaac's future by getting him a wife from his own people. It also should be taken into account that the trip to Haran could have taken much time. The journey proved to be very successful, however, and Isaac was provided with a beautiful wife in short order. This left Abraham alone. He still felt strong and vigorous, so he took one of his slave girls, Keturah, as his wife to provide him with companionship in his declining years.

With respect to Abraham's descendants by Keturah, the following can be pointed out. The Midianites lived in the Sinaitic Peninsula, between the northern arms of the Red Sea and the Gulf of Aqaba, to the east of the Gulf of Aqaba to the Syrian-Arabian desert. Shuah is mentioned in connection with one of Job's friends, Bildad the Shuhite (Job 2:11). In the clay tablets there is a reference to a land called Shuho, located in the upper drainage of the Euphrates, southwest of Haran. We have already commented about Sheba and Dedan under 10:7.

It is striking that in Genesis 10 these latter names appear as descendants of Ham, while here they are introduced as descendants of the Semitic Abraham. We must remember, however, that the name Sheba appears in two different contexts in Genesis 10. In verse 7 he appears among the Hamites, but in verse 28 he is listed as a descendant of Heber's son, Joktan, while Abraham descended from Heber's other son, Peleg (Gen. 11:16–26). We need not view these references as conflicting with each other, however. As we mentioned in our introduction to chapter 10, the same name was probably used for two different tribes or territories. It is also possible that, in some instances, one tribe or family group absorbed another. The Asshurites could be the same people as the tribe of Asshur which, according to some early inscriptions, lived near the borders of Egypt. The name "Ephah" also appears in Isaiah 60:6, where it is applied to a tribe of traders that dealt in gold and incense. "Zimran" can possibly be identified with Sabram in Arabia. "Ishbak" may be the same as a northern Syrian name, "Jashbok." Regarding the other names we have no further information.

25:5, 6 *Abraham left everything he owned to Isaac. But while he was still living, he gave gifts to the sons of his concubines and sent them away from his son Isaac to the land of the east.*

In connection with these sons of Keturah the writer of Scripture emphasizes the fact that Isaac inherited Abraham's empire. The sons born to Keturah were given gifts while the patriarch was still alive and thereupon were sent away to the east—that is to the area of the Syrian-Arabian desert.

These sons of Keturah are here called the sons of "his concubines." The use of the plural for "concubine(s)" can be explained as follows: the plural is often used in Hebrew when two words are closely related, even though only one of them has a plural reference. The second word serves only to qualify the first. Thus the word here could refer to only one concubine, but when it is joined with the word "sons" we would get a reading like "concubine-sons." These would then be distinguished from Isaac, the son of Abraham's primary wife.

25:7–10 *Altogether, Abraham lived a hundred and seventy-five years. Then Abraham breathed his last and died at a good old age, an old man and full of years; and he was gathered to his people. His sons Isaac and Ishmael buried him in the cave of Machpelah near Mamre, in the field of Ephron son of Zohar the Hittite, the field Abraham had bought from the Hittites. There Abraham was buried with his wife Sarah.*

Thereupon we are told about the death of Abraham. He came to the end of his life at the age of 175. "He was gathered to his people" can be related to 15:15, "You will go to your fathers. . . ." He was buried by his two sons, Isaac and Ishmael, in the cave in which Sarah had been buried, in the field Abraham himself had purchased as a burial plot (see ch. 23).

An interesting sidelight here is that Ishmael joined Isaac for the burial of their father. Some feel that this is in conflict with 21:10ff., and they hold that his presence here implies that Ishmael was still a part of Abraham's household. This need not be the case, however. It is possible that Ishmael had been notified of his father's approaching death and that he came to his bedside before he died. Ishmael had established his residence in the wilderness of Paran, which was just to the south of the land of Canaan. We can even assume that the message about Abraham's approaching death had been sent to Ishmael by Isaac. This would then portray Isaac as being sympathetic and understanding toward his half brother. It should be noted that Isaac had also moved out of the family household since he was married and had children of his own. In this connection see 25:19–28 and chapter 26.

74

The fact that the children of Keturah were not included in the funeral can be explained as follows. Hagar was Sarah's personal servant who had been given to Abraham as a wife by Sarah herself. Thus the child of this union, according to Eastern custom, was legally recognized as the son of Abraham and Sarah. The sons of Keturah were on a slightly different level. In this connection see our interpretation of 16:2.

25:11 *After Abraham's death, God blessed his son Isaac, who then lived near Beer Lahai Roi.*

This episode closes with the information that, after the death of Abraham, God blessed Isaac. He made his home at Beer Lahai Roi. How this information is to be related to 26:19–22 will be discussed when we treat those verses.

21. *The Descendants of Ishmael* (25:12–18)

25:12–18 *This is the account of Abraham's son Ishmael, whom Sarah's maidservant, Hagar the Egyptian, bore to Abraham.*
These are the names of the sons of Ishmael, listed in the order of their birth: Nebaioth the firstborn of Ishmael, Kedar, Adbeel, Mibsam, Mishma, Dumah, Massa, Hadad, Tema, Jetur, Naphish and Kedemah. These were the sons of Ishmael; and these are the names of the twelve tribal rulers according to their settlements and camps. Altogether, Ishmael lived a hundred and thirty-seven years. He breathed his last and died, and he was gathered to his people. His descendants settled in the area from Havilah to Shur, near the border of Egypt, as you go toward Asshur. And they lived in hostility toward all their brothers.

With the exception of verse 18, this passage is ascribed to "P" by those who divide the sources. As basis for this designation mention is made of the detailed data about Ishmael's life span, the expansive style of the narrative, and the use of the expression "this is the account of." These aspects of the narrative are supposedly characteristic of "P." How reliable these conclusions are can be judged on the basis of our many discussions of such alleged characteristics of a given source in previous chapters.

Ascribing verse 18 to "J" is likewise supported with no convincing evidence. Some have tried to relate this passage to chapter 16 as a continuation of Hagar's experience, but there is no evidence for this connection either.

The genealogy of Ishmael, like that of Abraham and Keturah earlier, does not consist only of personal names. In verse 16 specific mention is made of "their settlements and camps." This clearly indicates that some of these names refer to tribal groups.

It is not possible to identify all of these tribal groups. Nabaioth and Kedar are also mentioned in Isaiah 60:7. Kedar appears also in Psalm 120:5; Song of Songs 1:5; Isaiah 21:16; 42:11; Jeremiah 2:10; 49:28; Ezekiel 27:21. From Isaiah 21:16 and Ezekiel 27:21 we can conclude that this was an Arabian tribe. In some cases the name is used interchangeably with "Arabians." Adbeel has been identified with a tribe mentioned by Tiglath-pileser called "Idibi-il," which was located on the borders of Egypt. Dumah can be related to an oasis in northern Arabia that is now known as el Gof. (It should be noted that Isa. 21:11 does not refer to this tribe but rather to the Edomites.) Tema is mentioned also in Job 6:19; Isaiah 21:14; and Jeremiah 25:23. This may refer to the modern Taima in northwestern Arabia. Jetur and Naphish were among the Transjordan tribes against which the Israelites fought (1 Chron. 5:19).

Of all of these Ishmaelite tribes, twelve in number in accordance with God's promise in 17:20, we are told that they lived from Havilah to Shur, in the direction of Assyria. Just where Havilah was located cannot be determined with certainty. Shur, we are told, was near the border of Egypt. It is also mentioned in Genesis 16:7; 20:1; 1 Samuel 15:7; 27:8. The note "as you go toward Asshur," when compared with Genesis 10:19, can be understood as a direction, thus in the direction of Assyria, which would be a northeasterly direction. This does not imply that the Ishmaelites spread all the way to the Assyrian border. It simply indicates in what general direction these tribes settled.

The statement, "And they lived in hostility toward all their brothers," refers, of course, to the Ishmaelites and is a fulfillment of Genesis 16:12 (see our commentary on that verse).

In the midst of this record of Ishmael's descendants, we are told that Ishmael died at the age of 137. The reference to "he was gathered to his people" is the same as that used in 25:8. We have discussed it under that verse.

22. *Isaac and Rebekah—the Birth of Their Children* (25:19–28)

According to those who divide the sources, this passage had its origin in various sources. Verses 19, 20, and 26b are ascribed to "P" because they include expressions that allegedly are characteristic of that source. The rest of the passage is ascribed to "J" because there the name "Jahweh" is used for God, except for a few words in verse 27 which are ascribed to "E." This is defended by describing the terms "a skillful hunter" and "a man of the open country" as doublets. The same is claimed for "a quiet man" and a man "staying among the tents." It is concluded, therefore, that these expressions must come from different sources, but even a casual reading of these expressions indicates that they are not repetitions at all. All we have is a further description that augments what has already been said.

In more recent times there has been an attempt to ascribe verses 21–26a to a fourth source, which was supposedly absorbed into "J," while verses 27 and 28 are considered to be pure "J." There is, however, no basis for this maneuver.

One Roman Catholic scholar has suggested that verse 19 was inserted by a redactor in order to establish a relationship between verses 11 and 21. He also ascribes verses 20 and 26b to a chronological editor. These suggestions also have no basis in the biblical text.

This passage does not follow chronologically on what immediately precedes it. Since Abraham reached the age of 175 (25:7), and was 100 years old when Isaac was born (21:5), he was still alive when Isaac's sons were born. He would have been 160 at that time. The death of Ishmael (25:17), who was born when Abraham was 86 (16:16), naturally falls much later than the event recorded in our present passage.

25:19, 20 *This is the account of Abraham's son Isaac.*

Abraham became the father of Isaac, and Isaac was forty years old when he married Rebekah daughter of Bethuel the Aramean from Paddan Aram and sister of Laban the Aramean.

At this point we get a new heading. This also was the case in Genesis 11:27, after the history of Noah and the new humanity which stemmed from him. A new period of history was introduced in which one specific family is brought into focus for the ongoing revelation. In the same way another period is introduced here with focus on the family of Isaac. We are told, "This is the account of Abraham's son Isaac." After the death of Abraham, the history of God's chosen people is carried forward in Isaac.

Obviously the writer of Scripture does not group all the material that pertains to Isaac into one concise package. We are told about Isaac's marriage in chapter 24. Then, after starting the account about Isaac, he soon moves on to record the event of the birth of the sons of the second patriarch. The line must move on. Eastern narrative style does not follow strict chronological order, the way Western style is apt to do, when it comes to all the historical details of a narrative.

The history of Isaac, then, begins with a reminder about his marriage to Rebekah. We are told that he was 40 years old at the time. The land from which Rebekah came is here called "Paddan Aram." In Genesis 24:10 it was called "Aram Naharaim." This raises the question whether the same territory was called by two different names. It is usually thought that

Paddan Aram, or just "Paddan," as it is called in 48:7, was a smaller district within the larger kingdom of Aram Naharaim. It has been suggested that the word *paddan* in Aramaic means a yoke of oxen. This would suggest that it refers to a piece of land that could be plowed by a yoke of oxen within a specified time. Others have suggested that Paddan Aram was the grain district of Aram.

In more recent times a newer hypothesis has been advanced. Based on the Akkadian language, the word *padānu* is a synonym for *harrānu*, which means caravan or road. It is then suggested that Paddan was another name for Haran which in Hebrew is *hārān*. Paddan Aram would then be the same as "Haran in Aram." Since this name appears only in those sections of Genesis that are usually ascribed to "P," it has been concluded that this is a distinguishing characteristic of this source. But this conclusion is a bit hasty because the name "Aram Naharaim," which is usually ascribed to "J," appears only once in the entire book of Genesis (24:10). With respect to "Aram," which appears in both of these names, Rebekah's father and brother are both described as Arameans, which has been translated as Syrians.

25:21 *Isaac prayed to the Lord on behalf of his wife, because she was barren. The Lord answered his prayer, and his wife Rebekah became pregnant.*

At first it appeared that the marriage of Isaac and Rebekah was also doomed to be childless as Rebekah seemed to be barren. (Remember that Abraham and Sarah's began that way too.) God does not fulfill His promises according to human plans and expectations. Isaac's faith also was tested, but he found refuge in prayer and his prayer was answered. Rebekah became pregnant.

25:22, 23 *The babies jostled each other within her, and she said, "Why is this happening to me?" So she went to inquire of the Lord.*

The Lord said to her,

"Two nations are in your womb, and two peoples from within you will be separated; one people will be stronger than the other, and the older will serve the younger."

Then something remarkable happened. The young mother was carrying twins in her womb, and the babies were very active. She interpreted this as something foreboding and cried to God for help. The Hebrew expression seems to be incomplete, for literally it would read, "If it is so, why do I?" There is considerable difference of opinion regarding the meaning of Rebekah's cry. Some interpret it as "Why am I pregnant?" Others on the basis of the Syrian Peshitta, read it as "Why do I live?" The most accepted reading, however, seems to say, "Why does this happen to me?" This is the way our translators have rendered it. It would then be an expression of her anxiety because of what she considered to be a threatening situation that was developing within her own body.

In her anxiety Rebekah turned to the Lord. Although we cannot be sure just what the meaning of her cry was, what is significant is that she received an answer. The Lord spoke to her with the message, "Two nations are in your womb, and two peoples from within you will be separated." The two children that would be born would form two nations, but these two nations, although stemming from the same source, would not live together in peace. The one nation would be stronger than the other. There would be strife between these two peoples and the one would overcome the other. She was even informed, before the children were born, that "the older will serve the younger." This implied that, in contrast to the normal order and the natural expectation, in this case the older son would not be given the preference. When we consider the special promises that were involved, this has enormous implications. Isaac was the child of promise, and now the one who was to become the child of promise in the next generation was not the older but the younger of Isaac's two sons.

This announcement, made to Rebekah, also involved another revelation of a very significant truth. Man's place in God's plan of redemption and grace is not determined by human actions or position. Paul emphasizes this in Romans 9:11: "before the twins were born or had done anything good or bad." Thus we have a clear reference to God's sovereign election of His own people.

We need not dwell on the fulfillment of this prediction made to Rebekah. The people of Israel became the people of promise. From them the Messiah became incarnate. They were the descendants of Isaac's younger son, Jacob. The descendants of the elder son, Esau, became the Edomites and they stood outside the line of God's covenant promises.

There is considerable data in Scripture regarding the descendants of the younger son defeating and subjugating the people who stemmed from the elder son. David utterly defeated and subjugated the Edomites (2 Sam. 8:14; 1 Kings 11:16; 1 Chron. 18:13). Later Amaziah thoroughly humiliated them again (2 Kings 14:7; 2 Chron. 25:11–12). Then, during the Intertestamentary period, King John Hyrcanus I crushed them in the year 126 B.C. He compelled them to be circumcised, to keep the laws of Moses, and to accept a Jewish governor—as had been predicted in Obadiah 18.

It is true that Edom frequently humiliated Israel also. This was especially true in the year 586 B.C., when Judah was subdued. We read of this in Ezekiel 25:12; 35:5, 12; 36:5; Lamentations 4:21; Psalm 137:7; and especially in Obadiah 10–14. But in the long and bitter struggle between these two peoples, the descendants of Jacob finally triumphed.

25:24–26 *When the time came for her to give birth, there were twin boys in her womb. The first to come out was red, and his whole body was like a hairy garment; so they named him Esau. After this, his brother came out, with his hand grasping Esau's heel; so he was named Jacob. Isaac was sixty years old when Rebekah gave birth to them.*

Equally remarkable is the account of the birth of Rebekah's two sons. When it was time for her to deliver, literally in Hebrew, "when her days were fulfilled," she gave birth to twins. The first baby that was born manifested a very unusual characteristic: his whole body was covered with hair. In medical terminology this is called hypertrichosis, and this gave him a reddish brown color. The Hebrew uses the word *'admônî* here. Some interpreters have tried to relate this to the name "Edom," but this is most unlikely, since the name Edom does not appear in this connection. The child is named Esau. Some have tried to relate this name to the term "hairy" but this connection is also very doubtful, even when we resort to the Arabic word.

The second twin also made an unusual entrance into this world. We are told that his hand grasped the heel of his brother, almost as if he was trying to hold his brother back. This child was named Jacob. Whether his name relates in any way to the peculiar circumstance of his birth cannot be determined with certainty. It is true that the name can be seen as a form of the verb that has the same root letters as the word for "heel." Thus some have interpreted the name as meaning "he who grasps the heel." It should be noted, however, that the text does not establish such a connection. It may well be that this similarity in the sound of the two words was wholly unintentional at the time. Then later when this was discovered it led to the forming of this connection (cf. 27:36).

Isaac was 60 years old when the twins were born. This indicates that he and Rebekah had waited 20 years for the blessing of children.

25:27, 28 *The boys grew up, and Esau became a skillful hunter, a man of the open country, while Jacob was a quiet man, staying among the tents. Isaac, who had a taste for wild game, loved Esau, but Rebekah loved Jacob.*

As the twins grew they manifested great differences in temperament and character. Esau was an outdoorsman and became a skilled hunter. Jacob, on the other hand, was more the domestic type, and was more inclined to stay close to home. He probably became involved in raising cattle as his father and grandfather had done.

It also became evident that the parents each favored a different son. Isaac favored Esau because he loved the tasty venison that Esau would bring to him. This would seem to be inconsistent with his qualities as a peacemaker (25:9) and a man of prayer (25:21). Rebekah on the other hand favored Jacob. This favoritism on the part of the parents was a critical mistake and later led to tragic consequences.

23. *Esau Sells His Birthright* (25:29–34)

Those who divide the sources generally ascribe this passage to "J." In recent years a number of scholars have considered this passage, along with 21–26a, to have been derived from a fourth source, which has been added to the more familiar three. A few even ascribe this section to "E." They argue that these verses contradict verses 21–23. Both sections supposedly deal with the relationship between Jacob and Esau. In one treatment this relationship is based on a declaration by God. In the other, the relationship is based on the experience of the sale of the birthright. But there is no conflict between these two presentations. The selling of the birthright is no more than a fulfillment of what God had declared.

25:29–34 *Once when Jacob was cooking some stew, Esau came in from the open country, famished. He said to Jacob, "Quick, let me have some of that red stew! I'm famished!" (That is why he was also called Edom.)*

Jacob replied, "First sell me your birthright."

"Look, I am about to die," Esau said. "What good is the birthright to me?"

But Jacob said, "Swear to me first." So he swore an oath to him, selling his birthright to Jacob.

Then Jacob gave Esau some bread and some lentil stew. He ate and drank, and then got up and left.

So Esau despised his birthright.

One day Jacob had cooked a pot of stew, made with lentils, a vegetable that is still cultivated in Palestine today. The stew also included onions, rice, and olive oil. Sometimes a few pieces of meat were also included.

Esau was returning home from the open fields, tired and hungry. In a very crude way he asked Jacob for some of his stew. The word which our translators have rendered "famished" appears nowhere else in the Old Testament. We feel that it expressed his eagerness to "gulp down" some of "the red." The lentils probably gave the stew a reddish brown color.

Undoubtedly Rebekah had told Jacob that God had declared he was to obtain the birthright (v. 23). Therefore when Esau made his request Jacob saw his opportunity to secure the birthright with Esau's concurrence. So he offered the exhausted, famished Esau the pot of stew in exchange for the birthright.

Esau's reply has been variously interpreted. Some insist, and this seems to be the intent of our translators also, that Esau claimed that, since he was dying of starvation anyway, the birthright would be of no value to him if he didn't get something to eat immediately. I feel that this is an exaggeration of the actual facts. I prefer to read Esau's statement as an expression of his careless and indifferent attitude toward life as a whole. What he said, then, was that since life ends in death anyway, the birthright would be of no value to him when he was dead. It was thus a very short-sighted, materialistic view of life. He attached no value to the rich promises of God that had been given to Abraham, Isaac, and their descendants. He thought only of satisfying his own immediate physical desires. Fulfilling these physical desires in this present life meant more to him than the blessing of God in the future.

Jacob insisted that the transfer of the birthright be sealed with an oath. Thereupon he gave Esau some stew and added bread and water for his brother's refreshment. After Esau had eaten, he left. He was seemingly wholly indifferent to the enormous loss he had sustained in selling his birthright. The writer of Scripture makes specific reference to the fact that Esau despised his birthright.

All of this does not imply that Jacob was justified in this shrewd deal. He took advantage of his brother's hunger and exhaustion in order to buy the priceless birthright blessing for the price of a bowl of stew.

Verse 30 mentions that this reference to "the red" of the stew explains Esau's name—"Edom." There is a remarkable similarity in the sound of "Edom" and the Hebrew word *'adōm* which means "red." No etymological connection between the two words can be established, however. The actual meaning of the word "Edom" is unknown to us. All we have in this statement is a typical Hebrew stylistic device, a play on words. (See our interpretation of Gen. 11:9.) The author seems to say that Esau's descendants were accurately called "Edom" because their tribal father had set such a value on *'adōm*—the red.

24. *Isaac and Abimelech* (26:1–33)

Those who divide the sources generally ascribe this passage to "J." Their primary basis for this is the use of the name "Jahweh" for God. It is also claimed that there are several typical Jahwistic expressions to be found here. There is no need for us to discuss these arguments again at this point.

The critics have claimed that verses 1–11 are a parallel to 12:10–20 and chapter 20. We have already discussed the impossibility of reading these three passages as descriptive of one and the same event in our treatment of Genesis 20. We can add to that the obvious fact that the narrative recorded here differs in almost every particular from the other two with which it can allegedly be identified. The only similarities are that Isaac, like Abraham his father, presented his wife as his sister, which was obviously a useful ploy, and that he, like Abraham, left his home during a time of famine. It should be noted, however, that the famine mentioned here in verse 1 is clearly distinguished from the famine of Abraham's time. The critics, as could be expected, avoid this inference by ascribing the statement in verse 1 to a redactor even though there is no textual justification for doing so.

If these three accounts indeed do describe the same event, as the critics claim, the dividing of the sources runs into serious problems, since two of these accounts are generally ascribed to the same source—"J." Various attempts have been made to get around this by ascribing 12:10–20 to a secondary source, or ascribing 26:1–11 to the alleged "fourth source." But all of these efforts find no support in the actual text.

It is generally accepted that 26:1–11 does not follow chronologically on what immediately precedes it. It would have been very difficult for Isaac to present Rebekah as his sister if she was accompanied by her children. We must therefore place this narrative between the time of Isaac's marriage to Rebekah and the birth of the children recorded in 25:24–26. This does not mean that the entire passage (26:1–33), must be placed before chapter 25. For instance, verse 18 mentions something that took place after Abraham's death. When we remember that Abraham died 15 years after the birth of Isaac's children, the events of verse 18 must have taken place more than 15 years after what is recorded in 26:1–11. This also implies that Isaac must have stayed in Gerar for a considerable period of time.

Verses 26–33 have also been looked upon as a doublet to 21:22–34. The scholars who hold to this theory are by no means agreed as to the sources to which the two passages must be ascribed. Some want to divide 21:22–34 between "J" and "E." Others think this section should be ascribed to the alleged "fourth source." Without entering into the whole argument regarding sources, we do want to point out that there is no substantial evidence for making these two passages parallel accounts of the same event. In both cases, it must be granted, it is King Abimelech and the commander of his armies, Phicol, who come to make an alliance. But the differences between the two accounts are considerable. In the one case, the alliance is made with Abraham, while in the other it is with Isaac. Before the alliance with Abraham could be sealed, there was a difference of opinion regarding a well that had to be settled. In Isaac's case there was some discussion about wells earlier in the chapter, but no connection is established between the matter of the wells and the alliance with Abimelech. In Abraham's case the alliance was sealed with the slaying of animals in a formal ceremony for making a covenant agreement. But in the case of Isaac, there is mention only of the swearing of an oath. In the instance with Abraham, the making of the alliance took place immediately and then Abimelech and his party took their leave. In the case of Isaac a feast was prepared and the agreement was not made until the next morning, and only after that did Abimelech and his group leave.

That there are certain similarities of expression is, of course, to be expected. The making of covenants was common in that period of history and there were certain formalities that were standard procedure in the making of such covenants.

Probably the strongest argument adduced for making this a doublet of a former passage is the use of the name "Beersheba" in verse 33. It would be highly improbable that the same place would be officially named on two occasions with the same name. In this connection the following should be considered.

In the Hebrew text the name that is given to the well here is different from that given in 21:31. The name used here, as is indicated by our translators, is "Shibah." Some translations have simply made this "Sheba" to make it agree with the name of the town that was near Isaac's reopened well. But this is not how the original text reads. Here, in 26:33, the name Beersheba applies only to the town, while Isaac's well is called "Shibah."

There evidently were a number of wells in that area. One of these wells was named "Beersheba" by Abraham. That was where Abraham and Abimelech made their alliance. The name of the well was later also given to the town that was nearby, and probably to that entire district. Now Isaac and his servants uncovered another well and they called it "Shibah," which means "seven." But this well was also in the same district, which by this time, was known as Beersheba. (See our interpretation of 21:31.)

Finally, a word about Abimelech and Phicol, who appear in both of these narratives. It should be noted, however, that here in chapter 26 a third man participates in the discussions, Ahuzzath, the king's personal adviser. He is not mentioned in Genesis 21. Although there is a lapse of some 70 years between the two events under discussion, it is possible that Abimelech and Phicol are the same individuals in both instances. If we accept the possibility that other people in that era reached ages similar to Abraham's 175 years, a span of 70 years would not be excessive for these wo men. It is also possible, that we are dealing with other persons with the ,ame names, or that these names were titles of office, similar to "Pharaoh")f Egypt.

:6:1–6 *Now there was a famine in the land–besides the earlier famine of Abra-*
•am's time–and Isaac went to Abimelech king of the Philistines in Gerar. The LORD
•ppeared to Isaac and said, "Do not go down to Egypt; live in the land where I tell
•ou to live. Stay in this land for a while, and I will be with you and will bless you.
⁷or to you and your descendants I will give all these lands and will confirm the oath
swore to your father Abraham. I will make your descendants as numerous as the
tars in the sky and will give them all these lands, and through your offspring all
tations on earth will be blessed, because Abraham obeyed me and kept my re-
tuirements, my commands, my decrees and my laws." So Isaac stayed in Gerar.

Just as Abraham found it necessary to leave his homeland in Canaan when famine struck the land, so Isaac was driven from his home in a time)f famine. He went to the land of the Philistines, to the territory of Abimelech, king of Gerar. Some have charged that it is an anachronism to speak of the Philistines at the time of the patriarchs. We have already liscussed this in our treatment of 21:32. (Regarding "Gerar," consult our reatment of 20:1.)

In Gerar Isaac received a revelation from God. He was warned not to go nto Egypt, which probably had been his intended destination. He was nstructed to stay in Gerar. A promise was added to these instructions, which was, in essence, a repetition of the covenant promise given to Abraham (15:5; 22:17). The Lord would be with him and bless him, and nis descendants would be as numerous as the stars of the heavens. He was further assured that his seed would inherit all the land of Canaan. Also idded was the great spiritual promise that all the nations of the earth would)e blessed through his offspring (see 12:3 and 22:8). God specifically stated that Isaac would inherit all the blessings of Abraham because the first patriarch had been obedient to the Lord. At God's instruction, then, Isaac ind his entourage stayed in Gerar.

26:7–11 *When the men of that place asked him about his wife, he said, "She is my*
sister," because he was afraid to say, "She is my wife." He thought, "The men of
his place might kill me on account of Rebekah, because she is beautiful."

When Isaac had been there a long time, Abimelech king of the Philistines looked
down from a window and saw Isaac caressing his wife Rebekah. So Abimelech
summoned Isaac and said, "She is really your wife! Why did you say, 'She is my
sister'?"

Isaac answered him, "Because I thought I might lose my life on account of her."

Then Abimelech said, "What is this you have done to us? One of the men might well have slept with your wife, and you would have brought guilt upon us."

So Abimelech gave orders to all the people: "Anyone who molests this man or his wife shall surely be put to death."

Like his father, Isaac was afraid in this strange environment. He slipped into the same sin that Abraham had committed by lying about his wife and declaring that she was his sister. (See 12:11–12; 20:2, 11.) Abimelech looked out of his window one day and saw Isaac caressing Rebekah in a manner which made it evident that she was actually his wife. Abimelech called Isaac to account and rebuked him for his foolish ploy. This could have had disastrous consequences if one of Abimelech's servants had taken sexual liberties with Rebekah. Thereupon Abimelech gave orders to his people that they were not to molest this stranger in their midst, or his beautiful wife, under penalty of death.

26:12–14 *Isaac planted crops in that land and the same year reaped a hundredfold, because the LORD blessed him. The man became rich, and his wealth continued to grow until he became very wealthy. He had so many flocks and herds and servants that the Philistines envied him.*

The blessing of God upon Isaac soon became evident. When he planted crops he was granted a superabundant harvest. This was the more remarkable because this area was not known for its fertility. The rainfall was so sparse that there were frequent crop failures. Thus, Isaac's success was seen as a special blessing from the Lord. The same blessing applied to his abundant herds of cattle and his large coterie of slaves. Isaac became very wealthy and the people of the land envied him.

26:15–18 *So all the wells that his father's servants had dug in the time of his father Abraham, the Philistines stopped up, filling them with earth.*

Then Abimelech said to Isaac, "Move away from us; you have become too powerful for us."

So Isaac moved away from there and encamped in the Valley of Gerar and settled there. Isaac reopened the wells that had been dug in the time of his father Abraham, which the Philistines had stopped up after Abraham had died, and he gave them the same names his father had given them.

There is considerable difference of opinion on how verse 15 should be related to the context. Our translators, with others, suggest that the Philistines expressed their envy of Isaac by stopping up the wells and filling them with dirt. This, however, seems unlikely. The wells mentioned in verse 18 must be different wells because at Abimelech's request Isaac had moved to another area.

We propose another approach to verse 15. We feel that verse 15 gives an explanation of verse 18. Moreover, the verb form can also be translated in the past perfect tense, instead of a simple past tense. It would then read that the Philistines "had closed" the wells at some time in the past. It has been argued that this explanatory note then appears in the wrong place; it should come after verse 17. This is possible. We find a similar placement of an explanatory note in 1 Samuel 9:9, where it should actually appear after verse 11. It is not necessary to insist that verse 15 is in the wrong place, however. It can also be accepted as a parenthetical statement which explains what is later recorded in verse 18.

More radical is the interpretation of those who hold that both verse 15 and verse 18 are interpolations into the text, inserted in order to harmonize material from two different and conflicting sources. There is no basis in the text for this position, however. In Genesis 21:30 we read of Abraham digging a single well. Here we are told that Isaac dug at least four wells.

The intent of the passage, in our view, is that the jealousy of the Philistines led Abimelech to ask Isaac to relocate to a place where there would be less tension. Isaac agreed to this request and moved further up the valley, but the Philistines obviously anticipated this move and tried to create difficulty for Isaac by closing the wells Abraham had dug there earlier. As long as Abraham was alive the alliance was in force, and this restrained the Philistines. By this time Isaac had lived in their land some 15 years. It must have taken him some time, also, to accumulate the vast possessions mentioned in verse 14.

When Isaac didn't let the stopped-up wells deter him but simply had his men open them up again, the Philistines gave him no further trouble. They were obviously not of a mind to resort to violence. They were aware of the alliance made with Abraham and manifested at least some respect for Isaac, Abraham's son (see 21:23). They did not go beyond the harassment of closing a few wells with the hope that this might induce Isaac to move further from their area.

26:19–22 *Isaac's servants dug in the valley and discovered a well of fresh water there. But the herdsmen of Gerar quarreled with Isaac's herdsmen and said, "The water is ours!" So he named the well Esek, because they disputed with him. Then they dug another well, but they quarreled over that one also; so he named it Sitnah. He moved on from there and dug another well, and no one quarreled over it. He named it Rehoboth, saying, "Now the LORD has given us room and we will flourish in the land."*

Isaac did not limit himself to opening the wells his father Abraham had dug, to which the Philistines had no rightful claim. He proceeded to dig an additional well and this was what caused strife. The herdsmen of Gerar claimed this well as theirs because it had been dug on their land. Once again Isaac proved himself to be a peace-loving man and moved to another location in order to avoid open conflict. But there the same problem developed. Once again, Isaac moved still further. In each case Isaac gave a name to the well he had dug and then relinquished. These names, "dispute" and "opposition," were descriptive of what had happened at each location. The third time he moved and dug a well there was no more hostility on the part of the Philistines. They probably recognized the fact that Isaac had now moved beyond the area they could rightfully claim as their territory. This time Isaac gave the well the name "Rehoboth," which means "room." He fittingly acknowledged the favorable hand of God in providing him room for his family and his flocks. This location can probably be identified with the modern er-Rochebah, which lies about 18 miles southwest of Beersheba.

We want to add a few comments regarding the statement in 25:11 that after his father's death, Isaac lived at the well of Lahai Roi. This well lay a little to the west of Kadesh Barnea (see our commentary on 16:14). The territory of Gerar, according to 20:1, lay between Kadesh and Shur, which was close to the Egyptian border. Thus, since Gerar also lay to the west of Kadesh, there is no conflict between these two references. We will have to assume that the location of the well of Lahai Roi (25:11) must be taken in a broad sense as indicating a general area. We can also understand this as implying that, as Isaac moved from well to well, he also stopped for a while at the well of Lahai Roi.

26:23–25 *From there he went up to Beersheba. That night the Lord appeared to him and said, "I am the God of your father Abraham. Do not be afraid, for I am with you; I will bless you and will increase the number of your descendants for the sake of my servant Abraham."*

Isaac built an altar there and called on the name of the Lord. There he pitched his tent, and there his servants dug a well.

From Rehoboth Isaac moved still further to the north until he reached Beersheba. There he received another revelation from God (see our commentary under 12:7 regarding the nature of these revelations). The fact that this revelation came to him during the night does not necessarily imply that it came in the form of a dream or a vision. Again Isaac is promised that the Lord will be with him and that therefore he need not be afraid. For the sake of his father Abraham, God would continue to bless him and would make his descendants increase in number. Thereupon Isaac built an altar and worshiped God publicly. (Regarding the expression, "called on the name of the Lord," see our commentary on 4:26. Also see under 12:8.)

Isaac remained in this location for a time, although we do not know exactly how long. Some time later we find him in Mamre, near Hebron (see 35:27).

26:26–31 *Meanwhile, Abimelech had come to him from Gerar, with Ahuzzath his personal adviser and Phicol the commander of his forces. Isaac asked them, "Why have you come to me, since you were hostile to me and sent me away?"*

They answered, "We saw clearly that the LORD was with you; so we said, 'There ought to be a sworn agreement between us' –between us and you. Let us make a treaty with you that you will do us no harm, just as we did not molest you but always treated you well and sent you away in peace. And now you are blessed by the LORD."

Isaac then made a feast for them, and they ate and drank. Early the next morning the men swore an oath to each other. Then Isaac sent them on their way, and they left him in peace.

While Isaac was at Beersheba, he was visited by Abimelech, king of Gerar, Ahuzzath, his personal adviser, and Phicol, the commander of his armies. Although the nature of their visit was friendly, Isaac expressed amazement at this visit since the Philistines previously had shown considerable hostility toward him and had sent him away from their territory. Abimelech and his companions assured Isaac that they had changed their attitude toward him and that this change had been brought about by their realization that the Lord was blessing Isaac in a most remarkable way. They had therefore come to establish an alliance with him, similar to the alliance that had been made with Abraham. The Philistines, however, did not refer to this earlier alliance, probably because their observance of the terms of that agreement had left much to be desired. Now they asked Isaac for an alliance of friendship to be sealed with an oath. They appealed to their favorable attitude toward Isaac as evidenced by the fact that they had not harmed or molested him while he lived among them, although Isaac probably thought about the stopped-up wells that had repeatedly caused him to move. But being a peace-loving man, Isaac indicated his willingness to discuss the terms for peaceful coexistence with the Philistines. So he prepared a feast for them, and the following morning the alliance was completed and sealed with an oath. Thereupon Abimelech and his associates returned to their homeland.

26:32, 33 *That day Isaac's servants came and told him about the well they had dug. They said, "We've found water!" He called it Shibah, and to this day the name of the town has been Beersheba.*

On that very day some of Isaac's servants reported to him that they had dug another well and had found an abundant supply of water. That well was called "Shibah," which means "seven." In reply to the question why this name was chosen for this well, the obvious answer would seem to be that this was the seventh well they had dug. Although a review of the text does not indicate the actual digging of seven wells, only five, it can readily be assumed that other wells were dug that were not specifically mentioned in the text. Regarding the relationship between this name and the name "Beersheba" we have already commented on this in the introduction to this section.

25. *Esau's Wives* (26:34, 35)

These two verses obviously do not relate to what immediately precedes. Although they do give some perspective on the two chapters that follow, they do not relate directly to those narratives either. Therefore we will take them by themselves.

These verses are usually ascribed to "P" by those who divide the sources. The reason given for this assignment is the presentation of chronological details in verse 34, and this is supposedly a characteristic of "P." We have discussed this basis for delimiting the sources earlier and we need not repeat our comments in this regard at this point.

26:34, 35 *When Esau was forty years old, he married Judith daughter of Beeri the Hittite, and also Basemath daughter of Elon the Hittite. They were a source of grief to Isaac and Rebekah.*

Esau had already gained some reputation for being indifferent to the religious convictions of his parents. He therefore had no scruples about taking two wives from the native people who occupied the land of Canaan. It was precisely because of the low religious level of these people that Abraham had sought a wife for Isaac from his own family in Haran. But such considerations did not concern Esau.

It has been argued that the names of these two women and also the names of their fathers were typically Hebrew names. This assumption has by no means been firmly established, however. We will return to a consideration of these names when we treat 36:2, where there is a similar use of names.

Questions have also been raised about the presence of the Hittites in southern Palestine at this time. We have given this some attention in our treatment of 20:1. Some have concluded that the presence of these people near Isaac's location implies that Isaac was living near Hebron at this time, but this conclusion is not convincing. Although there is no mention of the Hittites in the Book of Genesis in areas other than near Hebron, these nomadic people could have been present in other areas as well.

We are told that Esau was forty years old at this time. This means that Isaac was 100 years old when Esau entered into these marriages. It is specifically mentioned that Isaac and Rebekah were grieved by these marriages of Isaac's favorite son.

26. *Jacob Steals the Birthright Blessing* (27:1–40)

Those who divide the sources usually ascribe this narrative to a combination of two sources—"J" and "E." There is no agreement however on how the material should be divided between these two sources, and many scholars agree that it is not possible to determine this with certainty.

The primary reasons for accepting the composite nature of this section are the following:

1) It is claimed that there are two descriptions of how Jacob disguised himself. In verses 11–13 and 16 he did this by fastening parts of goat skins to his hands and neck. But in verse 15 he disguised himself by wearing Esau's clothes. In the same vein it is argued that in verses 22 and 23 Isaac was deceived by feeling Jacob's hands, while in verses 26 and 27 it was the smell of Esau's clothes that misled him. The critics also claim that according to verses 35–37 Isaac knew who had deceived him, since he recognized Jacob's voice, but according to verse 33 he did not know who had stolen the blessing.

The support for these assertions is very weak indeed. The disguise was effected, obviously, by using both the skin of a goat and Esau's clothing. Moreover, the interpretation given to verse 33 is, to put it mildly, naive. Certainly Isaac knew who had deceived him, but at the first shock of discovering what had happened he cried out, "Who was it, then . . . ?" Immediately following that he said, "Your brother came deceitfully. . . ." The question, thus, was not an expression of ignorance but of shock and dismay.

2) The critics claim that verses 21–23 and verses 24–27 are parallel accounts, both of which close with "so he blessed him." An attempt has been made to maintain the unity of the passage by translating the expression "so he blessed him" at the close of verse 23 as "so he greeted him." But this rendering clearly does violence to the text. Others have attempted

to remove the difficulty by declaring that the statement in verse 23 is an insertion into the text. The correct way to read this statement, however, is "So he *would* bless, or *decided* to bless him." In other words, after Isaac had felt Jacob's hands and was convinced that it was Esau, he decided to bless him. Thereupon, he ate the meat that had been prepared for him.

3) It is claimed that verses 35–38 are a duplication of 33–34. These verses, however, form a coherent unit. The repetition of Esau's complaint and his begging for a blessing can be readily explained by Esau's becoming emotionally upset when he realized what had happened.

There are also many different views regarding the assigning of various expressions to one source or another. Some examples are expressions such as "wild game" and "tasty food," but there is no need for us to discuss all of these different points of view.

There has also been an attempt to prove that there is a conflict between this passage and 25:29–34. It is argued that in chapter 25 Jacob and Esau act as independent adults, while in this present chapter they are still under the supervision of their father and mother. In chapter 25 we have the record of a definite sale of the birthright and that would have ended the matter. There was no need for Jacob to go through all the trouble of the disguise and deceit to obtain what he already had. Moreover, at the close of 25:29–34 we are told that Esau got up and left. This is interpreted as indicating that the two brothers parted company and from that point on Esau had no more association with his father's household. It is even claimed that the original text says that "he went to Seir" and that this statement was deleted when it was later combined with chapter 27. From all of this the critics conclude that 25:29–34 must be assigned to the so-called "fourth source."

But there is no substantial reason for establishing such a sharp conflict between these two passages. The independence of the two brothers indicated in chapter 25 certainly does not preclude all communication with their father and mother from that point on. The selling of the birthright, if Isaac indeed knew about it, certainly does not mean that Isaac had decided to withhold the birthright blessing from Esau. There was indeed one part of the birthright blessing that Isaac should have withheld from Esau according to God's pronouncement in 25:23, but since this did not deter Isaac from wanting to transmit the birthright blessing to Esau, then Jacob's subtle purchase of the right certainly would not have deterred him either. From what we have learned about Esau, he certainly would not be the one to say to his father, "I don't have a right to the blessing because I sold it to my brother." The fact that he pleaded for a blessing, even after Jacob had received the birthright blessing, indicates where Esau stood on this matter.

Moreover, given Isaac's and Esau's attitudes in this regard, there is nothing in Rebekah's and Jacob's actions that conflicts with 25:29–34 either.

Finally, the interpretation of Esau's departure in 25:34 as given by the critics is obviously tendentious. There is nothing in the text that even suggests that Esau left the country. The expression merely indicates that this ended the immediate encounter and Esau probably went hunting again.

Positively, the text strongly suggests that 25:29–34 and our present passsage complement each other without any conflict. In 27:36 Esau declares, ''He has deceived me these two times.'' This clearly refers to the incident in 25:29–34 and the incident in our present passage as two distinct happenings. Although critics have tried to relate the ''two times'' to two aspects of this present narrative, this is unconvincing. Esau's statement in 27:36 offers indisputable proof that the two passages in question complement each other logically.

Several interpreters suggest that the biblical narrator treats the deceit and trickery in which Rebekah and Jacob were involved too favorably. They note that there is no implication of wrongdoing here. We reply by observing that the objective narration of an event in no way expresses approval or excuse for that which was done. Besides, it should be noted that there are definite implications of a sense of guilt in the narrative. In verses 12 and 13 Jacob and Rebekah discuss this very factor with respect to their plan. Moreover, Isaac specifically refers in verse 35 to the ''deceitful'' nature of what had been done. Of special note is the clear portrayal of the results of this sinful act in the rest of the narrative as being a punishment of God upon what had been done.

On the other hand, the sacred writer intends to let us see how God's prediction in 25:28 actually was fulfilled, in spite of Isaac's prejudiced favoritism toward Esau. When it is claimed that this is not mentioned in the text, this is true. But when the various parts of the narrative are placed side by side, it is perfectly obvious that Isaac's attempt to give the birthright blessing to Esau was contrary to God's expressed intent. Although this in no way excuses Rebekah and Jacob for their trickery, it does clarify the fact that they did not manage to obtain something to which Jacob had no right. Jacob had a divine right to that blessing. But Rebekah and Jacob should have left the bestowal of that blessing in the hands of God in the faith that He would provide.

27:1–4 *When Isaac was old and his eyes were so weak that he could no longer see, he called for Esau his older son and said to him, ''My son.''*

''Here I am,'' he answered.

Isaac said, ''I am now an old man and don't know the day of my death. Now then, get your weapons–your quiver and bow–and go out to the open country to hunt some wild game for me. Prepare me the kind of tasty food I like and bring it to me to eat, so that I may give you my blessing before I die.''

The narrative begins with a description of Isaac's failing eyesight in his old age, to the extent that he could no longer see. We are not told, at this point, how old Isaac was at the time. In 27:46 we are told that Esau was already married. When we compare 26:34 with 25:26, we notice that Isaac was 100 years old when Esau was married. The events recorded here must be placed considerably later.

When we compare 41:46–47; 45:6; 47:9, we learn that Joseph was born when Jacob was 91 years old. When we relate this fact to 30:25 and 29:20, 27, we see that this birth took place in the 14th year of Jacob's stay with Laban. Thus when Jacob fled from Esau he was 77. This would fix Isaac's age at the time of these happenings at 137. Obviously, at that age he was showing some serious signs of weakness because of his advanced age.

From 35:28 we learn that Isaac lived to be 180. Naturally, Isaac had no way of knowing that the Lord was going to add another 43 years to his life. He had begun to feel, with his failing eyesight, that the end of his days was approaching. In the light of this awareness he decided that it was time to bestow the birthright blessing on his oldest son. (Regarding the nature of the birthright blessing, see our treatment of Genesis 9:25–27. In this case there is the added factor that the birthright blessing included the Covenant promise that had been given to Abraham and that had been confirmed to Isaac.)

That Isaac intended to give this special blessing to his oldest son would be completely understandable if there had been no specific direction to the contrary. But God had definitely revealed to Rebekah that the elder son would serve the younger (25:23). It would be unthinkable to feel that Rebekah had not informed her husband of this revelation from God. Therefore, we must assume that Isaac, motivated by his preference for Esau and his wild game (25:28), decided to bestow the blessing on his elder son contrary to the divine revelation. It is hard to believe that Isaac really wanted the Covenant blessing of Abraham to go to this indifferent hunter who was married to two heathen women, and who had already caused him considerable grief (26:35). Just what the aging Isaac had in mind is difficult to determine. It is clear, however, that Isaac gave in to his own weakness for Esau and thereby flaunted the expressed revelation of God.

In verse 4 we find an unusual expression, ''That my soul may bless you.'' Our translators have rendered this simply, ''That I may give you my blessing.'' This is a possible translation, but I would suggest that the statement should be a bit stronger. I have therefore chosen to translate it, "that I may bless you with my whole heart." Isaac asked Esau to bring him some wild game and to prepare it just the way he relished it. This expression of Esau's love for his father would in turn set the stage for Isaac's wholeheartedly bestowing his blessing on his favorite son.

27:5–10 *Now Rebekah was listening as Isaac spoke to his son Esau. When Esau left for the open country to hunt game and bring it back, Rebekah said to her son Jacob, "Look, I overheard your father say to your brother Esau, 'Bring me some game and prepare me some tasty food to eat, so that I may give you my blessing in the presence of the LORD before I die.' Now my son, listen carefully and do what I tell you: Go out to the flock and bring me two choice young goats, so I can prepare some tasty food for your father, just the way he likes it. Then take it to your father to eat, so that he may give you his blessing before he dies."*

Rebekah overheard this conversation between Isaac and Esau. As soon as Esau left to go hunting, she called Jacob to discuss with him a plan she had conceived. She told him to get a few choice goats from the flock. She would make of these a tasty meal, the kind she knew Isaac enjoyed. Jacob would then bring this dish to Isaac, posing as Esau, and Jacob would receive the blessing from his blind father. Thus Rebekah intended to nullify Isaac's plan, which he had kept from her. Although Rebekah undoubtedly was concerned about the revelation God had given to her about her two sons, this method of bringing it to pass was definitely wrong. Also, her motivation was influenced, undoubtedly, by her motherly favoritism for her younger son. This made the whole plan questionable.

The expression, "in the presence of the LORD," which she ascribes to Isaac's instruction to Esau, indicates that Rebekah definitely was thinking about the divine revelation regarding the one who was to receive the special blessing. How sad it is that she did not then also leave the carrying out of that divine pronouncement in God's hands, instead of trying to achieve it by her own deceitful scheme.

27:11–13 *Jacob said to Rebekah his mother, "But my brother Esau is a hairy man, and I'm a man with smooth skin. What if my father touches me? I would appear to be tricking him and would bring down a curse on myself rather than a blessing."*

His mother said to him, "My son, let the curse fall on me. Just do what I say; go and get them for me."

Jacob immediately raised some objections to the plan his mother proposed. He seemed to have no scruples about the deceit involved, but he was afraid of the consequences if the plan should prove to be unsuccessful. He reminded his mother that Esau was a hairy man while he himself was smooth-skinned. If Isaac would touch him and discover his deceit, he might well bring a curse upon Jacob's head instead of the blessing his mother and he sought. But Rebekah reassured him and agreed to take full responsibility for what might happen. Jacob was to leave it all in her hands.

27:14–23 *So he went and got them and brought them to his mother, and she prepared some tasty food, just the way his father liked it. Then Rebekah took the best clothes of Esau her older son, which she had in the house, and put them on her younger son Jacob. She also covered his hands and the smooth part of his neck with the goatskins. Then she handed to her son Jacob the tasty food and the bread she had made.*

He went to his father and said, "My father."

"Yes, my son," he answered. "Who is it?"

Jacob said to his father, "I am Esau, your firstborn. I have done as you told me. Please sit up and eat some of my game so that you may give me your blessing."

Isaac asked his son, "How did you find it so quickly, my son?"

"The Lord your God gave me success," he replied.

Then Isaac said to Jacob, "Come near so I can touch you, my son, to know whether you really are my son Esau or not."

Jacob went close to his father Isaac, who touched him and said, "The voice is the voice of Jacob, but the hands are the hands of Esau." He did not recognize him, for his hands were hairy like those of his brother Esau; so he blessed him.

Rebekah's plan was now put into action. The tasty meat dish was prepared and Jacob was disguised as effectively as possible. He put on Esau's clothes, and his smooth hands were covered with the skin of the goats. Thus disguised, he carried the tasty dish into his father's room.

In reply to Isaac's question, "Who is it?" Jacob asserted that he was indeed Esau and that he had prepared a tasty dish for his father. He invited his father to sit up and to eat of the meat and then asked him to bestow the coveted blessing. Isaac was apparently a bit suspicious and expressed his amazement at the speed with which the wild game had been brought in. Jacob cleverly replied that this was the special favor of God on his mission. It is interesting that Jacob here used the expression, "the Lord *your* God," and not "my" God. Must we conclude from this that, under the circumstances, Jacob hesitated to refer to God as "his God"? Or was this an attempt on his part to try to imitate the irreligious Esau?

Isaac's uncertainty, however, was not wholly removed. He asked Jacob to come closer to him so that he could feel him to make sure he was actually Esau. When Isaac felt the hair of the goats that had been fixed to

acob's hands, he made his famous declaration, "The voice is the voice of
acob, but the hands are the hands of Esau." Although the blind man's
loubts had not been fully alleviated, Rebekah's plan had succeeded in
ringing him to his decision to proceed with the blessing.

27:24–29 *"Are you really my son Esau?" he asked.*
"I am," he replied.
*Then he said, "My son, bring me some of your game to eat, so that I may give
you my blessing."*
Jacob brought it to him and he ate; and he brought some wine and he drank.
Then his father Isaac said to him, "Come here, my son, and kiss me."
*So he went to him and kissed him. When Isaac caught the smell of his clothes, he
blessed him and said,*
*"Ah, the smell of my son is like the smell of a field that the LORD has blessed. May
God give you of heaven's dew and of earth's richness—an abundance of grain and
new wine. May nations serve you and peoples bow down to you. Be lord over your
brothers, and may the sons of your mother bow down to you. May those who curse
you be cursed and those who bless you be blessed."*

Isaac had one last question, "Are you really my son Esau?" When he
received an affirmative answer, he asked for the food that had been prepared in order that he might proceed with bestowing the blessing. Jacob set
the food before his father and also gave him some wine to drink. In doing
so he came close to his father and also gave him a kiss of greeting. Isaac
then smelled the distinctive odor of Esau's clothes, and thereupon pronounced the blessing.

He began the blessing by musing about the smell of the fields that the
Lord had blessed. This obviously referred to Esau's love for the wilderness. He then proceeded to speak of abundance of harvests of grain and
wine, which really were not Esau's area of interest. He made special
mention of "heaven's dew" that was so important for the raising of crops
in that arid country. He spoke of fertile soil that was needed for abundant
harvests.

He then moved on to predict what position his son and his descendants
would hold. It is noteworthy that "lordship" is here predicted, not only
over other peoples but also over his own brothers. Thus the use of the
plural when Isaac had only two sons suggests that the reference is to a
broader group of kindred. It should be remembered that the blessing of
25:23 mentioned that "one people will be stronger than the other." Although Isaac intended to give this position of rulership to Esau, he now
bestowed it upon Jacob, just as it had been in the original pronouncement,
"the elder shall serve the younger."

The blessing closed with a repetition of the promise made to Abraham in 12:3 (see our interpretation of that verse). "May those who curse you be cursed and those who bless you be blessed." In making this pronouncement Isaac was inspired by the Holy Spirit. Although he thought he was blessing Esau, the words that came from his mouth were intended for Jacob, by divine revelation. This is evident from the reference to abundant crops. Thus Jacob is blessed with the blessing that God Himself had ordained for him. This did not happen, it should be emphasized, because of Jacob's deceit. It should be seen, rather, as happening in spite of Jacob's deplorable method of acquiring this blessing. Thus we see that God can fulfill His own purposes in spite of all kinds of human sins and errors. On the other hand, this does not mean that the sinful actions of men which serve to achieve God's appointed ends are thereby any less sinful. Sin remains sin. As is evident from the ensuing history, such sin will receive its deserved punishment.

27:30–38 *After Isaac finished blessing him and Jacob had scarcely left his father's presence, his brother Esau came in from hunting. He too prepared some tasty food and brought it to his father. Then he said to him, "My father, sit up and eat some of my game, so that you may give me your blessing."*

His father Isaac asked him, "Who are you?"

"I am your son," he answered, "your firstborn, Esau."

Isaac trembled violently and said, "Who was it, then, that hunted game and brought it to me? I ate it just before you came and I blessed him—and indeed he will be blessed!"

When Esau heard his father's words, he burst out with a loud and bitter cry and said to his father, "Bless me—me too, my father!"

But he said, "Your brother came deceitfully and took your blessing."

Esau said, "Isn't he rightly named Jacob? He has deceived me these two times: He took my birthright, and now he's taken my blessing!" Then he asked, "Haven't you reserved any blessing for me?"

Isaac answered Esau, "I have made him lord over you and have made all his relatives his servants, and I have sustained him with grain and new wine. So what can I possibly do for you, my son?"

Esau said to his father, "Do you have only one blessing, my father? Bless me too, my father!" Then Esau wept aloud.

Isaac had finished speaking and Jacob had barely left the scene when Esau returned from his hunt. He also had prepared a tasty meal and now brought it to his father, with his request for the blessing. Isaac's immediate question, naturally, was, "Who are you?" When Esau told him who he was Isaac realized he had been deceived. The old man was very upset and trembled and cried out, "Who was it, then . . . ?" He told Esau what had happened and that he had given the imposter the blessing and that this could not be changed. At this Esau broke out in a bitter cry and begged his father to give him a blessing also. By this time Isaac was fully aware of what had happened and Jacob was specifically named as the one who had deceitfully received the blessing. The Hebrew word *ya'aqōb* can be understood as a verb form that means "he deceives." Esau, therefore, bitterly declared that his brother had been rightly named "the deceiver." Twice he had deceived him, first when he cajoled him into selling the birthright, and now when he had secured the blessing by deceit. That this was not the intent of the parents when they named Jacob must be clear. What we have here then is an instance of the use of a name similar to that which we met in the case of Nabal (see our discussion under Gen. 11:9). It obviously did not occur to Esau that he himself had shown the greatest of disdain for the birthright blessing (see 25:32–34). Now he considers himself to be the one who was mistreated.

Esau continued to beg his father for a blessing. Isaac responded by pointing out the nature of the blessing he had already pronounced on Jacob, with the question, "What can I possibly do for you" after that? Isaac's attitude at this point strongly suggests that he realized he had been wrong in his effort to bestow the birthright blessing on Esau. He seemed to imply that God Himself had seen to it that the blessing had gone to Jacob. But Esau resorted to weeping aloud as he pleaded with his father to give him a blessing also.

27:39, 40 *His father Isaac answered him, "Your dwelling will be away from the earth's richness, away from the dew of heaven above. You will live by the sword and you will serve your brother. But when you grow restless, you will throw his yoke from off your neck."*

Isaac was finally persuaded and then pronounced a separate blessing on Esau. Again inspired by the Spirit of God, he predicted the lot of Esau and his descendants. Esau's dwelling would be away from the fertile farm land and he would not be favored with the abundant dew. Actually, the mountain country that the descendants of Esau later occupied was largely unproductive and lacking in moisture. As a result the Edomites made their living primarily by raiding caravans that traveled through their territory and by poaching on neighboring countries who were better supplied with food. Thus the Edomites lived by the sword.

As far as the relationship of Esau's descendants to the descendants of Jacob was concerned, Isaac repeated that "you will serve your brother." That yoke, however, was not to rest on the descendants of Esau without interruption. There would be times when the yoke would be eased and even thrown off. This did not imply that Edom would be completely liberated from the yoke of Israel, since this would be in conflict with the blessing to Jacob (see 25:23; 27:29). It means only that there would be times when Edom would rise to oppress Israel. Examples of this would be found during the reign of Joram, king of Judah (2 Kings 8:20–22; 2 Chron. 21:8–10) under Ahaz (2 Chron. 28:17); in the days of the Maccabees (1 Macc. 5:3) and finally, in the reigns of the Herods as kings of the Jews since the Herods were Edomites, both by blood and by temperament.

27. *Jacob's Flight From Esau's Fury* (27:41–28:9)

Verses 41–45 of chapter 27, like the first 40 verses of the chapter, are generally divided between "J" and "E" by those who split the sources. As alleged evidence for the mixing of these two sources it has been proposed that in verse 41 the hostility of Esau seems to be mentioned twice. First we are told that "Esau held a grudge against Jacob," and then we read of his determination to kill his brother. It would seem obvious, however, to an objective reader, that the latter flowed naturally from the former.

Critics also argue that the statement in verse 45, "When your brother is no longer angry," is a repetition of what we read in verse 44, "until your brother's fury subsides." But this form of repetition is characteristic of Hebrew narrative style, and therefore offers no evidence for more than one source.

The section from 27:46–28:9 is generally ascribed to "P." It is argued that this section includes certain expressions which supposedly are characteristic of "P," but it is also charged that this section offers a different account of the separation between Esau and Jacob. It is claimed that, according to this section, the two brothers parted company in full harmony with each other and there was no malice between them. Jacob, supposedly, received the blessing not by trickery and deceit but by being obedient to his father when Isaac urged Jacob to seek a wife among Rebekah's people in Haran. Esau, on the other hand, it is claimed, forfeited the birthright by marrying two Hittite women. Esau, moreover, was not at all disturbed by this, but tried to remove to some degree the offense, which had caused his parents grief, by marrying a third wife who was a daughter of Ishmael. According to this interpretation, Esau remained content in his parental home until Jacob returned and then later moved to Seir since Canaan was not large enough to contain both families (36:6–8).

We need not comment here about the stylistic characteristics that supposedly point to a specific source. The presentation of what took place, however, is nothing more than an artful contrivance. When this passage is ead without preconceived prejudices, it is obvious that Jacob left for Paddan Aram to escape from Esau's anger and vengeance. Although Isaac was not aware of this, since Rebekah did not share her motives with him, her whole plan was conceived in order to get Jacob safely out of the country for she had been made aware of Esau's threat to kill his brother. The idea of getting a wife for Jacob from her own people was her method of achieving her goal to save Jacob's life until Esau's anger would subside. She found it easy, moreover, to convince Isaac of the advisability of Jacob's departure on the grounds that he could then secure a godly wife.

Generally 27:46 is ascribed to the redactor and this weakens the connection between 27:41–45 and 28:1–9. But there is no firm basis for thus ascribing this verse. The blessing that Jacob received before he departed was no more than a confirmation of what had been pronounced in 27:27–29. We will discuss 36:6–8 when we reach that point in the commentary. It should be noted that many of the scholars who hold, in principle, to the theory of divided sources admit that there is no essential conflict between the two sections of this narrative. This admission, moreover, removes the primary ground for dividing this material.

27:41–45 *Esau held a grudge against Jacob because of the blessing his father had given him. He said to himself, "The days of mourning for my father are near; then I will kill my brother Jacob."*

When Rebekah was told what her older son Esau had said, she sent for her younger son Jacob and said to him, "Your brother Esau is consoling himself with the thought of killing you. Now then, my son, do what I say: Flee at once to my brother Laban in Haran. Stay with him for a while until your brother's fury subsides. When your brother is no longer angry with you and forgets what you did to him, I'll send word for you to come back from there. Why should I lose both of you in one day?"

The blessing bestowed on Jacob became a source of increasing aggravation to Esau. He became so bitter about the whole development that he determined to kill his brother. To spare his father further grief he decided to wait with his plan to murder his brother until after his father's death. Esau did not keep his plan a secret but obviously discussed it with someone and word of his plan inadvertently came to Rebekah.

On learning of Esau's threat, she immediately devised a plan to save Jacob's life. She called for her favorite son, and informed him about what she had learned. She urged him to go to Haran and to stay with her brother Laban until Esau's anger had subsided. As she expressed it, the burden of her heart was that if Esau would indeed kill Jacob she would be deprived of both of her sons in one day. The obvious intent of this remark was that if

Esau committed murder justice would demand that Esau also be killed (Gen. 9:6).

27:46–28:5 *Then Rebekah said to Isaac, "I'm disgusted with living because of these Hittite women. If Jacob takes a wife from among the women of this land, from Hittite women like these, my life will not be worth living."*
So Isaac called for Jacob and blessed him and commanded him: "Do not marry a Canaanite woman. Go at once to Paddan Aram, to the house of your mother's father Bethuel. Take a wife for yourself there, from among the daughters of Laban your mother's brother. May God Almighty bless you and make you fruitful and increase your numbers until you become a community of peoples. May he give you and your descendants the blessing of Abraham, so that you may take possession of the land where you now live as an alien, the land God gave to Abraham." Then Isaac sent Jacob on his way, and he went to Paddan Aram, to Laban son of Bethuel the Aramean, the brother of Rebekah, who was the mother of Jacob and Esau.

After her conversation with Jacob, Rebekah went to Isaac to convince him of the wisdom of her plan. She did not mention Esau's murder threat, however. She probably realized that Isaac would not have believed such a report about his beloved Esau. Moreover, even if he did accept it, the peace-loving Isaac would, no doubt, have considered a gentle reprimand to be adequate to restore peace to the family. Therefore, Rebekah used an entirely different approach in order to secure Isaac's approval for her plan to send Jacob away.

Rebekah reminded Isaac of the grief that had been caused by Esau's Hittite wives. She then threw up the specter of what life would become for her if Jacob also should marry one or more of these Hittite women: this would make life completely unbearable. Since Isaac shared her grief with respect to Esau's wives, her appeal struck a responsive chord with the elderly patriarch. He called Jacob to him and told him that he must not take a wife from among the Canaanites. Instead, he must go to Paddan Aram, to the household of Bethuel, and there seek out a wife from the family of Laban, his mother's brother. (Regarding the use of Paddan Aram, see the discussion under 25:20.)

The fact that Isaac now repeated the blessing he had given to Jacob earlier is wholly understandable. This blessing included the promise that God had given to Abraham and to his descendants. The line of those descendants was of utmost importance for the fulfillment of the promise, and thus seeking out a suitable wife for Jacob also was most significant. Therefore Isaac pronounced God's blessing on Jacob in his mission to seek a wife because this stood in close relationship to the promise made to Abraham and to Isaac. The details of this promise have been treated earlier ιn this commentary. The innumerable descendants were mentioned in 12:2; 13:16; 15:5; 17:2, 4–6, 16; 18:18; 22:17. Also, compare 26:4, 24.

The inclusion in this blessing of the promise of "a community of peoples" reminds us of 17:4–6, 16. In this connection the objection has been raised that Jacob's descendants never became more than one nation. Mention can be made of the twelve tribes of Israel, but this hardly fulfills the promise of "many nations." We must bear in mind that the covenant made with Abraham was a spiritual covenant. In Christ all nations would share in the blessings of Abraham and thus also of Jacob. (See our comments under 17:4–5.)

Mention has also been made of the land of Canaan in which Isaac and Jacob now lived as strangers. The inheritance of this land had been promised in 17:8; 13:14–17; 15:7, 18. (See also 26:3.)

It is noteworthy that Isaac made no mention of the deceit that Jacob had used in order to secure the blessing. No doubt Isaac was sensitive to the fact that he had not been without fault in this whole matter himself. He had tried to withhold the blessing from Jacob, even after God had announced that Jacob was the one who should receive it (25:23). Moreover, Isaac must have recognized that God had so directed the affairs of his household that, in spite of the deceit and jealousy that were present, God's purpose with respect to that blessing had been realized. In view of all of this, Isaac now determined that it would be best to remain silent about the sinful aspects of the whole process of bestowing that blessing. So Jacob is sent forth on his way to Paddan Aram.

28:6–9 *Now Esau learned that Isaac had blessed Jacob and had sent him to Paddan Aram to take a wife from there, and that when he blessed him he commanded him, "Do not marry a Canaanite woman," and that Jacob had obeyed his father and mother and had gone to Paddan Aram. Esau then realized how displeasing the Canaanite women were to his father Isaac; so he went to Ishmael and married Mahalath, the sister of Nebaioth, and daughter of Ishmael son of Abraham, in addition to the wives he already had.*

When Esau learned what had happened and he became aware of the reasons why his father had sent Jacob to Paddan Aram to get a wife, and in so doing had blessed Jacob, he began to rethink his own actions. He now realized how grievously displeasing his own action of marrying two Hittite women had been to his father. Whether Isaac had frankly discussed this matter with Esau we do not know. At any rate, Esau now decided to alleviate his father's displeasure in this regard by marrying a daughter of Ishmael, by the name of Mahalath. This woman at least met the requirement of being a descendant of Abraham. Whether she held to Abraham's religion was probably a matter of no concern to Esau, and he still did not understand the nature of Isaac's grief in this whole matter. His mother's displeasure also was apparently of no concern to him.

28. *Jacob at Bethel* (28:10–22)

Those who divide the sources generally ascribe this section to the two sources "J" and "E." With a few variations on minor points, the division is usually made as follows: "J"—verses 13–16, 19; "E"—verses 10–12, 17–18, 20–22. The primary basis for this allocation is the change in the use of the name for God from "Jahweh" to "Elohim." Also stressed by the critics is the alleged parallel between Jacob's vow in verses 20–22 and God's promise in verses 13–15. This charge, however, carries no weight at all. Jacob's vow simply stated that when God had fulfilled His promise, Jacob would perform what he had pledged at the close of verse 21 and in verse 22. There is no doubt or uncertainty in Jacob's statement. It rather constituted a believing acceptance of God's promise and his own response in the form of a sacred commitment. It is noteworthy that the name "LORD" is used in verse 21, even though this verse is supposed to be an Elohist passage. The critics get around this by ascribing this statement to a redactor's change. We cannot accept such playing with the text of Scripture.

28:10 *Jacob left Beersheba and set out for Haran.*

After the interlude dealing with Esau's marriage, the biblical narrative returns to Jacob. A specific incident that took place on his journey to Paddan Aram is recorded with some detail.

Jacob left Beersheba where, according to 26:23–25, Isaac had established his residence. The Hebrew text says that "he went to Haran." Our translators have correctly rendered this as he "set out for Haran." The event that is recorded in the following verses took place while he was still within the borders of Canaan.

28:11 *When he reached a certain place, he stopped for the night because the sun had set. Taking one of the stones there, he put it under his head and lay down to sleep.*

Since Bethel is about 80-90 km. (about 150 miles) from Beersheba, Jacob must have been on the way for a few days when he chose this place for an overnight stop.

In the Hebrew the definite article is used with the word "place." This has led some interpreters to conclude that this was a well-known place.

Some have even gone so far, on the strength of the use of the definite article, as to call it a "holy place." This results, however, from a misunderstanding of the use of the definite article in Hebrew, for in many instances it is used where we would use the indefinite article. A classic example of this Hebrew usage can be found in Amos 5:19. In that verse the definite article is used for "the lion," "the bear," "the house," and "the snake." Our translators have rendered all of these terms with the indefinite "a," and correctly so. In the same way, our translators in this verse have used "a certain place," thereby indicating that it was an otherwise undesignated place at which Jacob decided to spend the night. There is then no basis linguistically for reading something special or something holy into the use of the definite article in this instance. At this particular spot Jacob made himself as comfortable as possible, using a stone as a pillow on which to recline.

28:12–15 *He had a dream in which he saw a stairway resting on the earth, with its top reaching to heaven, and the angels of God were ascending and descending on it. There above it stood the Lord, and he said: "I am the Lord, the God of your father Abraham and the God of Isaac. I will give you and your descendants the land on which you are lying. Your descendants will be like the dust of the earth, and you will spread out to the west and to the east, to the north and to the south. All peoples on earth will be blessed through you and your offspring. I am with you and will watch over you wherever you go, and I will bring you back to this land. I will not leave you until I have done what I have promised you."*

While Jacob was sleeping, he had a dream. He saw a ladder, or stairway, which reached from the earth to heaven. Angels were ascending and descending this ladder, and at the top stood the Lord Himself. The Lord presented Himself to Jacob as the God of Abraham and of Isaac. He promised Jacob that all the blessings He had promised to Abraham and to Isaac would be bestowed upon him and upon his descendants. Once again, these blessings were enumerated: possession of the land of Canaan (see 13:14–17; 15:7, 18; 17:8; 26:3); innumerable descendants (see 12:2; 13:16; 15:5; 17:2, 4–6, 16; 18:18; 22:17; 26:4, 24); and that all nations of the earth would be blessed through his seed (see 12:3; 18:18; 22:18; 26:4). What had been promised to Jacob even before his birth (25:23) and had been confirmed to him in the blessing pronounced by his father (27:27–29; 28:3–4) now was promised to him by God Himself.

Besides the repetition of the covenant promises, God also assured Jacob that He would go with him, would take care of him, and would prosper him in this journey and bring him back to his homeland. Then the Lord added the overarching promise, "I will not leave you until I have done what I have promised you."

28:16, 17 *When Jacob awoke from his sleep, he thought, "Surely the Lord is in this place, and I was not aware of it." He was afraid and said, "How awesome is this place! This is none other than the house of God; this is the gate of heaven."*

When Jacob awoke, he was overwhelmed with a deep sense of awe. What a remarkable place this had become for him! He was not aware that this campsite he had chosen had become a place of sacred importance. This was a place where God was present in a very special sense. This was "the house of God," "the gate of heaven." This statement of Jacob has been misunderstood in two ways. On the one hand, it has been charged that this indicates that Jacob had a limited, localized concept of God, or that God's revelation, at least, was limited to specific localities. This is not tenable since God almighty, the God of his father's blessing (28:3), certainly had given Jacob abundant reason to believe in the infinite greatness of God. On the other hand, it has been charged that Jacob's amazement stemmed from his conviction that it would be impossible to meet God away from his parental home and the places where his father had built altars. In reply it should be observed that Jacob certainly had no doubts, as expressed in his words, that this was indeed a very special place for the presence of God.

When Jacob's words are seen in their true perspective, they indicate that, although Jacob does not deny the omnipresence of God, in his own experience this place had a special significance for him. It was here that he had been brought into the very presence of God and had received a revelation from God that was especially important for him at this time in his life. It was here that he had his first clear communication with God. Although we may raise some questions about Jacob's theology, as to whether he was altogether clear on the infinity and omnipresence of God, the biblical narrative simply records the experience he had and his immediate reaction to it. To conclude from this that the Holy Scriptures here teach a limited concept of God's Being is altogether facetious.

28:18, 19 *Early the next morning Jacob took the stone he had placed under his head and set it up as a pillar and poured oil on top of it. He called that place Bethel, though the city used to be called Luz.*

Jacob wanted to mark this spot with a suitable token. Therefore, he took the stone he had used for a pillow and set it on end as a memorial or marker. He then dedicated this memorial by pouring oil on it. This stone has given rise to a great deal of discussion, both in Jewish tradition and in biblical exposition.

One tradition dwells on the fact that setting this stone on end was a demonstration of superhuman strength on Jacob's part. However, nothing in the text suggests that the stone was of such great size that it required enormous strength to move it. The fact that Jacob used it for his pillow would suggest that it was a rock of normal size that could readily be moved by one person.

Others have charged that the upright stone was intended as an object of worship, a sacred stone. A similar expression is used in other passages, however, to designate a memorial to some event or person without any suggestion of this becoming an object of worship. For example, we see a memorial to Jacob's covenant with Laban (Gen. 31:45); the gravestone of Rachel (Gen. 35:20); the memorial to Absalom (2 Sam. 18:18). It is true that the upright stone or pillar (Hebrew *massēbâ*), became a common object of worship for the Canaanites. But such objects of worship were strictly forbidden for the Israelites (see Exod. 23:24; 34:13; Lev. 26:1; Deut. 7:5; 12:3; 16:22). It must be granted that Israel did not always obey this commandment (see 1 Kings 14:23; 2 Kings 17:10; 18:4; 23:14; 2 Chron. 14:3; 31:1; Hos. 10:1–2; Micah 5:13). But this does not warrant interpreting Jacob's stone at Bethel as a ''sacred stone'' and then deducing from that a certain approval of the use of such objects of worship during this period of Israel's history.

So also, there is no evidence that the pouring of oil on the stone had some religious significance for Jacob as some kind of offering. All we have here is the placing and designation of a memorial stone or a marker.

Jacob also memorialized this place by giving it the name ''Bethel,'' which means ''house of God.'' In this way he gave expression to the deep impression that this experience made on him (v. 17).

At this point an explanatory note is added in the text, ''though the city used to be called Luz.'' The narrative suggests that Jacob spent the night out in the desert country, rather than in a city. What we have here, no doubt, is that the place where Jacob spent the night was near the city of Luz. Originally, only that immediate spot was called Bethel. Later, however, this name was also given to the city. As a consequence, we find Bethel and Luz distinguished in Joshua 16:2, while they are identified in other passages such as Genesis 35:6; Joshua 18:13; Judges 1:23. We had a similar situation in the case of Beersheba, which was first applied to a well and then later became the name of the city that was nearby. (See our discussion of 21:31 and the introduction to 26:1–33.) Moreover, in earlier references, such as 12:8 and 13:3, the name ''Bethel'' is used in anticipation of its later naming, just as was done with "Beersheba" in 21:14.

It appears that Jacob was moving to the north from his father's home in Beersheba. This can be explained by the fact that at certain times of the year the Syrian desert was impassable on foot.

28:20–22 *Then Jacob made a vow, saying, "If God will be with me and will watch over me on this journey I am taking and will give me food to eat and clothes to wear so that I return safely to my father's house, then the LORD will be my God. This stone that I have set up as a pillar will be God's house, and of all that you give me I will give you a tenth."*

Jacob also made a vow that he would keep after the Lord had fulfilled His promise to him (v. 15). This is the first time we read of a vow in the Old Testament. Such a vow was not the fruit of doubt that God would keep His promise (see our discussion of v. 9). It was, rather, an expression of thanksgiving for the help God promised to provide. When compared with the promise God had given him (vv. 13–14), Jacob's expectation was remarkably modest. All he asked for was God's protection on his journey, food to eat and clothes to wear, and a safe return to his father's house.

The content of Jacob's vow is also worthy of note. He began by saying, "then the LORD will be my God." We would be inclined to say that there was nothing significant about that statement. Certainly, we are supposed to serve God and honor Him in all circumstances and at all times. This was Jacob's responsibility before the fulfillment of God's promise as well as after. A few interpreters, therefore, want to make these words part of the conditional statement that begins in verse 20 with "If God will be with me . . . ." Then Jacob's commitment would begin with verse 22. This presents some real grammatical difficulties, however, so most interpreters read this as the opening statement of Jacob's commitment to God. Some of the critics try to remove the statement altogether by branding it as a later insertion into the text.

We are convinced that the statement should remain just as it is in the text and in our translation of the verse. It then indicates that Jacob had not yet reached the point of unconditional commitment to God as his God. It evidences that he is still somewhat selfish in his service of God. He has not yet fully surrendered his life to God's service. He does not reach that point of dedication until later (see 32:24–30). We have already noted that in verses 16–17 Jacob's commitment to God was somewhat deficient.

What this vow declares, further, "This stone that I have set up as a pillar will be God's house," has caused even more discussion among biblical scholars. There has been a strong effort to establish the fact that these

108

words suggest a kind of "fetishism" which believes that deity is incorporated in this or that object. In this case it is the stone that represents "God" for Jacob. It is claimed that, although the narrator has tried to remove this fetishism from the account, it is still clearly obvious. This interpretation, however, loses sight of the fact that Jacob declares that this *will be* the house of God at some time in the future. Fetishism would demand that this stone itself, on the basis of Jacob's experience there, would be a sacred object at that moment. This is not indicated in the narrative.

Opinions differ widely regarding the term "God's house." One interpretation holds that Jacob declares that he will honor this place as a dwelling place of God. This will not do because Jacob did not speak about the place but about the stone. Others think that this stone would be used to build a house of God. The words of Jacob are then related to the "holy place" that Jeroboam later built at Bethel, for the worship of the golden calves. But this is reading more into these words than they actually say.

This leaves a third possibility. We hold that the term "house of God" must be taken in a broader sense as being somewhat symbolic. The stone would always serve to remind Jacob of God's favor and blessing and would inspire him to worship and praise God. This would also harmonize with what we read in 35:7 when Jacob fulfilled his vow and built an altar to the Lord at this place. Thus the stone was a memorial with great religious implications and inspiration for Jacob in years to come.

Many of the critics see a second meaning to the name "Bethel" as given here. They want to use this as justification for ascribing this passage to two sources. The text, however, in no way relates the term "house of God" to the name "Bethel."

Finally, Jacob vowed that he would give God a tenth of all he would acquire. Note that he now changed to the second person and addressed God directly. Tithing was an ancient practice, and we discussed it earlier under 14:20 where we read of Abraham giving a tithe to Melchizedek.

29. *Jacob in Haran* (29:1–30:43)

Those who divide the sources ascribe these two chapters to an interweaving of the parallel records of "J" and "E." The only exceptions to this are 29:24, 28b, 29, and 30:4a and 9b, which are assigned to "P." In more recent years some scholars have also given the so-called "fourth source" some credit for these chapters. We need not go into a lengthy discussion of the grounds that have been advanced for this splintering of these chapters. The entire narrative forms an obvious unit. Even some of the advocates of dividing the sources will grant this. The primary basis for dividing the sources is again the names used for God. We have repeatedly discussed this and pointed out the weakness of this basis. Here also there is the very striking instance in 30:18, which is ascribed to "E" because the name "Elohim" is used for God, where we find the characteristic Jahwistic word for "slave woman." This confirms, once again, that assigning a given passage to a specific source on the basis of the use of one word, even if that word is a name for God, is completely untenable.

There is, however, one item in this passage that appears to give strength to the recognition of the "fourth source." A seemingly natural interpretation of 29:20–21 would conclude that Jacob married Leah and Rachel after having been in Haran seven years. This, the critics feel, would have been impossible. They argue that Joseph was born at the close of the second seven-year period, according to 30:25–26. Thus the 12 children who are introduced in 29:31–30:24 would have been born in a period of less than seven years. This, the critics feel, would have been impossible. They therefore ascribe the reference to two seven-year periods to the so-called "fourth source," in distinction from the source that tells about the birth of all those children.

The difficulty presented here is a formidable one. Some scholars who deny the theory of divided sources suggest that in this case we should probably think of two different traditions. The one tradition would take its departure from the marriage occurring seven years after Jacob's arrival and the children being born during the second seven-year period plus the six years Jacob stayed in Haran beyond this point. The other tradition, according to these scholars, would hold that Jacob married soon after his arrival and that the children were born during the 14 years Jacob worked for Laban. It is suggested that both of these traditions were introduced into the text. This would explain why there is some chronological inconsistency here. Some fine conservative scholars accept the position that the marriage took place at the beginning of the first seven-year period. They then try to remove the further difficulties in various ways.

As we mentioned above, the most natural reading of this passage would place the marriage after the first seven-year period. The statement in 29:21, "my time is completed," can hardly refer to anything else than Jacob's term of service. The question we must ask frankly is whether it is actually impossible to fit the birth of this many children into the space of seven years. We should bear in mind that these eleven children were conceived by four different women. Certainly we need not insist that all of these children were born in the exact chronological order as they are introduced in the text. It is altogether possible, and even probable, that the pregnancies of these four women overlapped and this would, of course, reduce the time required in a marked way. Moreover, it is likely that Rachel did not wait very long before giving her slave girl to Jacob as a secondary wife, after she learned of Leah's prompt pregnancy. She may well have resorted to this as soon as Judah was born to Leah. The narrative also suggests that Leah's four children were born in rapid succession so this could have been accomplished in less than four years. Moreover, the lapse in time during which Leah failed to become pregnant probably was not very long either. With the strong spirit of competition between these two sisters in the matter of producing children, Leah probably gave her slave girl to Jacob soon after she learned she had not become pregnant again. In the light of all of this, it is possible that Joseph was born within that seven-year period. This would leave Dinah, but the text specifically states that she was born some time later. Thus the birth of Jacob's children can be harmonized with the data as it is given in the text, and this does not offer a substantial basis for ascribing this material to more than one source.

29:1–3 *Then Jacob continued on his journey and came to the land of the eastern peoples. There he saw a well in the field, with three flocks of sheep lying near it because the flocks were watered from that well. The stone over the mouth of the well was large. When all the flocks were gathered there, the shepherds would roll the stone away from the well's mouth and water the sheep. Then they would return the stone to its place over the mouth of the well.*

The inspired narrator now tells us about the continuation of Jacob's journey after he left Bethel. A few scholars have made quite a point of the Hebrew expression that literally reads, "then Jacob lifted up his feet." It is argued that this expression indicates that Jacob started his journey at this point. It is then held that the material about the incident at Bethel is an insertion into the text from another source. It is claimed that the expression has the same connotation as "he lifted up his voice." This is really unconvincing. To be sure, to lift up the voice indicates a beginning of an expression of praise, but it certainly does not imply that there could not have been an expression of praise previously. Thus the expression in verse 1 can correctly be translated, "Then Jacob continued on his journey," as our translators have rendered it.

The direction Jacob took is indicated by the term, "to the land of the eastern peoples." This is a very broad term. Sometimes it refers to all the territory east of the Jordan River (Judg. 6:3, 33; Isa. 11:14; Jer. 49:28). It is also used to designate the Syrian desert east of Damascus and that is probably its intent here. It appears, then, that Jacob traveled north from Bethel to the area of Damascus and then headed northeast to Haran. It should be noted that Hebrew narration does not give as precise designations for compass directions as are common today. Thus, the term "east" may indicate that he traveled northeast or even north-northeast.

We are told nothing else about the journey itself. The next episode finds Jacob in the area of Haran (29:4), and there his attention fell on a well with three flocks of sheep lying nearby. It has been noted that this well probably was not the same one mentioned in 24:11ff., for there certainly would be several wells in the immediate proximity to a city as prominent as Haran. The following details are given regarding this particular well. The opening was covered with a large stone. It was customary to wait until all the flocks had gathered at the scene before the stone was removed, and after all the flocks had been watered the well would again be covered. Such community wells can still be found in Eastern countries.

That the stone was large enough to cover the well does not necessarily imply that it would require superhuman strength for one man to remove it, as Jacob did according to 29:10. Usually two or three men would remove the stone and replace it again. The fact that Jacob removed it alone would suggest that he possessed above average physical strength. (See also our comment under 28:18.)

29:4–8 *Jacob asked the shepherds, "My brothers, where are you from?"*
"We're from Haran," they replied.
He said to them, "Do you know Laban, Nahor's grandson?"
"Yes, we know him," they answered.
Then Jacob asked them, "Is he well?"
"Yes, he is," they said, "and here comes his daughter Rachel with the sheep."
"Look," he said, "the sun is still high; it is not time for the flocks to be gathered. Water the sheep and take them back to pasture."
"We can't," they replied, "until all the flocks are gathered and the stone has been rolled away from the mouth of the well. Then we will water the sheep."

Jacob spoke to the herders and asked whether they knew his uncle Laban and whether he was well. His questions were answered rather curtly but he did get the information he sought. The herders then added that at that very moment Rachel, Laban's daughter, was arriving with her father's flock.

But before Rachel arrived, Jacob had more communication with these shepherds. Since he himself was a shepherd, he expressed surprise that they brought their flocks to the well so early in the day. If the animals needed water they could bring them in for that purpose, but there would still be plenty of time to allow the flocks to graze. The shepherds, in reply, informed Jacob that the policy that had been agreed upon was that each one would wait until all the flocks had gathered, then the stone would be removed and all the flocks would be watered. Some have read this statement, "we can't," as indicating that it required the strength of all the shepherds to remove the stone. We do not accept this. We are convinced that this was just a matter of community agreement.

29:9–14a *While he was still talking with them, Rachel came with her father's sheep, for she was a shepherdess. When Jacob saw Rachel daughter of Laban, his mother's brother, and Laban's sheep, he went over and rolled the stone away from the mouth of the well and watered his uncle's sheep. Then Jacob kissed Rachel and began to weep aloud. He had told Rachel that he was a relative of her father and a son of Rebekah. So she ran and told her father.*

As soon as Laban heard the news about Jacob, his sister's son, he hurried to meet him. He embraced him and kissed him and brought him to his home, and there Jacob told him all these things. Then Laban said to him, "You are my own flesh and blood."

While Jacob was speaking to the shepherds, Rachel arrived at the well, because she had been assigned the duty of shepherdess of her father's flock. Jacob immediately saw an opportunity to make a favorable impression on the lovely Rachel and also on her father. Making use of his great physical strength, he removed the stone from the well and proceeded to water Laban's flock. As a stranger he was not bound by the local agreement and he did not hesitate to demonstrate his physical prowess in removing the large stone. Thereupon he introduced himself to his cousin Rachel, and she hurried home to share the exciting news with her father, Laban.

Thereupon, Laban hurried out to meet Jacob. He greeted his nephew in typical Eastern style and brought him to his home. We read that Jacob told him "all these things," but just what was included in this communication is difficult to determine. It probably referred, first of all, to the events at the well. Further, he must have told them about his family. This can be deduced from Laban's response, "You are my own flesh and blood." Jacob then stayed with Laban for a month.

29:14b–20 *After Jacob had stayed with him for a whole month, Laban said to him, "Just because you are a relative of mine, should you work for me for nothing? Tell me what your wages should be."*

Now Laban had two daughters; the name of the older was Leah, and the name of the younger was Rachel. Leah had weak eyes, but Rachel was lovely in form, and beautiful. Jacob was in love with Rachel and said, "I'll work for you seven years in return for your younger daughter Rachel."

Laban said, "It's better to give her to you than to some other man. Stay here with me." So Jacob served seven years to get Rachel, but they seemed like only a few days to him because of his love for her.

We have already come to know Laban as a shrewd, avaricious man (see 24:30). Laban soon recognized Jacob's great skill as a herdsman, so he sought to devise some way to keep this young man in his employ. To achieve this, Laban assumed the role of the beneficent uncle. He seemed to take for granted that Jacob would continue in his service but he now declared that he should be paid for his services. He asked Jacob what wages he should receive, probably hoping that his nephew would not be demanding. Jacob, however, had been continually mindful of his purpose for coming to Haran. Consequently, when Laban made his request, Jacob was ready with an immediate offer. He offered to work for his uncle Laban for seven years for the hand of Rachel, with whom he had fallen in love.

At this point the narrator includes some details about Laban's family that are necessary in order to understand what follows. Rachel was not the only daughter in the family. She had an older sister, Leah, who was afflicted with weak eyes. This was a serious handicap for a young lady in the East where lovely eyes were a mark of true beauty. Rachel, on the other hand, was blessed with a beautiful face and an attractive figure. Now Laban recognized the advantages he would gain by accepting Jacob's offer, for he would gain an outstanding young man who stemmed from his own kindred as a husband for his daughter. At the same time he would have the long-term service of an unusually capable herdsman. So the agreement was made. Jacob worked for seven years in order to gain his beloved Rachel as his wife. We read that the time seemed very brief to Jacob because of his great love for Rachel.

29:21–30 *Then Jacob said to Laban, "Give me my wife. My time is completed, and I want to lie with her."*

So Laban brought together all the people of the place and gave a feast. But when evening came, he took his daughter Leah and gave her to Jacob, and Jacob lay with her. And Laban gave his servant girl Zilpah to his daughter as her maidservant.

When morning came, there was Leah! So Jacob said to Laban, "What is this you have done to me? I served you for Rachel, didn't I? Why have you deceived me?"

Laban replied, "It is not our custom here to give the younger daughter in marriage before the older one. Finish out this daughter's bridal week; then we will give you the younger one also, in return for another seven years of work."

And Jacob did so. He finished out the week with Leah, and then Laban gave him his daughter Rachel to be his wife. Laban gave his servant girl Bilhah to his daughter Rachel as her maidservant. Jacob lay with Rachel also, and he loved Rachel more than Leah. And he worked for Laban another seven years.

At the end of the seven-year period Jacob asked Laban to let him have Rachel as his wife. Laban, of course, could not refuse this request. He called his friends and his neighbors to a feast in honor of his daughter's marriage, but he conceived a clever trick whereby he could keep the service of Jacob for another seven years. That this was his objective, and not merely marrying off his unattractive older daughter, is clear from the fact that the proposal that Jacob work for another seven years came from Laban.

Laban now took advantage of a custom of that time, namely, that the bride, completely veiled, would be brought in to her husband on the evening of the first day of the seven-day feast. Instead of Rachel, the tricky father gave Leah to Jacob as his bride. It is obvious that this could not have been arranged without Leah's willing cooperation. It is probably not true, however, that Leah had collaborated with her father in the whole plan, for young women had nothing to say in the choice of their husbands. They were simply ''given'' to a man as a wife. Leah can be faulted only for not informing Jacob about what was going on. At any rate, on the first night of the feast the marriage of Jacob and Leah, not Rachel, was consummated.

We are told that in the morning Jacob discovered that his new bride was not his beloved Rachel but her sister, Leah. Understandably, Jacob had some harsh words for his uncle Laban because of his deceit, but Laban had a ready answer. To give the younger daughter in marriage before the older one was not in keeping with their custom. Although this probably was true, it certainly did not excuse Laban. He should have told Jacob about this at the time they made their agreement with respect to Rachel. Laban deceitfully violated a formal contract.

Jacob, however, did not want to bring shame on the house of Laban by returning Leah to her father after he had sexually consummated the marriage with her. She was his legal wife. Undoubtedly Laban had anticipated that Jacob would honor this marriage even though it had not been his choice. Laban was now ready with a renewed proposition. Jacob was to complete the week of the marriage feast with Leah, and thereupon Laban would give him Rachel also. The only condition was that Jacob had to agree to work for his uncle for another seven years.

Jacob may have felt that being made a victim of Laban's trickery was a retribution for his own deception of his blind father. At any rate, he agreed to Laban's proposal, and a week later he married Rachel also. In this connection we read that he loved Rachel more than Leah. Thereupon Jacob served Laban as chief herdsman for another seven years.

Laban gave each of his daughters a slave woman to serve as a personal servant. To Leah he gave Zilpah and to Rachel, Bilhah. The names of these women are introduced at this point because they later played significant roles in Jacob's family life.

The kind of marriages into which Jacob entered were later specifically forbidden by Mosaic Law (Lev. 18:18), but this commandment had not yet been given in Jacob's day. His marriages were, however, in conflict with the creation ordinance that limited marriage to one man or one woman (Gen. 2:21–24).

29:31–35 *When the LORD saw that Leah was not loved, he opened her womb, but Rachel was barren. Leah became pregnant and gave birth to a son. She named him Reuben, for she said, "It is because the LORD has seen my misery. Surely my husband will love me now."*

She conceived again, and when she gave birth to a son she said, "Because the LORD heard that I am not loved, he gave me this one too." So she named him Simeon.

Again she conceived, and when she gave birth to a son she said, "Now at last my husband will become attached to me, because I have borne him three sons." So he was named Levi.

She conceived again, and when she gave birth to a son she said, "This time I will praise the LORD." So she named him Judah. Then she stopped having children.

To compensate for the lack of love Jacob showed for Leah, God blessed her with fertility while Rachel remained childless. In this we see both the mercy and the righteousness of God. His mercy was evident because Leah was certainly not without guilt with respect to this unhappy marriage relationship. God's righteousness was evident in that Jacob certainly was not justified in making Leah unhappy after he had accepted her as his wife.

In rapid succession Leah bore Jacob four sons. These were given the names Reuben, Simeon, Levi, and Judah. That these names were given by the mother is not an indication of a matriarchal society, as some have claimed (see our discussion under Gen. 4:1).

The statements that are made in conjunction with the naming of each of these sons do not express an etymological description of the names as such. The names are given, rather, in connection with a certain similarity in sound between the names themselves and certain words included in these statements. Thus the name of the first-born son was Reuben—Hebrew *re'ûbēn*. This sounds like the combination of two of the words Leah spoke, "seen"—Hebrew *rā'āh*, and "my misery"—Hebrew *be'onyî*. The name of the second son was Simeon—Hebrew *šimôn*. This has a sound similar to the word translated "heard"—Hebrew *šāma'*. The third name was Levi—Hebrew *lēwî*. This relates to the word translated "attached"—Hebrew *lāwāh*. The fourth son was Judah—Hebrew *yehûdâ*. This has the same sound as the word for "praise"—Hebrew *yādāh*. After the birth of this fourth son there was an interruption in Leah's prolificacy.

30:1–8 *When Rachel saw that she was not bearing Jacob any children, she became jealous of her sister. So she said to Jacob, "Give me children, or I'll die!"*

Jacob became angry with her and said, "Am I in the place of God, who has kept you from having children?"

Then she said, "Here is Bilhah, my maidservant. Sleep with her so that she can bear children for me and that through her I too can build a family."

So she gave him her servant Bilhah as a wife. Jacob slept with her, and she became pregnant and bore him a son. Then Rachel said, "God has vindicated me; he has listened to my plea and given me a son." Because of this she named him Dan.

Rachel's servant Bilhah conceived again and bore Jacob a second son. Then Rachel said, "I have had a great struggle with my sister, and I have won." So she named him Naphtali.

Leah's amazing fertility was, however, a source of deep jealousy on the part of Rachel. She confronted Jacob with the lament that if he didn't give her any children she would die. Jacob responded to her demands in anger, and impressed on Rachel that it was God who was withholding children from her and that he, as her husband, was not capable of playing God in this matter. Thereupon Rachel resorted to the same device Sarah had employed (16:2). She gave her slave girl, Bilhah, to Jacob for conjugal relationships in order that he might produce children by her.

In this connection Rachel used a very interesting expression when she said that Bilhah could bear children "on my knees." This expression, which also appears in Genesis 50:23, has been interpreted by some as a symbolic reference to the "adoption" of children. Although the expression does apply in this sense in some cases, it probably must be taken more literally here. Rachel actually wanted to participate in the process of the birth of the children of her slave girl. Rachel also used the expression Sarah had used, "that through her I too can build a family." (For the interpretation of this statement see our discussion of 16:2.)

Rachel's plan was soon effective and Jacob conceived two sons by Bilhah in rapid succession. Rachel assumed the role of mother and named the children, and the names have the same characteristics as those of Leah's children (see on page 116). The name of the first son was Dan, which in Hebrew has the same sound as the verb "vindicated"—Hebrew *dîn*. The second son was called Naphtali, which relates to the Hebrew word for "struggle"—*năptûlîm*. It should be remembered that when Rachel declared that God "vindicated" her through the birth of a son, this was Rachel's own feeling only and does not constitute a revelation from God. All that the Scripture tells us here is that this is what Rachel said. After what we learn about Rachel in 29:31, it would be difficult to interpret Rachel's barrenness as an act of wrong against her.

Rachel's statement at the birth of the second son, about a great struggle she had endured, can be readily understood. The situation of a childless woman, inflamed by jealousy toward her abundantly productive sister, with whom she had to share her husband, determined not to be outdone in this apparently ultimate function of bearing children, certainly provided all the ingredients for an enormous personal struggle. Literally the Hebrew uses the term "a struggle unto (or before) God." Some have interpreted this as indicating that Rachel wrestled with God for His blessing in this regard. This, however, gives Rachel too much credit, especially when we consider her statement in verse 1.

The expression "before God," or however it may be translated, is a typical Hebraism which indicates something exceptional or great. Thus in Jonah 3:3 godless Nineveh is called a city "important to God." In Psalm 68:15 the mountains of Bashan are described as "majestic mountains," while in the next verse they are contrasted with Mount Zion where God dwelt. Thus the term indicates no more than an exceptionally large city or exceedingly high mountains. Similar usage of this term can be found in 1 Chronicles 12:22 of an army, in Psalm 80:10 of cedar trees, and in Psalm 36:6 of mountains. Our translators have consistently rendered this term by the word "great" or "mighty," and correctly so. Thus, in the case of Rachel's struggle, the term indicates a struggle beyond ordinary human limitations.

30:9–13 *When Leah saw that she had stopped having children, she took her maidservant Zilpah and gave her to Jacob as a wife. Leah's servant Zilpah bore Jacob a son. Then Leah said, "What good fortune!" So she named him Gad.*

Leah's servant Zilpah bore Jacob a second son. Then Leah said, "How happy I am! The women will call me happy." So she named him Asher.

When Leah's child-producing ability was temporarily interrupted, she promptly resorted to the same device her sister had used. She was determined to stay ahead of her sister at all costs in this matter of producing children by Jacob, so she gave her slave girl, Zilpah, to Jacob so he could have conjugal relations with her also. Zilpah thereupon also bore two sons by the patriarch. Their names bear the same characteristics as the names mentioned above. The first was named Gad, which resembles the Hebrew word *gād,* and means good fortune. Some have tried to relate this to the Semitic god of fortune, also called Gad, but there is no substantial basis for this. It is interesting that there is a reference to this god of fortune in

Isaiah 65:11 and there our translators have correctly rendered the term "Fortune."

The second son was named Asher, which has a sound similar to the Hebrew word *'ōšer*—happy, or the verb *'āšar* which means to be considered happy.

30:14–18 *During wheat harvest, Reuben went out into the fields and found some mandrake plants, which he brought to his mother Leah. Rachel said to Leah, "Please give me some of your son's mandrakes."*

But she said to her, "Wasn't it enough that you took away my husband? Will you take my son's mandrakes too?"

"Very well," Rachel said, "he can sleep with you tonight in return for your son's mandrakes."

So when Jacob came in from the fields that evening, Leah went out to meet him. "You must sleep with me," she said. "I have hired you with my son's mandrakes." So he slept with her that night.

God listened to Leah, and she became pregnant and bore Jacob a fifth son. Then Leah said, "God has rewarded me for giving my maidservant to my husband." So she named him Issachar.

In these verses an incident is recorded which casts a definite light on the relationship between the two sisters who were Jacob's wives. During the wheat harvest, probably during the months of May and June, Leah's oldest son, Reuben, brought some mandrake plants to his mother. Reuben must have been a little fellow of about five at this time. (See our introduction to this section.) These plants were abundant in the Mediterranean region and belonged to the nightshade family. Among some peoples they were considered to have magic powers and they were also known as "love apples," or "May apples." In ancient times it was believed that the fruit of this plant was a stimulant to sexual desire or served as an aphrodisiac. Some prepared a drink from the fruit, which was considered to be a love potion.

When Rachel saw the mandrakes Reuben had brought to his mother, Leah, she asked her sister for some of her mandrakes. She probably hoped that they would help her to become pregnant. But Leah snapped back at her, accusing Rachel of first taking her husband from her, and now also wanting to take her son's mandrakes or "love apples." Rachel was willing to make a deal, however, and she offered Leah the privilege of sleeping with Jacob that night if she would allow Rachel to have some of her "love apples." To this Leah agreed. When Jacob returned from the field that evening, Leah went out to meet him and told him about the deal she had made with Rachel. Jacob complied with the plan of his wives and slept with Leah that night, but all of this is not very uplifting revelation. It gives us a glimpse into Jacob's family life that is not very inspiring.

We now read that after this God heard Leah's prayer and she again became pregnant and bore Jacob her fifth son. It has been suggested that Rachel put so much faith in the "love apples" that she was willing to let her sister sleep with Jacob. God, as it were, taught her that the birth of children was not brought about by some magic potion, but that God Himself bestowed this blessing. "Sons are a heritage from the LORD" (Ps. 127:3). For that reason God responded to Leah's prayer and granted her another son. Leah herself interpreted it as a reward for giving her slave girl to Jacob for conjugal relations. The Scripture does not indicate that she was correct in this assumption, however. The name Issachar—Hebrew *yiś-śakār,* relates to the word "reward"—Hebrew *śākār.*

30:19–21 *Leah conceived again and bore Jacob a sixth son. Then Leah said, "God has presented me with a precious gift. This time my husband will treat me with honor, because I have borne him six sons." So she named him Zebulun.*
Some time later she gave birth to a daughter and named her Dinah.

After the birth of Issachar, Leah again became pregnant and bore Jacob her sixth son. She recognized this child as a gift from God, and felt sure that now her husband would treat her with honor because she had borne him six sons. The name Zebulun—Hebrew *zebulûn*—has a similarity in sound to the Hebrew verb, *zābal* which Leah used, and which means to continue with, or as our translators have it, "treat with honor." Finally, Leah also gave birth to a daughter, who was named Dinah. There is no interpretation given for this name.

30:22–24 *Then God remembered Rachel; he listened to her and opened her womb. She became pregnant and gave birth to a son and said, "God has taken away my disgrace." She named him Joseph, and said, "May the LORD add to me another son."*

During all this time Rachel remained childless. Finally God also heard her prayers and in His grace He granted her a son. When we read that God "heard her," it is evident that she had not trusted only in the love apples but that she had also prayed to God for a child. Although the religious life of Jacob's family left much to be desired, it was not wholly neglected. Rachel looked upon the birth of her son as the removal of the shame of being childless, for in the ancient East a childless woman was not looked upon with pity but with disdain. Following the birth of her son, she immediately expressed the hope that she would have another son. Joseph—Hebrew *yôsēp*—sounds like the optative form of the verb "to add"—

Hebrew *'āsap̄*. This seems to be almost a play on words. Some critics claim that the name Joseph is given two different interpretations in the text, leading, in turn, to two different sources, but we find no basis for this.

The manner in which the birth of Jacob's children is recorded affords a strong proof that the heads of the twelve tribes were historical people and not creations of fantasy, as some have claimed. If the sons of Jacob are to be understood as having been fantasized by the twelve tribes of Israel at a later date, how can it be explained that Jacob is given only twelve "mythical" sons and not thirteen. It should be noted that there were two tribes that stemmed from Joseph: Ephraim and Manasseh. Furthermore, what possible reason could there have been for fantasizing a daughter, Dinah, since obviously no tribe descended from her.

It should also be noted that even after the division of Joseph's descendants into two tribes, Israel is consistently spoken of as the "twelve tribes" (Exod. 24:4; 28:21; 39:14; Num. 17:2, 6; Ezek. 47:13; etc.). This is unquestionably based on the historical reality that Jacob had twelve sons. For practical purposes the number twelve could be maintained because the Levites were an exception. In Ezekiel 48:1–7 and 23–28 this is clearly spelled out. The land of Canaan was to be divided into twelve portions for twelve tribes. In the center of the land there was to be a special section set aside for the Lord and this was where the sanctuary was to be located. This would then also be the area where the Levites would live.

There are also other serious objections to describing the sons of Jacob as creations of later, popular fantasy. It would have been unthinkable for the creator of such a fantasy to ascribe four of Jacob's sons to slave women with whom Jacob cohabited. This certainly cannot be explained by ascribing lesser importance to those four tribes. Any objective historian would have to grant that the entire grouping of the twelve sons as they are here presented could not possibly have been fantasized during a single period of Israel's history. There simply was no one historical situation in the entire account of the people of Israel that would lend any credence to such a fantasy. The only conclusion that can be reached, then, is that this narrative is factual and reliable.

Some have claimed that Jacob's two wives and two slave women should also be considered as tribal heads. This must be rejected, however, since there is no evidence of such tribes at any time in Israel's history.

30:25–30 *After Rachel gave birth to Joseph, Jacob said to Laban, "Send me on my way so I can go back to my own homeland. Give me my wives and children, for whom I have served you, and I will be on my way. You know how much work I've done for you."*

> *But Laban said to him, "If I have found favor in your eyes, please stay. I have learned by divination that the Lord has blessed me because of you." He added, "Name your wages, and I will pay them."*
>
> *Jacob said to him, "You know how I have worked for you and how your livestock has fared under my care. The little you had before I came has increased greatly, and the Lord has blessed you wherever I have been. But now, when may I do something for my own household?"*

After the birth of Joseph, Jacob decided that the time had come for him to return to the land of Canaan. He reminded Laban that he had worked for his wives and also suggested that Laban knew very well how hard he had worked for him. So he asked his uncle for permission to leave and return to his own country, but Laban was very reluctant to let Jacob leave because he realized that he and his household had been richly blessed because of Jacob's presence. He asked Jacob to continue to work for him, and told Jacob he could name his own wages.

Many interpreters, including our translators, are of the opinion that the word Laban used to describe how he had come to this awareness of God's blessing via Jacob means "divination." In a sense it should not surprise us to find the practice of certain forms of divination in Laban's household. From 31:19, 30, we learn that he kept "teraphim" or family idols in his house. In spite of this, however, we are convinced that this interpretation is not correct. The word can also have a broader meaning, such as "take notice" or "to deduce from certain facts." The actual meaning of the word will be considered under 44:5, 15. The reason for coming to this conclusion is that divination usually was used to predict the future rather than to form a conclusion regarding events of the past, as was the case here.

Naturally, Laban realized that he could not continue to have Jacob work for him without providing further wages, for Jacob had fulfilled the terms of his contract for his two wives. Even though this was hard for the avaricious Laban to accept, he asked Jacob to state his wages and they would be paid, if only Jacob would continue to work for him. Jacob, rather diplomatically, avoided a direct answer. He once again reminded Laban of his faithfulness to him and the resulting increase of Laban's possessions. Laban had had a relatively modest household, but he had gained great wealth as the direct fruit of Jacob's work. In this way Jacob impressed on Laban how advantageous it would be for him to have him continue to run his business. But, Jacob continued, the time had come when he had to think of his own family and had to provide for his own security as well. This could be done either by leaving and setting up his own economic household, or by acquiring a fair share of Laban's possessions.

30:31–36 *"What shall I give you?" he asked.*

"Don't give me anything," Jacob replied. "But if you will do this one thing for me, I will go on tending your flocks and watching over them: Let me go through all your flocks today and remove from them every speckled or spotted sheep, every dark-colored lamb and every spotted or speckled goat. They will be my wages. And my honesty will testify for me in the future, whenever you check on the wages you have paid me. Any goat in my possession that is not speckled or spotted, or any lamb that is not dark-colored will be considered stolen."

"Agreed," said Laban. "Let it be as you have said." That same day he removed all the male goats that were streaked or spotted, and all the speckled or spotted female goats (all that had white on them) and all the dark-colored lambs, and he placed them in the care of his sons. Then he put a three-day journey between himself and Jacob, while Jacob continued to tend the rest of Laban's flocks.

Laban now repeated his offer to provide Jacob with a fair wage. Jacob's response obviously caught Laban completely off guard, because he made the following proposal. He would go through Laban's flocks and herds and set apart every speckled and spotted sheep and every dark-colored lamb. These would become Jacob's possession and would serve as his wages. It should be noted that sheep in that area were usually white in color and speckled and spotted ones were exceptions to the general rule. Likewise goats were generally of a solid dark color and those with white stripes or spots were unusual. Realizing this, Laban quickly agreed to Jacob's proposal. Jacob offered to do the work of culling out Laban's herds and assured him of impeccable honesty in this process. If any normally colored animals were found in Jacob's flocks they would be considered stolen.

The crafty Laban, however, decided to cull the irregular animals out of his flock himself, thereby showing his distrust of Jacob. Laban further placed the flock of spotted and speckled animals under the care of his own sons and removed them three days' journey from the rest of the flocks that remained under Jacob's care. This was Laban's shrewd method of insuring that Jacob's share of the herds would be as small as possible. By removing all of the abnormally colored animals from the flock, the possibility of the main herds producing more of such colored lambs and kids was greatly reduced.

30:37–43 *Jacob, however, took fresh-cut branches from poplar, almond and plane trees and made white stripes on them by peeling the bark and exposing the white inner wood of the branches. Then he placed the peeled branches in all the watering troughs, so that they would be directly in front of the flocks when they came to drink. When the flocks were in heat and came to drink, they mated in front of the branches. And they bore young that were streaked or speckled or spotted.*

Jacob set apart the young of the flock by themselves, but made the rest face the streaked and dark-colored animals that belonged to Laban. Thus he made separate flocks for himself and did not put them with Laban's animals. Whenever the stronger females were in heat, Jacob would place the branches in the troughs in front of the animals so they would mate near the branches, but if the animals were weak, he would not place them there. So the weak animals went to Laban and the strong ones to Jacob. In this way the man grew exceedingly prosperous and came to own large flocks, and maidservants and menservants, and camels and donkeys.

But Laban's cleverly devised plan did not work out as he intended. He did not take into account the fact that Jacob was an exceptionally knowledgeable herdsman and knew the tricks of the trade far better than he did himself. Jacob knew of a method whereby he could get solid-colored animals to bring forth spotted or striped young. He took branches of trees and peeled off the bark in strips, thus leaving a striped effect. He placed these peeled branches in the water troughs when the flocks were in season and they would mate before them. By looking at the striped branches a physiological factor was set into motion which caused the animals to produce striped or spotted young. This has been a well-known technique among stock breeders and has been used with varying results.

Thus far the meaning of the passage is clear. The statement in verse 40, however, causes considerable difficulty. Without going into detailed discussion of all the varied and conflicting interpretations, let us proceed immediately to what we consider to be the correct understanding of these lines.

It is of utmost importance that we distinguish between the "setting apart" at the beginning of the verse, and the statement at the close of the verse that speaks of "making separate flocks." If we confuse these two expressions the verse becomes unintelligible. What we are told here is that when spotted lambs were born Jacob separated these, not from the flock, but from their mothers, which was done as soon as possible. His intent obviously was to have these spotted animals mix with the solid-colored ones. Then he would encourage the solid-colored ones to mate with the spotted ones and thus increase the possibility of producing more spotted ones. It is obvious that this clever stockbreeder knew all the tricks for getting mating sheep and goats to produce the kind of young he wanted to acquire. He actually used two methods, according to this account. First, there was the use of the striped branches that were put in the water troughs. Then, second, there was the judicious placing of spotted animals within the herd to further increase the production of spotted young.

The last part of the verse tells us that he placed this rapidly growing number of spotted animals in a separate herd for himself, since they had served the purpose of diminishing the flock of solid-colored animals. One note should be added here. The fact that this verse speaks only of white animals indicates that this refers only to sheep. Undoubtedly Jacob used the same strategies with goats also.

Verses 41 and 42 mention still another aspect of Jacob's strategy. He did not use the striped branches in the case of all the mating sheep. He would use these branches when the stronger animals would mate at the water troughs, but not when the weaker animals paired off. By this method he managed to build up a herd of strong, robust animals for himself, while Laban's flocks increasingly became made up of weaker, less healthy animals.

In all of this Jacob outsmarted his crafty and avaricious uncle. Within a few years Jacob acquired enormous flocks of sheep and goats. Mention also is made of the fact that he acquired slaves and slave women, as well as camels and donkeys. In other words, the man became very wealthy in a short time.

We need not comment at length on the morality of what Jacob did. He observed the terms of his agreement with Laban to the letter. Moreover, Laban got only what he deserved. We cannot avoid the conclusion, however, that Jacob's methods were questionable from the point of view of acquiring his neighbor's goods by the use of clever tricks. As such, Jacob's behavior would fall under the judgment of the principle set forth in Lord's Day 42 of the Heidelberg Catechism. In Laban we see the deceiver deceived, but the method used to achieve that end can hardly stand the test of God's law.

30. *Jacob's Secret Departure From Haran and His Covenant With Laban* (31:1–55)

According to those who divide the sources, only a small section of this chapter (v. 18) is ascribed to "P." The reason given for this is the use of the word "Paddan Aram" in this section. We have discussed the use of this name earlier, under 25:19–20. The rest of the chapter is generally considered to be a mixture of material from "E" and "J." There is considerable uncertainty, however, regarding the proper division of the material between these two sources. More recently the picture has become even more confused since some scholars have ascribed some sections to the so-called "fourth source." Moreover, a few references formerly ascribed to "E" are now being assigned to "J."

It is claimed that the chapter includes a number of duplications that point to more than one source. Verse 1 allegedly gives a different motivation for

Jacob's flight than verse 2 does; his departure with all of his possessions is recorded twice, in verses 17–18 and in verse 21; we are told twice that Laban overtook Jacob, in verses 23 and 25; Jacob gave two different replies to Laban, verses 31 and 32; two different symbols are used, a stone pillar in verse 45 and a pile of stones in verse 46; two different names are given, Galeed in verse 48 and Mizpah in verse 49. It is further alleged that two different agreements are recorded. The one in verse 50 deals with Jacob's wives and children, while the one in verse 52 fixes the boundary between Israel and Syria. It is also charged that two different names are used for God, ''The Fear of Isaac'' in verses 42 and 53, and, in the same verses, ''The God of Abraham and the God of Nahor.''

The main point emphasized by the critics is that there is a marked difference between the narrative about Jacob's increase in possessions in chapter 30 and the account Jacob gives to his wives in 31:6–13. These passages supposedly offer clear evidence that we are dealing with two different accounts concerning the way in which Jacob acquired his huge flocks and herds. Thus, chapter 30 is ascribed to ''J'' and the so-called ''fourth source'' while chapter 31 is assigned to ''E.''

Most of the arguments outlined above need little rebuttal. We have repeatedly pointed out, for instance, that what appears to us as a duplication or repetition may be no more than a typical Hebrew narrative style. As such, these apparent duplications provide no basis for discovering multiple sources. The other allegations, which deal more specifically with differences in content, will be considered when we treat the material in our commentary following.

31:1, 2 *Jacob heard that Laban's sons were saying, ''Jacob has taken everything our father owned and has gained all this wealth from what belonged to our father.'' And Jacob noticed that Laban's attitude toward him was not what it had been.*

The amazing increase of Jacob's wealth aroused the growing jealousy of Laban and his sons. One day Jacob overheard Laban's sons discussing this. They were accusing Jacob of taking their father's possessions as his own and in this way gaining his great wealth. Jacob also detected that Laban's attitude toward him was no longer friendly.

31:3 *Then the Lord said to Jacob, ''Go back to the land of your fathers and to your relatives, and I will be with you.''*

As the situation became more uncomfortable for him in Haran, Jacob began to think that the time had come for him to return to Canaan, as he had planned to do earlier (see 30:25–26). It was then that he received a revelation from God instructing him to leave Haran and assuring him that God would be with him.

31:4–13 *So Jacob sent word to Rachel and Leah to come out to the fields where his flocks were. He said to them, "I see that your father's attitude toward me is not what it was before, but the God of my father has been with me. You know that I've worked for your father with all my strength, yet your father has cheated me by changing my wages ten times. However, God has not allowed him to harm me. If he said, 'The speckled ones will be your wages,' then all the flocks gave birth to speckled young; and if he said, 'The streaked ones will be your wages,' then all the flocks bore streaked young. So God has taken away your father's livestock and has given them to me.*

"In breeding season I once had a dream in which I looked up and saw that the male goats mating with the flock were streaked, speckled or spotted. The angel of God said to me in the dream, 'Jacob.' I answered, 'Here I am.' And he said, 'Look up and see that all the male goats mating with the flock are streaked, speckled or spotted, for I have seen all that Laban has been doing to you. I am the God of Bethel, where you anointed a pillar and where you made a vow to me. Now leave this land at once and go back to your native land.' "

Jacob's first challenge lay in convincing his wives that he should leave Haran and return to Canaan. When he spoke of leaving earlier (30:25) everything was peaceful and his departure would have caused no serious problems. But now the relationship with Laban's family was under considerable strain. Jacob therefore had to ascertain what the attitude of his wives, who were Laban's daughters, would be toward a possible move to Canaan. Although there had been no open conflict between Jacob and Laban, there was obviously a good deal of tension. Jacob would now have to determine on which side the sympathies of his wives were inclined to fall.

Jacob called his wives out to the field where he was caring for the sheep, for he wanted an opportunity to speak with them in complete privacy. It was there he told them about the growing hostility on the part of their father toward him. He insisted that there was no good reason for their father's unfriendly attitude, and the increase in his wealth had been due solely to the favor of his father's God. He reminded them that he had served their father diligently and faithfully, while Laban had constantly tried to cheat him by changing his wages "ten times." This number was no more than a figure of speech indicating repeated action. First the speckled animals were to be his wages, then the striped animals, etc. over and over again. But whichever animals were designated, God would intervene and cause the flocks to produce that color predominantly. So God had gradually given Laban's flocks to him.

Jacob added an account about a dream he had during the breeding season of the flocks. In his dream he saw that all the rams that were mating were striped, spotted, and speckled. Then the angel of the Lord (regarding this term see 16:7; 21:17; 22:11; this is a reference to God Himself) declared that the God of Bethel (28:12–22) was intervening in his behalf against Laban's trickery. He added that God had also told him that he should leave Haran and return to his native country.

Obviously there is considerable difference between what Jacob told his wives and what is recorded in chapter 30. Here he said nothing about how he had used his skills as a breeder of livestock for his own advantage. He simply ascribed all of his success to the favor of God. Here he also mentioned the repeated changes in his wages and the special revelation received in a dream, which are not found in chapter 30. As a consequence, many scholars are convinced that we are dealing with two narratives derived from different sources. That there is a textual problem here is obvious. Whether ascribing these chapters to different sources resolves that problem is another matter.

It will hardly do to describe Jacob's presentation to his wives as a cleverly conceived falsehood. His mention of the repeated changes of his wages could readily be verified by his wives. It would seem unlikely, moreover, that he would create the account of the dream and its revelation from God out of his own fantasy. Naturally he was eager to win his wives to his side in this controversy with Laban, and it is understandable that he would not tell them about the clever manipulations in animal breeding that he had employed. At the same time there is no justification for branding his account to his wives as a clever falsehood.

How then are we to reconcile these two accounts? In the first place, it must be granted that the use of the skills, of which Jacob was a master, to acquire Laban's herds, and then ascribing the results to the favor of God, are not necessarily exclusive. God's control extends over everything, also over human efforts that may be ethically questionable. Jacob may well have been convinced in his own mind that his success in building up his herds was due more to the favor and blessing of God than to his own skill in raising livestock. In presenting this matter to his wives, he obviously decided that the emphasis should be placed on God's favor, to the exclusion of his own skill.

In the second place, although chapter 30 does not mention the repeated changes that Laban manipulated in Jacob's wages, the capability of such manipulation was certainly in full accord with Laban's character as it comes to light in the entire narrative. Chapter 30 records only the end result of this whole process of negotiations between Laban and Jacob. Now, in his account to his wives, Jacob includes details that are simply omitted in chapter 30. This, however, does not constitute a conflict between the two records.

This leaves the problem of Jacob's alleged dream, which is not mentioned in the earlier account. It certainly will not do to ascribe Jacob's dubious methods of livestock breeding to God's direct instruction since these methods were morally questionable. Moreover, Jacob would certainly not have mentioned the dream to his wives if he suspected that this would lead his wives to conclude that his operation had been shady at best.

What, then, was the purpose of the dream and why would Jacob recount it to his wives? Some have suggested that God intended to teach Jacob that his great wealth was produced, not by his own cleverness, but by the blessing and favor of the Lord. Others go even farther and suggest that God was telling Jacob that there was no need for any manipulation on his part, but that the production of animals of a given color was exclusively a matter of divine control and arrangement. Both of these explanations imply, however, that Jacob's reference to the dream would point directly to his own manipulation, and this was precisely what he didn't want to bring to the attention of his wives. Even so, these interpretations do lead us in the right direction.

If we assume that Jacob received this dream at an early time of his stay with Laban, before he put his own maneuver into action, there need be no conflict. In that case he was not being altogether truthful with his wives, to be sure. In verse 13 he implied that the dream had occurred only recently. Obviously, it is not possible, on the basis of the text as we have it, to set up an exact time schedule for the various items in the record. This may be a reference to a dream that he had much earlier while the revelation from God telling him to leave Haran had only recently been received. In his effort to convince his wives, Jacob then presented these two events as taking place simultaneously.

31:14–16 *Then Rachel and Leah replied, "Do we still have any share in the inheritance of our father's estate? Does he not regard us as foreigners? Not only has he sold us, but he has used up what was paid for us. Surely all the wealth that God took away from our father belongs to us and our children. So do whatever God has told you."*

Jacob received a very sympathetic response from his wives. They declared themselves to be wholly on his side. Considering the way their father had treated them in the past, they felt that they could expect little consideration from him in the future. They declared that he had treated them like strangers, had sold them like slaves, and in exchange Laban had received all of the benefits of Jacob's effective service. This he had selfishly appropriated for himself. They therefore considered everything that Jacob had acquired from their father as rightfully belonging to them and to their children. They were thus wholly in agreement with his plan to leave Haran.

31:17-21 *Then Jacob put his children and his wives on camels, and he drove all his livestock ahead of him, along with all the goods he had accumulated in Paddan Aram, to go to his father Isaac in the land of Canaan.*

When Laban had gone to shear his sheep, Rachel stole her father's household gods. Moreover, Jacob deceived Laban the Aramean by not telling him he was running away. So he fled with all he had, and crossing the River, he headed for the hill country of Gilead.

Jacob wasted no time in carrying out his plan, for he immediately started making preparations for their departure. Since he anticipated opposition from Laban, he decided to leave without his knowledge. He waited for Laban and his sons to leave home to shear their sheep, an activity that evidently was carried out some distance from home (see also 30:36). Jacob placed his wives and children on camels, and driving his vast herds of livestock, they set out to return to the home of his father Isaac in Canaan.

Their first major effort was to cross the river, which probably was the great river Euphrates. If they could succeed in crossing this major obstacle, they would be well on their way. After making the crossing, they headed for the hills of Gilead, in the area that lay east of the Jordan.

Since her father was away from home when they left the family household, Rachel managed to make off with the family "teraphim." Just exactly what the nature of these "teraphim" was is difficult to determine. We can deduce from Laban's words, in verse 30, that they were some kind of family idols. The term implies this also in other Old Testament passages where it appears (Judg. 17:5; 18:14ff.; 1 Sam. 15:23; 19:13, 16; 2 Kings 23:24; Ezek. 21:21; Hos. 3:4; Zech. 10:2). The references in Ezekiel and in Zechariah suggest that "teraphim" were used in connection with fortune telling. The passage in 1 Samuel 19 suggests that they were used to create false illusions. As a result, some scholars have considered them to be idols that portrayed the human form. Others consider them to have been some kind of mask. It is apparent, especially from verse 34, that the objects were not large.

The incident gives us an interesting insight into Rachel's religious tendencies, which definitely leaned toward idolatry. One Jewish Midrash has suggested that Rachel took the idols in order to prevent her father from worshiping them. Such noble motivations are not supported by the biblical text, however.

31:22–25 *On the third day Laban was told that Jacob had fled. Taking his relatives with him, he pursued Jacob for seven days and caught up with him in the hill country of Gilead. Then God came to Laban the Aramean in a dream at night and said to him, "Be careful not to say anything to Jacob, either good or bad."*

Jacob had pitched his tent in the hill country of Gilead when Laban overtook him, and Laban and his relatives camped there too.

Due to the fact that Laban's herds were grazing a great distance from home at that time, there was a lapse of three days before Laban was informed about Jacob's departure. As soon as he learned of it, he gathered his forces and set off in hot pursuit. After seven days he caught up with Jacob and his entourage, who had already reached the hill country of Gilead. Laban's intentions toward Jacob were obviously not friendly, but God was watching over Jacob. In a dream God sternly warned Laban not to harm Jacob in any way. The expression the Lord used, "Be careful not to say anything to Jacob, either good or bad," seems to imply that Laban was not to try to prevent Jacob from continuing his journey by any means, either good or bad. Even though Jacob had not been honest and forthright in all his dealings, God evidenced His grace to him by protecting him from any harm that Laban might seek to do to him.

We can assume that God's warning came to Laban shortly before he overtook Jacob's traveling company. Consequently, when Laban saw Jacob's camp in the hills of Gilead, he pitched his camp nearby. Some scholars hold that a name has been omitted here. They claim that the hill on which Jacob was camped must be a different hill than the one on which Laban had marshaled his forces. However, since verse 23 already indicated that Jacob was in the hill country of Gilead, there was no need to repeat that fact in verse 25. Certainly the hill country of Gilead allowed ample room for two extensive campsites with some space between them.

A far more serious problem is that this "hill country" of Gilead is some 600 km. (about 360 miles) from Haran and, it is claimed, it would have been physically impossible for Jacob to travel that distance with all his possessions in a mere 10 days. It might have been possible for Laban, riding hard on camels, to cover the distance in seven days, but not for Jacob with all his flocks and herds. The only resolution to this difficulty is

131

to assume that Laban did not initiate his pursuit immediately after he learned of Jacob's flight. He knew that Jacob would be compelled to move slowly, and thus he was in no hurry to gather his forces and launch his pursuit. Just how many days Jacob would need to reach the hills of Gilead with all his flocks and his family is not certain. Some scholars have estimated that he must have been underway for some 40 days by this time. This may be a bit exaggerated, but in any case, if we allow sufficient time between Laban's learning about the departure of his nephew and his launching of his pursuit, we need not conclude that there is an error in the text.

31:26–30 *Then Laban said to Jacob, "What have you done? You've deceived me, and you've carried off my daughters like captives in war. Why did you run off secretly and deceive me? Why didn't you tell me, so I could send you away with joy and singing to the music of tambourines and harps? You didn't even let me kiss my grandchildren and my daughters good-by. You have done a foolish thing. I have the power to harm you; but last night the God of your father said to me, 'Be careful not to say anything to Jacob, either good or bad.' Now you have gone off because you longed to return to your father's house. But why did you steal my gods?"*

When Laban confronted Jacob he rebuked him angrily for leaving secretly and deceptively. He accused him of carrying off his daughters and his grandchildren like so many captives of war. He told Jacob that if he had only let it be known that he wanted to return to his own country, they would have been sent off with a feast of joy and music. One can only wonder how Jacob received that pious boast from his crafty uncle.

Laban implied that he had had intentions of violence against Jacob, but, he said, the God of Jacob's father had prevented him from this. He then added the burning charge that Jacob had stolen the family "gods."

31:31–35 *Jacob answered Laban, "I was afraid, because I thought you would take your daughters away from me by force. But if you find anyone who has your gods, he shall not live. In the presence of our relatives, see for yourself whether there is anything of yours here with me; and if so, take it." Now Jacob did not know that Rachel had stolen the gods.*

So Laban went into Jacob's tent and into Leah's tent and into the tent of the two maidservants, but he found nothing. After he came out of Leah's tent, he entered Rachel's tent. Now Rachel had taken the household gods and put them inside her camel's saddle and was sitting on them. Laban searched through everything in the tent but found nothing.

Rachel said to her father, "Don't be angry, my lord, that I cannot stand up in your presence; I'm having my period." So he searched but could not find the household gods.

In reply to Laban's charge that his departure had been improper, Jacob insisted that he had been afraid that Laban would have taken his wives from him. With respect to the alleged theft of the family idols, Jacob was obviously completely ignorant of what Rachel had done. He therefore strongly declared his innocence in this regard. He offered Laban the freedom to search all his belongings before witnesses, and if anything was found that belonged to Laban the objects stolen would not only immediately be returned, but the person who was guilty of the theft could be sentenced to death. This stern penalty was not uncommon in that day, especially for a thief who had stolen "holy things."

Laban accepted Jacob's offer and proceeded to search Jacob's tents, including the tents of Leah and the two slave women. Finally he came to Rachel's tent. Rachel, however, had hidden the stolen objects in a saddle on which she was seated while the search went on. When Laban searched her tent, Rachel asked that she be excused from getting up because, she claimed, she was having her menstrual period. Thus, even though Laban searched the rest of the tent, he did not discover the idols.

31:36–42 *Jacob was angry and took Laban to task. "What is my crime?" he asked Laban. "What sin have I committed that you hunt me down? Now that you have searched through all my goods, what have you found that belongs to your household? Put it here in front of your relatives and mine, and let them judge between the two of us.*

"I have been with you for twenty years now. Your sheep and goats have not miscarried, nor have I eaten rams from your flocks. I did not bring you animals torn by wild beasts; I bore the loss myself. And you demanded payment from me for whatever was stolen by day or night. This was my situation: The heat consumed me in the daytime and the cold at night, and sleep fled from my eyes. It was like this for the twenty years I was in your household. I worked for you fourteen years for your two daughters and six years for your flocks, and you changed my wages ten times. If the God of my father, the God of Abraham and the Fear of Isaac, had not been with me, you would surely have sent me away empty-handed. But God has seen my hardship and the toil of my hands, and last night he rebuked you."

Now it was Jacob's turn to express his anger. First he derided Laban for his charge of stealing and defied him to place any stolen object on display before the relatives who were present and could serve as witnesses. Then Jacob set the record straight regarding the twenty years of sacrificial, faithful service he had given to Laban. He pointed out how petty and self-seeking Laban had been throughout this time. He declared that if the God of Abraham and Isaac had not taken care of him, Laban would have sent him back to Canaan empty-handed. But God had given heed to Jacob's miserable treatment at Laban's hands and had rebuked Laban for his misdeeds.

31:43, 44 *Laban answered Jacob, "The women are my daughters, the children are my children, and the flocks are my flocks. All you see is mine. Yet what can I do today about these daughters of mine, or about the children they have borne? Come now, let's make a covenant, you and I, and let it serve as a witness between us."*

Laban had little to say in defense. He certainly expressed no word of apology or regret. He maintained his haughty attitude. He claimed that Jacob's wives and children and flocks were really his, but he would press his claims of ownership no farther. In this display of false magnanimity he further proposed that he and Jacob enter into a covenant of peace and friendship. Several interpreters have found difficulty with the last phrase of verse 44, "Let it serve as a witness between us." The point of the text, however, is that the covenant they were to make would serve as a witness between them that they would henceforth live in peace with each other. To insist that the stone pillar should be the "witness" and therefore should have been mentioned here is wholly unnecessary.

31:45–50 *So Jacob took a stone and set it up as a pillar. He said to his relatives, "Gather some stones." So they took stones and piled them in a heap, and they ate there by the heap. Laban called it Jegar Sahadutha, and Jacob called it Galeed.*
Laban said, "This heap is a witness between you and me today." That is why it was called Galeed. It was also called Mizpah, because he said, "May the Lord keep watch between you and me when we are away from each other. If you mistreat my daughters or if you take any wives besides my daughters, even though no one is with us, remember that God is a witness between you and me."

Jacob was willing to agree to making such a covenant and immediately proceeded with the appropriate ceremony for covenant making. He set a stone on end to serve as a memorial stone (see 28:18) and invited his relatives (Laban's family who had become his relatives by marriage) to add stones that they had selected. Thus they unitedly built a marker in the form of a carefully selected heap of stones.

Thereupon they ate a ceremonial meal at the site of this stone marker. This meal was to seal their covenant. Laban declared that the pillar of stones would serve as a "witness" for him and Jacob and he called it "Galeed," which means "the pillar of witness." It was also called "Mizpah," which means "the place of watch." The scene was dedicated with the words, "May the Lord keep watch between you and me while we are away from each other."

Laban then added the warning that if Jacob should mistreat his daughters or take other wives in addition to them, the Lord would surely judge him for this.

In the Hebrew text, which is followed by our translators also, there is a line in verse 47 that declares that Laban named the place "Jegar Sahadutha," while Jacob named it "Galeed." The name "Jegar Sahadutha" consists of two Aramaic words that are practically equivalent to the Hebrew word "Galeed." Both expressions mean something like "a heap of witness." The presence of these Aramaic words in the text causes some difficulty. It is claimed that the Aramaic language developed at a later date, but later research has discovered that Aramaic writings go back as far as 1500 B.C. (See our commentary on 10:22.) There is no reason for assuming that Aramaic could not have been spoken at the time of Jacob.

Others have insisted that the Aramean people had not moved into the area of Mesopotamia at this time. Thus when Laban and his father Bethuel were called "Arameans" in 25:20, this would be in conflict with the historical data. This name could have been given to them, however, not to indicate that they were part of the Aramean people as such, but rather that they lived in an area that was called by that name. Paddan Aram was also known as Aram-Maharaim.

Others have suggested that the different names given to the place by Laban and Jacob indicate that they did not speak the same language. It would have been possible, however, that Laban and his family still spoke the language that Abraham's family spoke, although at the same time they could have gained some acquaintance with the language spoken by other people living in their area.

The real difficulty with this name "Jegar Sahadutha" comes from the fact that these Aramaic words appear in the Old Testament only after the Babylonian Captivity, in the Books of Ezra and Daniel. The only earlier reference in which they appear is in Jeremiah 10:11, and that is obviously an insertion into the text (see our commentary on Jeremiah). This does not mean that the language was not spoken at all prior to this, but there is good reason to question that these words would have appeared in this form at this early date. This leads to the conclusion that these two words were not part of the original text. In accord with the position that is held by many scholars, verse 47 as a whole was probably inserted in the margin by a later hand and then erroneously found its way into the text itself.

This position regarding verse 47 is confirmed by two other considerations. In the first place, the verse appears at the wrong place in the text. It is certainly doubtful that the term "pillar of witness" would be used before that which is witnessed is recorded in verse 48. Second, as the text now stands, Laban named the place twice—in verse 47 he gives it the Aramaic name "Jegar Sahadutha" and in verse 48 he gives it the Hebrew name "Galeed," which was the same name Jacob had given it in verse 47.

Some have tried to remove this difficulty by translating the line, "They named . . . ," but this only confuses matters further. In verse 49 we have the verb "said" with no subject but the implied subject is the same as that for the verb "named" in verse 48 and this can only be Laban. Thus changing the subject to "they" is highly improbable. On the other hand, when verse 47 is seen as a later insertion into the text, the passage reads logically. Laban is introduced as the subject at the beginning of verse 48 and he remains the subject of the verbs in all of verses 48 and 49.

It would be understandable that verse 47 was placed as a marginal note by a later Scribe who could not accept the fact that Laban gave a Hebrew-sounding name to this marker. He probably did not understand the close relationship, also linguistically, between Laban and Jacob. This marginal note then later slipped into the Hebrew text through an error of a copyist.

31:51–55 *Laban also said to Jacob, "Here is this heap, and here is this pillar I have set up between you and me. This heap is a witness, and this pillar is a witness, that I will not go past this heap to your side to harm you and that you will not go past this heap and pillar to my side to harm me. May the God of Abraham and the God of Nahor, the God of their father, judge between us."*

So Jacob took an oath in the name of the Fear of his father Isaac. He offered a sacrifice there in the hill country and invited his relatives to a meal. After they had eaten, they spent the night there.

Early the next morning Laban kissed his grandchildren and his daughters and blessed them. Then he left and returned home.

The covenant included more than Laban's demand that Jacob treat his daughters well. Laban continued by stressing the fact that they should pledge to each other that all future contacts between them should be peaceful and cordial. The pile of stones that had been erected should serve as a token that neither of them would pass this way with evil intentions toward the other. The all-knowing God was again called to witness. In this connection it is worthy of note how Laban refers to God. He seems to distinguish between the God of Abraham, whom Jacob served, and the God of Nahor, whom he served. The expression our translators have rendered "the God of their father," can also be read "the God of each one's father." This would imply that Laban looked on God as two distinct objects of worship. In verse 49 Laban did use the term "Lord," but this seems to refer only to Jacob's God. However in verse 29 he specifically spoke of "the God of your father" and in verse 42 Jacob refers to "the God of my father.'' Laban obviously was aware that he did not serve the same God as Jacob did, and Jacob realizes this also. In Laban's family the knowledge of the true God had degenerated. This is also confirmed by the presence of the ''teraphim.''

The covenant was confirmed with an oath, and in taking the oath Jacob used the name of ''the Fear of his father Isaac'' in referring to his God. (See also v. 42.) What ''God'' Laban used for the purpose of his oath is not mentioned, but he probably referred to the God of his father Nahor. Thereupon Jacob brought a sacrifice and then invited Laban and his company to join in the sacrificial meal. Thus the covenant was sealed. Laban and his associates spent the night there on the hills of Gilead. Early the next morning, after a hearty farewell, they returned to their own country.

31. *Jacob Prepares for His Meeting With Esau* (32:1–21)

This passage is also divided between two sources by those who split the sources of the Genesis record. Verses 3–13a are ascribed to ''J'' while verses 1–2 and 13b–21 are placed with ''E.'' It has been suggested that the division of Jacob's caravan into two groups and the sending of gifts in advance are parallel accounts regarding the way in which Jacob prepared the way for his impending meeting with Esau. The ''night'' mentioned in verse 13a would then be the same as the one mentioned in verse 21. There is no justification for this proposal, however. There is no reason why Jacob could not have used both of these preparatory measures. Moreover, the night in verse 21 can well be the night following the one mentioned in 13a.

32:1, 2 *Jacob also went on his way, and the angels of God met him. When Jacob saw them, he said, ''This is the camp of God!'' So he named that place Mahanaim.*

After Laban's departure, Jacob continued his journey. In this connection we are told that ''the angels of God met him.'' We are not informed how this encounter took place and what the purpose of this meeting was. Some have proposed that the nature of this announcement suggests that it was some kind of heading or title for the episode recorded in chapter 32— Jacob's wrestling at Peniel. This cannot be correct, however. Even though the announcement is made simply, it definitely refers to a separate incident. Since there is no suggestion of a vision here, and the possibility of its being a dream is out of the question, this meeting with the angels must be seen as an actual happening. We can surmise that this manifestation of God's angels was intended to reassure Jacob that the Most High would protect him on his continuing journey by means of His heavenly messengers (see Heb. 1:14). When Jacob saw the angels he said, ''This is the camp of

God!'' Thereupon he called the name of the place ''Mahanaim,'' which actually means ''two camps.'' The precise location of this scene is not known, but the name is mentioned later in Joshua 13:26, 30; 21:38; 2 Samuel 2:8–12, 29; 17:24, 27; 19:32; 1 Kings 2:8; 4:14; 1 Chronicles 6:80. It became a well-known town in Transjordan.

32:3–5 *Jacob sent messengers ahead of him to his brother Esau in the land of Seir, the country of Edom. He instructed them: ''This is what you are to say to my master Esau: 'Your servant Jacob says, I have been staying with Laban and have remained there till now. I have cattle and donkeys, sheep and goats, menservants and maidservants. Now I am sending this message to my lord, that I may find favor in your eyes.' ''*

As Jacob approached the homeland of his father, he thought it would be well to try to effect a reconciliation with his brother Esau. During Jacob's absence Esau had established his residence in the land of Seir. The narrator mentions, for the benefit of the readers of his time, that this area later was known as Edom. This lay to the south of the Dead Sea. It was to this location that Jacob now sent messengers to inform his brother of his return. When Jacob refers to the wealth he had acquired, this was not intended as boasting. He wanted to assure Esau that he was not returning as a poor wanderer in desperate need of his father's inheritance. It should be noted that Jacob addressed Esau in a very humble tone, calling himself Esau's servant, and calling Esau his master. Jacob seemed to realize that it would be well for him to make up for what he had done in the past. He therefore made it clear that he was eager to stimulate a favorable attitude on the part of Esau.

32:6–8 *When the messengers returned to Jacob, they said, ''We went to your brother Esau, and now he is coming to meet you, and four hundred men are with him.''*

In great fear and distress Jacob divided the people who were with him into two groups, and the flocks and herds and camels as well. He thought, ''If Esau comes and attacks one group, the group that is left may escape.''

When the messengers returned to report on their mission, they brought a very disturbing message. Esau was on his way to meet Jacob accompanied by an army of 400 men. Jacob immediately concluded that Esau's intentions were hostile. Jacob therefore took some hasty measures to save what he could of his possessions and family in case of an attack by Esau's forces. He divided both his people and his flocks into two companies. In this way, if Esau should attack one group, the other group could escape.

32:9–12 *Then Jacob prayed, "O God of my father Abraham, God of my father Isaac, O LORD, who said to me, 'Go back to your country and your relatives, and I will make you prosper,' I am unworthy of all the kindness and faithfulness you have shown your servant. I had only my staff when I crossed this Jordan, but now I have become two groups. Save me, I pray, from the hand of my brother Esau, for I am afraid he will come and attack me, and also the mothers with their children. But you have said, 'I will surely make you prosper and will make your descendants like the sand of the sea, which cannot be counted.'"*

But Jacob did more than take a few obvious precautions. He knew there was One who was able to help him in his hour of need, so he prayed earnestly to the God of his grandfather Abraham and of his father Isaac. God had told him earlier to return to his own country, and had promised that He would prosper him in his journey. Jacob acknowledged that he was not worthy of God's favor, but what undeserved blessings the Lord had already bestowed on him! He had crossed the Jordan twenty years before with only his staff. Now he was returning with the wealth of a family and with great possessions, to the extent that they formed two large companies. He prayed that the Lord would deliver him from the threat of Esau's power. He called on God to have mercy on him. He pleaded on God's promises that his descendants would be as the sand of the seashore—innumerable. How could these promises be fulfilled if Esau would now wipe him out?

The expression, "the mothers with their children" has somewhat of a proverbial quality. It is descriptive of a total annihilation from which no one would escape. It is equivalent to our statement "with no survivors."

32:13–21 *He spent the night there, and from what he had with him he selected a gift for his brother Esau: two hundred female goats and twenty male goats, two hundred ewes and twenty rams, thirty female camels with their young, forty cows and ten bulls, and twenty female donkeys and ten male donkeys. He put them in the care of his servants, each herd by itself, and said to his servants, "Go ahead of me, and keep some space between the herds."*

He instructed the one in the lead: "When my brother Esau meets you and asks, 'To whom do you belong, and where are you going, and who owns all these animals in front of you?' then you are to say, 'They belong to your servant Jacob. They are a gift sent to my lord Esau, and he is coming behind us.'"

He also instructed the second, the third and all the others who followed the herds: "You are to say the same thing to Esau when you meet him. And be sure to say, 'Your servant Jacob is coming behind us.'" For he thought, "I will pacify him with these gifts I am sending on ahead; later, when I see him, perhaps he will receive me." So Jacob's gifts went on ahead of him, but he himself spent the night in the camp.

When morning came, Jacob decided to send Esau a gift, in an effort to create a more favorable attitude on his brother's part. He chose an assortment of animals out of his flocks and placed these under the care of some of his trusted servants. These were divided into separate groups which would then be delivered to Esau as a series of gifts, with a space between the several groups. As each group was presented to Esau the same message was to be communicated, namely, "They belong to your servant Jacob. They are a gift sent to my lord Esau, and he is coming behind us." In this way Jacob hoped to break his brother's hostility and soften his heart. As the animals intended as gifts for Esau went ahead, Jacob and the rest of his entourage remained in camp and tried to get a night's rest.

32. *Jacob at Peniel* (32:22–32)

Although most of the scholars who divide the sources ascribe this section to "J," a few insist that the material must be divided between "J" and "E." In support of two sources the following arguments are advanced. The crossing of the stream is allegedly mentioned twice, in verses 22 and 23. Jacob's wrenched hip, acquired while he wrestled with the "man," according to the first half of verse 25, was caused by a jerk from his opponent, while according to the last half of the verse it was the result of accidentally twisting it during the encounter. The giving of the name "Israel" is presented as a blessing, in verse 28, while it was not in accord with the blessing expressed in verse 29. The outcome of the struggle according to verse 28 was a victory for Jacob, while according to verse 30, he barely escaped with his life.

The most charitable judgment that can be made regarding these arguments would be that they are rather far-fetched. It is not surprising, then, that many modern scholars hold to the unity of this passage and then ascribe it to the so-called "fourth source." But there is no strong reason for this latter position either. It is based primarily on the supposed nature of the struggle in which Jacob engaged. These scholars hold that this was a struggle with a demon of some kind. This, of course, does not agree with the facts that are presented in verses 1–21 of this chapter. We will not discuss this in detail at this point but it will be taken up when we enter into the interpretation of the passage itself.

32:22, 23 *That night Jacob got up and took his two wives, his two maidservants and his eleven sons and crossed the ford of the Jabbok. After he had sent them across the stream, he sent over all his possessions.*

After Jacob had sent the gifts ahead to Esau, he remained in camp. That night he tried to get some rest (v. 21), but during the night he got up with a deep concern about Esau's approach. He was camped near the Jabbok River, which probably is the same stream that today is known as Nahr-ez-Zerka—the Blue River. This was a branch of the Jordan that cut through a deep canyon and entered the Jordan about 40 km. (24 miles) north of the Dead Sea. Jacob was terrified at the thought that Esau might attack while he was fording this river with his vast company of people and flocks. He therefore decided to take the great risk of crossing the river during the night. Obviously he felt that this was less dangerous than a possible attack by Esau's forces during a daylight crossing of the river. So he sought out the best location to ford the river and brought his wives and concubines and children, together with his entire company, across the river. Since he was traveling from the north this would indicate that he crossed to the south side of the Jabbok.

Among his children mention is made only of his eleven sons. The fact that his daughter Dinah is not mentioned need not surprise us, since daughters often are omitted from family registers. Genesis 37:35 and 46:7, 15, suggest that Jacob actually had more daughters than the one who was introduced earlier. At any rate, at this point mention is made only of his eleven sons.

32:24 *So Jacob was left alone, and a man wrestled with him till daybreak.*

After successfully sending the rest of the company across the river, Jacob remained behind. There has been some discussion as to whether this means that he stayed on the north bank of the river or whether he simply allowed his caravan to proceed while he stayed on the south bank of the river. This question is not easy to answer. The actual location of Peniel, whether on the north side or the south side of the Jabbok River, is usually determined by what position is taken on Jacob's activity at this point. Although this is not a matter of great importance, we are convinced that the opening statement of this verse suggests that Jacob remained on the north side of the river and that is, then, where Peniel should be located also.

Jacob's purpose in remaining behind while his caravan moved forward has been variously explained. Some have argued that he wanted to make sure that any stragglers who had fallen behind could be directed as to the route they had to take. This, however, does not seem likely. It is understandable that Jacob wanted to spend some time alone in order to pour out his burdened heart to the Lord. While he was there alone, he suddenly was confronted by a man who wrestled with him and this struggle continued until the day began to dawn.

Who was this "man" with whom Jacob had this encounter in the night? Without exception, interpreters are agreed that this was not an ordinary man. This is, of course, completely obvious from what follows in the text. In verse 26 Jacob asked his opponent for a blessing. In verse 28 we are told that his opponent gave him a new name. Moreover, it is specifically stated that he had "struggled with 'Elohim'." This word can refer to God but it can also be used of any other heavenly being. Opinions differ widely with respect to this "being." He is presented as a demon, a local god, such as the god of the river or of the district, a very primitive concept of Jacob's God, an angel, or even Jacob's guardian angel or, for that matter, Esau's guardian angel. Many of these presentations are, of course, in sharp conflict with the biblical context, both here in this passage and in the Bible as a whole. All concepts about a demon or an area god can rest only on the ingenuity of those who invent these tales. So, too, the thought that this might be an ordinary angel finds no support in the text. The idea that this might have been an angel rests entirely on Hosea 12:4 where we read that Jacob "struggled with the angel." It cannot be ignored, however, that in the preceding verse Hosea says that he wrestled "with God." This strongly suggests that the angel mentioned here would be "the angel of the LORD," who appears more often in the Book of Genesis (see 16:7ff.; 21:17; 22:11; 31:11). "The angel of the LORD" is then distinguished from God, but at the same time is identified with God. Many interpreters are of the opinion that it is this "angel of the LORD" with whom Jacob wrestled at Jabbok, and in the light of Hosea 12:3-4, we would agree with this interpretation. That the angel of the Lord appeared in the form of a man must be understood in the same way as the Lord appearing in human form in Genesis 18:1ff. Thus we are dealing here with a "theophany" or an "appearance"—in this case of the angel of the Lord. We refer our readers to what we have said about such "theophanies" under 12:7 and 18:2 and 8.

32:25 *When the man saw that he could not overpower him, he touched the socket of Jacob's hip so that his hip was wrenched as he wrestled with the man.*

This verse describes the progress of the struggle. The first part of the verse does not indicate who is subject and object, but this becomes clear from the latter part of the verse. Jacob's antagonist noticed that he was not overcoming the patriarch. Thereupon he gave a violent twist to Jacob's hip joint with the result that the hip was dislocated. Some interpreters have turned this around and insist that Jacob was the one who dislocated his opponent's hip, but this is in obvious conflict with the text. The fact that Jacob's divine opponent was not able to win this fight simply suggests that he did not make use of his divine strength but limited himself to the normal strength of the human form he had assumed for this appearance.

32:26 *Then the man said, "Let me go, for it is daybreak."*
But Jacob replied, "I will not let you go unless you bless me."

After Jacob had been crippled, his opponent wanted to end the struggle and said, "Let me go, for it is daybreak." This statement has led some to describe the heavenly visitor as some kind of ghost who had to disappear as soon as daylight appeared. This has then been substantiated by various examples from secular literature, but this is not supported by the text. Others have suggested that since the heavenly visitor was not able to win the fight he wanted to sneak off while it was still dark before Jacob could stand forth in the daylight as the winner. This too has no basis. Still another view is that God wanted to test Jacob, or again, that God wanted to spare Jacob from seeing Him since this could spell death for Jacob (see Exod. 33:20). This last suggestion fails to recognize the fact that Jacob would not have looked upon God Himself, but only on a "theophany," which represented no real threat to a man, as evidenced by Abraham's meeting with such a visitor (in ch. 18).

The most natural interpretation, offered by a number of Roman Catholic scholars, is that the struggle had gone on so long, throughout the night, and had not come to any definite conclusion, and therefore the angel of the Lord decided that it was time to call a halt to this conflict. Jacob's reply was most striking: "I will not let you go unless you bless me." This statement indicates that Jacob recognized the divine nature of his adversary. In spite of his crippled hip, Jacob wanted to persist until his heavenly adversary granted him a blessing. Just what led Jacob to conclude that he had been contending with God is not indicated. It is possible that the way in which his opponent had crippled his hip may have revealed that he was struggling with a being with more than human strength. Jacob's request for a blessing lifts this entire encounter above the realm of a mere physical conflict. Some interpreters go so far as to suggest that the entire struggle at Peniel was an exceptionally intense experience of prayer on Jacob's part. Some hold the the inspired author is simply giving an unusually vivid description of fervent prayer.

We cannot accept the view that this was no more than a deeply spiritual experience. The narrative gives a definite description of a physical encounter, a man-to-man conflict, in which physical strength was involved.

The dislocation of Jacob's hip was specifically a physical phenomenon. We are willing to grant that deep psychological experiences can have amazing physical consequences. Even so, the biblical narrative vividly described a physical encounter. This physical struggle was just as real as the eating of food was on the part of the three men who visited Abraham.

Even though we cannot ignore the reality of the physical struggle as it is described here, we must emphasize the fact that this was more than a mere physical wrestling match between two men. This is evidenced especially by Jacob's asking for a blessing. Hosea 12:4 even strengthens this by declaring that "he wept and begged" for a blessing.

Since Jacob made this plea for a blessing after he realized that his antagonist was a manifestation of God Himself, we see the progress of the encounter somewhat as follows: Jacob, in the dead of night, wrestled with his unknown antagonist with all of his great physical strength. When he realized that he was actually contending with the Lord, he turned to fervent prayer and petition for a blessing. He must have come to an awareness that he had been fighting against God, whom he had offended so deeply with his grievous sins. He recognized in his nighttime opponent his righteous Judge who had come to contend with him. If the Almighty had crushed him in that conflict, instead of merely crippling his hip, he would have received only what he deserved. Although he had put forth much effort to obtain God's blessing, he had gone at it in the wrong way. He had taken advantage of his brother's weariness and hunger. He had deceived his blind father. He had cleverly outfoxed Laban. God would have been justified in withholding that blessing from him. So Jacob pleaded for mercy. As a penitent he cast himself on God's grace. He held fast to God's promise. He begged for the blessing, not because he had any right to it, but because God had promised it, and therefore he pleaded, "I will not let you go unless you bless me."

We believe that this is the perspective from which this unique theophany at Peniel should be seen. It was not intended to reveal to Jacob that he still had many hardships to face, as some claim. Nor was it to reassure him that he would not be overcome by Esau when his brother would meet him. This certainly would not have required such an intense physical struggle. It was, rather, through the bitterness of that physical struggle and the resulting dislocation of his hip, that Jacob was brought to the full realization that he deserved to be overcome, certainly by the angel of the Lord who wrestled with him in the night, but also by his brother Esau when he met him on the morrow. Jacob had to be brought to a point of penitence for his sins and of trust only in God's grace. As several interpreters have pointed out, Jacob at Peniel reached a point of spiritual crisis which was equivalent to a conver-

sion experience, a point of spiritual renewal and purification. It was here
that Jacob experienced what Jesus meant when He said, "whoever loses
his life will preserve it" (Luke 17:33).

32:27, 28 *The man asked him, "What is your name?"*
"Jacob," he answered.
Then the man said, "Your name will no longer be Jacob, but Israel, because you
have struggled with God and with men and have overcome."

The answer to Jacob's prayer came in the form of a question—"What is
your name?" This question did not indicate that Jacob's opponent did not
know his name. It was simply a way of introducing what was to follow.
The angel announced that Jacob's name would be changed to "Israel." We
previously have noted such changes in names, in the case of Abraham
(17:5) and Sarah (17:15). Just as the change in those names was related to
the promises of God, so here Jacob's new name was related to the tremendous change that had taken place in his life. Whereas his name formerly
was "Jacob," which means "deceiver" (see our discussion under 27:36),
from this point forward his name would be "Israel," which means "one
who wrestles with God." Obviously the reference is not first of all to
Jacob's physical struggle, but rather to his spiritual struggle. Mention is
made of the fact that Jacob had "overcome" in this struggle and this would
then indicate that his prayer for a blessing had been answered. Jacob would
receive God's blessing because he had humbled himself before Him.

32:29 *Jacob said, "Please tell me your name."*
But he replied, "Why do you ask my name?" Then he blessed him there.

Thereupon Jacob inquired about the name of his antagonist. This must
not be interpreted as though Jacob did not know the name of God. Jacob
wanted to be reassured that he had indeed had an encounter with God. The
reply to his question included a mild rebuke, "Why do you ask my name?"
Was Jacob's faith so weak that, after all of this, he still needed reassurance
that he had actually met God? To confirm the whole encounter as indeed a
meeting with God, Jacob is now given the blessing he had requested.

32:30 *So Jacob called the place Peniel, saying, "It is because I saw God face to*
face, and yet my life was spared."

After his nighttime visitor had disappeared Jacob, moved by the life-
transforming experience he had had there, called the name of the place
"Peniel," which means "the face of God." He added the words, "and yet

my life was spared.'' Many interpret this as Jacob's amazement that, having seen God face to face, he did not die, on the basis of Exodus 33:20. We question this interpretation. We think of it, rather, as an expression of Jacob's joy and gratitude that he had not been overcome in his struggle with his divine antagonist, as he certainly would have deserved. Moreover, he had obtained the blessing he sought, and as such he was given the assurance he needed that he would not be overcome when he met his brother Esau.

32:31 *The sun rose above him as he passed Peniel, and he was limping because of his hip.*

Jacob now decided to rejoin his caravan. This was not easy for him because from this point on he walked as a cripple. But as the sun rose, Jacob left Peniel behind him to resume his place with his traveling company.

32:32 *Therefore to this day the Israelites do not eat the tendon attached to the socket of the hip, because the socket of Jacob's hip was touched near the tendon.*

The sacred writer closes this section with mention of a practice, which was observed by later Israelites, of not eating the tendon of the hip joint, as an enduring reminder of Jacob having been touched by the messenger of the Lord at this part of his body. We reject the interpretation that this was some kind of a superstitious taboo adopted by Jacob's descendants. Certainly the night visitor who contended with Jacob had touched him in other parts of his body also. Thus the whole body could have been made taboo. Moreover, the Israelites never were cannibals, eating human flesh. As such it was a practice that dealt only with animals, and that changes the whole implication. This practice of not eating this particular tendon is mentioned nowhere else in the Bible. Obviously it was still in vogue at the time Genesis was written, and some strict Jews still maintain the practice today. The kosher slaughter of animals requires that this particular part of the body of an animal be carefully removed before the meat can be used for human consumption.

Attempts have been made to relate the remarkable events of this pericope to the mythological material of other peoples. Various parallels are supposedly to be found. There are tales about nighttime struggles with various kinds of demons, monsters, evil spirits, and ghosts. Some even try to describe the event at Peniel as a nightmare. It goes without saying that there is a vast difference between what is recorded here in Genesis and

hese pagan sagas. Most serious scholars give no credence to these efforts
to establish such a connection.

Others have tried to find parallels with accounts in which a human being
wrestled with deity and was able to compel the god to give in to his wishes.
An example would be the page in Homer's *Odyssey,* in which King
Menelaus forcefully detained the sea-god Proteus until he got all the information he wanted from him. This, of course, assumes that Jacob's "overcoming" at Peniel actually was a physical victory in hand-to-hand combat.
But, as we have seen in our treatment of verse 25, this assumption finds no
basis in the biblical text.

Finally, even if we could find an exact parallel to the events of Peniel in
secular literature, this would not prove that this narration is no more than a
myth or saga. The nature of this narrative, as myth or historical fact, is
determined only by the reality that this is not merely a human tale but is the
very word of God. It is not a matter of scientific proof, but a matter of
unwavering faith. We accept the Bible as the word of God and therefore we
accept, without any reservations, the historical and factual reality of
Jacob's experience at Peniel.

33. *Jacob's Meeting With Esau and His Return to Canaan* (33:1–20)

Those who divide the sources generally ascribe this chapter in its entirety
to "J," with the exception of verses 5, 10, 11, 18–20, which are given to
"E." There is some uncertainty regarding the exact portions within these
verses that are to be assigned to "E," however. Then, because the name
"Paddan Aram" appears in verse 18, some are convinced that a few words
in that verse come from "P." We have already discussed this last matter in
our treatment of 25:20. More recently some scholars have suggested that a
few words in verses 18–20 should be ascribed to the "fourth source."

It should be noted that the name "Jahweh" does not appear in the entire
chapter, while the name "Elohim" is found in verses 5, 10, 11, and 20. In
the light of this it would be expected that the chapter would have been
assigned to "E." But to do this would have conflicted with the theory that
the term "maidservants," in verses 1, 2, 6, is a Jahwistic word. We have
already discussed this theory in our introduction to 21:8–21.

When we consider all of the maneuvers of those who insist on dividing
the sources of the Genesis account, it becomes obvious that everything
depends on the prejudgments with which a given passage is approached. If
they start with the position that the names of God must be the determining
factor, this chapter must be given to "E." On the other hand, if the use of a
word such as "maidservant" is adopted as their standard of judgment, it is
clearly a Jahwistic passage. The only conclusion to which objective schol-

arship can come is that neither of these bases for assigning a passage to thi or that source actually carries any weight. To split up a passage such as thi between two or more sources merely on the basis of such flimsy evidence is certainly something less than substantial scholarship.

The basis for assigning verses 18–20 to the "fourth source" is the use of the name "Israel," which was given Jacob in 32:28. Since that section ha been assigned to this source by these scholars, they then use this as a basi for assigning this section to the same source. But since there is no basis in the text for the assignment in 32:28, both positions collapse together.

33:1–3 *Jacob looked up and there was Esau, coming with his four hundred men so he divided the children among Leah, Rachel and the two maidservants. He put the maidservants and their children in front, Leah and her children next, and Rachel and Joseph in the rear. He himself went on ahead and bowed down to the ground seven times as he approached his brother.*

After Jacob's experience at Peniel he rejoined his traveling household Soon they saw Esau and his 400 men (32:6) coming into view. Now tha the critical moment had arrived, Jacob took one more measure of precau-tion. He had already separated his entire company with the flocks and herds into two groups, but now he also divided up his family, placing his two slave wives with their children in front, then Leah and her children, and finally Rachel and her son Joseph in the rear. It is surprising that those who divide the sources do not point out a slight difficulty in harmonizing 32:7 with what we are told here. Even so, the two passages present no real conflict. Obviously, when Jacob divided his entire company into two groups, he kept his family together within one of these groups.

The usual interpretation of this arrangement has been that Jacob placed his slave wives and their children at the point of greatest danger, in case of an attack by Esau's forces, while Rachel and Joseph were placed in the safest position in the caravan. This interpretation raises some real difficul-ties regarding Jacob's motivation in this matter. We are convinced that this matter of safety had no bearing on the order in which the members of his family were placed in the caravan. It would seem to be more reasonable to assume that Jacob was thinking of the order in which he wanted to present the members of his family to Esau. If he would succeed in placating his brother, Jacob would then have the opportunity to introduce his wives and his children to Esau. He wanted to do this in the most impressive order he could think of, so he arranged his family in the order of their importance to him, first the slave wives and their children, then Leah and her children, and finally, as his chief pride and joy, the beautiful Rachel and her son.

Jacob himself went to the head of the caravan. He wanted to be the first
ɔ meet Esau and to seek a reconciliation with his brother. In case Esau's
ostility could not be assuaged, Jacob would be the first to be attacked. As
1e two brothers approached each other, Jacob bowed to the ground seven
imes, probably moving a few steps forward with each bow. In those days
1is was the highest form of expression of esteem and honor to another
·erson. Actually one bow would have sufficed, even in the presence of a
·erson of great position and honor (see Gen. 18:2; Exod. 18:7; 2 Sam.
·:6). The Amarna Tablets repeatedly refer to those who bowed before
.ings. Mention is made of some who bowed seven times and even "sev-
nty times seven times." Undoubtedly this is an exaggeration, but Jacob
.ctually bowed before Esau seven times in an all-out effort to court his
·rother's favor by a show of deep humility.

3:4 *But Esau ran to meet Jacob and embraced him; he threw his arms around his*
eck and kissed him. And they wept.

The meeting of the two brothers was very favorable. Esau didn't wait for
acob to say anything, but ran to him, threw his arms around him, em-
·raced and kissed him. Both of them were moved to tears. It was a deeply
·motional scene. Obviously during Jacob's twenty years of absence all of
ᴣsau's hostility had vanished. His army of 400 men had no hostile inten-
ions. Jacob's anxiety had been without cause. All that Esau had in mind
vas to provide a display of his own success.

3:5–7 *Then Esau looked up and saw the women and children. "Who are these*
ɔith you?" he asked.
Jacob answered, "They are the children God has graciously given your servant."
Then the maidservants and their children approached and bowed down. Next,
⸃eah and her children came and bowed down. Last of all came Joseph and Rachel,
ɩnd they too bowed down.

While the two brothers were engaged in their emotional reunion, the
vives and children, detecting that all was well, also had moved forward.
Vhen Esau saw them he said, with some amazement, "Who are all of
hese people with you?" Jacob then introduced his family to his brother,
ιcknowledging God's favor in providing him with his wives and children.

3:8–11 *Esau asked, "What do you mean by all these droves I met?"*
"To find favor in your eyes, my lord," he said.
But Esau said, "I already have plenty, my brother, Keep what you have for
ourself."

"No, please!" said Jacob. "If I have found favor in your eyes, accept this gift from me. For to see your face is like seeing the face of God, now that you have received me favorably. Please accept the present that was brought to you, for God has been gracious to me and I have all I need." And because Jacob insisted, Esau accepted it.

Esau then asked, "What do you mean by all these droves I met?" Certainly Esau knew that these were intended as a gift (see 32:13ff.). His question indicated that he wanted Jacob to know that such an elaborate gift was wholly unnecessary. When Jacob pointed out that this gift was intended to find favor with his brother, whom he called, "my lord," Esau refused to accept the gift. He made no mention of what had transpired between them in the past. He stressed the fact that now this was wholly unnecessary. He had done very well and had plenty of his own, so Jacob should keep the flocks and herds he had sent as a gift.

Jacob, thereupon, urged his brother to accept the gift. He expressed his deep gratitude to his brother for receiving him so graciously and spoke of his joy at seeing his brother again. On this basis Esau had to accept the gift. This was in keeping with the custom of the time as a means of expressing appreciation for a distinguished visitor.

Jacob compared his joy at seeing his brother with that of "seeing the face of God." This was not intended to indicate the fear that the face of God should instill in a person, as some have claimed. It referred, rather, to the love and comfort that radiated from the presence of God. Seeing his brother in such a favorable attitude was for Jacob like the comforting radiance of God's presence. This was no exaggeration or flattery on Jacob's part. After the deep anxiety through which he had passed, his sense of relief was so great that he could hardly find words to express his joy. He added that Esau need not hesitate to accept the gift from him because God had favored him with great abundance. Esau was persuaded and accepted the gift in good spirit.

33:12–14 *Then Esau said, "Let us be on our way; I'll accompany you."*

But Jacob said to him, "My lord knows that the children are tender and that I must care for the ewes and cows that are nursing their young. If they are driven hard just one day, all the animals will die. So let my lord go on ahead of his servant, while I move along slowly at the pace of the droves before me and that of the children, until I come to my lord in Seir."

Since they could not stay at the place where they had met, Esau proposed that they move on and that he and his men would accompany Jacob's caravan. Jacob had some reservations on this score, however. There is ıothing in the text that indicates that Jacob still nurtured a certain fear of ɔsau which caused him to decline Esau's offer, as some have suggested. We can accept as wholly genuine Jacob's suggestion that Esau and his men ɔould travel far more rapidly than Jacob's party could. Jacob's children were still young, the oldest could not have been more than 12 years old (see 29:20ff. and 31:41). Moreover, Jacob had great flocks and herds which undoubtedly included young sucklings. These had to be herded along gently and consequently Jacob's party had to move slowly. It would be a burden for Esau and his men to travel at such a slow pace.

Some scholars have suggested that Jacob's offer that he would meet Esau in Seir was evasive since he later did not keep this commitment. According to verse 17 Jacob settled in Succoth for a considerable period of time. He built a house there, and from there he moved to Shechem (v. 18). Even so, we do not consider the charge, that Jacob was intentionally misleading Esau with regard to his plan to meet him in Seir, to be justified.

It should be noted, in the first place, that Esau had not mentioned going to Seir. He suggested only that they travel on together. It would have been logical for him to assume that Jacob would head for his father's home in Canaan. Had Jacob really intended to settle in Seir, this could have been upsetting to Esau since this was the area he had chosen for his home. In the second place, Esau knew full well that Jacob was the heir to the promised land of Canaan. Esau could therefore have understood Jacob's intent to come to Seir as a reference to a fraternal visit and no more than that. In the third place, such a proposed visit need not have been carried out immediately upon Jacob's return. It would be far more likely that he would first establish a home for his family and for his flocks and herds. Furthermore, it is not at all sure that Jacob did not, in fact, keep his word and visit Esau in Seir. Although there is no record of such a visit in the Genesis account, it goes without saying that Genesis does not begin to include everything Jacob did. But even if Jacob did not find occasion to visit his brother in Seir, this still does not warrant the conclusion that Jacob intentionally misled Esau. If this had been the case the writer of Genesis probably would have indicated this in the narrative (cf. 27:18ff. and 30:31ff.).

33:15–17 *Esau said, "Then let me leave some of my men with you."*
"But why do that?" Jacob asked. "Just let me find favor in the eyes of my lord."
So that day Esau started on his way back to Seir. Jacob, however, went to Succoth, where he built a place for himself and made shelters for his livestock. That is why the place is called Succoth.

Esau understood Jacob's reservation, and offered to leave part of his men with Jacob's caravan to serve as a guard along the way. But Jacob also refused this. Why should he accept such a guard, for God had protected them throughout their journey from Haran. However, he respectfully asked Esau, addressing him again as "my lord," not to be offended by his refusal. Thereupon Esau departed and returned to Seir, while Jacob moved on to the place that from then on would be known as "Succoth."

The location of Succoth is uncertain. It probably lay in the area east of the Jordan (cf. Josh. 13:27 and Judg. 8:4-5). Jacob chose this location for an extended stay, and there he built a house for his family and pens for his livestock. We do not know exactly how long his stay at Succoth was, but it probably extended over a period of several years. We can surmise that while he was there he made a visit to his parental home in Canaan. Why he did not immediately move to Canaan we do not know; probably the area of Succoth provided good pasture for his huge flocks and herds. He probably realized that the area where his father lived would not be able to provide adequate grazing for both his herds and those of his father. It is possible also that during this time Jacob paid a visit to his brother Esau in Seir.

The name "Succoth" means "huts" or "shelters" and is taken from the "huts" that Jacob built there for his livestock. Whether Jacob himself gave this name to the place or whether this was done by others is not clear from the text. The Hebrew text would allow either reading, and it is a matter of no significance.

33:18-20 *After Jacob came from Paddan Aram, he arrived safely at the city of Shechem in Canaan and camped within sight of the city. For a hundred pieces of silver, he bought from the sons of Hamor, the father of Shechem, the plot of ground where he pitched his tent. There he set up an altar and called it El Elohe Israel.*

After Jacob had lived in Succoth for several years he moved to Shechem and set up his camp within sight of that city. Shechem was actually a part of Canaan, and lay at about the same altitude as the valley through which the Jabbok flows. Thus Jacob had finally crossed the Jordan, making his crossing at a ford that was slightly to the south of where the Jabbok joins the Jordan. For the first time after his departure from Canaan, the patriarch had returned to the Promised Land. The inspired writer uses the term "safely" to indicate that the Lord had spared Jacob through all of his travels and finally had brought him home. Obviously Jacob intended to make this his permanent home, since he bought a piece of ground from the sons of Hamor, the father of Shechem, and there he pitched his tent and set up his camp. This Hamor was the ruler of that area (see 34:2), and his son

Shechem is mentioned because he was to play an important role in the life of Jacob and his family in the future (ch. 34). The term "the sons of Hamor" refers to the tribe over which Hamor was the ruler. Thus Jacob established a legal residence in that area, and the price he paid is given in pieces of silver known as "kesitahs." This type of coin is also mentioned in Joshua 24:32 and Job 42:11. It seemed to have the value of fifteen shekels, although its exact weight and value is not known (see 20:16). Whether the price was as exhorbitant as Abraham paid for the cave of Machpelah is difficult to determine since we do not know how large a plot of ground Jacob purchased.

Some scholars are convinced that in Jacob's case it was also his intent to purchase a place to bury his dead. This is in no way suggested in the text, however. His only purpose seems to have been to have a definite, legal home where he could operate his animal raising industry.

Now that he had acquired a home, Jacob built an altar to the Lord, following the example of Abraham in 12:7 and 13:18, and Isaac in 26:25. He gave the altar the name "El Elohe Israel" which can be translated either "mighty is the God of Israel" or "God is the God of Israel." On the basis of all the experiences through which he had passed, Jacob now testifies to the amazing power of God that had kept him and prospered him through every difficulty. It is significant that Jacob used his new name "Israel" which had been given to him by God at Peniel (32:28). In essence what Jacob confessed here was, "God, my God, is mighty."

34. *Dinah and the Shechemites* (34:1–31)

This chapter places those who divide the sources, by their own admission, before a very difficult problem. In general, however, they have come to the conclusion that this unusual narrative contains two traditions. The one has been called the "Hamor tradition." According to this Hamor is the leading figure in the narrative. He is the one who asks for the hand of Dinah to be given in marriage to his son Shechem, and in that connection also proposes general intermarriage between the two peoples. According to this tradition, then, all of Jacob's sons appear as avengers of their sister's honor. To achieve this they pretend to accept the intermarriage proposal with the condition that all the men of Shechem must be circumcised with the secret intent of murdering them.

The other tradition can be called the "Shechem tradition," in which Shechem is the leading figure. Shechem wanted Dinah for his wife. He faced the obstacle that he was not circumcised. His love for Dinah brought him to submit to circumcision for himself and for his household. Simeon and Levi took advantage of the wounded condition of the men in

Shechem's family, entered the house, killed the men of Shechem's immediate family, and brought Dinah back to her father's household.

The Hamor tradition formerly was ascribed to "E," while the Shechem tradition was traced to "J." Both traditions, however, were thought to have gone through considerable redaction. This editing of the original traditions allegedly was done in the spirit of "P." In more recent studies by the critics the Shechem tradition has been ascribed to the "fourth source."

The bases for this position of the two distinct traditions are somewhat as follows. In verses 6 and 8–10 the negotiations were carried on by Hamor while in verses 11 and 12 they were carried on by Shechem. Hamor was the one who introduced the idea of general intermarriage while Shechem was interested only in securing Dinah as his wife. According to verse 14 the proposal was rejected, while in 15–17 it was accepted with a specified condition. According to verse 19 Shechem acted without delay, while according to verses 20–24 he took time to persuade the other men of Shechem to cooperate. According to verse 26, Simeon and Levi departed, while according to verse 27 all of the sons of Jacob were on the scene.

It should be observed that none of these factors presents substantial contradictions in the facts of the narrative. The entire narrative can readily be read as a unified account (see our interpretation below). One factor that makes the two-tradition theory especially vulnerable is that the proponents of this theory have found it necessary to make several changes in the text in order to maintain the credibility of their theory.

34:1–3 *Now Dinah, the daughter Leah had borne to Jacob, went out to visit the women of the land. When Shechem son of Hamor the Hivite, the ruler of that area, saw her, he took her and violated her. His heart was drawn to Dinah daughter of Jacob, and he loved the girl and spoke tenderly to her.*

After Jacob had lived near Shechem for a while, his daughter Dinah, one of Leah's children, decided to make the acquaintance of the young women of the city. We can surmise that she also had some natural desires to be seen by the young men of the city as well. So Dinah ventured into the city, by herself, unaware of the danger to which she was exposing herself in this pagan environment. She soon caught the attention of Shechem, the son of the chief of this tribal community, Hamor. Shechem, in complete accord with the custom of the day, considered this lovely stranger to be fair game, picked her up, and promptly defiled her. This, however, became more than a momentary fling for Shechem. He fell deeply in love with Dinah and tried to persuade her to become his wife.

A question has been raised about Dinah's age at this time. Some have argued that she could not have been old enough for marriage. This has been based on Joseph's age (17) when the events of chapter 37 occurred, and Dinah was allegedly younger than Joseph. In reply, it should be observed that in Eastern countries girls were considered marriageable at an earlier age than is common in our Western cultures. Furthermore, the events that are recorded in chapter 35 could have developed over a period of as much as a year. It is possible that some 10 years had passed since Jacob's return from Haran. He had spent some time at Succoth before moving to Shechem. The events recorded in chapter 37, concerning Joseph and his brothers, need not have followed in strict chronological order on what is recorded in previous chapters. Thus Dinah could have been at least 15 or older at this time.

Hamor, the ruler of the area, is called a Hivite in this verse. We refer our readers to what we have said about this tribal group of Canaanitish people under 10:17.

34:4–7 *And Shechem said to his father Hamor, "Get me this girl as my wife."*
When Jacob heard that his daughter Dinah had been defiled, his sons were in the fields with his livestock; so he kept quiet about it until they came home.
Then Shechem's father Hamor went out to talk with Jacob. Now Jacob's sons had come in from the fields as soon as they heard what had happened. They were filled with grief and fury, because Shechem had done a disgraceful thing in Israel by lying with Jacob's daughter—a thing that should not be done.

Because of his deep love for Dinah, Shechem wanted to marry this stranger in the community and, therefore, asked his father to make the customary arrangements with her family. Meanwhile, word of what had happened to Dinah had reached Jacob. Since his sons were away from home taking care of the family flocks, Jacob took no immediate action in the matter. He planned to await the return of his sons before entering into the issues involved in this sticky situation.

At the same time Hamor was on his way to visit Jacob with a proposal of marriage for his son to Jacob's daughter, Jacob's sons learned of what had happened, and they quickly returned home. Thus, when Hamor paid his visit to Jacob he was confronted not only by the patriarch himself but also by his indignant sons. These young men had been aroused to great anger by what had been done to their sister. The writer of the narrative adds the comment that what Shechem had done was "a disgraceful thing in Israel . . . a thing that should not be done." The expression that is used is found more often in the later books of the Old Testament (Deut. 22:21; Josh. 7:15; Judg. 20:10; 2 Sam. 13:12; Jer. 29:23). It implies that what had happened was a very serious offense that should under no circumstances be tolerated in Israel. That this statement was not part of the words of Jacob's sons is obvious from the use of the term "Israel." This refers to the descendants of Jacob as a nation or people which was not possible at that point of time. The charge that the writer engaged in an anachronism or that he stepped out of his role as narrator is, of course, ridiculous. All he does is offer a word of explanation to his readers regarding the disturbance and anger of Jacob's sons. What had happened Dinah was considered by Jacob's family to be of the same nature as what later was known as "a disgraceful thing in Israel."

34:8–12 *But Hamor said to them, "My son Shechem has his heart set on your daughter. Please give her to him as his wife. Intermarry with us; give us your daughters and take our daughters for yourselves. You can settle among us; the land is open to you. Live in it, trade in it, and acquire property in it."*

Then Shechem said to Dinah's father and brothers, "Let me find favor in your eyes, and I will give you whatever you ask. Make the price for the bride and the gift I am to bring as great as you like, and I'll pay whatever you ask me. Only give me the girl as my wife."

Hamor began by telling Jacob and his sons that his son Shechem had his heart set on Dinah, and he asked for her hand in marriage to the young man. He further proposed a general policy of intermarriage that would open the way for Jacob's family to the full rights of citizenship in this land, including the rights of acquiring property and settling in the location of their choice.

Shechem also entered into this conversation. In an attempt to gain favor with Jacob and his sons, he assured them that he was ready to pay whatever price they might require, in accordance with the custom of that time (see 24:53), if only he could have Dinah as his wife.

34:13–17 *Because their sister Dinah had been defiled, Jacob's sons replied deceitfully as they spoke to Shechem and his father Hamor. They said to them, "We can't do such a thing; we can't give our sister to a man who is not circumcised. That would be a disgrace to us. We will give our consent to you on one condition only: that you become like us by circumcising all your males. Then we will give you our daughters and take your daughters for ourselves. We'll settle among you and become one people with you. But if you will not agree to be circumcised, we'll take our sister and go."*

The sacred writer indicates that the reply given by Jacob's sons was intentionally deceptive. They pretended to accept the proposals of Hamor and Shechem. At the same time they insisted that before there could be any intermarriage between them, all the males of the Shechemites would have to be circumcised. To marry an uncircumcised man would be a disgrace for any woman from Jacob's family. If the Shechemites would be willing to accept this condition, the way would be open for intermingling and intermarriage between the two tribes. If, on the other hand, the Shechemites would not agree to this condition, they would proceed to get Dinah from Shechem's house, where she seems to have stayed during the interim, and then leave the country. This is what they said, but what their actual intentions were became evident from what followed.

34:18–24 *Their proposal seemed good to Hamor and his son Shechem. The young man, who was the most honored of all his father's household, lost no time in doing what they said, because he was delighted with Jacob's daughter. So Hamor and his son Shechem went to the gate of their city to speak to their fellow townsmen. "These men are friendly toward us," they said. "Let them live in our land and trade in it; the land has plenty of room for them. We can marry their daughters and they can marry ours. But the men will consent to live with us as one people only on the condition that our males be circumcised, as they themselves are. Won't their livestock, their property and all their other animals become ours? So let us give our consent to them, and they will settle among us."*

All the men who went out of the city gate agreed with Hamor and his son Shechem, and every male in the city was circumcised.

Hamor and Shechem, not suspecting the deceptive motives of Jacob's sons, agreed to the proposal. They, however, first had to convince the other men of Shechem to go along with the plan. Shechem, a very popular young man in his city, immediately exercised all of his best powers of persuasion on his fellow townsmen. No mention was made of Shechem's personal interest in the matter. Shechem and Hamor appealed only to the selfish interests of the Shechemites. Meeting with their townsmen at the gate of the city, the customary meeting place, they pointed out all the benefits that would accrue to the Shechemites if they would go along with the plan. Intermingling and intermarrying with the family of Jacob would prove to their advantage, they argued. Certainly the land was large enough to accommodate all of them. They could then share in the wealth that so obviously marked the family of Jacob. They suggested that submitting to the rite of circumcision was a small price to pay for all the advantages they would gain from allowing this new people to live among them.

The Shechemites were convinced by these arguments and they proceeded to be circumcised. The term that is used is "all the men who went out of the city gate." This suggests that it included all those who were mature enough to come and go at will. Thus the rite of circumcising small children was not introduced among the Shechemites at this time.

34:25–29 *Three days later, while all of them were still in pain, two of Jacob's sons, Simeon and Levi, Dinah's brothers, took their swords and attacked the unsuspecting city, killing every male. They put Hamor and his son Shechem to the sword and took Dinah from Shechem's house and left. The sons of Jacob came upon the dead bodies and looted the city where their sister had been defiled. They carried off all their wealth and all their women and children, taking as plunder everything in the houses.*

By the third day after this mass operation, all the men of the city were in great pain and the resulting inflammation and fever that was a usual consequence was at its worst. Thus all the men of the city who were capable of bearing arms were temporarily incapacitated. Jacob's sons had obviously anticipated this when they made their original proposal. Two of them, Simeon and Levi, took this opportunity to arm themselves and to raid the city, killing all the men of the city in a vengeance blood bath, starting their slaughter by killing Hamor and Shechem. Then they seized Dinah from Shechem's house and brought her back to her father's household. Then, accompanied by the rest of the brothers, they plundered the city, stripped the bodies of the dead of all valuables, and captured all the livestock both inside the city and out in the fields. They also took all the possessions of the Shechemites and carried away the women and children as captives.

A few interpreters are convinced that the "sons of Jacob" in verse 27 also refers only to Simeon and Levi, but this is not likely. Nor can this be made to refer to the other sons of Jacob to the exclusion of Simeon and Levi. The most logical explanation is that Simeon and Levi, after their massacre of the men of Shechem, called on their brothers to join them in plundering the city.

34:30, 31 *Then Jacob said to Simeon and Levi, "You have brought trouble on me by making me a stench to the Canaanites and Perizzites, the people living in this land. We are few in number, and if they join forces against me and attack me, I and my household will be destroyed."*

But they replied, "Should he have treated our sister like a prostitute?"

When Jacob learned what his sons had done he was very angry. He poured out his wrath especially upon Simeon and Levi, the actual perpetrators of this vile deed. Jacob insisted that their actions would bring the entire family into disrepute in the land, and he accused his sons of actually bringing this about. The Canaanites and the Perizzites (see 15:20) would certainly repay the house of Jacob with the same kind of vengeance. How were they, as a small family tribe, to defend themselves against the fury of all the people of the land who had been provoked by their vicious conduct? The result could very well be that Jacob's whole family would be annihilated. But Jacob's sons showed no remorse or repentance. They sullenly defended their crimes by charging that Shechem had treated their sister as a common whore.

The narrative recorded in this chapter is certainly one of the most distressing in the history of the Israelites. It was disturbing that Dinah would so flippantly expose herself to the men of this pagan city, and that Jacob did not take proper steps to prevent such folly on the part of his daughter. It was distressing that Jacob did not overrule the vicious scheme his sons had so deceptively foisted on the Shechemites. Although they had reason to be disturbed because their sister had been defiled, this certainly did not justify their vengeful treatment of Shechem, especially after he had put forth a sincere effort to compensate for his actions. Even though the proposal for intermarriage was unacceptable, since this would have resulted in the dissolution of the chosen race, this gave no warrant for Simeon and Levi's treachery. They certainly deserved no praise for preserving the purity of the elect bloodline by resorting to the vicious murder of the defenseless people of Shechem. Even though their young prince was guilty of a serious indiscretion, his action was in accord with the customs of the time, and the other citizens of the city were in no way involved in that incident. As a matter of fact, Dinah was far more at fault for what had happened than anyone else in the city of Shechem.

Some have charged that Jacob displayed a characteristic weakness in the way he rebuked his sons. They argue that he seemed more concerned about the unfavorable consequences of his sons' actions for him and his family than about their guilt and sinfulness. Dealing with such a vicious crime with no more than a verbal rebuke was certainly an evidence of Jacob's moral weakness as a father and authority in his family. Even so, Jacob cannot be rightfully charged with implicity in or sanction of the crimes of his sons. He charged his sons with having made him, and his family, "a stench to the Canaanites and the Perizzites." He thereby declared that he considered their action to be worthy of the strongest condemnation and disdain.

This unvarnished account, revealing such glaring moral weaknesses in Jacob and his family, certainly rules out any possibility of this being a prejudicially laundered history, as some have charged. If later generations of the Hebrews indulged in fantasizing about their forefathers, they most certainly would have omitted this account from the annals of their patriarchal history. Thus we have here another example of the almost cruel objectivity of the biblical narrative. There is no glorification of leading figures and no glossing over of their faults and their crimes.

Others have charged that this simply cannot be a factual, historical record. They declare that it would have been impossible for two men to kill off an entire city. In reply, it should be noted that these ancient cities did not have large populations when judged by modern standards. The Amarna Tablets are very revealing in this regard. It is also possible that Simeon and Levi were accompanied by a number of their servants when they made their terrorist raid on Shechem. It must also be remembered that the men of Shechem were in a weakened and defenseless condition which kept them confined to their homes. It would have been possible for a few well-armed men to stealthily move from house to house and carry out this bloody mission.

Still others suggest that this account deals with tribes rather than with individuals. It is then argued that the Hivite tribe of Shechem subdued the Israelitish tribe of Dinah, and in response the tribes of Simeon and Levi went to war to liberate them. This suggestion must be rejected because there is no reference anywhere to a "tribe of Dinah."

Some have altered this position somewhat and suggest that since 35:1 tells us that Jacob and his family moved to another location, the battle against Shechem by the two tribes of Simeon and Levi was unsuccessful. But this is in direct conflict with the facts as given in the narrative.

The idea that we are here dealing with a fantasized saga of tribal history cannot be accepted. Why should these two tribes be singled out for such infamy? Simeon's territory later was at some distance from Shechem. Levi, the priestly tribe, did not receive an assigned territory and thus would have no direct dealings with Shechem.

Finally, the attempt to interpret this narrative as a myth based on the rescue of a disgraced sister, similar to the Greek myth about the rescue of Helena by the Twins, Castor and Pollux, cannot be taken seriously. The similarities to the Greek saga are completely overshadowed by the vast differences in almost every part of the narrative before us.

35. *Jacob's Return to Bethel* (35:1–15)

Those who divide the sources have assigned this section to two sources, after doing considerable realigning of the passage. Verses 1–5, 6b–8 and 14 are assigned to "E," while 9–13 and 15 are given to "P." Later scholars assign verse 15 to the "fourth source."

The reasons given for assigning the designated passages to "E" are the use of the name "Elohim" for God, and the similarity of these verses to other passages that have been assigned to "E" such as chapters 28 and 34. Verse 3 is supposedly similar to the vow made by Jacob in 28:20. The reference to the sons of Jacob ("them") in verse 5 is allegedly similar to references in 34:13 and 27. To us these similarities indicate only that the narrative continues in a consistent style.

Why then is not the entire narrative ascribed to "E"? The critics insist that verse 6 gives the kind of minute detail about the location of Luz that is characteristic of "P" and therefore must be assigned to that source. Similarly the use of names such as "Paddan Aram" supposedly points to "P." We have emphasized repeatedly in this work that such arguments carry no weight.

One specific reference that allegedly gives strong evidence for more than one source is the naming of "Bethel" described in verse 15. It is claimed that this must be related to Jacob's previous naming of "Bethel" in 28:19. We consider this to be no more than a confirmation of that name when Jacob revisited the place, after an interval of some 30 years, and not a parallel to the previous passage. Still another point that is raised by the critics is the change of Jacob's name in verse 10. This is then related to a similar reference in 32:28 and is considered to establish a twofold transition of the Peniel incident. We would expect that verse 14 would also be considered to be a parallel to 28:18 and consequently ascribed to another source. However, since this does not fit the theory of the critics this reference is avoided.

In order to maintain their theory the critics hold that verses 9–13 are an insertion from another source and that verse 14 follows verse 8. Such manipulation of the text, however, changes the meaning of the entire passage and therefore we consider it to be wholly unacceptable.

35:1 *Then God said to Jacob, "Go up to Bethel and settle there, and build an altar there to God, who appeared to you when you were fleeing from your brother Esau."*

After the blood bath that the sons of Jacob had carried out at Shechem, the word of the Lord came to Jacob to warn him to move out of the area. To remain in the district of Shechem would, as Jacob had already suggested (34:30), expose them to great danger. The Lord instructed him to move his household to Bethel, the place where he had received a special revelation when he was fleeing from Esau (see 28:12ff.).

It should be noted that this revelation, which in chapter 28 was described as a "dream," is here called an "appearance." In this case the "appearance" did not include an outwardly real presence, as in the other cases in which we had references to this phenomenon (see 12:7; etc.). We will have to interpret the expression as it is used here as indicating that what was experienced in other appearances as a physical presence, was experienced in a dream in the case of God's revelation at Bethel. This is not unusual. We often experience things in dreams that are as realistic as experiences in real life.

Jacob was now instructed to settle at Bethel. He was to build an altar to the Lord there. In this way he was reminded of the commitment he made there (28:22), and at long last the time had come for him to fulfill that commitment.

35:2–4 *So Jacob said to his household and to all who were with him, "Get rid of the foreign gods you have with you, and purify yourselves and change your clothes. Then come, let us go up to Bethel, where I will build an altar to God, who answered me in the day of my distress and who has been with me wherever I have gone." So they gave Jacob all the foreign gods they had and the rings in their ears, and Jacob buried them under the oak at Shechem.*

Jacob therefore announced to his entire family that they were moving to Bethel. It was in this connection that Jacob also faced another serious responsibility with respect to his family. Up to this time he had shown great tolerance and even compromise with respect to traces of idolatry within his family. This was seen in his attitude toward his wives as we witnessed Rachel's theft of the family teraphim (31:19). It was also true of his attitude toward the religious life of some of his servants. It must be admitted that Jacob was not a strong leader in the normal activities of his family. We can refer to his laxness with respect to his wives, which we have discussed under 29:14–18. We have also observed this with respect to his children in our treatment of 34:1, 13. All of this now had to change.

Now that Jacob was returning to Bethel he was reminded forcefully of the commitment he had made to God there many years before. In the light of that commitment he could no longer tolerate the practice of idolatry within his household. He had vowed that the Lord would be his God (28:21). The residues of idolatry that were still evident within his family could not be harmonized with this vow. Therefore, Jacob now took a courageous stand. He announced that all "foreign gods" that were present in his family had to be removed. As a further evidence of his religious reform, his family was ordered to purify themselves and also to change their clothes.

Jacob's reform movement proved effective. All of the idols, presumably also the teraphim stolen by Rachel, and the earrings that probably served as amulets, were turned over to Jacob. In an impressive act of purification these were buried in the ground under the oak at Shechem. Whether this was the same oak tree as the one mentioned in 12:6 is not certain (see our comment under that verse).

35:5 *Then they set out, and the terror of God fell upon the towns all around them so that no one pursued them.*

After this act of purification, Jacob and his whole company set out for Bethel. The Lord provided a special protection for them against the threat of attacks from their neighbors. The expression used is that ''the terror of God fell upon the towns. . . .'' Although this could possibly be interpreted as the intimidation of the Canaanites by the show of strength which the sons of Jacob had displayed at Shechem, it was undoubtedly far more than this. The Canaanites obviously were impressed with the way the Lord had blessed and protected and cared for these people. This, in turn, struck fear in their hearts. This does not imply that the Lord had set His approval on the bloody revenge that the sons of Jacob had wreaked on Shechem. Jacob's sons certainly deserved to be subjected to the full revenge of the people of Canaan, but God, in His grace, spared them from this. Once again it became crystal clear that God's special care for His chosen people was not a matter of merit but a matter of grace.

35:6–8 *Jacob and all the people with him came to Luz (that is, Bethel) in the land of Canaan. There he built an altar, and he called the place El Bethel, because it was there that God revealed himself to him when he was fleeing from his brother.*
Now Deborah, Rebekah's nurse, died and was buried under the oak below Bethel. So it was named Allon Bacuth.

And so Jacob and all the people with him arrived at Bethel, or ''Luz'' as it was formerly known (28:19). In keeping with the command of the Lord (v. 1) and his own earlier commitment (28:22) Jacob built an altar there. We are told that he renamed the place ''El Bethel,'' the name he had given to it when God revealed Himself to Jacob there when he was fleeing from his brother Esau.

At this point the biblical narrator inserts a reference to the burial of Rebekah's nurse, Deborah. This is the only reference we have to this woman by name, and here we are simply told that she was buried under an oak tree and that the name of the place was ''Allon Bacuth'' which means ''oak of weeping.'' This reference has given rise to many questions.

If this implies that the death of this woman occurred at this time, how can it be explained that she was in Jacob's company? Had she gone to

Haran and then returned to Canaan with Jacob's family? How old would she have been at this time? When she came to Canaan with Rebekah until Jacob's return to Bethel would be about 130 years. If she was 30 years old when she first came, she would now be 160, which would not be inconsistent with the ages people reached at that time. All of these questions can be resolved, however, if we accept the possibility that Deborah had died here at an earlier date. The reason for mentioning it in this connection was that the location was near Bethel and this was a matter of historical interest with respect to this location.

There is therefore no need to resort to the position that there is an error in the text and that this should read "Rachel" instead of "Rebekah." Likewise, we reject the interpretation of those who hold that the spirit of this woman was believed to have resided in this oak tree. Nor is there any basis for the assumption that this oak tree was the same tree as the "palm tree" under which the prophetess Deborah lived (Judg. 4:5).

35:9–13 *After Jacob returned from Paddan Aram, God appeared to him again and blessed him. God said to him, "Your name is Jacob, but you will no longer be called Jacob; your name will be Israel." So he named him Israel.*

And God said to him, "I am God Almighty; be fruitful and increase in number. A nation and a community of nations will come from you, and kings will come from your body. The land I gave to Abraham and Isaac I also give to you, and I will give this land to your descendants after you." Then God went up from him at the place where he had talked with him.

At Bethel Jacob received another revelation from God in the form of a theophany. (For the nature of these revelations see our discussion under 12:7.) We are told that God appeared to Jacob *again* and that this was related to his return from Paddan Aram. This can be interpreted in two ways. It can mean that the first appearance was recorded in 28:12ff. What we have here then would be the second appearance to Jacob at Bethel—the first when he was on his way to Paddan Aram and the second after his return from there. It can also mean that the first appearance was the one recorded in 32:24ff. This would then mean that this was the second appearance of God to Jacob after his return from Paddan Aram, first at Peniel and now at Bethel. This latter interpretation is supported by the repetition of the giving of Jacob's new name, which points to Peniel. The first interpretation is supported by the repetition of the promise given to Abraham and Isaac and now to Jacob. This would then point back to the earlier scene at Bethel. Either interpretation is textually acceptable.

The blessing bestowed on Jacob at the time of this theophany begins with a repetition and confirmation of the change of Jacob's name (see

32:28). This is a simple recalling of that event with no comment regarding the significance of the change of his name. After that we have a renewal of the promise to Abraham and Isaac. "I am God Almighty" (see 17:1); "be fruitful and increase." This refers not so much to Jacob himself as to his descendants (see 28:3). When he is promised, "a nation and a community of nations will come from you," we refer to what we have said under 28:3 regarding the difficulty this presents when it is applied to the direct descendants of Jacob. It has been suggested that the word used here for "nations" is a different word from the one used in 28:3, and that this word cannot refer to the various tribes that stemmed from Jacob. In that case we will have to consider this reference as a renewal of the promise given to Abraham in 17:5. We do not consider the word used here for "nations" to necessarily exclude the possibility that it could refer to the tribes of Israel, however. It is interesting that when Jacob recounts this "appearance" to Joseph years later in Egypt (48:4), he uses the same term. This suggests that the two terms are synonymous. The "kings" mentioned here would then be the kings that later ruled over Israel. It may well be that the division of the people into two kingdoms may also have been in this prophetic perspective.

Finally, Jacob is specifically promised that he will receive the land of Canaan as an inheritance for himself and his descendants, in keeping with the promise to Abraham and Isaac (see 13:14–17; 15:7, 16; 17:8; 26:3).

After giving this promise God again "went up" from him. (Regarding this statement, compare our comment under 17:22.) It is worthy of note that in this case we have the added comment, "at the place where God had talked with him." Some interpreters consider these words to be a later insertion, although there is no basis for this. The intent probably was to indicate that the "form" in which God appeared to Jacob ascended directly up from the place where God had appeared to Jacob. Thus it indicated to Jacob that he had had an encounter with a heavenly visitor.

35:14, 15 *Jacob set up a stone pillar at the place where God had talked with him, and he poured out a drink offering on it; he also poured oil on it. Jacob named the place where God had talked with him Bethel.*

Once again, Jacob set up a memorial stone to mark the place where he had received this revelation, as he had done previously (see 28:18). This certainly does not indicate that the stone he had erected at that place previously was no longer there. We are simply told that Jacob set up a memorial related to this particular revelation, as it is recorded in verses 1–12. In this case the stone was dedicated, not only by pouring oil *on* it, but mention is made also of pouring *out* or "spilling." This is usually interpreted as the offering of a drink offering, as our translators also have done. However, it is hard to believe that if Jacob offered a drink offering, he would further dedicate the stone by pouring oil on it. Some have considered this to be an insertion into the text but there is no firm basis for this conclusion. We are inclined to think that this so-called "drink offering," which probably consisted of wine, was also part of Jacob's dedication of the memorial stone.

After this Jacob again named the place, which, when compared with verse 7, would constitute a confirmation of what he had already done.

36. *The Birth of Benjamin and Rachel's Death* (35:16–20)

Those who divide the sources ascribe this portion to "E." Basis for this is supposedly found in the use of the word *massebâ* or "pillar" in verse 20, which served as a grave marker. This is then related to verse 14 where there is also a reference to such a pillar, and that passage is usually assigned to "E." It should be noted, however, that the reference in verse 14 does not indicate that the pillar served as a grave marker for the grave of Deborah, as some have claimed. Thus there really is no textual basis for assigning this passage to this particular source.

35:16–18 *Then they moved on from Bethel. While they were still some distance from Ephrath, Rachel began to give birth and had great difficulty. And as she was having great difficulty in childbirth, the midwife said to her, "Don't be afraid, for you have another son." As she breathed her last—for she was dying—she named her son Ben-Oni. But his father named him Benjamin.*

We do not know how long Jacob and his company stayed at Bethel. When they left there they obviously moved in a southerly direction to the area of "Ephrath" (v. 19), which later became Bethlehem. While they were still some distance from Ephrath Rachel began to have birth pains. The word used in the Hebrew to express the distance from Ephrath is an unknown measurement for us today. Some translators, as ours, have rendered this "a considerable distance," while others are convinced that they actually were near the area of Ephrath.

It had been many years since the birth of Joseph before Rachel again became pregnant. The delivery of her baby was very difficult and Rachel died in childbirth. The midwife tried to comfort her in her agony by assuring her that she had borne Jacob another son, thus fulfilling her lifetime longing (see 30:24). With her last breath Rachel named her child *Ben-Oni* which means "son of trouble." In essence this name would have characterized the boy as a child of misfortune. Jacob, in spite of his deep grief at the passing away of his beloved Rachel, did not want this child to carry such a negative name. He therefore changed the name to "Benjamin," which means "son of my right hand." This would then characterize this child as a "fortune child" for the rest of his days.

35:19 *So Rachel died and was buried on the way to Ephrath (that is, Bethlehem).*

Since burial of necessity took place soon after death in this desert country, Rachel was buried there on the way to Ephrath. The sacred writer inserts the note that this later became Bethlehem, but many have called this editorial note into question. They think of it as a marginal note which was improperly brought into the text. The basis for this position is allegedly found in two other references that supposedly locate the grave of Rachel farther to the north. These references are 1 Samuel 10:2 and Jeremiah 31:15. The latter passage pictures how the weeping of Rachel for her children, who were then in captivity, was heard in Ramah. This indicates, it is claimed, that the grave of Rachel was near Ramah, but if we read the passage in Jeremiah with care we will note that there is no reference of any kind to the grave of Rachel. (For an objective interpretation of the passage in Jeremiah see the commentary in this series on the Book of Jeremiah.)

The other passage, 1 Samuel 10:2, does make mention of Rachel's grave. It is located on the borders of the tribal inheritance that was occupied by the tribe of Benjamin. This does present some difficulty, since Bethlehem lies a few hours to the south of that location. It should be remembered, however, that Rachel's death and burial did not occur at Ephrath itself. We are specifically told that it was on the way to Ephrath. As we observed under verse 16, we do not know how far they were from Ephrath at the time. Add to this the fact that the location mentioned in 1 Samuel 10:2 can well indicate a general area near the borders of Benjamin's inheritance. Thus, we are left with no substantial basis for the alleged conflict between these two passages.

35:20 *Over her tomb Jacob set up a pillar, and to this day that pillar marks Rachel's tomb.*

It is understandable that Jacob wanted to place a suitable marker on the grave of his beloved Rachel. He erected a stone pillar *(massebâ)* on the spot (see 18:18). This marker was still at that location at the time when this biblical narrative was written. It is evident from 1 Samuel 10:2 that it was there also during the time of Samuel and Saul.

37. *Reuben's Scandalous Behavior* (35:21, 22a)

35:21, 22a *Israel moved on again and pitched his tent beyond Migdal Eder. While Israel was living in that region, Reuben went in and slept with his father's concubine Bilhah, and Israel heard of it.*

This brief account of Reuben's shameful conduct is generally ascribed to "J," although some later scholars assign it to the "fourth source." There is no need for us to discuss the arguments for this assignment at this time. The passage supposedly has similarities to chapters 37–50, which are assigned to "J," and on the strength of that the verses before us are likewise assigned. Whether there is any justification for this will be discussed when we study those chapters later in this commentary.

There has been considerable discussion about the location where this incident occurred. The text describes it as being "beyond Migdal Eder." That name means "shepherd's tower" and such towers were common among sheepherders for guarding their flocks in the rugged terrain. Mention of such towers is also made in 2 Chronicles 26:10. This particular tower has often been identified with a reference in Micah 4:8, but this identification is questionable. We will have to recognize the fact that we do not know the location of Migdal Eder.

Moreover, since we do not know its location it is also impossible to determine which direction is indicated by the term "*beyond* Migdal Eder," whether this is to the north or to the south.

We do not know how long Jacob was camped there, but while there Reuben had sexual relations with his father's concubine, Bilhah. This was a very serious offense since it was not only adultery but it was also a shameful offense against his own father. Jacob learned of Reuben's scandalous actions, but we are not told what Jacob did about it. The seriousness of the offense does become evident from a reference in Genesis 49:4.

38. *Jacob's Sons* (35:22b–26)

35:22b–26 *Jacob had twelve sons:*
The sons of Leah: Reuben the firstborn of Jacob, Simeon, Levi, Judah, Issachar and Zebulun.
The sons of Rachel: Joseph and Benjamin.
The sons of Rachel's maidservant Bilhah: Dan and Naphtali.
The sons of Leah's maidservant Zilpah: Gad and Asher.
These were the sons of Jacob, who were born to him in Paddan Aram.

Just why the biblical narrator provides a list of Jacob's sons at this point is difficult to say. It is possible that the account of the birth of Benjamin, the last of Jacob's children, which is recorded earlier in this chapter, could have occasioned this list. It is surprising, however, that this list was not given immediately following verse 20. Those who divide the sources generally ascribe this passage to "P." They also have no explanation to offer for the strange location of this list. If a later redactor assembled all of this material, why should he not have placed this in a more logical sequence in the text?

The twelve sons of Jacob (note that his daughter, Dinah, is not mentioned) are grouped according to their mothers. Leah is mentioned first since she gave birth to Jacob's first-born—Reuben. Then Rachel, Jacob's other primary wife, is mentioned. Thereupon Jacob's two concubines are introduced with their children, with Bilhah mentioned first since she was the first to cohabit with Jacob. The last to be mentioned is Zilpah.

The closing clause, "who were born to him in Paddan Aram," has been ascribed to another tradition by the critics. There is no real agreement as to which source is to be identified here, but most of the scholars seem to prefer "P." Many scholars are bothered by the omission of some exceptive clause with reference to Benjamin since he was not born in Paddan Aram. This is, however, in keeping with Hebrew narrative style which gives far less attention to such details than is common among us today. The reference to the name Paddan Aram has also been used to support "P" as the source for this material. (In this connection see our treatment of 25:20.)

39. *The Death and Burial of Isaac* (35:27–29)

35:27–29 *Jacob came home to his father Isaac in Mamre, near Kiriath Arba (that is, Hebron), where Abraham and Isaac had stayed. Isaac lived a hundred and eighty years. Then he breathed his last and died and was gathered to his people, old and full of years. And his sons Esau and Jacob buried him.*

Those who divide the sources also ascribe this brief narrative to "P." The following grounds are offered for this assignment. The name "Kiriath Arba" is used here and this is found also in 23:2, a passage that is generally ascribed to "P." We find a brief chronology here and this supposedly is a characteristic of "P," but the main basis is that this passage implies that Isaac was still alive up to this time and, according to the critics, the other sources imply that he was already dead when Jacob returned from Haran.

Regarding the first two arguments, it is obvious that these serve only to beg the question. To assign this passage to a given source on the basis of having assigned another passage to the same source, of course raises the question of the validity of that assignment, etc. As we have already seen, there is no firm basis for those previous assignments, and thus the scholars have no case.

The third argument, namely that "J" and "E" assume that Isaac had passed away by the time Jacob returned from Haran, has been considered in some detail earlier. It might be well, however, to look at these claims once again in this context of the account of Isaac's death and burial.

The critics hold that Isaac was already on the point of death when Jacob acquired the birthright blessing by posing as his brother Esau. They argue, further, that when Jacob returned from Haran, he did not return to his parental home, nor is there any mention of him even visiting his father in the entire narrative up to this point. Even Esau is brought into this argument. It is pointed out that in 32:3 and 33:14, 16 it is obvious that Esau was living at Seir. Supposedly, Esau moved to Seir after his father's death, while here in our present passage it is implied that he was still living in his father's household (35:29).

In reply to these arguments we would offer the following. First of all, the fact that Isaac, and members of his family, were convinced that he was approaching death (ch. 27) does not warrant the conclusion that he could not have lived for some years after that time, as our present passage clearly implies.

Further, the silence of Scripture regarding a visit by Jacob to his father, after his return from Haran, cannot be used to establish the fact that such a visit was not actually made. The biblical narrative certainly does not record every detail and every movement of its leading figures. The same argument could be used, for instance, to prove that Rebekah must have died before Jacob's return from Haran since there is no reference to a visit by Jacob to his mother either. But the narrative clearly establishes the fact that Rebekah was still alive and well at that time.

With respect to the argument of Esau establishing his home in Seir, this certainly could have occurred long before Isaac's death. Isaac himself did not continue to live with his father Abraham after he was married, yet he participated in his father's burial. Moreover, if 35:29 implies that Esau was still living in his father's house, then 25:9 would imply the same for Ishmael when Abraham died and we know that this was not the case. Thus, when all of the arguments are examined, there is no substantial basis for accepting two distinct traditions for this biblical narrative.

When we read that Jacob "came home to his father Isaac," this does not imply that this was his first visit to his father's house after his return from Haran. It suggests, rather, that Jacob now moved his residence to this location. During the interim he may well have visited his father from time to time while maintaining his own residence elsewhere.

The location is given as "Mamre," near Kiriath Arba or Hebron. When Jacob left for Haran his father was living at Beersheba, according to 26:23–25. Therefore he must have moved to the same location where his father Abraham had lived previously. (Regarding this location and the names used for it, see our treatment under 13:18; 23:2, 19.)

We are now told that Isaac had reached the age of 180 years. Thereupon we are told about his death and burial. This does not imply that Isaac died as soon as Jacob arrived at Mamre. Jacob was born when Isaac was 60 years old (25:26), thus he had reached the age of 120 when Isaac died. We have already observed that he must have been 77 when he went to Haran (21:1), and he stayed there about 20 years. If we add another ten years during which he lived in Canaan after his return from Haran, he would have been 107 when he moved to Mamre. Thus, he could have lived there some 13 years before his father died.

The expression, "he was gathered to his people," has been discussed under 25:8 and 17. (See also 15:15.)

We are told that Esau was present for his father's funeral, so Jacob had probably notified his brother of their father's impending death. Esau was living in Seir, which was not too far away to allow his traveling to Mamre on rather short notice. (See our discussion under 32:3.)

It is striking that there is no mention of Rebekah at this time. We probably must assume that she had died before Isaac did. On his deathbed (see 49:31), Jacob says that both Isaac and Rebekah had been buried in the cave of Machpelah, where Abraham and Sarah had also been buried. (For other interpretations of 49:31, see our treatment of that passage in this commentary.)

40. *The Descendants of Esau* (36:1–43)

This chapter consists of a number of lists of names, each of which is given a heading, as in verses 1, 9, 31, 40. There are some explanatory comments given in verses 5, 6–8, 19, 24, 35, and 43, which also includes a concluding summary statement.

These lists of names are obviously of early origin and cannot possibly be ascribed to later fantasy. This is also acknowledged by those who divide the sources. The exceptions are verses 1–8 and 40–43, which generally are ascribed to "P," the latest of the generally accepted sources. The bases for this assignment are the following: 1) There are similarities to other passages that they have ascribed to "P." Mention is made of the similarity between verses 2 and 28:1, 6, 8, between verse 5 and 35:26, between verse

6 and 12:5 and 31:18, and between verse 7 and 13:6. 2) Certain expressions are used that are allegedly characteristic of "P." Both of these arguments are, however, without cogency since they rely entirely on the presuppositions of the critics which, in turn, cannot be substantiated by the biblical text. Thus there is no substantial basis for assigning sections of this chapter to a later source. The entire chapter is old material that was gathered, collated, and transcribed by the biblical narrator.

36:1 *This is the account of Esau (that is, Edom).*

Verse 1 offers a title or heading for this entire collection of lists. After having recorded the death of Isaac at the close of chapter 35, the narrator obviously intended to provide a brief sketch of Esau's descendants before proceeding with the history of God's chosen people, the descendants of Jacob. He provides this overview of what is here called the people of "Edom," by using certain genealogical lists that were available to him.

36:2, 3 *Esau took his wives from the women of Canaan: Adah daughter of Elon the Hittite, and Oholibamah daughter of Anah and granddaughter of Zibeon the Hivite–also Basemath daughter of Ishmael and sister of Nebaioth.*

The first data recorded is the names of Esau's wives. As we observed briefly in our treatment of 26:34–35, we face a difficulty in that the names of these women and, in part, of their fathers given here, are different from those given in 26:34 and 28:9. No satisfactory resolution to this problem has been found. Even those who appeal to multiple sources for the Genesis record have failed to find a possible source to which they can ascribe these names. The suggestion that there could be two conflicting sources that were incorporated into the account is wholly unlikely. There would be no possible reason for the author to borrow material from another source on a matter of such insignificance. Moreover, if we are dealing here with a copy of an older document in which the redactor hesitated to make any changes, why would he not have made the material in 26:34 and 28:9 agree with what is given here?

One attempt to explain this change of names suggests that it was not unusual for persons to have more than one name and that women were often given a new name when they were married. It would be amazing, however, to find such a large number of name changes in one brief passage. It would be even more doubtful that one of the newly selected names, for the daughter of Ishmael, would be the same as that given to another of Esau's wives in 26:34, Basemath.

Another suggestion is that this was a later corruption of the text. It is true that the Septuagint translation used many variations of names from those in the original Hebrew text. It can be expected that names were especially liable to alteration in the process of translation and copying. Genesis 36 is a striking example of this. Another clear example of this phenomenon is found in Jeremiah 39:3 where a list of Babylonian officials is given. (See our commentary on that passage.)

We can therefore conclude that the resolution to this difficulty must be found in this direction. Precisely which names have been altered and what their original reading was cannot be determined with certainty. We have therefore given the names as they are in the Hebrew text, both here and in the earlier passages (26:34 and 28:9).

One other point of conflict that probably should be pointed out is that Esau's wives are called Hittites in 26:34, while one of them is introduced as a "Hivite" in our present passage. (Cf. 34:2.) Most interpreters are convinced that this should read "Horite" rather than "Hivite." They point out, with considerable justification, that in verse 25 Oholibamah is placed among the Horites. Another difficulty is that Anah, Oholibamah's father, is called the brother of Dishon in verse 20 while he is presented as his father in verse 25. There is a difference in spelling, however, which our translators have indicated by using the names Dishan and Dishon.

36:4, 5 *Adah bore Eliphaz to Esau, Basemath bore Reuel, and Oholibamah bore Jeush, Jalam and Korah. These were the sons of Esau, who were born to him in Canaan.*

We are then given the names of the sons which these wives bore to Esau. The information that is added is that they were born to Esau in Canaan. This agrees with what we are told in chapters 26 and 27, which suggest that Esau remained in Canaan for some time after his marriages.

36:6–8 *Esau took his wives and sons and daughters and all the members of his household, as well as his livestock and all his other animals and all the goods he had acquired in Canaan, and moved to a land some distance from his brother Jacob. Their possessions were too great for them to remain together; the land where they were staying could not support them both because of their livestock. So Esau (that is, Edom) settled in the hill country of Seir.*

Many interpreters are convinced that these verses conflict with what we are told in 32:3 and 33:14, 16. In keeping with their interpretation of 35:29, where, according to these scholars, it is implied that Esau still lived with his father, this passage would then describe Esau's move to Seir after his father's death. We would respond that this is not necessarily what these verses describe. The sacred writer does not tell us at what point in time Esau moved to Seir. All we have here is the information that he made this move after the birth of his sons mentioned in verses 4 and 5. Since Esau was obviously living in Seir at the time of the events described in the previous chapters, we should give the verb in verse 6 a past perfect tense and this is grammatically wholly possible.

The one difficulty that remains, then, is the statement in verse 7 that the land was too limited to accommodate the livestock of both Jacob and Esau. Various attempts have been made to circumvent this difficulty. Some have suggested that the references in 32:3 and 33:14 do not necessarily imply that Esau had already taken up his permanent residence in Seir. He could have gone there as a frequent visitor or to temporarily range his cattle, while he maintained his residence in Canaan. But this would be an unnatural reading of these earlier references. The implication is clear that this was actually Esau's home.

Others have suggested that Esau had anticipated that when Jacob returned to claim his father's inheritance and added to that everything he had accumulated in Haran, the land would be far too small to accommodate both of their households. But this is purely an arbitrary assumption, and not a likely one at that. Verse 7 specifically states that the limitations of this area of the land of Canaan were the occasion for Esau's move to Seir. The most acceptable interpretation seems to be that this must be seen as a divine intervention which motivated Esau to leave Canaan before Jacob returned from Haran. We have a precedent for this in the division of the land between Abraham and Lot, in chapter 13. God provided adequate room for His chosen people to develop as a separate people. Now, once again, since that region was too limited for the descendants of both Jacob and Esau, God moved Esau to establish his home elsewhere. It is possible that Esau had his own reasons for moving to Seir as well. If one of his wives was indeed a Horite (v. 2), this could have motivated him to settle in that area. At any rate, Esau lived in the hills of Seir and the sacred writer adds that this became known as "Edom."

36:9–14 *This is the account of Esau the father of the Edomites in the hill country of Seir.*

These are the names of Esau's sons: Eliphaz, the son of Esau's wife Adah, and Reuel, the son of Esau's wife Basemath.

The sons of Eliphaz: Teman, Omar, Zepho, Gatam and Kenaz. Esau's son Eliphaz also had a concubine named Timna, who bore him Amalek. These were grandsons of Esau's wife Adah.

The sons of Reuel: Nahath, Zerah, Shammah and Mizzah. These were grandsons of Esau's wife Basemath.
The sons of Esau's wife Oholibamah daughter of Anah and granddaughter of Zibeon, whom she bore to Esau: Jeush, Jalam and Korah.

Under a new heading, the narration now proceeds with a second list that includes Esau's sons and some of his grandsons. The names of the sons given here are the same as those given in verses 4 and 5.

36:15–19 *These were the chiefs among Esau's descendants: The sons of Eliphaz the firstborn of Esau: Chiefs Teman, Omar, Zepho, Kenaz, Korah, Gatam and Amalek. These were the chiefs descended from Eliphaz in Edom; they were grandsons of Adah.*
The sons of Esau's son Reuel: Chiefs Nahath, Zerah, Shammah and Mizzah. These were the chiefs descended from Reuel in Edom; they were grandsons of Esau's wife Basemath.
The sons of Esau's wife Oholibamah: Chiefs Jeush, Jalam and Korah. These were the chiefs descended from Esau's wife Oholibamah daughter of Anah.
These were the sons of Esau (that is, Edom), and these were their chiefs.

Thereupon we are given a list of the tribal chiefs of the Edomites. These are the same names as those given to Esau's grandsons and the sons he had by Oholibamah in verses 10–14. The intent seems to be that these were the first heads of families which then later became tribes.

The tribe headed by Teman settled in the northeastern section of Edom. This tribe is also mentioned in Ezekiel 25:13 and in Habakkuk 3:3. They later became so prominent that the name is sometimes used to designate the whole kingdom of Edom (see Jer. 49:7, 20; Amos 1:12; Obad. 9).

The "Amalek" who is introduced here must not be considered to be the tribal head of what came to be known as the Amalekites. He is presented as the head of a tribe of Edomites, while the Amalekites were a different people who were already present at the time of Abraham (see 14:7). Some have suggested that since he was the son of a concubine of Eliphaz (v. 12), this tribe could have had some Amalekite elements within it. This is pure conjecture, however.

36:20–30 *These were the sons of Seir the Horite, who were living in the region: Lotan, Shobal, Zibeon, Anah, Dishon, Ezer and Dishan. These sons of Seir in Edom were Horite chiefs.*
The sons of Lotan: Hori and Homam. Timna was Lotan's sister.
The sons of Shobal: Alvan, Manahath, Ebal, Shepho and Onam.
The sons of Zibeon: Aiah and Anah. This is the Anah who discovered the hot springs in the desert while he was grazing the donkeys of his father Zibeon.

> *The children of Anah: Dishon and Oholibamah daughter of Anah.*
> *The sons of Dishon: Hemdan, Eshban, Ithran and Keran.*
> *The sons of Ezer: Bilhan, Zaavan and Akan.*
> *The sons of Dishan: Uz and Aran.*
> *These were the Horite chiefs: Lotan, Shobal, Zibeon, Anah, Dishon, Ezer and Dishan. These were the Horite chiefs, according to their divisions, in the land of Seir.*

In these verses we are given two lists of names of the Horites, previously mentioned in 14:6. They were the original occupants of the land of Edom. The first list begins with Seir, after whom the area and its hills were named. His immediate descendants are listed. The fact that two of the names, "Anah" and "Dishon," are mentioned twice need not surprise us since it was common for two people to have the same name. With respect to the second "Anah," in verse 24, an incident is recorded which apparently was familiar to the readers of this account. We, however, have no record of this incident. There is a further difficulty in that the meaning of the word translated "hot springs" is uncertain because it appears nowhere else in Scripture.

If "Oholibamah" indeed was the wife of Esau (see v. 2), mention of a woman by the same name among the Horites establishes a strong connection between Esau's descendants and the Horites. Later the Edomites drove out the original dwellers of this land and wiped them out as a distinct people (Deut. 2:12, 22).

The second list mentions the tribal heads of the Horites. These tribal chiefs were the seven sons of Seir (see v. 21). Thus we have to accept a similarity between this list and the record of the sons and grandsons of Esau, as observed under verses 15–19.

36:31–39 *These were the kings who reigned in Edom before any Israelite king reigned: Bela son of Beor became king of Edom. His city was named Dinhabah.*

When Bela died, Jobab son of Zerah from Bozrah succeeded him as king.

When Jobab died, Husham from the land of the Temanites succeeded him as king.

When Husham died, Hadad son of Bedad, who defeated Midian in the country of Moab, succeeded him as king. His city was named Avith.

When Hadad died, Samlah from Masrekah succeeded him as king.

When Samlah died, Shaul from Rehoboth on the river succeeded him as king.

When Shaul died, Baal-Hanan son of Acbor succeeded him as king.

When Baal-Hanan son of Acbor died, Hadad succeeded him as king. His city was named Pau, and his wife's name was Mehetabel daughter of Matred, the daughter of Me-Zahab.

In these verses we are given a list of Edomite kings. We are told that these kings ruled before Israel was ruled by kings. This would then establish what we mentioned in our Introduction, namely, that this record could have been written no earlier than the time of King Saul. Some scholars have tried to make this read that these kings of Edom ruled before any Israelite king ruled over Edom. This would push the date when this was written at least to the time of David. This interpretation is not substantiated by the text, however.

One objection raised to this list is that it includes only eight kings. By comparing Numbers 20:14 and Judges 11:26 it could be concluded that this period covered some 300 years—from Moses to Jephthah. Consequently a series of eight kings would hardly suffice to cover such a long period of time. There is, however, nothing in the text that dictates the conclusion that these kings followed each other in immediate succession. None of them are introduced, for instance, as sons of their predecessors. It is therefore possible that their reigns were separated by shorter or longer periods of time.

With respect to some of these kings we are also told *where* they ruled. Mention is made of "his city was named. . . ." In some cases the place of their origin is also mentioned, as "from Bozrah." This "Bozrah" later apparently became the capital (see Isa. 34:6; 63:1; Jer. 49:13, 22; Amos 1:12). When mention is made of Rehoboth as being "on the river," some insist that this must refer to the Euphrates, but this is most unlikely. It probably refers to one of the rivers that ran from the mountains of Seir into the Dead Sea.

Some scholars have tried to identify "Bela, son of Beor" with the later Balaam, who is also called "son of Beor," but there is no basis for this identification. When mention is made of "Bedad" as the one "who defeated Midian" (v. 35), no further information about him has come down to us. The fact that the names of the wife and mother of "Pau," the last king on the list, are mentioned suggests that these women held some political position in their day.

36:40–43 *These were the chiefs descended from Esau, by name, according to their clans and regions: Timna, Alvah, Jetheth, Oholibamah, Elah, Pinon, Kenaz, Teman, Mibzar, Magdiel and Iram. These were the chiefs of Edom, according to their settlements in the land they occupied.*
This was Esau, the father of the Edomites.

Finally, we are given a second list of Edomite tribal leaders. This list differs radically from the one given in verses 15–19. Here we are given only eleven names while in the previous passage we were given thirteen.

Only two names, Teman and Kenaz, appear in both lists. Some modern scholars are convinced that this list is nothing more than a collection of names taken from other lists and that as such it has no historical value. Other scholars suggest that the list in 15–19 is genealogical while this list in 40–43 is geographically arranged. To support this view, it is pointed out that the term "according to their regions" appears both in verse 40 and 43. It should be noted, however, that it does not state that these were their locations, but rather that these were their names. Even so, the statement "according to their locations" is interesting. It probably indicates that the names of these tribal groups are geographically arranged, even though it is not possible for us today to determine what these actual locations were on the basis of the information we have at hand.

This second list undoubtedly refers to a later time than the earlier list does. Some have suggested that these could have been tribal leaders after David brought an end to the Edomite kings and their reigns. Some of these tribal leaders could well have lived during the time of the Edomite kings, however. There is no basis for the claim that this list covers the time immediately before the Babylonian exile. We must grant, however, that this list in 40–43 represents a later time than the list in 15–19, especially since the later list reduces the number of these leaders by two. This could suggest that two of the earlier tribes had already become extinct or had been absorbed by some of the other tribes.

There is still a real question raised by the reference to two of these tribal leaders with names that earlier had been ascribed to women, Timna in verse 12 and Oholibamah in verse 2. It has been concluded from this that these are names of places rather than of persons, since women's names can be used for places. It should be observed, however, that such names could well have been used for men as well as for women. Even today it is not uncommon to use the same name for girls and boys.

This section concludes with the summary that looks back over the record with, "This was Esau, the father of the Edomites."

41. *Joseph Sold as a Slave Into Egypt* (37:1–36)

Chapter 37 introduces a new episode in this particular period of the history of God's revelation. Here we are told about the preparation for the development of the chosen people of God from a family to a nation. There had been no trace of this in the narratives of Abraham and Isaac. These dealt purely with personal and family matters. Now with the third patriarch, Jacob, events began to point in the direction of Israel becoming a nation. Verse 2 gives a new heading for the history that is to follow, "This is the account of Jacob." Even though the preceding chapters give much information about Jacob, we are now introduced to a new period that begins during the life of Jacob. The emphasis now shifts from Jacob's personal struggles to receive the blessing promised to Abraham and Isaac, to the events in Jacob's life that lead up to the formation of Israel as a nation. Here we are told about Joseph's dream that occurred before Isaac's death; this is recorded earlier in 35:29. Isaac died when Joseph was 29 years old, and he had already spent some time in Egypt. Thus the whole of chapter 37 deals with events that chronologically preceded 35:29.

But this raises the question whether the death of Isaac is the only event that happened after the events recorded in chapter 37. What about the death of Rachel, for instance? It is worthy of note that in verse 10 Jacob asks, ''Will your mother and I and your brothers actually come and bow down to the ground before you?'' This implies that Rachel, Joseph's mother, was still alive at this time. Some have argued that this reference to ''your mother'' could also refer to Leah, but we consider this to be most unlikely. This is certainly not the same situation as a second marriage where the children would accept their father's new wife as ''mother.'' In the case of a polygamous marriage with simultaneous plural wives, each woman was called mother only by her own children (cf. Gen. 20:12 and 21:10). Thus Jacob would not have spoken of Joseph's mother bowing down before him after Rachel's death.

The fact that Joseph saw eleven stars—symbolizing his eleven brothers—need not imply that Benjamin had already been born at this time. This was a dream and the dream did not necessarily reflect the conditions of that moment. But Jacob's reply dealt with a real-life situation at that time and his inclusion of Rachel would seem to require that she was still alive.

Must we conclude from this that we must place the whole of chapter 37 before the death of Rachel? Certainly not. It is quite unlikely that all the events recorded in this chapter took place within a comparatively short space of time. What we are told in verses 2–4 seems to imply a considerable time sequence. There is, moreover, nothing that suggests that the two dreams were received in rapid succession. Furthermore, verse 11 tells us that Jacob ''kept the matter in mind,'' which suggests that this may have been for some time. It is possible, therefore, that the death of Rachel took place between the two dreams. This is verified by verse 14, where we are told that Jacob sent Joseph ''from the Valley of Hebron,'' and 35:27 informs us that Jacob did not settle in the area of Hebron until after the death of Rachel. If we place the death of Rachel after the two dreams and before Joseph's visit to his brothers we can avoid any chronological difficulties.

It should be understood that the narrator brings together in one coherent record the various events that led up to the sojourn in Egypt, which had already been announced to Abraham in 15:13, without concern for exact chronological progression. All emphasis is focused on Israel going into Egypt where God's promise to make of them a great nation was to be fulfilled. Attempts have been made to prove that the statement in verse 14, "from the Valley of Hebron," was an insertion from a secondary source, but we will consider this when we discuss verse 14.

Those who divide the sources generally ascribe verses 1 and 2 to "P," while the rest of the chapter, as also the further chapters that give the story of Joseph, is assigned to "J" and "E." It is claimed that verse 1 complements 36:8 and since that verse has been ascribed to "P" this one should also be given to this source. But the basis for ascribing 36:8 to "P" is questionable, so this certainly cannot be used as a basis for assigning another passage to this source. Concerning verse 2 it is argued, once again, that the chronological detail given there is characteristic of "P" and we have dealt with this argument repeatedly in the past and need not pursue it here.

As far as the division of the rest of the chapter between "J" and "E" is concerned, it is rather amusing that the usual basis for making this division, the names of God, falls away completely here because the name of God is not mentioned in the entire chapter. Some have argued that the use of the names "Jacob" and "Israel" points to separate sources. But even those who advocate separate sources are a bit shaky about the use of this argument and feel compelled to point out several "exceptions." Others point to various doublets and differences within the passage. A careful study of the passage, however, clearly establishes the essential unity of the entire narrative. Still others have made a point of the fact that the passing caravan is described on the one hand as Midianites and on the other as Ishmaelites. As we shall see, this usage in no way establishes two different sources for the narrative.

37:1 *Jacob lived in the land where his father had stayed, the land of Canaan.*

After the abbreviated history of Esau's tribal life in chapter 36, 37:1 brings us back to the family of Jacob. This chapter must not be seen as being in contrast to 36:8 only, but actually to the whole of chapter 36. While Esau left the land of promise and his descendants formed a separate people, the Edomites, who settled in the land of Seir, Jacob and his family remained in the same area where their father had lived, the land of Canaan, the Land of Promise that was to be the inheritance of his descendants.

37:2a *This is the account of Jacob..*

Here we are given a heading or title for the new episode which the sacred narrator is about to record. It has been asked why this heading reads "This is the account of Jacob," and not "This is the account of Jacob's sons." Although we cannot give a definitive answer to this question (see a similar usage in 11:27, where only Terah is mentioned), it is obvious that the period of sacred history that deals with the "chosen people of God" begins with Jacob.

37:2b–4 *Joseph, a young man of seventeen, was tending the flocks with his brothers, the sons of Bilhah and the sons of Zilpah, his father's wives, and he brought their father a bad report about them.*
Now Israel loved Joseph more than any of his other sons, because he had been born to him in his old age; and he made a richly ornamented robe for him. When his brothers saw that their father loved him more than any of them, they hated him and could not speak a kind word to him.

The account begins with mention of the strained relationships between Joseph and his brothers. This served to set the stage for the further drama that was to unfold. We are told that Joseph was 17 years old at this time. A comparison of 30:24–26 with 31:41, indicates that this was 11 years after Jacob returned from Haran.

Joseph was working as a shepherd boy in company with his brothers, especially the sons of Bilhah and Zilpah, who significantly are here called Jacob's "wives," without any qualification. Jewish scholars have argued that, since Joseph was favored by his father above the other sons, he must have been in a different position than his less-favored brothers. This has led some to change the text to indicate that Joseph was placed in a position of oversight over his brothers and that this in turn caused the animosity of his brothers toward him. The text, however, does not allow this differentiation in any way. Joseph simply worked as a shepherd alongside his brothers. Jacob's favoritism for his youngest son came out in other ways, as is indicated in verse 3.

As Joseph worked in close proximity with his brothers, he learned some rather unsavory things about them, and in turn, would carry tales to his father about them. This reveals a less favorable side of Joseph's character, which had undoubtedly been fostered by Jacob's favoritism toward his favorite son.

We are told that this favoritism was encouraged by the fact that Joseph was the son of Jacob's old age. This expression makes better sense if we assume that Benjamin had not yet been born and that, as such, Rachel was still alive. This would then also confirm what we observed above, that the events recorded in verses 2–10 should be placed chronologically before 35:16–20. Thus, Joseph was at this time still the youngest son, and literally, the son of Jacob's old age.

Jacob's favoritism toward Joseph was expressed by the gift of a "richly ornamented robe," as our translators have rendered it. Many pages have been written in defense of one or other interpretation of the precise description of this robe. The meaning of the term is, at best, obscure. We would do well not to become too dogmatic in describing this garment that Jacob gave to his beloved Joseph. Certain conclusions can be made on the basis of studies in the cultures of people in this area at that time in history, and it undoubtedly was a garment with bright colors and it served to indicate a position of special honor and distinction. Little wonder that Joseph's brothers became jealous and developed a hatred for their younger brother to the extent that we read they could not "speak a kind word to him."

37:5–8 *Joseph had a dream, and when he told it to his brothers, they hated him all the more. He said to them, "Listen to this dream I had: We were binding sheaves of grain out in the field when suddenly my sheaf rose and stood upright, while your sheaves gathered around mine and bowed down to it."*

His brothers said to him, "Do you intend to reign over us? Will you actually rule us?" And they hated him all the more because of his dream and what he had said.

The relationship between Joseph and his brothers deteriorated even further when Joseph had a remarkable dream and then told his brothers about it. He dreamed that he and his brothers were in the field binding sheaves of grain. (It can be concluded from this that Jacob not only raised livestock but that he also raised cultivated crops. This is confirmed on the part of his father Isaac in 26:12 and 27:28.) In his dream Joseph saw that his own sheaf stood upright and remained standing, while those of his brothers gathered around and bowed down to his sheaf. The brothers were ready with an immediate interpretation of this dream. They angrily demanded to know whether Joseph intended to rule over them. Thus the hostility of Joseph's brothers became more bitter, first because he had the dream, and further because he had the impropriety to tell them about it ("what he had said").

It should be noted that the text makes no mention of this dream being a revelation from God to Joseph, as had been the case on previous occasions (see 20:3–7; 28:12–15). It is true that in the ensuing history Joseph did reach a position where his brothers in fact bowed down to him. Looking back from that perspective, we could conclude that this dream was indeed a revelation from God in which He revealed, in symbol, what would later take place. But at the time Joseph had the dream there was no way for him to know that God was revealing the future to him. Nor did he present it as such when he told his brothers about it.

37:9–11 *Then he had another dream, and he told it to his brothers. "Listen," he said, "I had another dream, and this time the sun and moon and eleven stars were bowing down to me."*

When he told his father as well as his brothers, his father rebuked him and said, "What is this dream you had? Will your mother and I and your brothers actually come and bow down to the ground before you?" His brothers were jealous of him, but his father kept the matter in mind.

But Joseph did not stop with one dream, for he had another one in which the sun and the moon and eleven stars bowed down to him. This dream he also told to his brothers and then proceeded to tell his father as well. This brought a sharp rebuke from father Jacob, not so much because he had a dream but because he insisted on telling about his dream and thus deepening the bitter tension with his brothers. Jacob also interpreted the dream as indicating that Joseph would attain a position of authority. Although Joseph's brothers grew more heated in their hatred for Joseph, Jacob "kept the matter in mind." The dream had a revelatory significance.

As in the case of the first dream, no mention is made of this being a revelation from God. As far as a fulfillment of this dream is concerned, we would do well not to dwell on the details with too much emphasis. To do so could lead to serious difficulties. Jacob interpreted it as predicting that Joseph's father and mother and eleven brothers would bow down to him. If this is to be taken literally, the reference to his mother causes some difficulty. Both Rachel and Leah had died by the time Jacob and his family came into Egypt after Joseph had risen to power there, so all we can conclude, as far as the revelation that this dream provided is concerned, is that Joseph was to reach a position of power and authority above his entire family.

37:12–14 *Now his brothers had gone to graze their father's flocks near Shechem, and Israel said to Joseph, "As you know, your brothers are grazing the flocks near Shechem. Come, I am going to send you to them."*

"Very well," he replied.

So he said to him, "Go and see if all is well with your brothers and with the flocks, and bring word back to me." So he sent him off from the Valley of Hebron.

After the author explains the causes for the hatred of Joseph's brothers toward him, he goes on to describe how that hatred was expressed. As we have already indicated, some time must have elapsed between these stages of the narrative.

Joseph's brothers had gone to graze the family flocks in the region of Shechem. Obviously they no longer feared reprisals from the Shechemites as a result of their former encounter there (see ch. 34). This time Joseph was not with them, but this must not be ascribed to Jacob's concern for the young man's safety, however. If this had been the case, Jacob certainly would not have sent Joseph on the mission to which he now assigned him. It is not likely that Jacob even realized how deep-seated the hatred of his other sons for his favorite Joseph had become. They certainly would have kept their feelings in this regard from their father. Note that Jacob later did not suspect his sons of foul play in connection with Joseph's disappearance.

Nor can we conclude that Jacob was showing his favoritism for Joseph by allowing him to live a life of leisure at home while his brothers did all the work. To be sure, Jacob must be faulted for his favoritism toward Joseph, the more so since he himself had been a victim of such favoritism when he was a young man (see 25:28). But it would be unwarranted to conclude that Jacob carried this favoritism for Joseph to such extremes that he allowed this young man to live a life of pampered idleness. We would be more correct if we interpret the departure of Joseph's brothers to a distant grazing area without the presence of their younger brother as a providential circumstance under God's direction. It was precisely this circumstance that produced the far-reaching consequences for the family of Jacob that are recorded in the rest of the Book of Genesis.

After the brothers had been away for some time, Jacob decided to send Joseph to them to see whether all was well, both with them and with the flocks. Joseph agreed to accept this mission, so he left from the valley of Hebron, where Jacob was settled at that time, and made his way toward Shechem.

This reference to the valley of Hebron has raised the objection that this was too great a distance from Shechem to be feasible, and thus must be considered to be an interpolation. But it was the fact that it was at some distance that explains Jacob's method of keeping informed about the welfare of his sons and the flocks. If they had been somewhere in the immediate area, Joseph's mission would have been unnecessary and unlikely.

One charge that has been made is that Joseph was too young to accept such a demanding assignment. In response to this charge we would point out that verse 2 tells us that he was 17 years old and, as we have seen above, some years had passed since that time. There can be no reasonable question that Joseph was a responsible adult when he made this journey. Moreover, as becomes increasingly evident in our narrative, he was a young man with exceptional abilities and talents.

37:15–17 *When Joseph arrived at Shechem, a man found him wandering around in the fields and asked him, "What are you looking for?"*

He replied, "I'm looking for my brothers. Can you tell me where they are grazing their flocks?"

"They have moved on from here," the man answered. "I heard them say, 'Let's go to Dothan.'"

So Joseph went after his brothers and found them near Dothan.

When Joseph reached Shechem, his brothers were not there. He then proceeded to search for them in the open fields. There he met a man, probably a resident of the area, who was able to inform him that his brothers had left Shechem and had moved in the direction of Dothan. This was a town that lay about four hours walking distance to the north of Shechem. Some interpreters have concluded that the man who directed him was acquainted with Joseph and his brothers. From this, in turn, they have deduced that this is further evidence that the reference to Hebron in verse 14 is a later erroneous insertion. This claim has no basis, however. The fact that the man knew about the movement of Joseph's brothers with their large flocks is not at all surprising. Their arrival in the area and then their later departure undoubtedly caused a considerable sensation among the local residents. The conversation between Joseph and the local citizen, moreover, is recorded in an abbreviated form because it is not an important part of the narrative. Joseph simply asked someone for directions and, having received this information, immediately moved on toward Dothan, and there he found his brothers.

37:18–20 *But they saw him in the distance, and before he reached them, they plotted to kill him.*

"Here comes that dreamer!" they said to each other. "Come now, let's kill him and throw him into one of these cisterns and say that a ferocious animal devoured him. Then we'll see what comes of his dreams."

His brothers were able to identify him at some distance as he approached. When they saw him coming they devised a vicious plan to dispose of Joseph and thus to prevent the fulfillment of the dreams that had aggravated them so deeply. Their plan was to kill the young dreamer and to throw his body into one of the wells that were found in that area. They planned to report to their father that his beloved son must have been slain by some wild animal.

37:21, 22 *When Reuben heard this, he tried to rescue him from their hands. "Let's not take his life," he said. "Don't shed any blood. Throw him into this cistern here in the desert, but don't lay a hand on him." Reuben said this to rescue him from them and take him back to his father.*

Reuben, Jacob's firstborn, did not agree with the plot his brothers had conceived. He realized, however, that it would be futile for him to oppose the plan openly. He therefore resorted to a ruse by which he hoped to save Joseph's life. He pretended to agree with his brothers' evil designs, but proposed that they should not kill him but only throw him into an empty well where he would eventually die anyway. Then they would not have his blood on their hands. Reuben's intention was to return to the well later, haul Joseph out of the well, and send him back to his father unharmed.

37:23, 24 *So when Joseph came to his brothers, they stripped him of his robe—the richly ornamented robe he was wearing—and they took him and threw him into the cistern. Now the cistern was empty; there was no water in it.*

Reuben's proposal found favor with the rest of the brothers. Although they hated Joseph intensely, they did have some hesitation about resorting to murdering their brother with their own hands. Thus, when Joseph arrived on the scene, they seized him and threw him into a nearby dry well.

37:25–27 *As they sat down to eat their meal, they looked up and saw a caravan of Ishmaelites coming from Gilead. Their camels were loaded with spices, balm and myrrh, and they were on their way to take them down to Egypt.*

Judah said to his brothers, "What will we gain if we kill our brother and cover up his blood? Come, let's sell him to the Ishmaelites and not lay our hands on him; after all, he is our brother, our own flesh and blood." His brothers agreed.

We are told that the brothers then proceeded to sit down to a meal. This action revealed the character of these men. They were so hard-hearted that they could sit down to enjoy a meal, wholly insensitive to the cries of their younger brother from the well in which they had imprisoned him. Perhaps they moved a little distance from the well for their meal so that his cries for help would not be too disturbing to their own conversation.

While they were eating they noticed a caravan of Ishmaelites approaching, carrying various spices from Gilead to Egypt. (Dothan was situated on one of the great trade routes that ran from Syria to the Nile Valley.) The approach of the caravan gave Judah an idea. He proposed to his brothers that they should sell Joseph to the Ishmaelites so that they in turn could sell him as a slave in Egypt. In this way they would rid themselves of Joseph and his offensive dreams while not involving themselves in murder. To let him die in the well would not benefit them in any way. Judah, in what appears to be a display of conscience, pleaded the case for avoiding any violence against their brother since he was their own flesh and blood. Once again, the brothers agree to this change in their plans for disposing of Joseph.

It has been alleged by some scholars that this narrative is based on two different traditions. In the one tradition Reuben is presented as Joseph's deliverer and in the other Judah is portrayed in that role. But this does not agree with the text. Reuben wanted no part in disposing of Joseph at all, no matter how it was done. Judah, on the other hand, at first went along with the plan to kill Joseph. It was only later that he had some conscience qualms about murder and then proposed that they dispose of their hated brother by selling him as a slave.

37:28 *So when the Midianite merchants came by, his brothers pulled Joseph up out of the cistern and sold him for twenty shekels of silver to the Ishmaelites, who took him to Egypt.*

At this point, a new factor enters into the narrative. A few Midianite merchants happened to pass by. They heard Joseph's cries from the well, hauled him out, and quickly sold him to the Ishmaelites for twenty silver coins. This was about one-third lower than the price usually set for a slave (see Exod. 21:32). Obviously the Ishmaelites also wanted to realize something on the deal. Thus the Midianite merchants did what Joseph's brothers had intended to do, and this probably was made possible by the distance Joseph's brothers had moved from the well (see above). By the time they arrived at the well, the Midianites had already sealed the deal. The brothers offered no resistance since this would have been futile anyway. Even so, their objective was realized and the brother who had angered them so deeply was on his way to Egypt as a slave. They were confident that they were rid of him for good.

When we read the narrative in this way we have an answer for those who insist that mention of both Midianites and Ishmaelites indicates two separate traditions. Some have suggested that these two names actually indicate the same group of travelers. The text, however, introduces the Midianite merchants as a distinct group who enter the scene at a later point than the Ishmaelites. For this reason the subject for the verbs "pulled up" and "sold" must be the "Midianite merchants." This avoids the need for resorting to a theory of two traditions.

This reading is also in accord with Joseph's statement in Genesis 40:15, where he says that he was stolen out of the "land of the Hebrews." Joseph, of course, did not know about his brothers' plan to sell him as a slave. All he knew was that they had thrown him into the well. As far as he knew his brothers were in no way involved in pulling him out of the well and selling him as a slave. This was done by the Midianites and, as such, he thought he had been stolen out of the land of the Hebrews. It is true that in 45:4–5 we read that Joseph accused his brothers of having sold him into Egypt. However, this can be considered as an abbreviated account of what had happened in which he pointed out that his brothers were not without fault in the whole transaction.

37:29, 30 *When Reuben returned to the cistern and saw that Joseph was not there, he tore his clothes. He went back to his brothers and said, "The boy isn't there! Where can I turn now?"*

We must accept the fact that everything that is recorded in verses 25–28 took place without Reuben's knowledge. He probably found some pretense to leave the camp of his brothers immediately after the meal. He had hoped to take a circuitous route to the well where Joseph was imprisoned, release him, and send him home to his father. When he came to the well and found Joseph missing he was disturbed; his plan had obviously miscarried. Reuben was so grieved by what had happened that he tore his clothes as an expression of his sorrow. When he returned to his brothers he cried out, "The boy is not there, and I, what shall I do?" Undoubtedly he thought of the trauma of facing his father with the news of Joseph's disappearance.

37:31–35 *Then they got Joseph's robe, slaughtered a goat and dipped the robe in the blood. They took the ornamented robe back to their father and said, "We found this. Examine it to see whether it is your son's robe."*

He recognized it and said, "It is my son's robe! Some ferocious animal has devoured him. Joseph has surely been torn to pieces."

Then Jacob tore his clothes, put on sackcloth and mourned for his son many days. All his sons and daughters came to comfort him, but he refused to be comforted. "No," he said, "in mourning will I go down to the grave to my son." So his father wept for him.

The other brothers, however, thought of a plan for notifying Jacob about his missing son. They took the ornamental robe that they had stripped from Joseph, dipped it in the blood of a kid that they had butchered, and sent the bloody package to their father. In the message they sent along they did not state that Joseph had been slain by a wild animal. They claimed that they had found the blood-stained garment out in the field and thus left Jacob to draw his own conclusions.

Jacob, naturally, drew the conclusion that Joseph had been killed and devoured by wild animals, which was what his sons had anticipated. Thereupon Jacob adopted the customary methods of expressing deep grief. He tore his clothes and dressed in coarse sackcloth. (For similar expressions of grief see 2 Sam. 1:11; 13:31; Jer. 4:8; etc.) Jacob could not be consoled, even though his sons and daughters tried to comfort him. He said that he would go to his grave in sorrow, that is, he would grieve the rest of his days for his favorite son. It should be noted that this is the only reference to Jacob's daughters (plural).

Of special interest here also is the use of the Hebrew word "Sheol," which has caused much discussion and has been variously translated. We will not go into a detailed study of the use of this word in Scripture at this point. Suffice it to say, however, that the common translation for centuries, which was "hell," is certainly not correct in this instance. Here, as in many other places in Scripture, the word seems to refer to the state of death, or being placed in the grave, and no more than that.

37:36 Meanwhile, the Midianites sold Joseph in Egypt to Potiphar, one of Pharaoh's officials, the captain of the guard.

Meanwhile, Joseph, who had been sold to the Ishmaelites by the Midianites, was taken into Egypt. There he was sold as a slave to one of the high-ranking officers of the pharaoh, named Potiphar. He is introduced as the "captain of the guard." (Regarding this position see our discussion under 12:15 and 39:1.) Thus the chapter concludes with Joseph, Jacob's favorite son, as he begins his new life as a slave in Egypt.

42. *Judah and Tamar* (38:1–30)

The story of Joseph is now interrupted with a record of one of the adventures of Judah. The most obvious chronology for the events of this chapter would seem to be some time between Joseph's being taken to Egypt as a slave and the departure of the entire family of Jacob into Egypt. The latter event certainly is the outside limit when this event could have taken place since this episode definitely takes place while they were in Canaan. That it took place before Joseph's departure into Egypt cannot be determined with equal certainty.

The chapter begins with the phrase, "at that time." This need not be taken too literally since it is a general designation of time. Many interpreters, including Augustine, take this statement literally, however, and assume that Judah's exploits were taking place at the same time as the events described in chapter 37. This is not likely, however. When Joseph was sold to Egypt, Judah was present with his brothers taking care of the flocks. Judah's visit to Adullam and all the resulting events could hardly have been a momentary exploit. Moreover, our chapter begins with the statement that, "Judah left his brothers." In view of this it would seem more acceptable to place this entire narrative after Joseph was taken to Egypt.

But this time sequence raises another difficulty. Would it be possible for Judah to go through all of these experiences between the time Joseph went to Egypt and the time when Jacob's entire family left for Egypt? When we compare 41:46 and 45:10 we can conclude that Joseph was 39 years old when his father left Canaan for Egypt. From this follows that there was a time span of 20 years before the happenings in chapter 38. Would this allow enough time for Judah to get married, produce three sons, two of whom had reached marriageable age and had died, and for Judah to cohabit with his widowed daughter-in-law and produce twins by her? Although twenty years is a rather short time for all of this to take place, it would not be wholly impossible. Judah could have married within six months after Joseph's banishment into Egypt and then could have had three sons within three years. Young people married at an earlier age at that time than is usual today. Er, therefore, could have married Tamar when he was 15 or 16, and then could have died within six months. His brother Onan could have taken on his brotherly duty of trying to produce seed by his brother's widow shortly after that. With this rapid-fire sequence it would have been possible for the death of Onan to have occurred about 17½ years after Joseph's exile. This would then leave 1½ years for Tamar's widowhood and Judah's sensuous exploit with his disguised daughter-in-law. Judah could then have joined his brothers for their first trip to Egypt to buy food while Tamar was pregnant and the second trip could have come after Tamar had given birth to twin sons, fathered by Judah. Although this is a matter of conjecture, it does demonstrate that the time factor need not present an insurmountable difficulty.

Those who divide the sources generally ascribe chapter 38 to "J," because the name "Jahweh" appears three times in verses 7 and 10. More recent studies have ascribed the passage to the "fourth source." One argument that has been used to assign this material to a separate source is that Judah is presented here as living apart from his brothers, while in chapter 37 and in later chapters he was obviously living with his brothers. Some have even argued that 38:5 suggests that Judah acquired an immediate possession in Canaan and that this excluded him from a stay in Egypt. It is possible, however, that Judah's departure from the rest of the family, which is recorded here, was of short duration and that he later rejoined them. If this was the case, the events recorded in the latter part of chapter 38 must have taken place during the first few years of the great famine. It is even conceivable that it was precisely the crisis of the famine that drove Judah back into the company of his family. To suggest that verse 5 indicates that Judah at this time established a permanent home in Canaan is reading far more into the text than is there. This conclusion can be drawn only if we assume, as many of the critics do, that this entire chapter does not deal with individual persons but with events of a tribe. This, however, is wholly untenable. It cannot be denied that Judah and Tamar are presented here as actual persons. To present their experiences as personifications of tribal events is wholly unacceptable. Even the comments about some of the lesser figures in the narrative, such as Onan, can hardly be interpreted as referring to tribal groups. One of the strongest arguments favoring the position that this is actual history dealing with real persons is that Judah is presented here in a very unfavorable light. If this was a matter of Jewish myth or nationalistic fantasy, the later Israelites certainly would have laundered out such tales.

We want to offer a final word about the place of this chapter in the history of the Israelites. Actually the biblical narrative is masterfully composed. At the close of chapter 37 Joseph disappears from the scene of Jacob's family in Canaan. It would be many years before he would rejoin his father's household. At this point the author diverts the attention of the readers away from Joseph and turns his focus to events in the life of Judah that covered a considerable period of time. This chapter is then placed after chapter 37, not only because the events took place after Joseph's captivity in Egypt began, but also because of another factor involved. It is significant that it was Judah who is here brought under the spotlight of revelation. There certainly were many other happenings in the family of Jacob during this time that could have been incorporated into the narrative, but it was these events that especially bring to light the critical danger that threatened the "chosen seed" if they remained in Canaan at this time. Mixed marriages with the Canaanites could lead only to the people of Israel losing their identity among the Canaanites and eventually being absorbed by them. This chapter clearly indicates that Jacob's descendants had to leave Canaan if they were to develop as a separate and distinctive people. It was imperative that they be moved into a situation where they could not possibly mix with their countrymen. This, of course, happened in Egypt. This chapter therefore serves as a "filler" in the progressive narrative. It forms a significant part of the development of the history of redemption that began with chapter 37, and moves on with Israel's eventual sojourn in Egypt.

38:1–5 *At that time, Judah left his brothers and went down to stay with a man of Adullam named Hirah. There Judah met the daughter of a Canaanite man named Shua. He married her and lay with her; she became pregnant and gave birth to a son, who was named Er. She conceived again and gave birth to a son and named him Onan. She gave birth to still another son and named him Shelah. It was at Kezib that she gave birth to him.*

These verses tell how Judah separated himself from his brothers and moved from the region of Hebron where his father's household was residing at that time (see 37:14 and 35:27). Judah moved in a westerly direction. The word that is used says that he "descended," which suggests that he moved to a lower altitude closer to the Mediterranean Sea. He settled near Adullam and stayed with a man named Hirah. In Joshua 12:15 Adullam is mentioned as one of the Canaanitish city-kingdoms conquered by the Israelites. In Joshua 15:35 it is included among the places in the Shephelah, or the foothills that lay between the hill country, which later was inherited by the tribe of Judah and the coastal lowlands that were occupied by the Philistines.

We are not told what occupation Judah pursued in this location, but we are told that there he made the acquaintance of a Canaanitish girl. Although we are not given her name, she was the daughter of Shua. Judah married this girl and in quick succession she bore him two sons. When his third son was born, somewhat later, Judah was living at Kezib, which was another town in the Shephelah. This latter town must be distinguished from the coastal town of Aczib, which later became part of the territory of the tribe of Asher (Judg. 1:31).

38:6–11 *Judah got a wife for Er, his firstborn, and her name was Tamar. But Er, Judah's firstborn, was wicked in the LORD's sight; so the LORD put him to death.*

Then Judah said to Onan, "Lie with your brother's wife and fulfill your duty to her as a brother-in-law to produce offspring for your brother." But Onan knew that the offspring would not be his; so whenever he lay with his brother's wife, he spilled his seed on the ground to keep from producing offspring for his brother. What he did was wicked in the LORD's sight; so he put him to death also.

Judah then said to his daughter-in-law Tamar, "Live as a widow in your father's house until my son Shelah grows up." For he thought, "He may die too, just like his brothers." So Tamar went to live in her father's house.

As soon as Judah's oldest son, Er, reached marriageable age, his father chose a wife for him. Her name was Tamar and she is identified because she later played a very significant role in the narrative. She undoubtedly also was a Canaanite, although this is not specifically mentioned, and her father's house was evidently near Judah's location (see vv. 11 and 13ff.). Shortly after Er's marriage, we are told, he provoked the anger of God and died. It is striking that we are not told what the nature of his offense was. After his death, Judah asked his second son, Onan, to fulfill one of the Eastern customs or laws to produce children by his brother's widow. A child born of such a relationship would then be considered to be the child of the dead brother. This practice of levirate marriage later became a part of the Mosaic Law. This law did, however, allow the living brother to excuse himself from this responsibility, but not without some loss of honor (see Deut. 25:5–10). We have an example of such a levirate marriage in Ruth 4:5–8. Onan agreed to accept his brotherly responsibility with Tamar, but because he realized that the child that might be born from his relationship would not be considered to be his, he intentionally did not complete the sex act with Tamar to avoid impregnating her. Since this practice also displeased the Lord, Onan died too.

The death of his two oldest sons instilled a certain superstitious fear in Judah. He seemed to feel that this young widow, Tamar, had been the cause of the death of his two sons. He hesitated to risk the life of his third son, Shelah, by putting this woman in his arms also. Judah therefore urged Tamar to return to her father's house and live as a widow until Shelah would reach marriageable age. Although this was a delaying tactic on Judah's part, Tamar went along with it. It is likely that Shelah was too young to accept the responsibility of levirate marriage, although not by very much.

38:12–19 *After a long time Judah's wife, the daughter of Shua, died. When Judah had recovered from his grief, he went up to Timnah, to the men who were shearing his sheep, and his friend Hirah the Adullamite went with him.*

When Tamar was told, "Your father-in-law is on his way to Timnah to shear his sheep," she took off her widow's clothes, covered herself with a veil to disguise herself, and then sat down at the entrance to Enaim, which is on the road to Timnah. For she saw that, though Shelah had now grown up, she had not been given to him as his wife.

When Judah saw her, he thought she was a prostitute, for she had covered her face. Not realizing that she was his daughter-in-law, he went over to her by the roadside and said, "Come now, let me sleep with you."

"And what will you give me to sleep with you?" she asked.

"I'll send you a young goat from my flock," he said.

"Will you give me something as a pledge until you send it?" she asked.
He said, "What pledge should I give you?"
"Your seal and its cord, and the staff in your hand," she answered. So he gave
them to her and slept with her, and she became pregnant by him. After she left, she
took off her veil and put on her widow's clothes again.

When Shelah was mature enough to fulfill his responsibility to Tamar, Judah took no action in this regard. Then Tamar realized that she had been deceived by Judah, so she decided to take things into her own hands and put some pressure on Judah with respect to his responsibility to her. When her father-in-law went to Timnah for the shearing of the sheep, Tamar saw her opportunity and seized it with clever determination. Judah invited his friend, Hirah, to accompany him to the feast which customarily was associated with the shering of the sheep (see 1 Sam. 25:2–11). Later we find Absalom extending a similar invitation to the princes of the royal family (2 Sam. 13:23).

We are told that when Judah took this trip he had put aside his mourning for his dead wife. Timnah was situated at a higher altitude, so we are told that he "ascended" to Timnah, and this suggests that Timnah lay in the hill country. Tamar found out about Judah's trip, so she shed her widow's clothes and put on the garb usually worn by prostitutes. Then she covered her face with a veil and took her position at the gate of the city of Enaim, which was on the route that Judah would take on his way to Timnah.

Although Tamar's actions in this regard may seem strange to us, there is evidence that among ancient Assyrian and Hittite peoples, part of the custom was that the levirate responsibility could pass to the father of the widow's husband if there were no brothers to fulfill it. Thus Tamar was only trying to acquire that to which she had a legal right. Judah walked right into the trap she had set for him. When he spotted what he considered to be an attractive prostitute, he propositioned her and offered her a kid from his flock as payment for her services. Tamar, however, was not satisfied with a mere promise of future payment and asked for some pledge or surety. She wanted to have proof that the child she hoped to conceive from this intercourse with Judah was indeed his child. She therefore asked Judah to give her his signet ring and the cord with which this was carried around his neck, plus his shepherd's staff. Judah agreed to her demand and then proceeded to have intercourse with his daughter-in-law, who was disguised as a prostitute. Tamar did not wait for the payment Judah had promised her, but immediately returned home, removed her disguise, and again assumed the role of the widow. She soon realized that her scheme had worked and that she was carrying Judah's child.

38:20–23 *Meanwhile Judah sent the young goat by his friend the Adullamite in order to get his pledge back from the woman, but he did not find her. He asked the men who lived there, "Where is the shrine prostitute who was beside the road at Enaim?"*

"There hasn't been any shrine prostitute here," they said.

So he went back to Judah and said, "I didn't find her. Besides, the men who lived there said, 'There hasn't been any shrine prostitute here.' "

Then Judah said, "Let her keep what she has, or we will become a laughingstock. After all, I did send her this young goat, but you didn't find her."

Judah obviously had every intention of paying the girl the agreed price as soon as possible, and also to get his ring and staff back. He sent the kid by the hand of a friend, the Adullamite, but the prostitute, who had been so obvious when he entered the city, was nowhere to be found. In this connection the Adullamite referred to her as a "shrine prostitute." This refers to a practice that was widely used in the worship practices of the Canaanites and later also among the Greeks and Romans. Shrine prostitutes were a common factor in the religious exercises of many pagan peoples. It is not surprising, then, that Judah's Canaanite friend used this term in referring to Judah's sex companion.

When his friend returned and reported that the woman was nowhere to be found, Judah decided to let her keep his ring and his staff. To pursue this matter any farther could become very embarrassing for a man of Judah's position and would make him a laughingstock among the people of that area. He consoled himself with having put forth an effort to pay the woman, but since she could not be found, the whole matter was best forgotten.

38:24–26 *About three months later Judah was told, "Your daughter-in-law Tamar is guilty of prostitution, and as a result she is now pregnant."*

Judah said, "Bring her out and have her burned to death!"

As she was being brought out, she sent a message to her father-in-law. "I am pregnant by the man who owns these," she said. And she added, "See if you recognize whose seal and cord and staff these are."

Judah recognized them and said, "She is more righteous than I, since I wouldn't give her to my son Shelah." And he did not sleep with her again.

But Judah was not going to escape the consequences of his immoral activity that easily. After three months it was evident that Tamar was pregnant, and in order to force Judah into a public admission of his involvement in her pregnancy, she risked being charged as a prostitute. This charge was taken seriously in those days, and in her case the charge was especially serious since she supposedly was committed to become Shelah's wife. The customary penalty for women guilty of this sin was death by fire. Although there is some question about whether this penalty was practiced among the Canaanitish people of that era, there are evidences that it was used by some of the ancient civilizations for serious offenses. Thus, when Judah found out about Tamar's pregnancy and her conviction of prostitution, he, as the father of her previous husbands and her husband-to-be, exercised his right in this matter and demanded that the sentence be carried out.

Tamar played her role with great effectiveness. When she was led to the place of execution, she carried with her the ring, the cord, and the staff that Judah had given her as surety. At the crucial moment she had these items presented to Judah, accompanied by the message that the man who owned them was the father of her child. Judah, of course, immediately recognized his ring and his staff. At that moment he realized that the prostitute with whom he had indulged in sexual relations at Enaim was none other than his daughter-in-law, and that the child she was carrying in her womb was his own.

Judah admitted his guilt in the whole matter. He acknowledged that Tamar was more righteous than he. He had tried to deprive her of the levirate right to his son Shelah. Now she had, in her own surreptitious way, forced him to fulfill that levirate responsibility himself. It would be hard to determine how deep and sincere Judah's penitence for his sinful acts actually was, but we are told that he had no further sexual relations with the girl.

38:27–30 *When the time came for her to give birth, there were twin boys in her womb. As she was giving birth, one of them put out his hand; so the midwife took a scarlet thread and tied it on his wrist and said, "This one came out first." But when he drew back his hand, his brother came out, and she said, "So this is how you have broken out!" And he was named Perez. Then his brother, who had the scarlet thread on his wrist, came out and he was given the name Zerah.*

When the time came for Tamar to deliver her child it was found that there were twins in her womb. A strange incident is recorded regarding the birth of these two babies, which, in turn, explains the names they were given. The baby whose hand first came forth was marked by placing a red string around the hand. But then the other baby actually was born first. At this the midwife cried out, "So this is how you have broken out!" The exact reading is rather obscure. At any rate, the child who was born first was named "Perez." It was from this line that David was born (see Ruth

4:18–22; 1 Chron. 2:5–15), and, through David, the promised ''Seed of the woman,'' our Lord Jesus. Thereupon the other child, marked with the red string, was born. He was named ''Zerah,'' which means ''red'' or ''scarlet.''

43. *Joseph in the House of Potiphar and in Prison* (39:1–23)

After the interlude about Judah and his exploits in Canaan, the narrative returns to Joseph and how he fared in Egypt. The focus again turns to the preparation for the entrance of the patriarchal family into Egypt where the tribal family was to become a great nation.

Chapter 39 is generally ascribed to ''J'' by those who divide the sources. A few exceptions to this assignment are the description of Potiphar in verse 1, and the whole of verse 6. These sections are generally assigned to ''E.'' Some scholars hold that there is evidence of two distinct traditions within this narrative. They argue that according to ''E'' Joseph was bought as a slave by Potiphar, the captain of the guard, as soon as he arrived in Egypt. Since Potiphar also was in charge of the prison, Joseph would have served as keeper of the prison from the outset (see 40:3–4). The ''J'' tradition, according to these scholars, holds that Joseph was purchased by an unknown Egyptian official for whom he served as a house servant. Joseph gained a high regard and the complete confidence of this master, until he was trapped by his master's seductive wife. Thereafter he was thrown into prison.

Our interpretation as given below, as well as our treatment of chapter 40, will indicate that this critical analysis of the passage is not substantiated by the text. There is no textual evidence for two distinct traditions that contradict each other.

At this point it would be well to provide some historical data about this period, on the basis of secular historical records. One of our major difficulties is that the name of the pharaoh who was in power at the time Joseph came to Egypt is not mentioned in the biblical narrative. Some light has been shed on the use of the name ''Pharaoh'' in our earlier discussion of 12:15, but it is not possible to pinpoint or even approach the exact dates when Joseph was in Egypt on the basis of the narrative before us.

When we turn to secular histories of Egypt, there is considerable evidence that we are dealing with the period of the Hyksos dynasty. (See our treatment of 12:16.) Factors that point in this direction are the following: 1) In Joseph's time horses were referred to as being present in Egypt (47:17), and horses were introduced to Egypt by the Hyksos people. 2) Mention is made of a new king ''who did not know about Joseph'' in Exodus 1:8. This could refer to the restoration of a pure Egyptian dynasty, after the Hyksos were driven out. This could explain why Egyptian sources make no mention of Joseph and his work since the Egyptians tried to erase all references to the hated Hyksos from their historical records. 3) There is one record from the latter part of the Hyksos period that has been preserved in the tomb of Sekenenre, one of the Thebian rulers who were Egyptians, and who continued to rule in the southern part of Egypt, the so-called 17th Dynasty, during the Hyksos period. This record refers to rules that were set up for the gathering and storing of corn during a famine that continued for many years. Since periods of famine were very rare in Egypt, it is highly probable that this could be a reference to the famine in the days of Joseph.

4) The pharaoh under whom Joseph was active apparently had his residence in the Nile Delta. We note, for instance, that it was convenient for Joseph to present his father and his brothers to Pharaoh. This would have been the case since the land of Goshen where Joseph's family resided was in that same area. It is known that the Hyksos kings had their residence in Avanis, which probably was located in the northeastern section of the delta.

5) The reign of the Hyksos kings would have offered an opportune time for a Semite such as Joseph to attain a high position in the government. Likewise this was a favorable time for a Semite tribe such as Jacob's family to be offered a refuge in Egypt. 6) In this chapter, verse 1, Potiphar is described as ''an Egyptian.'' This strongly suggests that the pharaoh under whom he served was not an Egyptian, and this would also point to the Hyksos dynasty.

In spite of all these considerations, many scholars do not agree that Joseph's ascendancy in Egypt came during the rule of the Hyksos kings. They point to the strict segregation between the Egyptians and the Hebrews at the meal, mentioned in 43:32. This would have been most unlikely under a Hyksos government. Others have insisted, however, that the Hyksos rulers fully adopted the Egyptian culture. Even so, it is hard to believe that they accepted that culture so fully that they would refuse to eat with their fellow Semites, or that they would have permitted the Egyptians who were subject to them to practice this kind of segregation toward these Semite tribesmen.

Another objection that has been raised points to the argument that Joseph used to gain permission to have his family settle in Goshen (46:34). Joseph would hardly have speculated about the ancient Egyptian disdain for sheepherders in dealing with a Hyksos king.

In reply to the argument that Potiphar is designated as ''an Egyptian,'' it has been stressed that it was common in Egypt to promote men of foreign backgrounds to high official positions. The point to be emphasized in that reference would then be, not that this high official was an Egyptian, but rather that Joseph, as a Hebrew slave, gained such a high position of trust under an Egyptian ruling official.

It is further argued that the marriage of a prominent man such as Joseph to the daughter of the high priest of On (41:45) would be in conflict with the policies of the Hyksos kings, for the Hyksos people did everything in their power to break the domination of the Egyptian priests. This same factor would apply to the portion of the land assigned to the priests according to 47:22, 36.

A strong argument raised against placing these events in the time of the Hyksos kings is that the pharaoh of Joseph's time reigned over the whole of Egypt (see 41:41, 43, 44, 46; 47:20–21), whereas the realm of the Hyksos kings was limited to lower Egypt. On the other hand, it has been argued that some of the Hyksos kings also reigned over upper Egypt, as for instance, Apophis or Apepi III, who is identified with the pharaoh of Joseph's time by many scholars.

Another factor that comes into consideration, in this connection, is that among the records found of this period there are indications that Palestine also formed part of Egypt's domain under the Hyksos kings. If this were the case there would be a number of difficulties that should be faced: 1) Why did Joseph not then initiate an effort to find out about the welfare of his family? 2) Why did Joseph accuse his brothers of being spies when they came from Palestine to Egypt? 3) Why did the funeral procession that carried Jacob's body to Canaan take the long route around the Dead Sea (50:10)? 4) Why did the Egyptian escort that accompanied the procession to Canaan not cross the river Jordan (50:13)? 5) Why did Joseph make use of an interpreter in speaking to his brothers because during the Hyksos time it would have been altogether understandable that a high Egyptian official could understand the Semitic language?

When all of these arguments are put together, probably the most significant consideration involves the use of horses and chariots. It has been generally accepted that these were introduced to Egypt by the Hyksos people. Later excavations, however, indicate that horses may have been used long before the time that was formerly accepted by scholars. A skeleton of a horse was found at Gaza, which was dated at approximately 2500 B.C. This would indicate that horses were present in southern Palestine, which borders on Egypt, long before the time of the Hyksos kings. Egyptian records also cast some doubt on the thesis that horses were introduced to Egypt by the Hyksos. A papyrus has been discovered that tells of an Egyptian princess who rode a horse. Although the papyrus dates from approximately 1220 B.C., the narrative it records is much older than that.

One final question has been raised. If Joseph and his family stood in such close association with the Hyksos kings, why didn't the pharaoh of the 18th Dynasty, who drove out the Hyksos, immediately begin his oppression of Israel? Why did he wait for many years before resorting to this method of containing these foreigners in their midst? The oppression of Israel started under the reign of Thutmose III (1478–1447 B.C.), while the Hyksos were driven out in 1580 B.C.

From all of this it is evident that there are strong arguments both in favor of and in opposition to dating the coming of Israel into Egypt during the time of the Hyksos kings. There is the added difficulty that we do not know how long the Hyksos kings actually were in power in Egypt. An ancient Egyptian historian-priest, by the name of Manetho (c. 260 B.C.) sets the period of the Hyksos rule at five centuries. This has been strongly denied by later historians, however, and many set this period at no longer than one century. It is generally agreed that the period falls somewhere between these two figures. This period probably began after the 12th Dynasty or approximately 1790 B.C. In the light of biblical data concerning the dates of the building of Solomon's temple, the conclusion has been reached that the birth of Abraham must be set at 2169 B.C. (See introduction to 11:27–12:9.) If this is correct, the year of Joseph's arrival in Egypt would be 1899 B.C. Jacob was born 160 years after Abraham (cf. 21:5 with 25:26), and he was 130 when he arrived in Egypt (47:9). As we observed in our introduction to chapter 31, Joseph had been in Egypt some 20 years before Jacob arrived there. Thus, there was a space of 270 years between the birth of Abraham and Joseph's arrival in Egypt. If these dates are dependable, Joseph came to Egypt a century before the reign of the Hyksos kings.

Other scholars, such as Professor Noordzij, place the beginning of the Hyksos era much earlier, at about the year 2000 B.C. In that case, Joseph's time in Egypt would fall within the Hyksos period. It should also be noted that there are some questions about setting the date of Abraham's birth at 2169 B.C. as well, as discussed in our introduction to Genesis 11:27–12:9.

When everything is considered, we can say that there is a strong possibility that Joseph came into Egypt approximately 1900 B.C., and that the Hyksos kings probably were in power at that time, but these positions are by no means certain. It is also possible to defend the thesis that Joseph came to power long before the Hyksos period in Egyptian history.

39:1 *Now Joseph had been taken down to Egypt. Potiphar, an Egyptian who was one of Pharaoh's officials, the captain of the guard, bought him from the Ishmaelites who had taken him there.*

At the beginning of verse 1 our narrator picks up the thread of the story where he had left it at the end of chapter 37. He repeats what he had said in the closing verse of that chapter, namely, that Joseph had been taken to Egypt and had been sold there as a slave to Potiphar, who was captain of Pharaoh's guard. As we observed in our treatment of 37:36, Potiphar probably did not buy Joseph directly from the Ishmaelites who had brought him to Egypt. They probably sold him to a slave dealer from whom the actual purchase was made by one of Potiphar's subordinates. We have already made some comments about someone being called "an Egyptian." Although the term can be interpreted in various ways, it is obvious that Potiphar was indeed a pure-blooded Egyptian. His name also was Egyptian and it meant "he whom Ra (the sun god) has given."

39:2–6 *The Lord was with Joseph and he prospered, and he lived in the house of his Egyptian master. When his master saw that the Lord was with him and that the Lord gave him success in everything he did, Joseph found favor in his eyes and became his attendant. Potiphar put him in charge of his household, and he entrusted to his care everything he owned. From the time he put him in charge of his household and of all that he owned, the Lord blessed the household of the Egyptian because of Joseph. The blessing of the Lord was on everything Potiphar had, both in the house and in the field. So he left in Joseph's care everything he had; with Joseph in charge, he did not concern himself with anything except the food he ate. Now Joseph was well-built and handsome,*

Although Joseph was a slave in Egypt, the Lord did not forsake him but prospered him in his humble state in this foreign land. His first advantage was that he was not placed in the fields as a laborer, as was the lot of many slaves. Joseph became a house servant for Potiphar. His master observed that Joseph carried on his duties with unusual efficiency and dispatch. This was, of course, due to the blessing of the Lord. When we read that Potiphar observed this, this does not indicate that Potiphar ascribed Joseph's success to the blessing of the Lord. It indicates, rather, that he took note of the favorable consequences (of God's blessing) in the quality of Joseph's service. The pagan Potiphar obviously did not know Joseph's God.

Joseph gained such favor with his master that he was promoted step by step. First he was made his master's personal attendant. Then he was placed in charge of the entire household, that is, he was given supervision over all the other servants. Finally, he was promoted to being in charge of all of Potiphar's possessions, both in his house and in the fields. God blessed Joseph so abundantly that Potiphar's personal affairs prospered in a most remarkable way. So completely did Potiphar trust his distinguished servant that he left everything in Joseph's exclusive care, except the food he ate, which remained under his own surveillance.

This last statement has caused some discussion among interpreters. Some have insisted this indicates that the only thing Potiphar did anymore was to eat and drink. The term, however, does not refer to the activity as such but rather to the supervision of that activity. We would prefer an interpretation that says that since there were Egyptian rituals to be observed with respect to the preparation and the eating of food, Potiphar preferred to keep this aspect of his household life under his personal control, rather than placing this under the supervision of his foreign servant.

Then there is an added comment to the effect that Joseph was physically well-built and very handsome in appearance. This is, no doubt, added in preparation for what follows. It would explain why Potiphar's sensuous wife took a personal interest in her husband's attractive young slave.

39:7–10 *And after a while his master's wife took notice of Joseph and said, "Come to bed with me!"*

But he refused. "With me in charge," he told her, "my master does not concern himself with anything in the house; everything he owns he has entrusted to my care. No one is greater in this house than I am. My master has withheld nothing from me except you, because you are his wife. How then could I do such a wicked thing and sin against God?" And though she spoke to Joseph day after day, he refused to go to bed with her or even be with her.

In these verses we have a description of how the unfaithful spouse of Joseph's master tried to seduce this handsome young slave. Joseph, however, resisted her enticement by reminding her that his master had entrusted everything he had to him. He had been given such a position of trust that only his master's wife was not under his control. It was unthinkable for Joseph that he should violate that trust. But even more importantly, he could not yield to her seduction because to do so would be a sin against God. Potiphar's wife continued to lure Joseph to make love to her but Joseph steadfastly refused her advances and even avoided her company.

39:11–15 *One day he went into the house to attend to his duties, and none of the household servants was inside. She caught him by his cloak and said, "Come to bed with me!" But he left his cloak in her hand and ran out of the house.*

When she saw that he had left his cloak in her hand and had run out of the house, she called her household servants. "Look," she said to them, "this Hebrew has been brought to us to make sport of us! He came in here to sleep with me, but I screamed. When he heard me scream for help, he left his cloak beside me and ran out of the house."

One day Joseph came into the house to carry on his regular duties while none of the other servants were in the house. This was the opportunity Potiphar's wife had been seeking. She grabbed Joseph by his clothes (it was probably the outer cloak that hung over the shoulders) and begged him to make love to her. Joseph, however, pulled away from her embrace, leaving his cloak in her hands, and fled from the house. "No wrath so great as a woman spurned." Humiliated by Joseph's refusal to listen to her request to go to bed with her, she determined to get revenge. She screamed for help, and other servants came running to her aid. Her story was that Joseph had tried to physically assault her and that when she cried for help he had fled, leaving his coat behind in her hands. The other servants accepted the coat as condemning evidence and were ready to testify against Joseph before their master. When their spiteful mistress referred to Joseph as "this Hebrew" this only added fuel to the fire. No doubt the other servants were jealous of Joseph's rapid promotion and would be happy to assist in his downfall. Regarding the use of the term "Hebrew," see our treatment under 10:21 and our introduction to chapter 14.

39:16–20a *She kept his cloak beside her until his master came home. Then she told him this story: "That Hebrew slave you brought us came to me to make sport of me. But as soon as I screamed for help, he left his cloak beside me and ran out of the house."*

When his master heard the story his wife told him, saying, "This is how your slave treated me," he burned with anger. Joseph's master took him and put him in prison, the place where the king's prisoners were confined.

The woman kept the alleged evidence, Joseph's cloak, close at hand until her husband came home. She told her husband the same story she had related to the other servants. When Potiphar heard it, he believed it, became very angry, and threw Joseph into prison.

There are two matters in this connection that have caused a great deal of discussion among scholars. The first is the term used to describe the prison in which Joseph was placed. For many years there was great uncertainty about the proper translation of this term. More recently it has been generally agreed that it actually is an Egyptian term and should be translated, as our translators have done, "the place where the king's prisoners were confined." This probably was a special prison, set aside for those who were found guilty of political crimes. Since Potiphar was captain of the royal guard, it would seem logical that he was also in charge of this prison. Thus when he decided to imprison Joseph, this would have been the prison selected for his high-ranking servant.

A more critical question that has been raised is why Potiphar imprisoned Joseph and did not have him promptly beheaded. Many scholars are convinced that Potiphar was actually not fully convinced of Joseph's guilt. To avoid a public scandal and to satisfy his wife, he meted out a rather light sentence for Joseph. This of course raises the question about the statement that Potiphar "burned with anger." Some have tried to avoid this point by suggesting that he was angry, not so much with Joseph as with his wife, or just because his household had been publicly shamed. The obvious intent of the story, however, is that when his wife told him her story Potiphar believed her. After all, she had the evidence in her hand. The result of Potiphar's anger is Joseph's imprisonment. It is possible that being placed in that particular prison was considered to be a severe punishment. Some have suggested that Joseph was placed there only to await execution. There is, however, no textual evidence for this assumption.

A number of scholars have held that this prison was known as the "Prison of Tar, or Saru," based on the Egyptian term used here. This supposedly was located on the border between Egypt and Palestine. According to Egyptian records, this prison was used not only for political prisoners but also for those who were guilty of other serious crimes. In the light of this it would appear that Joseph was placed in this particular prison because his offense was considered to be very serious. It would be comparable to placing a prisoner in "maximum security" in our day.

There is a record in an ancient Egyptian papyrus about a legend that has certain similarities to this story of Joseph and Potiphar's wife. Similar sagas have also been found among the Greeks, in India, in Persia, in Germany, and in Arabia. In none are the similarities to the biblical narrative so strong that a case can be made for a common source, however. To be sure, the subject matter of an unfaithful wife who is jilted by her would-be lover is all too familiar everywhere in the world. But this cannot be made a basis for calling the historicity of this biblical account into question. If we accept the Bible as the Word of God, there is no need to question the truth of the event recorded here. If this was no more than a fable or a saga the outcome would certainly have been that the unfaithful wife would have been found out, and the hero, in this case Joseph, would have been exonerated and set free. The very fact that Joseph was kept imprisoned in the royal fortress argues for the historicity of this narrative.

39:20b–23 *But while Joseph was there in the prison, the LORD was with him; he showed him kindness and granted him favor in the eyes of the prison warden. So the warden put Joseph in charge of all those held in the prison, and he was made* *responsible for all that was done there. The warden paid no attention to anything under Joseph's care, because the LORD was with Joseph and gave him success in whatever he did.*

The first thing we are told about Joseph's experience in prison is that "the Lord was with [him]." This, of course, casts a special light on the whole event. Further, we are told that the Lord showed kindness to Joseph by granting him favor with the keeper of the prison. This probably was a gradual process, with Joseph first finding favor with some of the lesser officials in the prison, who in turn brought a good report about this prisoner to the warden or commander of the royal guard house. The latter was probably under the direct command of Potiphar who was captain of the guard.

In time the warden placed Joseph in a position of responsibility that involved supervision over the other prisoners and over the entire activity of the prison. The warden delegated full responsibility to Joseph so that he himself paid no attention to the details of the daily operation of the prison. It is again stressed that all of this occurred because the Lord blessed Joseph and prospered him in all he did.

44. *Joseph As the Interpreter of Dreams* (40:1–23)

This chapter is generally assigned to "E" by those who divide the sources. A few small sections in verses 1, 5, and 15, it is claimed, include a mixture of material from more than one source. Some of the arguments used in this connection are based on conclusions that these same scholars had already drawn with respect to chapters 37 and 39, since those chapters relate to the material recorded here. One example would be the theory that there are two different accounts of how Joseph came to Egypt. Another idea was that Joseph was actually not a prisoner but that his duty in the prison was part of his responsibility as Potiphar's slave. These critical theories were discussed when we treated the chapters mentioned and we need not repeat that discussion here.

There are a few other references in this chapter that allegedly point to more than one source for this material. There is the use of the expression, "after these things," which our translators have rendered "some time later." We have already discussed this in our introduction to chapter 22. In verse 4 of this chapter it appears as though Joseph was serving the cup-bearer and the baker while in 39:22 it is obvious that he was in charge of all the prisoners. Mention is also made, by the critics, of the fact that in verses 3, 4, and 7 another word is used for imprisonment than was used in 39:20–23. Our translators have used the term "custody" in this case.

Also, here we find the term "king of Egypt," while in the rest of the narrative the ruler is referred to as the "pharaoh."

In reply to these allegations, let it be said that there certainly is no conflict between a prison guard, such as Joseph was, on the one hand being "in charge" of the prisoners, and on the other hand "serving" them with their food and other needs. Further, the terms used to describe the state of being imprisoned are purely synonymous. The use of synonyms certainly does not, in itself, argue for multiple sources for the material at hand. It should be noted that in verse 15 Joseph used still another word for the prison, the word our translators have rendered "dungeon." Also, to change from the use of the term "pharaoh" to "king" certainly is not unusual. We find the same variety of expression in Egyptian literature, as well as in many other places in the Old Testament Scripture. Thus the arguments of the critics remain wholly unconvincing.

40:1–4a *Some time later, the cupbearer and the baker of the king of Egypt offended their master, the king of Egypt. Pharaoh was angry with his two officials, the chief cupbearer and the chief baker, and put them in custody in the house of the captain of the guard, in the same prison where Joseph was confined. The captain of the guard assigned them to Joseph, and he attended them.*

The chapter opens with the account of the arrival in the prison of the king's chief cupbearer and chief baker. What the nature of their offenses were we are not told and this is really of no consequence. Because they were officers of the king it was logical that they should be imprisoned in the king's guard house, where Joseph was also imprisoned. These officials were then placed under Joseph's supervision. It is worthy of note that this assignment was not made by the warden of the prison but by the captain of the guard himself. Verse 3 suggests that this prison was actually situated in the house in which the captain of the guard resided (see also v. 7). This would then be the house of Potiphar. When it came to making arrangements for the care of such high-ranking officials as these, the captain evidently made these arrangements himself. He probably consulted with the warden of the prison with whom Joseph had, by this time, found considerable favor (see 39:21–23). This would indicate, however, that Potiphar's anger against Joseph had cooled considerably since he now allowed these high officials to be placed under Joseph's personal care. Again we perceive how the Lord was favoring Joseph by opening the way for him to reach positions of great responsibility in the structure of the government of Egypt.

40:4b–8 *After they had been in custody for some time, each of the two men–the cupbearer and the baker of the king of Egypt, who were being held in prison–had a dream the same night, and each dream had a meaning of its own.*

When Joseph came to them the next morning, he saw that they were dejected. So he asked Pharaoh's officials who were in custody with him in his master's house, "Why are your faces so sad today?"

"We both had dreams," they answered, "but there is no one to interpret them."

Then Joseph said to them, "Do not interpretations belong to God? Tell me your dreams."

After these personal attendants of the king had been in custody for some time, both of them had dreams in the same night. It was to become evident later that these dreams were of great significance in the unfolding narrative. The cupbearer and the baker were convinced that their dreams had some special significance for them. In ancient Egypt, as in other ancient countries, there were strong beliefs and superstitions regarding the importance of dreams with respect to future events. So when these two Egyptian officials had dreams in the same night, which were strikingly similar, they felt sure that these dreams related somehow to their own destiny. Since they were in prison they did not have access to one of the interpreters of dreams who undoubtedly formed part of the royal court of Egypt. Thus, when Joseph made his usual morning visit to attend to their needs, he noticed immediately that they were disturbed and he inquired about the reasons for their dejection. These officials were ready to share the cause of their unrest with Joseph.

At this point Joseph pointed out to them that the interpretation of dreams is not a simple human skill but lies within God's power and is under His control. Even so, Joseph asked them to tell him about their dreams with the hope that his God would reveal their interpretation to him.

40:9–11 *So the chief cupbearer told Joseph his dream. He said to him, "In my dream I saw a vine in front of me, and on the vine were three branches. As soon as it budded, it blossomed, and its clusters ripened into grapes. Pharaoh's cup was in my hand, and I took the grapes, squeezed them into Pharaoh's cup and put the cup in his hand."*

First the cupbearer told Joseph his dream. In his dream he had seen a vine with three branches, and this vine produced buds and then grapes. Pharaoh's cup was in his hand and he took some of the grapes and squeezed the juice into the cup and gave it to Pharaoh.

40:12–15 *"This is what it means," Joseph said to him. "The three branches are three days. Within three days Pharaoh will lift up your head and restore you to your position, and you will put Pharaoh's cup in his hand, just as you used to do when you were his cupbearer. But when all goes well with you, remember me and show me kindness; mention me to Pharaoh and get me out of this prison. For I was forcibly carried off from the land of the Hebrews, and even here I have done nothing to deserve being put in a dungeon."*

God enabled Joseph to give an immediate interpretation of this dream. The three branches represented three days, and within three days the cupbearer would be restored to his former position and would again give the cup to Pharaoh. The expression "will lift up your head" refers to being raised up from a position of humiliation and dishonor to a position of honor and acceptance.

Joseph added an urgent personal request to his statement to the king's cupbearer. He asked the official that, when he was restored to his position with Pharaoh, he would not forget the one who had interpreted his dream for him in prison. He begged him to use his influence with Pharaoh to have him released from prison. He told them that he had been stolen from the land of the Hebrews (see our comments about the use of this term under 14:13). He further insisted that he had committed no crime that would warrant his being placed in this prison.

40:16–19 *When the chief baker saw that Joseph had given a favorable interpretation, he said to Joseph, "I too had a dream: On my head were three baskets of bread. In the top basket were all kinds of baked goods for Pharaoh, but the birds were eating them out of the basket on my head."*

"This is what it means," Joseph said. "The three baskets are three days. Within three days Pharaoh will lift off your head and hang you on a tree. And the birds will eat away your flesh."

The favorable outcome of the cupbearer's dream encouraged the baker also to tell his dream to Joseph. In his dream he was walking with three baskets of bread on his head. This practice of carrying baskets on the head can still be seen in the Middle East today. In the top basket there were all kinds of baked goods that were intended for Pharaoh, but before he could deliver them the birds came and devoured these baked goods.

The meaning of this dream was also immediately made clear to Joseph and he proceeded to give the interpretation. Again, there was a reference to three days, but the fortunes of the baker were the opposite of those of the cupbearer. In three days he would be executed and his body, hanging in a tree, would be eaten by birds of prey. When Joseph here also used the term "lift off your head," it was an obvious play on words, since in this case it meant that the man's head would be lifted up by hanging.

40:20-22 *Now the third day was Pharaoh's birthday, and he gave a feast for all his officials. He lifted up the heads of the chief cupbearer and the chief baker in the presence of his officials: He restored the chief cupbearer to his position, so that he once again put the cup into Pharaoh's hand, but he hanged the chief baker, just as Joseph had said to them in his interpretation.*

Everything happened exactly the way Joseph had predicted. The dreams accurately predicted the future and this clearly indicated that God had sent these dreams and had enabled Joseph to correctly interpret them.

Three days later Pharaoh had a birthday with an elaborate feast for all his officials. At that occasion he publicly restored the cupbearer to his honored position. The chief baker, however, was taken from the prison and hanged. In verse 20 the term "lifted up the heads" is again used as referring to both officials. The one was lifted up by being restored to his high position, while the other was hanged above the earth.

40:23 *The chief cupbearer, however, did not remember Joseph; he forgot him.*

We are told that the cupbearer promptly forgot all about the young Hebrew slave in the prison and his urgent request for intercession with Pharaoh in his behalf. This was probably no more than the usual lack of concern on the part of the high and mighty for the lowly and the disadvantaged.

45. *Joseph in the Court of Pharaoh* (41:1–57)

Even those who divide the sources recognize that this chapter presents a unified narrative. This, then, is generally ascribed to "E." Some scholars, however, still manage to point out certain traces of more than one source, especially in the latter part of the chapter, after verse 30, but there is little agreement among these scholars as to which references should be assigned to other sources. Some insist that the specific data about Joseph's age, etc., in verse 46, points to "P." Others have argued that verse 33 presents Pharaoh as restricting his order to one man, while verse 34 presents this as including a group of people. It has also been alleged that Joseph's special discernment is acknowledged twice, in verse 38 and again in verse 39. Moreover it is claimed that Joseph's promotion is mentioned twice, in verse 40 and again in verse 44. Further, there are supposedly two different presentations regarding the famine. The one suggests that the whole world suffered from hunger except for Egypt (v. 54), and the other suggests that Egypt also suffered from the famine.

It is not necessary to deal with each of these arguments individually. Each one of them will be discussed in the course of our commentary following. It will become evident that there are no true irregularities or contradictions in the text and, therefore, no substantial reasons for searching for more than one source.

41:1–7 *When two full years had passed, Pharaoh had a dream: He was standing by the Nile, when out of the river there came up seven cows, sleek and fat, and they grazed among the reeds. After them, seven other cows, ugly and gaunt, came up out of the Nile and stood beside those on the riverbank. And the cows that were ugly and gaunt ate up the seven sleek, fat cows. Then Pharaoh woke up.*

He fell asleep again and had a second dream: Seven heads of grain, healthy and good, were growing on a single stalk. After them, seven other heads of grain sprouted–thin and scorched by the east wind. The thin heads of grain swallowed up the seven healthy, full heads. Then Pharaoh woke up; it had been a dream.

Two years had lapsed after the release and restoration of Pharaoh's cupbearer. Then something happened that suddenly brought Joseph into the public eye in Egypt. This time it was the pharaoh himself who had a disturbing dream. In fact, he had two dreams, which were very similar. In his dreams he found himself on the banks of the Nile River. He saw seven cows, fat and sleek, come up out of the river and begin to graze along the riverbanks. It should be noted that the word used for "river" is of Egyptian origin. It was customary for the Egyptians to refer to the Nile simply as "the river." In the Old Testament the word also generally refers to the Nile, except in Daniel 12:5–7, where it refers to the Tigris. In the same way, the word that is used here for "grass" is an Egyptian term that actually means simply "the green."

After the seven fat cattle, Pharaoh saw in his dream seven other cows come forth. These were lean and scrawny. They approached the fat and sleek cows and ate them up. And there Pharaoh's dream ended abruptly and he awoke.

Soon Pharaoh went back to sleep and had another dream, similar to the first. This time he saw seven heads of grain that were full and abundant. Then he saw seven other heads of grain, which had sprouted very thin and then withered, and they were scorched by the "east wind." These lean ears again devoured the full, good ears. The "east wind," which was common to both Egypt and Palestine, was a hot wind that swept from the desert and scorched and withered all plant life. The Arabs actually distinguished between two "east winds." The "Chamsin" sometimes lasted as long as

210

fifty days and usually came in the spring of the year. The "Samoem," on the other hand, came at various times of the year and was of brief duration, sometimes just a few hours. The latter had the nature of a sudden violent storm and was extremely destructive for plant life, as well as for animals and humans.

41:8–13 *In the morning his mind was troubled, so he sent for all the magicians and wise men of Egypt. Pharaoh told them his dreams, but no one could interpret them for him.*

Then the chief cupbearer said to Pharaoh, "Today I am reminded of my shortcomings. Pharaoh was once angry with his servants, and he imprisoned me and the chief baker in the house of the captain of the guard. Each of us had a dream the same night, and each dream had a meaning of its own. Now a young Hebrew was there with us, a servant of the captain of the guard. We told him our dreams, and he interpreted them for us, giving each man the interpretation of his dream. And things turned out exactly as he interpreted them to us: I was restored to my position, and the other man was hanged."

The pharaoh was sure that his dreams had a special meaning, because the lean and ugly devoured the healthy and the strong. Moreover, it was obvious to him that the dreams portended something ominous and unfavorable. Consequently, the pharaoh was deeply disturbed. He immediately sent for those in his royal court who assumed responsibility for such things as interpreting dreams. Every royal court in those days, and especially those in Egypt, had a complement of "magicians" or "wise men," supposedly possessed with superior intelligence, who served as special advisors to the king. In Exodus 7:11, 22 and 8:7, 18, this word is used for those who performed miracles by magic and enchantments. Thus it referred to a class of people who were skilled in the secrets of wizardry and magic. Pharaoh told his dreams to these experts in his court, but none of them were able to interpret the dreams for him.

It was at this point that the king's cupbearer suddenly remembered his experience with the young Hebrew slave in the prison. He suggested to the king that Joseph might be able to interpret his dreams with the same skill he had demonstrated with his dreams and those of the baker. He recounted the entire incident of the king's anger against his officials, their imprisonment in the house of the captain of the guard, their dreams, and the amazing accuracy of the interpretation of their dreams given by the young "Hebrew slave" who was in the service of the captain of the guard.

41:14–24 *So Pharaoh sent for Joseph, and he was quickly brought from the dungeon. When he had shaved and changed his clothes, he came before Pharaoh.*

211

> *Pharaoh said to Joseph, "I had a dream, and no one can interpret it. But I have heard it said of you that when you hear a dream you can interpret it."*
> *"I cannot do it," Joseph replied to Pharaoh, "but God will give Pharaoh the answer he desires."*
> *Then Pharaoh said to Joseph, "In my dream I was standing on the bank of the Nile, when out of the river there came up seven cows, fat and sleek, and they grazed among the reeds. After them, seven other cows came up–scrawny and very ugly and lean. I had never seen such ugly cows in all the land of Egypt. The lean, ugly cows ate up the seven fat cows that came up first. But even after they ate them, no one could tell that they had done so; they looked just as ugly as before. Then I woke up.*
> *"In my dreams I also saw seven heads of grain, full and good, growing on a single stalk. After them, seven other heads sprouted–withered and thin and scorched by the east wind. The thin heads of grain swallowed up the seven good heads. I told this to the magicians, but none could explain it to me."*

Immediately a messenger was sent to bring Joseph from the prison to the royal court. Naturally, Joseph could not make his entrance before the king in the garb and appearance of a prisoner and a slave. The Semitic people allowed their hair and their beards to grow long, so to conform to Egyptian custom, Joseph had to shave and change clothes. After this preparation, Joseph was brought before the pharaoh of Egypt.

Pharaoh greeted Joseph by telling him about his dreams that no one had been able to interpret. With all due respect, Joseph insisted that he was not capable of interpreting dreams. He pointed out, however, that God sometimes revealed the future by means of dreams, and God could also reveal the meaning of such dreams. Joseph declared that God would give the king a favorable interpretation. Proper etiquette required that Joseph would avoid any suggestion that the dream might have an unfavorable implication for the king, for Joseph had been in Egypt long enough to be aware of proper court decorum.

So Pharaoh told Joseph his twofold dream. It is in keeping with the literary style of that period that the dreams are not told in exactly the same words each time they are recounted. Consequently a few stylistic changes are made as Pharaoh repeats his experiences in his dreams (cf. with vv. 1–7). Such stylistic changes are common in many of the narratives that have come down to us from that period.

41:25–32 *Then Joseph said to Pharaoh, "The dreams of Pharaoh are one and the same. God has revealed to Pharaoh what he is about to do. The seven good cows are seven years, and the seven good heads of grain are seven years; it is one and the same dream. The seven lean, ugly cows that came up after they did are seven years, and so are the seven worthless heads of grain scorched by the east wind: They are seven years of famine.*

"It is just as I said to Pharaoh: God has shown Pharaoh what he is about to do. Seven years of great abundance are coming throughout the land of Egypt, but seven years of famine will follow them. Then all the abundance in Egypt will be forgotten, and the famine will ravage the land. The abundance in the land will not be remembered, because the famine that follows it will be so severe. The reason the dream was given to Pharaoh in two forms is that the matter has been firmly decided by God, and God will do it soon.

Without any hesitation, Joseph immediately gave Pharaoh the interpretation he so urgently sought. The two dreams actually conveyed one message in which God revealed to Pharaoh what He would do. The number seven, which occurs repeatedly, referred to seven years. First there would be seven years of abundant harvests in Egypt. Following that there would be a period of seven years of severe famine, and so severe would the famine be that the years of abundance would soon be forgotten. The double presentation of this message indicated that God's purpose in this regard was firm, that He would certainly bring it to pass, and in the immediate future.

41:33–36 *"And now let Pharaoh look for a discerning and wise man and put him in charge of the land of Egypt. Let Pharaoh appoint commissioners over the land to take a fifth of the harvest of Egypt during the seven years of abundance. They should collect all the food of these good years that are coming and store up the grain under the authority of Pharaoh, to be kept in the cities for food. This food should be held in reserve for the country, to be used during the seven years of famine that will come upon Egypt, so that the country may not be ruined by the famine."*

Joseph did not limit his comments to an interpretation of Pharaoh's dreams, however. He took the liberty to advise the king as to what action should be taken in view of these impending events. He advised Pharaoh to appoint a qualified person who would be given broad authority over the whole of Egypt to control the food supply. By storing grain during the years of abundance an ample supply could be built up to provide food during the period of famine that would strike the land.

When verse 34 speaks of commissioners who would oversee this food conservation program, this does not conflict with verse 33, which suggests that one man would be put in charge of this operation. Obviously one man could not do all the work involved in such a huge project. He would need a staff of subordinates who would take care of gathering and storing all this food. The fact that Joseph recommended that only one fifth of the harvest be gathered during the years of plenty should not be seen as a weakness in his proposal. We should not conceive of this as meaning that Egypt would

213

have no crops at all during the years of famine. It should probably be seen as a period when the Nile would not overflow as extensively as it normally did. As a consequence the crops that depended on this annual overflow would be more limited than in normal years. At that time the stored reserves could supplement the diminished harvests. It should also be remembered that in a normal year Egypt produced far more grain than was needed for the country's use. Vast amounts of Egyptian grain were exported. In view of these facts, even one fifth of the grain produced in years of great abundance would provide an enormous supply for the storage plan that Joseph advocated.

Another factor that should be considered is that the people would be more apt to cooperate with the government if no more than one fifth of an abundant harvest was requisitioned, since they would still have an abundance for their own use.

The statement in verse 34 regarding "one fifth" of the harvest also is not in conflict with the reference in verse 35 to "all the food." This simply refers to all of the one fifth that would be stored.

Joseph further proposed that storage facilities be set up in the cities across the land.

41:37–40 *The plan seemed good to Pharaoh and to all his officials. So Pharaoh asked them, "Can we find anyone like this man, one in whom is the spirit of God?"*

Then Pharaoh said to Joseph, "Since God has made all this known to you, there is no one so discerning and wise as you. You shall be in charge of my palace, and all my people are to submit to your orders. Only with respect to the throne will I be greater than you."

Joseph's proposals were immediately accepted by Pharaoh and his advisors. Then something happened that Joseph had not anticipated when he gave his advice to the king. In considering the choice of a qualified person to place in charge of this entire venture, the king's eye fell on Joseph, himself. He first consulted with his advisors and officials and asked them whether there was anyone in Egypt who was better qualified for this assignment than this young Hebrew prisoner. With their concurrence he then addressed Joseph and declared that his wisdom and discernment had singled him out as the "man of the hour" for Egypt. When we read this in this way there is no evidence here for two distinct sources for this material. The reason for the repetition is completely obvious in the narrative.

It is striking that Pharaoh acknowledged that Joseph's wisdom and skill were more than natural human achievements. This, however, does not indicate that Pharaoh had become a believer in the one true God. The term, "one in whom is the spirit of God," can easily be taken in a polytheistic sense. When Pharaoh spoke to his officials he spoke of the spirit as being of "a god." Then when he addressed Joseph he showed respect for him, who was at that moment the center of honor and esteem, by referring to his God in the singular. Thus Joseph could think of this as the God of his people, while Pharaoh could consider this god as one of many.

After the declaration about Joseph's endowment with superhuman wisdom, Pharaoh proceeded to appoint Joseph to the highest position of power and authority in Egypt, next to the king himself. He put him in charge of the palace, which would include all of the other officials of the realm. His appointment as supervisor of the food supply was expressed in the statement, "all my people are to be fed by your orders." Our translators have slightly varied this reading by omitting the idea of all the people being fed and have simply said that all of the people would be under Joseph's authority. But the intent is clear in either reading. The word that is used probably has an Egyptian origin and has sometimes been translated "to kiss their food," which would then mean "to enjoy their food."

41:41–45 *So Pharaoh said to Joseph, "I hereby put you in charge of the whole land of Egypt." Then Pharaoh took his signet ring from his finger and put it on Joseph's finger. He dressed him in robes of fine linen and put a gold chain around his neck. He had him ride in a chariot as his second-in-command, and men shouted before him, "Make way!" Thus he put him in charge of the whole land of Egypt.*

Then Pharaoh said to Joseph, "I am Pharaoh, but without your word no one will lift hand or foot in all Egypt." Pharaoh gave Joseph the name Zaphenath-Paneah and gave him Asenath daughter of Potiphera, priest of On, to be his wife. And Joseph went throughout the land of Egypt.

After Pharaoh had appointed Joseph to his high position, he immediately proceeded to carry out the procedure for elevating this new official to the proper elegance and honor of his position. First of all, Joseph was given Pharaoh's signet ring as a symbol of royal honor and authority. Joseph was also dressed in the finest linen clothes and a gold chain was placed about his neck. In order to display his high position before all the people he was made to ride in a royal chariot with heralds running ahead shouting "Make way!" The term translated "make way" is an Egyptian word, *abrek.* It is worthy of note that even today in some Arab countries the word *balak,* which is an Arabic form of the same word, can be heard shouted in the streets. Thus Joseph was promoted to the position of a ruler of Egypt.

Verse 44 is not some needless repetition of what is recorded in verses 40 and 41, and thus an indication of multiple sources. We can visualize this as follows. After the spectacle of Joseph's sudden promotion, which was climaxed with a parade through the streets, Joseph returned to the palace for a personal audience with Pharaoh. Once again, Pharaoh impressed on Joseph the extent of the power and authority that had been conferred on him. This was expressed by the very colorful figure of speech, "without your word no one will lift a hand or foot in all Egypt." Joseph was also given a new name, Zaphenath-Paneah. All scholars are agreed that this was a pure Egyptian name, but there is little agreement about the meaning of that name. The last part of the term apparently means "life," but the meaning of the rest of the term is obscure. Some have interpreted it as "God speaks that he may live." Another reading, accepted especially by the scholar Yahuda, is "the food of the land is life." An older reading is, "sustainer of life."

Besides acquiring an Egyptian name, Joseph was also given an Egyptian wife who came from a high-ranking priestly family. It is worthy of note that the pharaohs also chose their wives out of this family and this is indicative of the high rank that Joseph was accorded, even in the selection of a wife. Joseph's wife's father was priest of On, also called Heliopolis, which lies north of Memphis and east of the Nile. His bride's name was Asenath, and her father was Potiphera. Both names are typically Egyptian. Asenath probably means "belonging to Noeth," an Egyptian goddess. Potiphera is a broad form of Potiphar and means "given by Ra, the sun god" (see our treatment of 39:1).

The scene closes with the statement "and Joseph went throughout the land of Egypt." This probably indicates that Joseph began his work in his new position of authority by conducting a survey of the entire agricultural situation in Egypt. He gathered the information that he would need for setting up his plan for storing all the surplus food that would be produced in the years of abundance. He had to determine what storage facilities were available and make provision for added storage space as needed for the gigantic program that was his responsibility.

41:46–49 *Joseph was thirty years old when he entered the service of Pharaoh king of Egypt. And Joseph went out from Pharaoh's presence and traveled throughout Egypt. During the seven years of abundance the land produced plentifully. Joseph collected all the food produced in those seven years of abundance in Egypt and stored it in the cities. In each city he put the food grown in the fields surrounding it. Joseph stored up huge quantities of grain, like the sand of the sea; it was so much that he stopped keeping records because it was beyond measure.*

We are told that when Joseph ascended to his position of great power in Egypt he was only 30 years old. He had now been in Egypt 11 years, of which at least 3 years had been spent in prison. Once again, the rather significant activity of investigating the whole food situation in Egypt is mentioned. This leads directly into a description of the years of abundance that had been predicted in Pharaoh's dream as interpreted by Joseph. The overflow of these abundant harvests was stored in the cities for the cities were obviously made collection points for the grain from the fields lying around them (see also v. 34). The volume of grain that was gathered was so great that it is recorded by the descriptive figure that it was "like the sand of the sea." In Egyptian fashion, at first careful records were kept of the amount of grain put into storage, but as the volume increased, keeping careful records became impossible and finally was abandoned. All of this reveals the eminent success of Joseph's plan and his effectiveness in his position as director of food supplies.

41:50–52 *Before the years of famine came, two sons were born to Joseph by Asenath daughter of Potiphera, priest of On. Joseph named his firstborn Manasseh and said, "It is because God has made me forget all my trouble and all my father's household." The second son he named Ephraim and said, "It is because God has made me fruitful in the land of my suffering."*

Before proceeding to a description of the years of famine, the narrator informs us that Joseph bore two sons by his Egyptian wife. Obviously these children were born during the years of plenty, and Joseph named his sons Manasseh and Ephraim. Regarding these names we take note of the same phenomenon that we mentioned in connection with the naming of Jacob's sons in chapters 29 and 30. The names were given in connection with certain expressions, based on similarities in sound between the name and one or more of the words in the expression used to describe the event of the birth of the child. Thus the name "Manasseh" (Hebrew *menaššeh*) was explained by the expression "God has made me forget all my trouble. . . ." The word "to forget" is *nāšāh*. It is somewhat surprising that Joseph makes such a point of having forgotten his father's household, and efforts have been made to explain this. Certainly Joseph is not priding himself on having forgotten his family in Canaan. It means, rather, that Joseph recognized that God had been so good to him in Egypt that all his grief endured at the hands of his brothers could now be forgotten. Joseph had now been fully accepted as an Egyptian and he could lay his unhappy childhood in Canaan behind him. Joseph looked on this as a providence of God in his life, which enabled him now to consider the rejection of his family as having "worked out for good." Of course, Joseph had no way of knowing about the contacts he would have with his family in the future. He certainly did not realize that God had sent him to Egypt for the purpose of saving his own family from famine. He could not have known that it was through him that God would fulfill His promise to make of Jacob's family a great nation and that this would become a reality in Egypt. For the present, all that Joseph knew was that God had given him a new life in Egypt, even though he was separated from his family.

Joseph's second son was named "Ephraim." The expression used in connection with that name was "Because God has made me fruitful in the land of my suffering." The word "fruitful" is *pārāh*, from which the sound "Ephraim" is taken. Joseph declared that God had made him fruitful in the birth of his sons in the very land where he had been a slave and a prisoner.

41:53–57 *The seven years of abundance in Egypt came to an end, and the seven years of famine began, just as Joseph had said. There was famine in all the other lands, but in the whole land of Egypt there was food. When all Egypt began to feel the famine, the people cried to Pharaoh for food. Then Pharaoh told all the Egyptians, "Go to Joseph and do what he tells you."*

When the famine had spread over the whole country, Joseph opened the storehouses and sold grain to the Egyptians, for the famine was severe throughout Egypt. And all the countries came to Egypt to buy grain from Joseph, because the famine was severe in all the world.

After the seven years of abundance, the bitter years of famine descended on the land, just as Joseph had predicted. The effectiveness of the program that Joseph had enacted soon became apparent. When other countries began to feel the agony of famine there was sufficient food in Egypt. It is evident that the severe drought was not limited to Egypt. Verses 56 and 57 speak of the famine as covering "all the world." Naturally, the reference is first of all to the lands that bordered on Egypt.

The scarcity of food among all the nations could not have been caused in the same way in every place. Egypt's harvests were dependent, to a great extent, on the annual overflow of the Nile. When, for one reason or another, this overflow did not follow its normal course there was bound to be a poor harvest in Egypt. Egyptian records mention periods of scarcity that sometimes lasted for a number of years. But in some of the neighboring countries times of famine were much more common due to a lack of rainfall. Because of Egypt's unique situation, other nations frequently turned to Egypt for relief in time of famine. This, in turn, would contribute to the depletion of Egypt's food supply even in times when Egypt itself had food enough to provide for its own needs.

There is no conflict between verses 54 and 55 in their accounts of the famine. Verse 55 informs us that there was no immediate need in Egypt at this time because the people could appeal to Pharaoh for help and he, in turn, referred them to Joseph who was able to supply them with food. While the rest of the world was agonizing because of the famine, Joseph opened the storehouses for the Egyptians and sold them grain from the vast resources that had been stored.

Further, when verse 56 says that "the famine was severe throughout Egypt" this is not in conflict with what was said in verse 54. The intent is to point out that the harvest in Egypt was inadequate to meet the needs of the people, but even though they felt the famine they had a recourse, since they could purchase food from the royal storehouses. Since neighboring countries were accustomed to coming to Egypt for food in time of famine, it could be expected that they would do so again in this instance. In this connection we can think of Abraham, in Genesis 12:10. The food supplies that Joseph had stored were obviously adequate to meet the needs of the Egyptians and still allow enough to sell to people from other countries who were in need.

46. *Joseph's Brothers Come to Egypt* (42:1–38)

Those who divide the sources generally divide the passage between "J" and "E." The reasons for this division of the material need not be discussed in detail at this time. We have previously discussed the use of the names "Jacob" and "Israel," in our introduction to chapter 37. Some of the other grounds for ascribing this to more than one source are discussed in the commentary following. The factor that is most frequently emphasized by these scholars is that the discovery of the money in the sacks is mentioned first in verses 27 and 28 and then is repeated in verse 35. Even some conservative scholars are convinced that verse 35 is an insertion into the text by a later redactor. The fact of the matter, however, is that at first only one of the brothers found money in his grain sack while the rest of the brothers didn't make this discovery until they reached home. This, moreover, does not conflict with 43:21, since both of these discoveries are there treated as one incident. When the brothers discovered the money after they reached home in Canaan, they concluded that it had already been in their sacks when they made their first stop on their return journey.

42:1, 2 *When Jacob learned that there was grain in Egypt, he said to his sons, "Why do you just keep looking at each other?" He continued, "I have heard that there is grain in Egypt. Go down there and buy some for us, so that we may live and not die."*

The news that there was grain for sale in Egypt (see 41:57) had also reached the family of Jacob in Canaan. So father Jacob urged his sons to go to Egypt to buy grain rather than to continue to complain about their plight in Canaan where there was no food available.

42:3, 4 *Then ten of Joseph's brothers went down to buy grain from Egypt. But Jacob did not send Benjamin, Joseph's brother, with the others, because he was afraid that harm might come to him.*

Ten of Joseph's brothers undertook the journey to the land of the Nile. Their reasons for going as a group were probably to enable them to jointly bring back a larger supply of food and also to provide protection for each other along the way. This latter consideration, moreover, motivated Jacob to keep Benjamin, Joseph's only full brother, safely at home.

42:5–9 *So Israel's sons were among those who went to buy grain, for the famine was in the land of Canaan also.*

Now Joseph was the governor of the land, the one who sold grain to all its people. So when Joseph's brothers arrived, they bowed down to him with their faces to the ground. As soon as Joseph saw his brothers, he recognized them, but he pretended to be a stranger and spoke harshly to them. "Where do you come from?" he asked.

"From the land of Canaan," they replied, "to buy food."

Although Joseph recognized his brothers, they did not recognize him. Then he remembered his dreams about them and said to them, "You are spies! You have come to see where our land is unprotected."

In this way, among the many people who came to Egypt to buy grain, Joseph's brothers also put in their appearance. This brought them into the presence of Joseph, who was the supreme authority in Egypt for the distribution of food. In keeping with the customs, Joseph's brothers bowed down before this august authority, with their faces to the ground.

It goes without saying that not all who came to buy grain appeared before Joseph personally. Much of the responsibility was of necessity delegated to lower officials. It is possible that Joseph involved himself personally with those who came from other lands to buy grain. There probably were special reasons why these ten men who arrived from Canaan were ushered into the presence of the supreme official in charge of this operation; the very size of the group would have attracted attention. It should be noted that Joseph immediately made the charge of espionage against this group who had come in such force from a foreign country.

As soon as Joseph saw his brothers, he recognized them but, as can readily be understood, they did not recognize this high Egyptian official as their younger brother. They had disposed of him as a slave bound for Egypt some years before. Joseph, moreover, gave no sign of recognition and did nothing to make himself known to them. He wanted to first determine whether they evidenced any remorse for the wrong they had done to him and to their father.

42:10–17 *"No, my lord," they answered. "Your servants have come to buy food. We are all the sons of one man. Your servants are honest men, not spies."*

"No!" he said to them. "You have come to see where our land is unprotected."

But they replied, "Your servants were twelve brothers, the sons of one man, who lives in the land of Canaan. The youngest is now with our father, and one is no more."

Joseph said to them, "It is just as I told you: You are spies! And this is how you will be tested: As surely as Pharaoh lives, you will not leave this place unless your youngest brother comes here. Send one of your number to get your brother; the rest of you will be kept in prison, so that your words may be tested to see if you are telling the truth. If you are not, then as surely as Pharaoh lives, you are spies!" And he put them all in custody for three days.

Joseph's brothers vociferously denied the charge of espionage. They tried to establish their good intentions by declaring that they were all sons of the same father. The argument seems to have been that no father would send all his sons on a dangerous spying mission to a foreign country. But Joseph gave the appearance of being unconvinced by their protestations of innocence. He repeated his charge that coming to buy grain was no more than a pretense for spying out the weaknesses of Egypt. In their defense the brothers gave more details about their family in Canaan. At one time there had been twelve brothers. The youngest had remained at home with his father and one of their brothers had passed away. They did not tell this august official in Egypt what they had done to their one brother, however.

At this point in the encounter Joseph declared that the truth of their words must be put to the test. He proposed that one of their number must return to Canaan to bring the youngest brother to Egypt. Meanwhile, the rest of them would be kept in prison in Egypt. In this way they could prove that they had indeed spoken the truth. With an oath, swearing by the life of Pharaoh, Joseph declared that if the youngest brother was not brought before him they would be considered as spies, and Joseph played his role very convincingly. After his pronouncement, he had the lot of them put in prison for three days. This imprisonment was intended to demonstrate a certain toughness on the part of this Egyptian official and to impress on the brothers the seriousness of their situation.

42:18–24 *On the third day, Joseph said to them, "Do this and you will live, for I fear God: If you are honest men, let one of your brothers stay here in prison, while the rest of you go and take grain back for your starving households. But you must bring your youngest brother to me, so that your words may be verified and that you may not die." This they proceeded to do.*

They said to one another, "Surely we are being punished because of our brother. We saw how distressed he was when he pleaded with us for his life, but we would not listen; that's why this distress has come upon us."

Reuben replied, "Didn't I tell you not to sin against the boy? But you wouldn't listen! Now we must give an accounting for his blood." They did not realize that Joseph could understand them, since he was using an interpreter.

He turned away from them and began to weep, but then turned back and spoke to them again. He had Simeon taken from them and bound before their eyes.

On the third day, Joseph brought his brothers before him for another interview. This time Jospeh appeared to be more considerate. The reason for this, he declared, was that he was a god-fearing man. His brothers must have understood this in a very general sense. Joseph announced to them that he would keep one of their number in prison while the rest of them returned to Canaan with a supply of food for their families, but he repeated his demand that their youngest brother must be brought to Egypt to verify their words. If they failed to bring their youngest brother they would all die. If they failed to return they would die of starvation and the one brother who was kept in prison would be executed as a spy.

Since Joseph's brothers were left no choice in this matter, nine of them prepared to return. They were deeply distressed by the predicament into which they had fallen, for they realized how reluctant their father, Jacob, would be to let Benjamin return to Egypt with them on the next trip. Their consciences also began to accuse them. They interpreted their distress as a consequence of the heartless treatment of their brother when they had turned deaf ears to his cries for mercy before they sold him as a slave into Egypt. Reuben, moreover, took this occasion to remind his brothers that he had warned them not to commit that evil against their brother but they had refused to listen to his warning. He insisted that now they were being called to account for his blood, which was on their guilty hands.

It appears that this conversation between the brothers took place in Joseph's presence. They naturally assumed that this Egyptian official could not understand their language, especially since he had communicated with them through an interpreter. Joseph, however, understood every word they spoke and their conversation stirred him deeply. Even so, he did not consider this to be the proper time to make himself known to his brothers.

Lest he make a public display of his emotions, Joseph withdrew momentarily into his private quarters, but when he returned he resumed his stern treatment of his brothers. He repeated his demand that only nine of them would be permitted to return and one of them would be kept in prison in Egypt. Joseph even selected the one who was to be detained. He passed by Reuben, who had revealed his concern for Joseph at the time he was banished as a slave into Egypt, and chose Simeon, Jacob's second son. He had Simeon bound before the eyes of the other brothers and led away to prison.

42:25–28 *Joseph gave orders to fill their bags with grain, to put each man's silver back in his sack, and to give them provisions for their journey. After this was done for them, they loaded their grain on their donkeys and left.*

At the place where they stopped for the night one of them opened his sack to get feed for his donkey, and he saw his silver in the mouth of his sack. "My silver has been returned," he said to his brothers. "Here it is in my sack."

Their hearts sank and they turned to each other trembling and said, "What is this that God has done to us?"

Joseph now gave orders with respect to the departure of his brothers for their homeland in Canaan. The containers they had brought for carrying food to their homes were all filled. The word used for these containers is a very general word, and can designate any kind of container in which material is transported. Our translators have rendered the word "sacks." Others use the term "packs" such as were commonly used on pack animals. They probably were some kind of sacks or bags. Since the word sacks is used later in a slightly different connotation, however, we might better use the word "packs" in this connection.

The money they had brought to pay for the grain was also put into these containers, although without their knowledge. Since each one probably transported more than one sack of grain, this money was then placed in one of the sacks of each of the brothers.

In addition, each one was given a supply of grain to be used as provision for men and beasts on their journey to Canaan. Finally the animals were all loaded and the caravan departed from Egypt and headed for Canaan.

After a day's journey, they camped for the night. When one of the brothers opened a sack of grain to feed his beast of burden, he was shocked to discover the money that had been used to pay for the grain in his sack. He immediately told his brothers about his discovery and they were all amazed. Completely confused by what had taken place, first in the presence of the official in Egypt and now by this mysterious development, they became frightened. They remarked to each other, "What is this that God has done to us?'' They had obviously interpreted the stern treatment they had received at the hands of that high official in Egypt as punishment from God for their misdeeds to their brother Joseph. Now they saw in their present predicament a further evidence of God's displeasure with them. Increasingly they were becoming afraid as one foreboding experience followed another. Some interpreters go so far as to try to explain the specific threat involved in this returned money. They insist that Joseph had planted this money so he could charge them with theft when they returned for more food. However, this is quite unlikely. When the brothers later returned to Egypt to buy more grain, no mention was made of this money. Even when they returned the money and offered an explanation of what had happened, the issue of possible theft was in no way suggested (43:18–23). The suggestion that Joseph had some hostile motive in returning the money is also nowhere supported in the text. It seems obvious that Joseph's motives lay in his unwillingness to accept money from his own family for the food he was able to supply them. Precisely what the cause of the brother's fear was is not indicated. If they feared being charged with theft they probably would have mentioned this. That specific fear seems to have been awakened in them when they prepared for their second journey to Egypt (see 43:18). At this point their fear was probably occasioned by the traumatic experience they had gone through in Egypt, much of which was completely beyond their comprehension. When this was coupled with the further mystery of the returned money they became increasingly apprehensive and afraid.

The use of another word for ''sack'' at this point is of no consequence since the words used are obviously synonymous.

42:29–34 *When they came to their father Jacob in the land of Canaan, they told him all that had happened to them. They said, ''The man who is lord over the land spoke harshly to us and treated us as though we were spying on the land. But we said to him, 'We are honest men; we are not spies. We were twelve brothers, sons of one father. One is no more, and the youngest is now with our father in Canaan.'*

''Then the man who is lord over the land said to us, 'This is how I will know whether you are honest men: Leave one of your brothers here with me, and take food for your starving households and go. But bring your youngest brother to me so I will know that you are not spies but honest men. Then I will give your brother back to you, and you can trade in the land.' ''

After the shocking discovery, recorded in verses 27 and 28, the rest of the trip to Canaan was uneventful. When the brothers arrived home, they naturally gave an account of their experiences to their father. They told him about the harsh treatment they had received at the hands of the Egyptian official and his charge of espionage. They reported how they had defended themselves against this charge by telling the official about their family and how he, in turn, had insisted that they would have to prove their claims by bringing their youngest brother to Egypt and how one of their number was kept in prison until such time as the youngest brother would be presented in Egypt.

42:35 *As they were emptying their sacks, there in each man's sack was his pouch of silver! When they and their father saw the money pouches, they were frightened.*

It goes without saying that when they returned home they all unloaded their pack animals and emptied their sacks of grain to provide food for their people and their animals. At that point they discovered that not just one of their number had his money returned but it had been returned to all of them. It is not too surprising that they had not discovered this earlier. All of the grain needed for the return trip could very well have been taken from the one sack that was opened on the first evening of their journey. Then when they arrived home, all of the sacks were emptied and it was not until then that they discovered that all of their money had been returned.

Some scholars have claimed that there is a conflict between verses 35 and 25, which, of course, points to a separate source. But this apparent conflict can be readily resolved if we accept the following chain of events. Although Joseph's intent was to place the money in the sacks of grain that would provide food for the families after they returned to Canaan, because of an oversight in one case, the money was actually placed in the sack that contained food for the journey. Thus, when they were on their return journey the money was discovered in this one sack. Meanwhile, the rest of the money was not discovered until they reached home and the animals were unloaded. It should be noted that this new discovery was an added reason for fear on the part of the brothers.

42:36–38 *Their father Jacob said to them, "You have deprived me of my children. Joseph is no more and Simeon is no more, and now you want to take Benjamin. Everything is against me!"*

Then Reuben said to his father, "You may put both of my sons to death if I do not bring him back to you. Entrust him to my care, and I will bring him back."

But Jacob said, "My son will not go down there with you; his brother is dead and he is the only one left. If harm comes to him on the journey you are taking, you will bring my gray head down to the grave in sorrow."

Upon hearing the report of his sons, Jacob broke out in a bitter lament. He bemoaned the fact that he was being deprived of all of his children.

Joseph was gone, Simeon had not returned with them, and now they wanted to take Benjamin from him also. Everything had turned against him. Actually, Jacob was being unfair to his sons. At this time he did not know what part they had played in the disappearance of Joseph, and they certainly could not be faulted for the harsh treatment they had received from the official in Egypt. Even so, Jacob's sons must have felt the sting of their father's lament because they realized that there was more truth in Jacob's words than Jacob did himself. They had indeed deprived him of Joseph, and when they were in Egypt they sensed that what happened to them there was a just punishment from God for their misdeeds. Indirectly they were also responsible for Simeon's imprisonment. And could they be certain that, if they took Benjamin to Egypt, they would be able to bring him back safely to his father?

In spite of all this, the brothers really had no choice. If they did not return to Egypt, Simeon would be killed as a hostage and their families would die of starvation. Therefore, Reuben made his plea before Jacob and asked his father to place Benjamin under his care. He guaranteed that he would bring Benjamin back safely. He went so far as to offer the lives of his own two sons as surety should he fail in his commitment. But Jacob was not to be persuaded. Benjamin was the only son of his beloved Rachel he had left. The thought of possibly losing him also was too much for the old patriarch to accept. If, for some reason, Benjamin would not be returned, he charged that his sons, who were urging him to allow Benjamin to accompany them, would bring his gray hairs with sorrow to the grave. The word that is translated "grave," just as in 37:35, is the Hebrew word "Sheol." (See our treatment of this word under 37:35.)

47. *The Second Journey to Egypt* (43:1–34)

Those who divide the sources generally give nearly all of chapter 43 to "J." The only exceptions are verse 14 and the closing words of verse 23, "Then he brought Simeon out to them." This line is ascribed to "E." Insofar as they consider part of this chapter as being derived from "E," these critics allege that there are certain conflicts between this chapter and the account in chapter 42. It is claimed that, as in the case of 42:27–28, the discovery of the money in the grain sacks took place when they camped for their first night on their return journey. But in 42:35 the discovery was not made until they arrived at home in Canaan. We have already discussed this alleged conflict in our treatment of chapter 42. The conversation between Joseph and his brothers allegedly also is different here from what is recorded in chapter 42. In 42:13, it is pointed out, Joseph's brothers offered the information that they had a younger brother at home, while here in verse 7 Joseph specifically asked whether they had another brother at home. We will indicate in our commentary below that there is no basis for the claim that this is evidence for two different sources for this material.

Another difficulty the critics have pointed out is that in chapter 42 it was Reuben who assumed responsibility for the safe return of Benjamin, while here it is Judah who accepts that role. But there is no conflict here, because it is obvious that we are dealing with two different occasions separated by some time. There is no reason why the one son could not offer to take this responsibility on one occasion while another son could do so at a later occasion.

The reason that is given for ascribing verses 14 and 23b to "E" is that mention is made of Simeon's imprisonment in Egypt, while the rest of chapter 43 makes no mention of this. This leads to a fourth point of alleged difference between the two passages. It is argued that the imprisonment of Simeon was intended to bring Joseph's brothers back to Egypt, but according to 43:3–5 Joseph told them that under no circumstance would they see his face again unless they brought their younger brother with them. Again, this offers no true conflict. Joseph could very well have surmised that his brothers would return without Benjamin and this he wanted to prevent with a strong condition. It has also been pointed out that according to chapter 43 Joseph's brothers made no mention of Simeon's imprisonment as motive for their return. But the fact that Simeon's imprisonment was well known to Jacob and his other sons made any further reference to this completely unnecessary. The primary issue was whether Benjamin was to go along or not. It has also been observed that Jacob's hesitancy to let Benjamin go had its background in what we are told in 43:36–38, and the imprisonment of Simeon had a definite bearing on that.

43:1–5 *Now the famine was still severe in the land. So when they had eaten all the grain they had brought from Egypt, their father said to them, "Go back and buy us a little more food."*

But Judah said to him, "The man warned us solemnly, 'You will not see my face again unless your brother is with you.' If you will send our brother along with us, we will go down and buy food for you. But if you will not send him, we will not go down, because the man said to us, 'You will not see my face again unless your brother is with you.'"

With the continued famine, also in Canaan, the provisions that Joseph's brothers had brought from Egypt soon were exhausted. Jacob therefore urged his sons to make another trip to Egypt to buy food, but his sons reminded him that they could not go to Egypt without Benjamin. This time it was Judah who served as spokesman for the brothers. He reminded Jacob that the Egyptian official had been very specific in his declaration that there would be no purpose in coming back to Egypt if they did not bring their younger brother with them. They would be willing to go only if Jacob would change his mind (42:38) and permit Benjamin to accompany them.

43:6 *Israel asked, ''Why did you bring this trouble on me by telling the man you had another brother?''*

No doubt Jacob had sheltered a hope that his sons would weaken and agree to go without Benjamin, but now he was under real pressure. On the one hand the family was beginning to feel the pangs of hunger and starvation. They had to have food and the only place it could be acquired was in Egypt. On the other hand Jacob was very reluctant to let Benjamin out of his sight for fear that some evil might befall him. Under this tension he burst forth with an accusation against his sons, charging them that they had betrayed him by telling the Egyptian official they had another brother at home.

43:7 *They replied, ''The man questioned us closely about ourselves and our family. 'Is your father still living?' he asked us. 'Do you have another brother?' We simply answered his questions. How were we to know he would say, 'Bring your brother down here'?''*

With Judah probably still serving as the spokesman, the brothers offered as their defense the fact that the Egyptian officials had asked them about the other members of their family and they had no choice but to tell him the truth. Moreover, they argued, there was no way for them to know that this cruel Egyptian would demand that they bring their younger brother to Egypt as a condition for being able to buy more food. What Jacob's sons said, according to this passage, is not wholly in accord with what we were told in 42:7–16. The differences, however, are so minor that the passages can easily be harmonized.

In the first place, it should be remembered that in 42:7–16 we have an account as given by the biblical narrator, while here in our present passage the report is given in the words of Jacob's sons. Not only was their report definitely subjective, but we can understand that in their eagerness to convince Jacob they shaded their report to defend themselves as much as possible. This does not imply that they intentionally falsified their account of what had happened. We can also conclude that their conversation with Jacob is not recorded verbatim, since there probably was a good deal more said than this brief report recorded here. Evidence for this conclusion can be found in 44:18–23 where Judah mentions other parts of the conversation. The biblical narrator gives us only an abbreviated version of what was said. Moreover, in 40:30–34, at the point of their return from Egypt, this account is even briefer. It should further be remembered that Joseph knew the family situation of his brothers full well. In his conversation with them he could well have led them on to reveal things that he was eager to know about, without his brothers being aware of his strategy. In any case, the difference between the two accounts is so slight that we can accept the fact that the brothers truthfully recounted what had happened the way they remembered it. This would also be true of their words to Joseph as recorded in 44:19.

43:8–10 *Then Judah said to Israel his father, "Send the boy along with me and we will go at once, so that we and you and our children may live and not die. I myself will guarantee his safety; you can hold me personally responsible for him. If I do not bring him back to you and set him here before you, I will bear the blame before you all my life. As it is, if we had not delayed, we could have gone and returned twice."*

Thereupon Judah put forth a strong effort to convince his father that he must let Benjamin go with them. He based his plea on the reality of the famine that would lead to starvation and death for them and their children. He argued that the journey was not actually so dangerous, and he was ready to offer himself as security for Benjamin and offered to assume full responsibility for the rest of his life for any evil that might befall his younger brother. He further argued the urgency of time. If they had not delayed so long they could have made two trips to Egypt by this time.

43:11–14 *Then their father Israel said to them, "If it must be, then do this: Put some of the best products of the land in your bags and take them down to the man as a gift—a little balm and a little honey, some spices and myrrh, some pistachio nuts and almonds. Take double the amount of silver with you, for you must return the silver that was put back into the mouths of your sacks. Perhaps it was a mistake. Take your brother also and go back to the man at once. And may God Almighty grant you mercy before the man so that he will let your other brother and Benjamin come back with you. As for me, if I am bereaved, I am bereaved."*

Finally Jacob reluctantly gave his consent. He could not withstand Judah's arguments. The expression "if it must be" indicates that Jacob finally realized that there was no alternative. He insisted, however, that they should spare no effort to insure the success of their mission.

Jacob told his sons that they should bring a gift to the high official in Egypt in order to soften his attitude toward them and seek to incur his favor. The gift was to consist of the finest products of the land of Canaan. Specific mention is made of the following products: "Balm"—probably must be considered to be a produce of the storax, which grew in northern Palestine and was used for medicinal purposes. (Think of the "balm of Gilead" mentioned in Jer. 8:22.) "Honey"—which was so abundant in Canaan that it was known as the land "flowing with milk and honey" (see Exod. 3:8, 17; etc.). Ezekiel 27:17 indicates that both honey and balm were exported from Palestine. "Gum"—which was made from the sap of a bush with long thorns and was used as an adhesive. In Egypt this product was used to strengthen the linen in which the mummies were wrapped. "Myrrh"—a clear substance that was derived from the leaves and branches of a type of rose plant and was used both in perfume and for medicinal purposes. Also included in the gift were to be pistachio nuts and almonds, which also were produced in Palestine.

In addition to the gift, Jacob's sons were to bring double money in their hands to compensate for the money that had been returned to them on their first journey to Egypt. Jacob prayed that God almighty would bless these measures and grant mercy in the presence of the official in Egypt, in order that Simeon might be released from prison, and that both he and Benjamin, whom Jacob reluctantly agreed to send along, might be returned to him.

Jacob closed his statement with another lament, which somewhat belies the faith in God he had expressed in his prayer. He assumed a rather fatalistic attitude when he said, "If I lose my children, then I lose them."

43:15–17 *So the men took the gifts and double the amount of silver, and Benjamin also. They hurried down to Egypt and presented themselves to Joseph. When Joseph saw Benjamin with them, he said to the steward of his house, "Take these men to my house, slaughter an animal and prepare dinner; they are to eat with me at noon."*

The man did as Joseph told him and took the men to Joseph's house.

Without further delay preparations were made for the journey and the caravan departed for Egypt. It goes without saying that when they arrived in Egypt they again had to make their appearance before Joseph. After the charge of espionage, which had been laid on them in their first visit, they would certainly be dealt with by the high official himself and not by some lesser agent. But when Joseph saw Benjamin with them, he ordered his assistant to bring the men into his own house and prepare a sumptuous meal for them. His assistant hurried to carry out Joseph's orders.

43:18–24 *Now the men were frightened when they were taken to his house. They thought, "We were brought here because of the silver that was put back into our* *sacks the first time. He wants to attack us and overpower us and seize us as slaves and take our donkeys."*

So they went up to Joseph's steward and spoke to him at the entrance to the house. "Please, sir," they said, "we came down here the first time to buy food. But at the place where we stopped for the night we opened our sacks and each of us found his silver—the exact weight—in the mouth of his sack. So we have brought it back with us. We have also brought additional silver with us to buy food. We don't know who put our silver in our sacks."

"It's all right," he said. "Don't be afraid. Your God and the God of your father has given you treasure in your sacks; I received your silver." Then he brought Simeon out to them.

The steward took the men into Joseph's house, gave them water to wash their feet and provided fodder for their donkeys.

Joseph's brothers, who did not know about the arrangements Joseph had made, looked on this order to be taken to the official's house as a trap that was somehow related to the money that had been returned in their sacks. They feared that once they were inside the man's house, they would be seized, sold as slaves, and their beasts of burden taken as booty. Before they entered the house, therefore, they approached Joseph's assistant with an urgent plea, hoping to avoid this trap. They told him that the return of the money on their first trip had been a complete surprise to them, and that they had brought double money this time for the food they hoped to buy. The steward, who obviously had received careful instructions from Joseph, reassured them and urged them not to be afraid. The money that they had brought had been received and they should look on the return of the money on their previous journey as a gift from their God and the God of their father. Gradually their fears subsided, especially when Simeon was brought out and permitted to join them. The steward brought them into the house and gave them water to wash their feet (see 18:4). He also provided food for their beasts of burden.

43:25–29 *They prepared their gifts for Joseph's arrival at noon, because they had heard that they were to eat there.*

When Joseph came home, they presented to him the gifts they had brought into the house, and they bowed down before him to the ground. He asked them how they were, and then he said, "How is your aged father you told me about? Is he still living?"

They replied, "Your servant our father is still alive and well." And they bowed low to pay him honor.

As he looked about and saw his brother Benjamin, his own mother's son, he asked, "Is this your youngest brother, the one you told me about?" And he said, "God be gracious to you, my son."

Now they were informed about the purpose for which they had been brought into Joseph's house. The high official had invited them to be his guests at dinner. The brothers could not understand the radical change in attitude on the part of the official. Perhaps he had decided to try to make up for the harsh treatment he had given them in the former visit. Probably he was convinced that they were not spies, since they had kept their word and brought Benjamin with them. At any rate, they were eager to show their gratitude and respect and prepared the gifts they had brought, so they would be ready to present them when the official made his entrance.

When Joseph arrived, they once again bowed before him to the ground, and presented their gifts to him. Joseph inquired about the welfare of their father, and the brothers responded in very humble terms, assuring him that their father was alive and well. Thereupon, they once again bowed before him to express appreciation for his expression of concern for their father.

Then Joseph's glance fell on Benjamin and he asked whether this was the younger brother about whom they had spoken. Joseph spoke kindly to Benjamin and wished him God's blessing, addressing him with a term of endearment, ''My son.''

43:30–34 *Deeply moved at the sight of his brother, Joseph hurried out and looked for a place to weep. He went into his private room and wept there.*

After he had washed his face, he came out and, controlling himself, said, ''Serve the food.''

They served him by himself, the brothers by themselves, and the Egyptians who ate with him by themselves, because Egyptians could not eat with Hebrews, for that is detestable to Egyptians. The men had been seated before him in the order of their ages, from the firstborn to the youngest; and they looked at each other in astonishment. When portions were served to them from Joseph's table, Benjamin's portion was five times as much as anyone else's. So they feasted and drank freely with him.

When Joseph made this contact with his brother Benjamin, the emotional impact was so powerful that he could not constrain himself. Since he did not want to reveal his true identity at this time, he quickly left the room and went into his own chambers to give vent to his tears. After he had composed himself, he washed his face and returned to his brothers. He then gave orders to proceed with the meal.

Here the narrator indicates that Joseph ate at a separate table from that at which his brothers were seated. This was undoubtedly in recognition of his high position. There was a third table set for the Egyptians in Joseph's household since Egyptian custom forbad them from eating with people from another country. This custom was based on a religious practice that did not permit Egyptians to eat the meat of certain animals that were commonly eaten by other peoples.

When they had been seated for the meal, Joseph's brothers were amazed that they had been seated in the exact order of their ages. Furthermore, Joseph had portions of the food he ate served to his guests. This was a display of honor for one's guests. Besides, when a guest was deemed worthy of very special honor, the portion served was made especially generous. In this case, that special honor was accorded to Benjamin who was served a portion five times larger than those given to the other brothers. In this way Joseph expressed his special love for his only full brother. It is also mentioned that they drank freely, and this indicates that this was considered to be a feast or a celebration. The Egyptians were known to imbibe freely of fermented liquors. Some translators have rendered this as that they became drunk. This, however, is more than the original text can rightly bear.

48. *The Silver Cup and Joseph Making Himself Known* (44:1–45:28)

These two chapters form one unit. Those who divide the sources, however, want to give chapter 44 to "J," while they divide chapter 45 between "J" and "E," with the larger portion going to "E." It is generally admitted among these scholars that making a proper division of this material presents some real difficulties. As a consequence there is little agreement among them as to the exact division of the material among the alleged sources. A few even want to bring in a third source, "P," especially in 45:17–21 and 25–27.

The bases for ascribing chapter 25 to more than one source are the following alleged repetitions. At the scene where Joseph makes himself known in verses 3 and 4; when Joseph tells his brothers to let his father know about his high position in Egypt in verses 9 and 13; when Joseph orders them to bring his father to Egypt in verses 13, 18, and 19. The critics also point to certain supposed contradictions. They charge that in verse 1 Joseph took certain measures to prevent the Egyptians in his court from learning about his family ties with these strangers from Palestine, while in verse 2 we are told that he wept so loudly that everyone in the court could hear him (see v. 16). It is further claimed that in verses 19 and 27 mention is made of wagons for bringing the family to Egypt, while in verse 23 it is implied that only donkeys were used.

None of these arguments carries much weight. The alleged repetitions can easily be explained by the vagaries of the narrative style of the ancient East. They can also be understood in the light of the emotional crisis described here. The repetition of the order to bring Jacob to Egypt, it should be noted, is actually one order given by Joseph and one by Pharaoh. The alleged contradictions obviously result from a misunderstanding of the text. Thus verse 1 merely says that Joseph did not want any of his Egyptian cohorts present when he made himself known to his brothers. The distinction between wagons and donkeys, which is a bit silly, can readily be explained when we assume that Jacob and his sons' families would be carried in the wagons while the provisions they brought with them would be loaded on donkeys and other beasts of burden. Taken as a whole, we once again come to the conclusion that there is no substantial evidence in the text for ascribing this material to multiple sources, which are then intermingled in the narrative we have before us.

44:1, 2 *Now Joseph gave these instructions to the steward of his house: "Fill the men's sacks with as much food as they can carry, and put each man's silver in the mouth of his sack. Then put my cup, the silver one, in the mouth of the youngest one's sack, along with the silver for his grain." And he did as Joseph said.*

Before making himself known to his brothers, Joseph wanted to put them to a final test of their sincerity. He sought an opportunity to place them under severe pressure by pretending that Benjamin would be kept in Egypt and they would have to return to their father without his precious youngest son. How would they react when they were placed before that eventuality? Would they calmly accept the inevitable and simply bring the crushing message to their aged father? Or would they do everything in their power to avoid this crisis for their father? Such a test of his brothers' true sincerity could be easily arranged. Joseph ordered his assistant to fill all the grain sacks to capacity. Then, once again, the money that they had brought was to be placed in the sacks. And finally, the supreme ploy, his own silver cup was to be placed in Benjamin's sack. In this way Benjamin could be charged with theft and be imprisoned in Egypt. Joseph's steward meticulously carried out all these orders.

Some interpreters have suggested that the reference to the money, in this case, is an insertion into the text. They argue that there is no further mention of this money in the rest of the narrative when the brothers are again confronted by Joseph, but this is certainly an arbitrary assumption. In the later incident the emphasis is on the silver cup which allegedly had been stolen. The money was not an issue. There is not a shred of evidence in the text that this was a later insertion. If we read Joseph's motive in returning the money as we did in our interpretation of 42:25–28, this same motive would be applicable here. Joseph's reason for returning the money, which had been such a mystery to his brothers, was simply that he refused to accept money from his own family for the food he was able to supply them.

Likewise, it is not necessary to insist that the phrase "mouth of the . . . sack" in verse 2 must be considered as a later insertion. It is argued that this is not possible since, had the cup been in the mouth of the sack, it would have been discovered immediately and would not have required the extensive search that Joseph's steward conducted. The inclusion of this statement can be readily explained, however. When the steward caught up with them and charged them with the theft of the cup, each man in turn lowered his sack from his beast of burden and these were opened one by one. The brothers were so sure they were innocent in this matter that they were eager to avoid any suggestion that they had quickly opened their sacks and then hidden the valued cup elsewhere. Each sack was opened under the watchful eye of Joseph's steward.

44:3–5 *As morning dawned, the men were sent on their way with their donkeys. They had not gone far from the city when Joseph said to his steward, "Go after those men at once, and when you catch up with them, say to them, 'Why have you repaid good with evil? Isn't this the cup my master drinks from and also uses for divination? This is a wicked thing you have done.'"*

Early the next morning Joseph's brothers departed for home with their heavily laden pack animals. They had barely left the city, however, when Joseph's steward caught up with them and accused them of stealing the silver cup of his master. It is of interest that the cup is described here as the cup from which the high official drank daily. Thus it was a very personal and intimate part of his life, and this was why its alleged theft was portrayed as a personal offense of serious proportions against this Egyptian ruler.

In this connection there is a difference of opinion among conservative scholars regarding the meaning of the term that our translators have rendered "uses for divination." Other scholars, including this commentator, feel that in this case the term should be read to say, "be sure to notice." The linguistic argument with respect to the word used in the original is not conclusive. A good case can be made for either reading, even when we compare this term as it is used here with other passages in which it appears. Little purpose is served in repeating all of the data and arguments that are available to us on this point. We suggest that it would be unlikely that Joseph would allow his personal drinking cup to be used as a "divination cup." It seems that in ancient times such a "divination cup" was filled with water and then oil was poured on the water. The future was then predicted on the basis of the forms and shapes that the oil took on the surface of the water. Although this ritual may well have been practiced in Joseph's court, it is not likely that a high official such as Joseph, would practice it himself. He would be more likely to delegate this to assigned magicians and soothsayers who were under his command. But it is even more unlikely that the high ruler's personal, silver drinking cup would be used for this unsavory purpose. Therefore we have concluded that the preferable reading would be, ''is not this the cup my master drinks from? He would be sure to notice'' (that is, the theft being alleged).

44:6–9 *When he caught up with them, he repeated these words to them. But they said to him, ''Why does my lord say such things? Far be it from your servants to do anything like that! We even brought back to you from the land of Canaan the silver we found inside the mouths of our sacks. So why would we steal silver or gold from your master's house? If any of your servants is found to have it, he will die; and the rest of us will become my lord's slaves.''*

Joseph's steward immediately carried out his master's orders and soon overtook them and made his accusations. Joseph's brothers strongly denied the charges of theft that were made against them. They appealed to the evidence of their honesty, which they had demonstrated by returning the money that had been put into their sacks. So sure were they of their innocence that they proposed that if the cup was found in the possession of one of their number, this person could be put to death and all would become slaves of the Egyptian official.

44:10–12 *''Very well, then,'' he said, ''let it be as you say. Whoever is found to have it will become my slave; the rest of you will be free from blame.''*

Each of them quickly lowered his sack to the ground and opened it. Then the steward proceeded to search, beginning with the oldest and ending with the youngest. And the cup was found in Benjamin's sack.

The steward, who had obviously received careful instructions from Joseph, declared that if the cup was found in the possession of one of their number, that person would be kept in Egypt as a slave while the rest of the brothers would be free to return to Palestine. The brothers quickly lowered the sacks of grain from their beasts of burden. Then, as we observed in our interpretation of verse 2, each opened his own sack as the steward moved from man to man to conduct his search. The search was systematic, starting from the oldest and moving down to the youngest. One can imagine the tension that built up as the search continued. And then, when the search came to the last man, there was the crushing revelation as the silver cup was discovered in Benjamin's sack.

44:13, 14 *At this, they tore their clothes. Then they all loaded their donkeys and returned to the city.*

Joseph was still in the house when Judah and his brothers came in, and they threw themselves to the ground before him.

In speechless horror the brothers tore their clothes. They reloaded their beasts of burden and all of them returned to the city. They obviously gave no thought to the freedom they had been offered to return to Palestine (v. 10). Since the catastrophe had fallen on Benjamin, their father's darling, they decided to face the crisis together. Evidently these brothers had changed their attitudes since the day when they ruthlessly disposed of their brother Joseph by selling him as a slave into Egypt.

Joseph had remained in his house to await the return of his steward, so the brothers were once again ushered into his presence. Once again they prostrated themselves before him in deep humiliation. Judah is mentioned specifically as the leader of the group, probably because he would now become their spokesman.

44:15, 16 *Joseph said to them, "What is this you have done? Don't you know that a man like me can find things out by divination?"*

"What can we say to my lord?" Judah replied. "What can we say? How can we prove our innocence? God has uncovered your servants' guilt. We are now my lord's slaves—we ourselves and the one who was found to have the cup."

While they were lying prostrate before him, Joseph began to rebuke them for their crime. He chided them for thinking that a man of his position would not notice the absence of the silver drinking cup he used constantly. Here, again, we have the use of the word our translators have rendered "to find out by divination." (Please see our discussion under v. 5 above.)

Judah now spoke for the brothers. He pleaded that there was no way they could prove their innocence. He confessed their guilt for which God was now punishing them, although it was not the guilt with which they were presently being charged. Judah declared that they were all prepared to become slaves of the Egyptian official. They were ready to share in Benjamin's lot. They would accept this as a punishment from God for their past sins.

44:17 *But Joseph said, "Far be it from me to do such a thing! Only the man who was found to have the cup will become my slave. The rest of you, go back to your father in peace."*

Judah's words revealed to Joseph that there had indeed been a great change in his brothers. Even so, he decided to pursue this matter a little farther. He wanted to be unmistakably sure of their changed attitude. He therefore repeated the condition that had been stated by his steward and assured them that the rest of them were free to return to Palestine with only Benjamin remaining as a slave in Egypt.

44:18–34 *Then Judah went up to him and said: "Please, my lord, let your servant speak a word to my lord. Do not be angry with your servant, though you are equal to Pharaoh himself. My lord asked his servants, 'Do you have a father or a brother?' And we answered, 'We have an aged father, and there is a young son born to him in his old age. His brother is dead, and he is the only one of his mother's sons left, and his father loves him.'*

"Then you said to your servants, 'Bring him down to me so I can see him for myself.' And we said to my lord, 'The boy cannot leave his father; if he leaves him, his father will die.' But you told your servants, 'Unless your youngest brother comes down with you, you will not see my face again.' When we went back to your servant my father, we told him what my lord had said.

"Then our father said, 'Go back and buy a little more food.' But we said, 'We cannot go down. Only if our youngest brother is with us will we go. We cannot see the man's face unless our youngest brother is with us.'

"Your servant my father said to us, 'You know that my wife bore me two sons. One of them went away from me, and I said, "He has surely been torn to pieces." And I have not seen him since. If you take this one from me too and harm comes to him, you will bring my gray head down to the grave in misery.'

"So now, if the boy is not with us when I go back to your servant my father and if my father, whose life is closely bound up with the boy's life, sees that the boy isn't there, he will die. Your servants will bring the gray head of our father down to the grave in sorrow. Your servant guaranteed the boy's safety to my father. I said, 'If I do not bring him back to you, I will bear the blame before you, my father, all my life!'

"Now then, please let your servant remain here as my lord's slave in place of the boy, and let the boy return with his brothers. How can I go back to my father if the boy is not with me? No! Do not let me see the misery that would come upon my father."

At this point Judah stepped forward and made a heartrending plea for the release of Benjamin. He offered to take Benjamin's place himself. He began by paying high respect to Joseph, declaring that he was equal to the pharaoh. He reminded Joseph that he had inquired of them whether they had a father and another brother, and that he was the one who had demanded that they bring their youngest brother to Egypt. Judah vividly pictured the scene in which the decision was made to come to Egypt to buy more food and how difficult this decision had been because of Joseph's condition that they must bring their youngest brother with them. He described the agony of their aged father as he finally yielded to the demand to let Benjamin accompany them. He told the Egyptian ruler that Benjamin was the only remaining child of their father's wife, the other having been lost, as Jacob thought, by being torn to pieces. He declared that if now the youngest son also would be taken from their father, the old man would certainly die of grief. Judah tried desperately to invoke the sympathy of the Egyptian official. Finally, Judah made his proposal. He mentioned the vow he had made to his father to serve as surety for Benjamin's safe return. If he failed to bring Benjamin back he would bear the blame the rest of his life. He therefore offered to take Benjamin's place and remain in Egypt as a slave if only Benjamin would be permitted to return to his father with the rest of the brothers. Judah concluded with an emotional appeal in which he stressed that he could not bear to go home to witness the misery of his father if Benjamin did not return.

45:1 *Then Joseph could no longer control himself before all his attendants, and he cried out, "Have everyone leave my presence!" So there was no one with Joseph when he made himself known to his brothers.*

Judah's plea had a tremendous emotional impact on Joseph. He now saw clearly how much his brothers had changed since that fateful day when they sold him as a slave into Egypt, without any concern for their father's broken heart. Now they were ready to pay any price to prevent the grief that would be heaped on their aged father if Benjamin did not return. Joseph was satisfied. At this point the emotional strain became so overpowering that Joseph could no longer contain himself. Before he made himself known to his brothers, he quickly dismissed everyone else from the room.

45:2, 3 *And he wept so loudly that the Egyptians heard him, and Pharaoh's household heard about it.*
Joseph said to his brothers, "I am Joseph! Is my father still living?" But his brothers were not able to answer him, because they were terrified at his presence.

Then Joseph broke out in open weeping. So loud was his crying that the servants heard him and even the court of Pharaoh heard about it. This must be understood as a report that was brought to Pharaoh's court by some of Joseph's servants. When he finally pulled himself together sufficiently to be able to talk, he approached his shocked brothers and cried out, "I am Joseph! Is my father still living?" This question was not superfluous, as some have claimed. As ruler of Egypt he had listened to the reports these men from Palestine had made about their father. But now the psychological situation was radically different. Now it was a deeply personal longing to hear about the well-being of his own father from whom he had been separated for so many years.

The reaction of Joseph's brothers was, at first, one of speechless terror. This was beyond belief. Joseph, their brother, the supreme ruler of Egypt! As the truth began to dawn on them their fears mounted also. From his present position of power he could now repay them for the scandalous way they had treated him in the past. They were so stunned by the whole experience that they could not say a word.

45:4–13 *Then Joseph said to his brothers, "Come close to me." When they had done so, he said, "I am your brother Joseph, the one you sold into Egypt! And now, do not be distressed and do not be angry with yourselves for selling me here, because it was to save lives that God sent me ahead of you. For two years now there has been famine in the land, and for the next five years there will not be plowing and reaping. But God sent me ahead of you to preserve for you a remnant on earth and save your lives by a great deliverance.*

"So then, it was not you who sent me here, but God. He made me father to Pharaoh, lord of his entire household and ruler of all Egypt. Now hurry back to my father and say to him, 'This is what your son Joseph says: God has made me lord of all Egypt. Come down to me; don't delay. You shall live in the region of Goshen and be near me—you, your children and grandchildren, your flocks and herds, and all you have. I will provide for you there, because five years of famine are still to come. Otherwise you and your household and all who belong to you will become destitute.'

"You can see for yourselves, and so can my brother Benjamin, that it is really I who am speaking to you. Tell my father about all the honor accorded me in Egypt and about everything you have seen. And bring my father down here quickly."

Joseph could understand both the amazement and the fear of his brothers. He therefore tried to put their hearts at rest. He assured them that he truly was their brother, Joseph, the one they had been instrumental in selling into Egypt (37:28). He did not intend this as an accusation because he immediately continued by telling them that they should not be distressed or angry with themselves for what they had done to him. God had sent him into Egypt in order that lives might be saved from the continuing famine. This was how God would save His chosen people from extinction. The famine that had been raging for two years was to continue for another five years. Thus it was God who had brought him into Egypt and not his brothers. Moreover, God had exalted him to this high position in order that he might be able to provide for the needs of his father and his family.

Joseph described his high position in Egypt by using a number of graphic terms. He had become "a father to Pharaoh." Attempts have been made to read this as an official title given to Joseph in Egypt. The Hebrew word for father is *'āb* and the Egyptian word for "vizier" is *abu,* so attempts have been made to relate these two words. It should be remembered, however, that at this point Joseph was not speaking to his brothers as an Egyptian but as a brother among his brethren, a Hebrew among Hebrews. It is more logical, then, to read this word "father" as a Hebrew expression indicating someone who was a trusted advisor and confidant (see Job 29:16; Isa. 22:21).

Joseph further described his position as "lord over Pharaoh's household." Pharaoh himself had also used this term when he promoted Joseph to this position (see 41:40). Third, he described himself as "ruler of all Egypt" (cf. 41:41, 43; 42:6).

Joseph now ordered his brothers to return to Canaan with haste with a message for Jacob from his son Joseph. He was to take his entire family and move into Egypt so that they could be spared from the ravages of the remaining years of famine. They could live in the land of Goshen. The exact location of Goshen has caused some question, but it is generally agreed that it was a strip of land that adjoined the Isthmus of Suez in the direction of the eastern arm of the Nile.

Joseph concluded his instructions to his brothers by appointing them, with special mention of Benjamin, as eyewitnesses to report to his father that he was still alive and that he had gained great power and honor in Egypt. They were to return to Canaan and lose no time in bringing Jacob and the entire family to Egypt.

45:14, 15 *Then he threw his arms around his brother Benjamin and wept, and Benjamin embraced him, weeping. And he kissed all his brothers and wept over them. Afterward his brothers talked with him.*

While Joseph was speaking, the first shock and fear that his brothers had experienced began to wane. The truth began to dawn on them that this mighty ruler of Egypt was actually their brother whom they had sold into Egypt. They also began to realize that Joseph had no intention of seeking revenge for the cruel treatment they had afforded him when he was a boy. Soon the tears began to flow and all the brothers were embraced with tears. Special mention is made of the greeting Joseph exchanged with his full brother, Benjamin. After that they began to talk, and there certainly was much for them to talk about.

45:16–20 *When the news reached Pharaoh's palace that Joseph's brothers had come, Pharaoh and all his officials were pleased. Pharaoh said to Joseph, "Tell your brothers, 'Do this: Load your animals and return to the land of Canaan, and bring your father and your families back to me. I will give you the best of the land of Egypt and you can enjoy the fat of the land.'*

"You are also directed to tell them, 'Do this: Take some carts from Egypt for your children and your wives, and get your father and come. Never mind about your belongings, because the best of all Egypt will be yours.'"

It goes without saying that what had taken place could not be concealed from the Egyptians. Nor had this been Joseph's intent, as some scholars have suggested on the basis of 45:1. The fact that he wanted to be alone with his brothers during the emotional scene in which he made himself known to them certainly can be understood. But once that intimate encounter had taken place, the time had come to inform the royal court about the arrival of Joseph's brothers. The report was received favorably by Pharaoh and his servants, and this also speaks well for the esteem Joseph had gained in his high position in Egypt.

When we read further that Pharaoh gave instructions to Joseph regarding the future of his family, we must assume that Joseph had personally communicated with Pharaoh about his contact with his brothers and the needs of his father Jacob's family in the foreseeable future. It is obvious that Joseph had made some kind of request to Pharaoh with respect to his family in Canaan, and Pharaoh now responded favorably to this request. Pharaoh instructed Joseph to tell his brothers to load their beasts of burden with food and to return to Canaan. Then they were to bring their father and their families to Egypt. Pharaoh added the promise that they would be given the best area in the land of Egypt to establish their residence and they would be given the best products of the land. It should be noted that the land of Goshen is not mentioned at this point. Obviously Joseph had not yet discussed his plan in this regard with Pharaoh. He reserved this for a later time (see 46:34 and 47:1, 4). In addition to these instructions, Pharaoh also ordered that wagons should be taken along from Egypt to facilitate the transporting of the women and children as well as the aged tribal father. Finally, Pharaoh generously offered that they should not be concerned about transporting their household belongings from Canaan since the best of Egypt would be placed at their disposal.

45:21–24 *So the sons of Israel did this. Joseph gave them carts, as Pharaoh had commanded, and he also gave them provisions for their journey. To each of them he gave new clothing, but to Benjamin he gave three hundred shekels of silver and* *five sets of clothes. And this is what he sent to his father: ten donkeys loaded with the best things of Egypt, and ten female donkeys loaded with grain and bread and other provisions for his journey. Then he sent his brothers away, and as they were leaving he said to them, "Don't quarrel on the way!"*

Joseph's brothers followed these instructions literally. Joseph provided them with carts, in accordance with Pharaoh's orders, and also gave them provisions for their journey. In addition, Joseph lavished his brothers with gifts. Each of his brothers received a gift of new clothes which probably were in the nature of festive robes, made of fine Egyptian linen. As was the case in 43:34, Benjamin was singled out for special favors. He was presented with 300 shekels of silver and five sets of new clothing. (See our discussion on the value of a shekel under 20:16.) For his father, Joseph sent ten donkeys loaded with costly products of Egypt and ten female donkeys loaded with food and provisions for the journey to Egypt.

So Joseph's brothers were sent on their way to Canaan. A striking final instruction from Joseph to his brothers was, "Don't quarrel on the way." Joseph had no doubt detected that there were signs of his brothers accusing each other regarding their past sins (see 42:22). It would have been easy for them to express bitterness toward each other after the intense emotional strain they had been under. Therefore, Joseph made his appeal for peace among his brethren.

45:25-28 *So they went up out of Egypt and came to their father Jacob in the land of Canaan. They told him, "Joseph is still alive! In fact, he is ruler of all Egypt." Jacob was stunned; he did not believe them. But when they told him everything Joseph had said to them, and when he saw the carts Joseph had sent to carry him back, the spirit of their father Jacob revived. And Israel said, "I'm convinced! My son Joseph is still alive. I will go and see him before I die."*

The journey from Egypt to Canaan was carried out without mishap. As the brothers arrived in Canaan they hurried to tell Jacob the news about Joseph—that he was still alive and that he was the highest ruler in Egypt. Jacob was so stunned that he remained incredulous until his sons showed him the wagons Joseph had sent. Finally the old patriarch accepted the message as authentic. He cried out, "My son Joseph is still alive. I will go and see him before I die."

49. *Jacob and His Family Move to Egypt* (46:1-47:12)

The entire narrative recorded in chapter 37 and in chapters 39-45 leads up to the critically important migration of the patriarchal family into Egypt. It was there, in a fertile valley in the land of the Nile, that God's chosen people would become a great nation. In order to achieve this historic development in the unfolding of God's redemptive plan, Joseph had been sent into Egypt, had been promoted to his high position of power and authority, and had prepared the way for the family of Jacob to become ideally situated in a favored location in Egypt. As long as Joseph was alive, and even for some years after he died, the family of Jacob was safe from attack and repression. This allowed them enough time and freedom to develop into a formidable national group.

Those who divide the sources ascribe the list of names of Jacob's descendants in 46:8–27 to one of the latest sections of "P." Some would even give it to a later source which was akin to "P." That a list such as this cannot be viewed as a characteristic of a specific source has been discussed on more than one occasion earlier in our commentary. In this particular instance, the list does present certain difficulties however, and these will be discussed in the course of our commentary following. From that discussion it will become clear that there are no adequate grounds for assigning this material to some other, unknown source.

The remainder of this passage is generally divided between the three usual sources. This division is usually made with the largest section being ascribed to "J," namely, 46:1, 4a; 46:28–47:4; 47:5a, 6b, 12. A few verses are assigned to "E," namely, 46:2–4b and 5. The rest is given to "P," namely, 46:6–7 and 47:5b, 6a, 7–11. This intermingling of the various sources is defended on the basis of certain alleged irregularities and repetitions that are pointed out.

It is charged that, according to 45:28, Jacob was immediately ready to undertake the journey to Egypt, while according to 46:3 he still had some misgivings about the whole venture. It is further claimed that two different audiences with Pharaoh are recorded. Allegedly five of Joseph's brothers made their appearance before the king as it is told in 47:2–4, while Jacob made a separate appearance according to 47:7–10. With respect to the place where Joseph's family settled in Egypt, 47:6 mentions the land of Goshen, while 47:11 speaks of the land of Rameses. We will not enter into these matters at this time. As we proceed with our commentary, however, it will become clear that there are no essential conflicts or repetitions here, and consequently there is no substantial basis for the arbitrary assignment of the material to multiple sources.

46:1–4 *So Israel set out with all that was his, and when he reached Beersheba, he offered sacrifices to the God of his father Isaac.*

And God spoke to Israel in a vision at night and said, "Jacob! Jacob!"

"Here I am," he replied.

"I am God, the God of your father," he said. "Do not be afraid to go down to Egypt, for I will make you into a great nation there. I will go down to Egypt with you, and I will surely bring you back again. And Joseph's own hand will close your eyes."

In response to the invitation of Joseph (45:27), Jacob now made plans to move his entire family and all his possessions to Egypt. According to 35:27 and 37:14, Jacob's last residence had been at Hebron. Since there is no reference to his having moved from there, we may assume that the starting point for their journey was Hebron. The first stop on their migration was made at Beersheba, which was on the southern border of Canaan. As Jacob stood at the point of leaving the Promised Land for an undetermined period of time, he paused to approach God through sacrifices. The fact that God is here described as the God of his father Isaac can be explained by the presence of the altar that was built by Isaac at Beersheba (26:25). It is altogether conceivable that this was the altar on which Jacob now offered his sacrifices.

That night Jacob received a vision. God spoke to him and assured him that he could move to Egypt without fear or apprehension. It would be in Egypt that God's promise to make of Jacob's family a great nation would be fulfilled. God promised to accompany them into Egypt and in due time to bring their descendants back to the Promised Land. Then was added a very tender personal assurance when Jacob was told that his beloved son Joseph would be at his side when his time came to leave this life.

Must we assume from the content of this vision that Jacob had some misgivings about moving to Egypt? It certainly would not be surprising if this had been the case. Nor would this be in conflict with what we are told in 45:28. Even so, this need not have been the purpose for the message God brought to Jacob in this vision. It is of considerable significance that Jacob felt the need for communicating with God at the very borders of the land of Canaan before leaving this land that had been promised to him and his fathers. The "fear" to which God referred in His statement, "Do not be afraid," need not have been a personal fear on Jacob's part. It could have been a concern for the future of the chosen people of God as they departed for Egypt. At the point of leaving the land that had been promised to them as an eternal inheritance, God reassured him that this promise would stand and would eventually be fulfilled.

46:5–7 *Then Jacob left Beersheba, and Israel's sons took their father Jacob and their children and their wives in the carts that Pharaoh had sent to transport him. They also took with them their livestock and the possessions they had acquired in Canaan, and Jacob and all his offspring went to Egypt. He took with him to Egypt his sons and grandsons and his daughters and granddaughters–all his offspring.*

The actual journey from Canaan to Egypt then proceeded from Beersheba. In this connection the caravan is first described and mention is also made of the wagons that Pharaoh had provided for transporting the women and children. This certainly does not imply that the wagons were not used until after they left the borders of Canaan. This happens to be the first description of the entire entourage, including Jacob and his children and grandchildren, as well as all their livestock and possessions. It becomes clear now that this was not to be a temporary sojourn or visit but that it was actually a migration of the entire tribe from Canaan to Egypt.

46:8–27 *These are the names of the Israelites (Jacob and his descendants) who went to Egypt:*

Reuben the firstborn of Jacob.

The sons of Reuben: Hanoch, Pallu, Hezron and Carmi.

The sons of Simeon: Jemuel, Jamin, Ohad, Jakin, Zohar and Shaul the son of a Canaanite woman.

The sons of Levi:.Gershon, Kohath and Merari.

The sons of Judah: Er, Onan, Shelah, Perez and Zerah (but Er and Onan had died in the land of Canaan). The sons of Perez: Hezron and Hamul.

The sons of Issachar: Tola, Puah, Jashub and Shimron.

The sons of Zebulun: Sered, Elon and Jahleel.

These were the sons Leah bore to Jacob in Paddan Aram, besides his daughter Dinah. These sons and daughters of his were thirty-three in all.

The sons of Gad: Zephon, Haggi, Shuni, Ezbon, Eri, Arodi and Areli.

The sons of Asher: Imnah, Ishvah, Ishvi and Beriah. Their sister was Serah. The sons of Beriah: Heber and Malkiel.

These were the children born to Jacob by Zilpah, whom Laban had given to his daughter Leah–sixteen in all.

The sons of Jacob's wife Rachel: Joseph and Benjamin. In Egypt, Manasseh and Ephraim were born to Joseph by Asenath daughter of Potiphera, priest of On.

The sons of Benjamin: Bela, Beker, Ashbel, Gera, Naaman, Ehi, Rosh, Muppim, Huppim and Ard.

These were the sons of Rachel who were born to Jacob–fourteen in all.

The son of Dan: Hushim.

The sons of Naphtali: Jahziel, Guni, Jezer and Shillem.

These were the sons born to Jacob by Bilhah, whom Laban had given to his daughter Rachel–seven in all.

All those who went to Egypt with Jacob–those who were his direct descendants, not counting his sons' wives–numbered sixty-six persons. With the two sons who had been born to Joseph in Egypt, the members of Jacob's family, which went to Egypt, were seventy in all.

It is at this point that the inspired writer lists the names of Jacob's immediate descendants. As has been mentioned earlier, this list presents certain difficulties. First of all, the list includes four sons of Reuben, which would seem to conflict with 42:37. The earlier passage indicates that a year before, when they returned from their first journey to Egypt, Reuben had only two sons. A second difficulty is that Judah's son, Perez, had two sons. But according to chapter 38, Perez and his brothers were themselves born shortly before the second trip to Egypt to buy grain (see our introduction to chapter 38). It has also been pointed out that two grandsons of Asher are listed. This would not be impossible, however, since Asher could have married some years before Judah did. If we check back in the record, Jacob was married at the age of 84 (see our discussion on 29:20, 27) and was now 130 (47:9). Asher could thus have been about 40 by this time and it would have been possible for him to have grandchildren. There is, admittedly, no evidence that Asher married at an early age.

A final difficulty is that we read here of no less than ten sons of Benjamin. In our introduction to chapter 37, we observed that Benjamin was born between Joseph's 17th and 19th birthdays. Thus, when the family moved to Egypt, Benjamin had reached the approximate age of 21. If we compare 41:46 with 41:47 and 45:6, we can conclude that Joseph was about 39 at this time. These facts would make it most unlikely that Benjamin could have had 10 children by this time.

In view of all of this evidence, we must conclude that some of the grandchildren who are listed here were born after the family moved to Egypt. This conclusion is strengthened by referring to Numbers 26, where we are given a list of names that includes all the male descendants of Jacob who are mentioned here, with the exception of Judah's two sons, who died childless. In the Numbers passage these men are introduced, moreover, as tribal heads. It would be hard to believe that all of those who later became tribal heads had been born before the family went into Egypt. We have therefore reached the conclusion that the purpose for the list given here in chapter 46 is to catalog the immediate descendants of Jacob who later became tribal and family heads, even though some of them were actually born in Egypt. To this must be added the observation that in the Numbers 26 account, the descendants of Manasseh and Ephraim, Joseph's two sons, are also included. This is undoubtedly because these later became heads of two of the twelve tribes of Israel.

If we assume this position, we are faced with another difficulty in verses 26 and 27. There we are told that the number of Jacob's direct descendants who went into Egypt numbered 66, and when Joseph and his family are added this number is given as 70 souls. These numbers are difficult to harmonize with the number of names in the list before us. After going through a rather involved process of juggling numbers, considering who should be included and who should not be included in this or that list, the only conclusion we have been able to reach is that the list before us is concerned primarily with the male descendants of Jacob, with the exception of Dinah and Serah. It is a list of those who later became family and tribal heads, regardless of whether they were born before or after the migration into Egypt. When the total number of those who went into Egypt is given, on the other hand, the female descendants are also included. The ultimate purpose of the list of names, then, is to establish the fact that the entire nation of Israel, which developed in Egypt, stemmed from the patriarch Jacob.

There are a few other matters of minor concern regarding this list of names, which probably should also be considered briefly. In the case of one of Simeon's sons, we are told that he was the "son of a Canaanite woman." Since there obviously were other Canaanite women who had become wives of Jacob's sons (see Gen. 38:2), the singling out of this particular instance would suggest that this particular woman was especially well-known. Just what the reason was for her notoriety we are not told. It is obvious that the remainder of Simeon's sons were not born of this woman and this would imply that Simeon had other wives as well.

The other point that demands our attention is that mention is made of a daughter born to Asher by the name of "Serah." It would be hard to believe that there were no other daughters among the children and grandchildren of Jacob. Verse 15 specifically refers to the daughters of Leah, for instance, without giving their names. Why, then, should Serah be the only girl mentioned in the list, with the exception of Dinah, who had gained some fame in her own right (ch. 34)? Since we are given no further information about Serah, there is no way for us to know why she was singled out for special mention. We have found a similar case in "Iscah" in 11:29, the daughter of Haran. There is a Jewish legend that Serah lived to see the Exodus of the Israelites from Egypt and that she was the one who pointed out the location of Joseph's bones (Gen. 50:26 and Exod. 13:19). This legend, of course, cannot be true to fact due to the lapse of time between their entrance into Egypt and the Exodus (Exod. 12:40).

46:28–30 *Now Jacob sent Judah ahead of him to Joseph to get directions to Goshen. When they arrived in the region of Goshen, Joseph had his chariot made ready and went to Goshen to meet his father Israel. As soon as Joseph appeared before him, he threw his arms around his father and wept for a long time.*

Israel said to Joseph, "Now I am ready to die, since I have seen for myself that you are still alive."

We now proceed to a description of the arrival in Egypt. Judah, who had become the designated spokesman for the family, was sent ahead to confirm the arrangements for settling the family in the land of Goshen and to serve as their guide when they entered the land of Egypt. As soon as Joseph heard of their arrival, he hurried to the land of Goshen to welcome his father whom he had not seen for many years. The reunion of the old patriarch with his favorite son was a deeply moving scene. As they embraced, Joseph wept openly and Jacob expressed the fulfillment he felt at seeing his son alive, after having counted him among the dead for all these years. He acknowledged that he was now prepared to die in peace.

46:31–34 *Then Joseph said to his brothers and to his father's household, "I will go up and speak to Pharaoh and will say to him, 'My brothers and my father's household, who were living in the land of Canaan, have come to me. The men are shepherds; they tend livestock, and they have brought along their flocks and herds and everything they own.' When Pharaoh calls you in and asks, 'What is your occupation?' you should answer, 'Your servants have tended livestock from our boyhood on, just as our fathers did.' Then you will be allowed to settle in the region of Goshen, for all shepherds are detestable to the Egyptians."*

Joseph had told his brothers that they could settle in the land of Goshen. (See our discussion of 45:10 for the location of Goshen.) The family evidently made this their destination upon their arrival in Egypt. Even so, before they actually proceeded to settle there, Joseph deemed it advisable to gain the approval of Pharaoh for this arrangement. He therefore told his family that he would inform Pharaoh about their arrival, stressing the fact that they were shepherds and that they had brought their flocks and herds with them. Since the land of Goshen was especially suitable for grazing livestock, Joseph advised them as to what they should say to Pharaoh when they appeared before the king. They were to declare that both they and their fathers had been shepherds.

Some scholars have suggested that this claim by Joseph's family was not altogether true and, therefore, was intended to mislead Pharaoh. It is true that the patriarchal family had also engaged in tilling the soil in Canaan (see 26:12; 27:28). Even so, their primary occupation was herding livestock (see 12:16; 13:2, 7; 20:14; 26:14; 30:43; 32:5; 37:2, 13). One of the factors that Joseph considered to be important in influencing Pharaoh was the dislike that the Egyptians traditionally had for shepherds. In view of this it was Joseph's conjecture that Pharaoh would agree to have them settle in Goshen, which was separated from the main centers of Egyptian life. This aversion to shepherds that is mentioned here is mentioned nowhere else. A disdain for cattle raisers is described vividly in Egyptian literature, and is also evident in artwork and monuments of various kinds. So too those who herded swine were held in low regard by the Egyptians. Although we find no similar references with respect to shepherds, this cannot justifiably be used to call the authenticity of verse 34 into question.

47:1–6 *Joseph went and told Pharaoh, "My father and brothers, with their flocks and herds and everything they own, have come from the land of Canaan and are now in Goshen." He chose five of his brothers and presented them before Pharaoh.*

Pharaoh asked the brothers, "What is your occupation?"

"Your servants are shepherds," they replied to Pharaoh, "just as our fathers were." They also said to him, "We have come to live here awhile, because the famine is severe in Canaan and your servants' flocks have no pasture. So now, please let your servants settle in Goshen."

Pharaoh said to Joseph, "Your father and your brothers have come to you, and the land of Egypt is before you; settle your father and your brothers in the best part of the land. Let them live in Goshen. And if you know of any among them with special ability, put them in charge of my own livestock."

Joseph proceeded to make arrangements for an audience with the pharaoh on behalf of his brothers. This included five of them. They carefully followed Joseph's instructions and emphasized the fact that they were shepherds by occupation. Then they added the request that they might be permitted to settle in the land of Goshen, to carry on this livelihood there. Their request was readily granted by Pharaoh. The king was unusually favorable to Joseph's family, another indication of the high regard he had for his high official. He assured them that the entire land of Egypt was at their disposal and that they were free to choose the best location in the country for their residence. Since they had expressed a preference for Goshen, he gave them his approval to establish their residence there.

It should be noted that Pharaoh did not speak directly to Joseph's brothers but rather addressed Joseph, his co-ruler, and ordered him to make the necessary arrangements for carrying out these plans. Pharaoh added another very interesting statement. Since Joseph's brothers were skilled in animal husbandry, Joseph was to choose the ablest of them and place them in charge of the royal herds, which conceivably were also kept in the grazing lands of Goshen.

Most interpreters have questioned the opening statement of Pharaoh's reply to Joseph's brothers. They argue that when Pharaoh addressed Joseph with the words, "Your father and your brothers have come to you," this was in no sense a reply to the request that had been made. Many scholars have therefore decided to follow the order of the Septuagint text, which arranged this material differently and also inserted another statement at this

250

point. This version then reads: "The Pharaoh said to Joseph, 'Let them live in the land of Goshen. And if you know of any among them with special ability, put them in charge of my own livestock.' Then Jacob and his sons came to Joseph in Egypt and Pharaoh, the King of Egypt, heard about it. And Pharaoh said to Joseph, 'Your father and your brothers have come to you. The Land of Egypt is before you. Let your father and your brothers live in the best section of the land.'"

It is obvious that the above reading cannot be the original text. This presentation gives the impression that Jacob and his family were just arriving in Egypt, while 46:48ff. clearly indicates that they were already there. Those who give preference to this order of the text, based on the Septuagint, hold that sources "J" and "P" are in even greater conflict at this point than the Hebrew text is. This would imply that even at the time when the Septuagint translation was made the various alleged sources had not yet been fully coordinated in the text. This, of course, is unthinkable.

Actually, there is no real need to question Pharaoh's opening statement. His intent obviously was to base his gracious attitude toward Jacob and his sons on the fact that they were Joseph's family. It was precisely for this reason that they were given this preferential treatment and were permitted to select the choice area of Egypt as their place of residence. It was only logical, therefore, that the king should begin his remarks by some reference to their arrival and this in no way indicates the time of their arrival.

47:7–10 *Then Joseph brought his father Jacob in and presented him before Pharaoh. After Jacob blessed Pharaoh, Pharaoh asked him, "How old are you?"*

And Jacob said to Pharaoh, "The years of my pilgrimage are a hundred and thirty. My years have been few and difficult, and they do not equal the years of the pilgrimage of my fathers." Then Jacob blessed Pharaoh and went out from his presence.

Pharaoh also gave an audience to the old patriarch, Jacob himself. This is not a duplication of verses 2–6 and, therefore, does not indicate a separate source. This is clearly a separate audience with the king. We probably should think of the sequence of events as follows. The first audience, which was more of a business nature, took place soon after the family arrived in Egypt. This cleared the way for the family to settle in the land of Goshen. When the family had actually settled there, then the old father was given a separate audience with Pharaoh. This would have allowed some time for the old man to rest from his long journey from Canaan. In this visit the Pharaoh wanted to show honor to Joseph's father and thus also to Joseph himself.

When Jacob was ushered into the presence of the king of Egypt, he stretched out his hands in blessing, gratefully acknowledging all that the great king had done for his son, for himself, and for the entire family. Pharaoh solicitously inquired about Jacob's age. In his answer Jacob revealed that all his life he had been a stranger and a pilgrim in the land in which he lived. He mentioned that he had suffered much grief and that consequently he had not reached the advanced age his fathers had attained. The implication seems to have been that Jacob felt that he would not live much longer (cf. 46:30); he seemed to feel that the end of his life was near. After this brief interview, Jacob left with a parting blessing for Pharaoh.

47:11, 12 *So Joseph settled his father and his brothers in Egypt and gave them property in the best part of the land, the district of Rameses, as Pharaoh directed. Joseph also provided his father and his brothers and all his father's household with food, according to the number of their children.*

In these verses two matters are mentioned. First, we are told that Joseph, in accordance with Pharaoh's orders, settled his family and gave them property in the best part of Egypt. This, of course, means that this area was best suited for their purpose as shepherds. Thus the people of Israel became residents of Egypt.

Second, Joseph provided food for his father and his brothers and their families. This undoubtedly applies to the duration of the famine. The supply of food was doled out according to the number of children they had. Thus Joseph's family did not receive preferential treatment over the Egyptians. The food was provided strictly in proportion to the number of mouths to be fed.

It is worthy of note that the area where the Israelites were permitted to settle is here called "the district of Rameses," rather than "the land of Goshen." It has been argued that the use of the name "Rameses" is evidence for a separate source for this section; but it should be noted that this is the only place where we read about the "land of Rameses." There are a few references to a city by that name in Exodus 1:11; 12:37; Numbers 33:3, 5, and this makes it difficult to offer any positive information about the "land" of Rameses.

It is possible that Rameses was simply another name for Goshen. Most interpreters have accepted this possibility or, at least, that Rameses was a part of the land of Goshen. A few scholars have held that Rameses refers to another area in Egypt altogether. If this were the case, we would have to accept the fact that there are two distinct traditions among the Jewish people as to where the Israelites lived in Egypt, and this would be very difficult to accept.

It has also been argued that there is a distinction here between "the sons of Israel," in a broader sense, and "Jacob and his sons" as an immediate family. This is not tenable, however, since in verses 6 and 11 we read of Joseph's father and brothers living, on the one hand in Goshen, and on the other hand in Rameses. Since both of these names refer to the same area, then, one use of the name "Rameses" offers no substantial basis for a separate source for part of this material. It is possible that the term "the district of Rameses" was an expression that was used for the area surrounding the city of Rameses, which was later built there (see Exod. 1:11). This would then be the same usage we observed regarding Beersheba in Genesis 21:14.

50. *Joseph's Relief Program During the Famine* (47:13-26)

47:13-26 *There was no food, however, in the whole region because the famine was severe; both Egypt and Canaan wasted away because of the famine. Joseph collected all the money that was to be found in Egypt and Canaan in payment for the grain they were buying, and he brought it to Pharaoh's palace. When the money of the people of Egypt and Canaan was gone, all Egypt came to Joseph and said, "Give us food. Why should we die before your eyes? Our money is used up."*

"Then bring your livestock," said Joseph. "I will sell you food in exchange for your livestock, since your money is gone." So they brought their livestock to Joseph, and he gave them food in exchange for their horses, their sheep and goats, their cattle and donkeys. And he brought them through that year with food in exchange for all their livestock.

When that year was over, they came to him the following year and said, "We cannot hide from our lord the fact that since our money is gone and our livestock belongs to you, there is nothing left for our lord except our bodies and our land. Why should we perish before your eyes—we and our land as well? Buy us and our land in exchange for food, and we with our land will be in bondage to Pharaoh. Give us seed so that we may live and not die, and that the land may not become desolate."

So Joseph bought all the land in Egypt for Pharaoh. The Egyptians, one and all, sold their fields, because the famine was too severe for them. The land became Pharaoh's, and Joseph reduced the people to servitude, from one end of Egypt to the other. However, he did not buy the land of the priests, because they received a regular allotment from Pharaoh and had food enough from the allotment Pharaoh gave them. That is why they did not sell their land.

Joseph said to the people, "Now that I have bought you and your land today for Pharaoh, here is seed for you so you can plant the ground. But when the crop comes in, give a fifth of it to Pharaoh. The other four-fifths you may keep as seed for the fields and as food for yourselves and your households and your children."

"You have saved our lives," they said. "May we find favor in the eyes of our lord; we will be in bondage to Pharaoh."

> *So Joseph established it as a law concerning land in Egypt–still in force today–that a fifth of the produce belongs to Pharaoh. It was only the land of the priests that did not become Pharaoh's.*

These fourteen verses are generally assigned to "J" by those who divide the sources. A few of these scholars hold that this section has been misplaced and should have followed 41:56, but this position has been strongly opposed by other scholars and lacks substantial support. The biblical narrator here describes Joseph's measures for dealing with the famine in Egypt during the period after his family had arrived in Egypt. As such, this pericope follows logically on what precedes in the text.

The passage begins by describing the severity and the extent of the famine. We are told that there was no food in the entire country and that Egypt and Canaan wasted away because of the drought. An added problem developed when the people ran out of money for buying the food that had been stored in the government storehouses. All of the available money gradually came into Joseph's hands and he deposited it in Pharaoh's bulging treasury.

When the people's money supply was exhausted, they asked Joseph for food to feed their families and he agreed to accept their livestock in exchange for food. It is interesting to note that mention is made of sheep and goats, cattle and donkeys, but there is also a reference to horses. (See our treatment under 12:14–16.) It is obvious that horses had been introduced into Egypt by Joseph's time. By this measure of exchanging their livestock for food Joseph was able to take the people through another year of the famine. Just which year this was cannot be determined because we do not know when the money ran out. From 45:6 we can conclude that it probably was one of the later years of the famine. The "following year" or "second year" mentioned in verse 18 was certainly not the second year of the famine. It could very well have been the last year of the famine.

During that year the Egyptians turned to Joseph again with a plea for food and seed for sowing their fields. Since their supplies of money and of livestock were now exhausted, all they had left to offer in exchange for food was their land and their own bodies for slavery. Joseph accepted this offer and consequently the entire land of Egypt became the possession of the pharaoh. The one exception to this was the priests who received a regular ration from Pharaoh for which they were not required to pay. Thus the priests were able to keep their land.

Joseph then made the land available to the farmers so that they could plant crops and also gave them seed for planting. He no doubt also made their beasts of burden available to them for working the fields. He then ordered that, of whatever crops would be produced, one-fifth would have to be given to Pharaoh while four-fifths could be kept for their own use and for further planting of crops. It would seem obvious that these measures were introduced when the land again began to yield crops and the famine was over. This suggests that the earlier reference took place during the last years of the famine. This regulation about one-fifth being given to Pharaoh was still in force when the Book of Genesis was written. It is observed that the Egyptians were content with this arrangement and they expressed gratitude to Joseph for having spared their lives during the famine.

From the secular writings, which have been unearthed in and about Egypt, it has become clear that the measures that Joseph took during the famine were consonant with conditions and practices in ancient Egypt. We don't want to go so far, however, as to say that the events concerning Joseph, as recorded in Genesis, are also described in these secular accounts. For instance, the Amarna Tablets refer to a certain "Janchamu" who exercised Egyptian authority over Syria and Canaan. We are told that he also had authority over grain warehouses in the Nile Delta from which he supplied the needs of certain Syrian cities, but we cannot identify this man with Joseph or claim that the biblical narrative was based on this secular source. The differences between the two accounts are far too great and the similarities far too meager to justify such identification.

There is also a passage in an Egyptian Papyrus, dated approximately 1200 B.C., in which mention is made of "a certain Syrian" who became commander of Egypt during a time of scarce food supplies and managed to make "the whole land tributary to himself" and "plundered all the possessions of the Egyptians." In this case, also, the differences between this "Syrian" and Joseph, as he is presented in Scripture, are so marked that the two cannot be identified.

Even so, there is considerable evidence in such writings that conditions in Egypt could readily have taken the turn that is described for us in the Genesis account. Such eventualities as having the pharaoh, together with the priests, take over all the land of the Egyptians or to have all their possessions appropriated by the pharaoh, the priests, and the military leaders, are not out of keeping with Egyptian history. Although we cannot relate such events directly to Joseph's regulatory measures during the famine, they do indicate that such measures are wholly conceivable for ancient Egypt.

The question has been asked whether Joseph's measures can be considered to be ethical. The answer to this question depends on whether we accept this narrative as historical or whether we look on it as a saga that is intended to be descriptive of conditions in Egypt in general at that time.

There are some interpreters who view this part of the narrative as no more than a product of the national vanity of the Israelites. This, in turn, has spawned a certain anti-Semitism that charges that a people who would exalt the kind of treatment Joseph foisted on the Egyptians can hardly be considered to be honorable people.

We, on the other hand, believe that what is here recorded in Scripture is historical fact, but this does not imply that the Scripture sets its stamp of approval on everything Joseph did. The account simply presents the facts as they actually took place and does not pass judgment on whether Joseph's conduct was either ethical or unethical. If we today want to evaluate the moral implications of Joseph's administrative measures we should not try to do this on the basis of present-day political insights and standards. Our bases for judgment must be restricted to the principles of moral conduct that are taught in Scripture as a whole. To be sure, the governmental policies that resulted from Joseph's regulatory measures can hardly be considered ideal when they are compared with the social and political implications of the Mosaic Law. We may not forget, however, that we do not know what the political situation was in Egypt prior to Joseph's administration. It could well be that Joseph's apparently stern measures were a great improvement over conditions that prevailed prior to his ascendancy. Moreover, the narrative makes a point of stressing the fact that the Egyptians themselves were happy with Joseph's administrative procedures and hailed him as the savior of the people during the bitter famine that swept across the land.

With respect to the requirement that the people had to pay rent on their land to the government to the extent of giving one-fifth of the yield from their efforts, this cannot be considered to be excessive by Egyptian standards. The unusual productiveness of the Nile Valley during normal years must be taken into account. Moreover, there are accounts from this part of the world where rents were as high as one-third, one-half, two-thirds, and even three-fourths of what was produced.

From an ethical point of view, the most questionable aspect of Joseph's administration would appear to be that the grain that he first requisitioned from the people for Pharaoh (41:34–48) was later sold back to the people, during the time of the famine, at the cost of all their possessions and even their freedom as they became slaves of the state. To offset the reprehensible nature of this procedure, there has been an attempt by Jewish scholars to prove that Joseph had informed the people in advance that this was what would be done. There is no basis for this claim, however. Regardless of what conditions may have prevailed in Egypt at that time of which we are uninformed, we cannot escape the conclusion that this whole procedure on Joseph's part cannot be ethically and morally justified.

Another question that has been asked is why these regulatory measures of Joseph are recorded in such detail here in the biblical narrative. We have already observed that we cannot accept the theory that this was a saga intended to describe conditions in Egypt. Likewise, we cannot accept the position held by some Jewish scholars that the writer of Genesis is trying to lay the groundwork for the use of the term "house of bondage" which is ascribed to Egypt in later books of the Pentateuch. It is argued that although the Israelites were a freedom-loving people, Egyptians were content to live as slaves, as long as they were provided with food. Thus, it is claimed, Egypt was, by the very nature of its people, a "house of bondage." In reply to this it must be obvious that the reason for Egypt being called "house of bondage" in the Old Testament was simply that this was where the Israelites lived as slaves for some 400 years.

It seems to us that the reason for giving these details regarding Joseph's regulatory measures was to graphically describe the severity of the famine in the land. It certainly becomes obvious that the only way the Israelites could have survived this famine was to come to Egypt. The reference to Canaan, in verses 13–15, was not an irrelevant insertion. It is brought into this context precisely to confirm the fact that Israel could not have survived if they had stayed in Canaan. The people of Canaan could buy corn in Egypt as long as they had money to exchange for food, but when their money ran out there was no other source of food for them. Joseph could not use the same measures with people from other nations that he used with the Egyptians. Since the Egyptians were willing to submit to such stringent measures in order to stay alive, it becomes abundantly clear what conditions would be in Canaan where there was no supply of food stored away. Thus this description of Joseph's regulatory measures in Egypt must be seen in direct relationship to the main point of this entire narrative in these chapters of Genesis, namely, the resettlement of God's chosen people from the land of promise to the land of Egypt. Moreover, it must be clearly seen that this resettlement was the direct consequence of the famine that God in His sovereign plan brought upon that part of the world. Jacob's family was destined to go into Egypt because it was there that God would make them a great nation. God literally compelled Israel to move to Egypt by force of circumstances in His sovereign control.

51. *Jacob's Last Years* (47:27–31)

47:27–31 *Now the Israelites settled in Egypt in the region of Goshen. They acquired property there and were fruitful and increased greatly in number.*

Jacob lived in Egypt seventeen years, and the years of his life were a hundred and forty-seven. When the time drew near for Israel to die, he called for his son Joseph and said to him, "If I have found favor in your eyes, put your hand under my thigh and promise that you will show me kindness and faithfulness. Do not bury me in Egypt, but when I rest with my fathers, carry me out of Egypt and bury me where they are buried."

"I will do as you say," he said.

"Swear to me," he said. Then Joseph swore to him, and Israel worshiped as he leaned on the top of his staff.

Those who divide the sources usually ascribe verses 27 and 28 of this section to "P," while the rest of the passage is given to "J." The reason for giving a few verses to "P" is that the details about Jacob's age are allegedly characteristic of the style of "P." We have repeatedly refuted this line of argument previously and need comment no further on it.

Verse 27 gives somewhat of a conclusion to what had been described in 46:1 to 47:12, regarding the resettlement of the patriarchal family. Chapter 47:13–26 related to that event very closely, as we have observed. The next section is then introduced with this summary statement about how Israel had come into Egypt and specifically into the land of Goshen.

The name "Israel" is used here in the plural and has rightly been translated "Israelites" in distinction from the personal name of the patriarch himself, which is the singular, used again in verses 29–31. This is the first time that the descendants of Jacob are called Israelites, except for Genesis 34:7, where we are dealing with a very special incident. At this time Israel was a nation only in embryo, but it was as a distinct people or nation that they were now established in Egypt. In this verse mention is made of the beginning of the phenomenal growth that the children of Jacob experienced in Egypt.

We are then told about the years Jacob continued to live, after he arrived in Egypt, which numbered seventeen years. Thus his total life span was 147 years.

One incident is singled out from these closing years of Jacob's life. As he began to feel his strength slipping from him and death approaching, he called his son Joseph to his side. He demanded that Joseph would promise, under oath, that when he died he would not be buried in Egypt but his remains would be taken to Canaan and placed in the family grave plot. We need not feel that Jacob was actually on his deathbed when he made this request. As Jacob began to feel that his end was approaching, he laid this charge on Joseph who was the only one who had enough authority and influence to carry out his request.

The expression regarding "putting his hand under the thigh" has been discussed under 24:2. The grave in which Jacob wanted to be buried was, of course, the plot that Abraham had purchased for this purpose in the cave of Machpelah (see 25:9 and 49:31) where both Abraham and Isaac had been buried. Some of the critics want to read this as "my grave" rather than "their grave" in order to tie this to Genesis 50:5. This change is made in order to support the case for separate sources. We insist that there is no textual justification for making this change and to do so is no more than arbitrary tampering with the biblical text.

Joseph was quite willing to agree to his father's request and gave his assurance to this effect by means of an oath. Thereupon Jacob bowed in worship and thanksgiving to God.

There has been considerable discussion about the expression that Jacob bowed down at the "head of his bed." Some modern critics have tried to read into this that Jacob had some type of teraphim on the head piece of his bed and that he worshiped by means of this idol. This would be in conflict with 35:2–4, and even so there is no basis for it in the text.

Our translators have rendered this statement "on the top of his staff," basing this reading on the Septuagint. This same translation is used in Hebrews 11:21. Although arguments can be offered for either reading, there really is no serious issue involved. If we think of an old man needing something on which to lean to support himself, it really is quite inconsequential whether he leaned on the head of the bed or leaned on his staff. The important point is that he bowed to worship God in praise and thanksgiving.

52. *Jacob and the Sons of Joseph* (48:1–22)

In this chapter those who divide the sources find all three sources, which are usually designated, represented. Verses 3–6 are assigned to "P." The rest of the chapter is usually divided between the other two sources as follows: 2b, 9b, 10a, 13, 14, 17–20 are ascribed to "J," while 1, 2a, 8, 9a, 10b–12, 15, 16, 21, 22 are given to "E."

Here it should be noted that this division does not include verse 7. This verse has at one time or another been ascribed to every conceivable source and has even been described as impossible to classify. It is apparent that this verse stands by itself. The reference to Rachel's death and burial can be related to Jacob's original wish that he might be buried beside his beloved Rachel. However, when we consider 47:30 and 49:29–32, it seems obvious that this wish was not realized. There is actually no reason why this verse must be considered as an unrelated fragment or must be moved to another position in the text, as some have done, by placing it after verse 10. It is wholly understandable that as Jacob was emotionally dwelling on his relationship to Joseph's sons his mind should recall their grandmother, his beloved and beautiful Rachel. For a moment the old man was painfully reminded of her untimely death and the continuing grief he felt as he remembered her burial there along the way, near Ephrath. Thus this verse can be logically accepted as a proper part of the text in its present position.

The assignment of verses 3-6 to "P" has been argued on the basis of a previous assignment of 35:6a, 9-13 to this source and the establishing of a certain connection with that passage. However, when we considered the passage in chapter 35 we observed that there is some real question about that assignment. Thus the basis for assigning our present passage to the same source falls away.

The assignment of the rest of the chapter to two separate sources is based on the following alleged conflicts or repetitions:

1) It is argued that in verse 1 we are told that Joseph learned his father was sick, while in 47:29-31 we are told that preparations were already made for his burial. But this presents no real conflict. We observed with respect to 47:28ff. that there is no call to look upon that incident as a deathbed scene. The old man felt his strength slowly waning and realized that he was not long for this life and therefore wanted to make some provisions for his eventual burial. Here in 48:1 his condition is presented as far more critical. He is now described as sick, and this sickness led to his death. It is also significant that in the incident in chapter 47 Jacob specifically called for Joseph. In this case Joseph learns of Jacob's serious illness and takes the initiative to go to his father's bedside. There is no evidence of conflict here in any way.

2) It is pointed out that according to verse 10a Jacob was no longer able to see. But in verses 8 and 11 we are told that he "saw" Joseph's sons. There is no real conflict here, either. As has been noted in our translation, verse 10 does not indicate that Jacob was blind, but merely that his eyesight was failing.

3) It is claimed that we are told twice, in verses 10 and 13, that Joseph brought his sons to Jacob and that this is repetition. But, as we will point out in our interpretation of the scene, it is apparent from the narrative that Joseph actually did bring his sons close to their grandfather twice in the course of the incident.

4) It has been argued that verses 15 and 16 break the connection between 14 and 17. Joseph's attempt to correct Jacob with respect to which child should receive the greater blessing, it is claimed, comes too late since the blessing has already been spoken. Thus it is suggested that verses 15 and 16 actually anticipate verse 20, but this is a nitpicking argument. There

was nothing in the words of Jacob, recorded in verses 15 and 16, that would indicate that Ephraim was being given a preferential blessing over his brother, Manasseh. There was no need for Joseph to panic and immediately jump into action as soon as the old man placed his hands on the heads of his sons. The whole scene is a very natural and tender one. When Jacob began to speak, Joseph gradually came to the realization that his father may have mistaken the elder for the younger of the two boys. So he interrupted his father and tried to correct the situation, but Jacob gently insisted that he knew what he was doing and thus the incident proceeded in a very natural way.

In the light of all of this it becomes clear that this chapter need not be broken up into little bits and pieces. It is a complete unit and graphically describes a tender, emotional scene in a very natural way. Even some of the scholars who insist on dividing the material between various sources have observed that the blending of this material into one coherent narrative is most effective in this chapter.

48:1–6 *Some time later Joseph was told, "Your father is ill." So he took his two sons Manasseh and Ephraim along with him. When Jacob was told, "Your son Joseph has come to you," Israel rallied his strength and sat up on the bed.*

Jacob said to Joseph, "God Almighty appeared to me at Luz in the land of Canaan, and there he blessed me and said to me, 'I am going to make you fruitful and will increase your numbers. I will make you a community of peoples, and I will give this land as an everlasting possession to your descendants after you.'

"Now then, your two sons born to you in Egypt before I came to you here will be reckoned as mine; Ephraim and Manasseh will be mine, just as Reuben and Simeon are mine. Any children born to you after them will be yours; in the territory they inherit they will be reckoned under the names of their brothers.

Some time after Joseph had visited his father (47:29–31), he was informed that Jacob was ill. Because of Jacob's advanced age, this news was genuine cause for alarm. Therefore, Joseph hastened to his father's side and took his two sons, Ephraim and Manasseh, with him. When Jacob heard about the arrival of his favorite son, his spirits were revived somewhat and he rallied his waning strength to the extent that he was able to sit up on his bed.

Jacob began his communication with Joseph by reviewing the "appearance" that God had made to him at Luz in the land of Canaan. (This incident is recorded in 35:9–13.) If we take into account the terms that are used here, there can be no doubt that it was specifically that appearance to which Jacob has referred. We can point to expressions such as "God Almighty" and "blessed." The specific elements are included in the blessing that is recorded, and even the order in which those elements are mentioned. Jacob added, further, that Joseph's two sons, Ephraim and Manasseh, who were born to Joseph in Egypt before Jacob resettled in the land of Goshen, would be counted as Jacob's own sons on the same level as his other sons, such as Reuben and Simeon.

The fact that Ephraim is mentioned before Manasseh is in anticipation of what was to follow. The rest of Joseph's children who might yet be born to him would be considered as Joseph's sons. They would receive no special inheritance but would share in the inheritance of Ephraim and Manasseh. This undoubtedly points to the eventual partitioning of the land of Canaan among the twelve tribes that would include the tribes of Ephraim and Manasseh. Each of them would receive a designated portion of the land of Canaan (see 35:11) when that land would be occupied. Scripture does not inform us about any other children born to Joseph, but that is immaterial since it was these two sons only who would become heads of tribes on a level with the other sons of Jacob.

48:7 *As I was returning from Paddan, to my sorrow Rachel died in the land of Canaan while we were still on the way, a little distance from Ephrath. So I buried her there beside the road to Ephrath'' (that is, Bethlehem).*

In addition to his blessing pronounced on the two sons of Joseph, Jacob referred to the death and burial of Rachel. This sad event is recorded in 35:16–20. The question that has caused much discussion is why Jacob brings this into this particular pronouncement. We have already rejected the idea that Jacob was expressing the hope that he himself might be buried in the same grave with Rachel. What then was Jacob's motive in inserting this reference to Rachel's death in this specific context? It is possible that there was a causal connection between Rachel's untimely death and Jacob's special provision for Joseph's two sons, Ephraim and Manasseh. Jacob could have decided to honor his beloved Rachel by adopting her two grandsons as his own sons and in that way increasing the number of her sons, for which she longed so desperately. This reference to her death would then present the motive for the special position that he now gave to Ephraim and Manasseh. The Latin Vulgate translation pointed in this direction by using a causal conjunction between the two statements.

It can be noted that Jacob referred to the country where he had gained his wives and his family with the shortened form of "Paddan" rather than the usual "Paddan Aram." (In this connection see our treatment of 25:20.) It goes without saying that the addition of the statement "that is, Bethlehem," when speaking of Ephrath, came from the hand of the sacred writer and was not part of Jacob's actual words. Thus our translators have correctly placed this as a parenthesis. We find a similar insertion in 35:19. Regarding the difficulty this identification presents, please refer to our treatment of 35:19.

48:8–11 *When Israel saw the sons of Joseph, he asked, "Who are these?"*
"They are the sons God has given me here," Joseph said to his father.
Then Israel said, "Bring them to me so I may bless them."
Now Israel's eyes were failing because of old age, and he could hardly see. So Joseph brought his sons close to him, and his father kissed them and embraced them.
Israel said to Joseph, "I never expected to see your face again, and now God has allowed me to see your children too."

It was at this point in the conversation that Jacob, whose eyesight was failing (v. 10), took note of Joseph's two sons who were present with him. In reply to Jacob's question regarding who these two young men were, Joseph introduced Ephraim and Manasseh to his father. Jacob asked the two young men to come close to him because he wanted to bless them. As they approached him he embraced them and kissed them. The old patriarch spoke warmly about the amazing miracle that, whereas he had expected never to see his beloved Joseph again, now God had given him the grace to see Joseph's two sons.

48:12 *Then Joseph removed them from Israel's knees and bowed down with his face to the ground.*

This verse presents some difficulty. First of all it could be asked whose knees are intended here. This can be readily answered because the context makes it clear that this refers to Jacob's knees and this is the way it has generally been accepted. Moving from one person to another in the course of a narrative without indicating this is in keeping with Hebrew narrative style.

The next question is just what the significance is of this reference to Jacob's knees. Some have held that Jacob took the two young men and placed them on his knees as a symbol of adopting them as his sons. But this will hardly do since these sons of Joseph, born before the time of the famine (41:50), were full-grown young men by this time. The Hebrew text, it should be noted, does not say that Joseph took his sons "off" his father's knees but rather that he took them "away from" his father's knees. We probably should picture this as follows: The feeble old man was sitting on the edge of the bed (v. 2). In order to embrace these two young men Jacob had to stand close to him, pressing against his knees. Then, at a signal from Joseph, they again withdrew to stand a bit further back. The reason for this is also apparent since we read that Joseph bowed down with his face to the ground before his father in order to express his gratitude for his father's gracious adoption of these two sons as his own. Of course, all of this had to be done in conformity with proper ancient, Eastern custom. In order that Joseph might properly perform his obeisance, it would have been necessary for his sons to step aside.

48:13–16 *And Joseph took both of them, Ephraim on his right toward Israel's left hand and Manasseh on his left toward Israel's right hand, and brought them close to him. But Israel reached out his right hand and put it on Ephraim's head, though he was the younger, and crossing his arms, he put his left hand on Manasseh's head, even though Manasseh was the firstborn.*

Then he blessed Joseph and said, "May the God before whom my fathers Abraham and Isaac walked, the God who has been my Shepherd all my life to this day, the Angel who has delivered me from all harm—may he bless these boys. May they be called by my name and the names of my fathers Abraham and Isaac, and may they increase greatly upon the earth."

Then Joseph put his sons into a position where his father could pronounce the blessing on them he had mentioned earlier (v. 9). He placed them before the old patriarch so that Manasseh was on the old man's right hand and Ephraim on his left, and he had the young men kneel so that Jacob could place his hands on their heads. Then an amazing thing happened. Jacob crossed his hands so that his right hand was on Ephraim's head and his left hand on Manasseh's, who was the firstborn, and then he began to pronounce the blessing.

We read that "he blessed Joseph." This does not mean, as some Jewish scholars have claimed, that Jacob pronounced a special blessing on Joseph that is not recorded here. It indicates, rather, that Joseph was blessed in the blessing pronounced on his sons. The Septuagint and the Vulgate try to improve on the text here by rendering this—"He blessed them" or "He blessed Joseph's sons." But there is no support for these readings in the Hebrew text.

The blessing is formulated as follows: God is described as the God of Jacob's fathers, Abraham and Isaac, who walked before this God (17:1), the God who had led Jacob all his life like a shepherd, and the God who was the Angel who had delivered him from all harm. It is obvious that the word "angel" does not here refer to a created angel, or a guardian angel. It refers, rather, to the Angel of the Lord who Himself was God (see our discussion under 16:7; 31:11; and 32:24ff.).

264

He specifically predicted in his blessing that these two young men would be called by his name and by the name of his fathers, Abraham and Isaac. He announced that they would increase in the earth as "fish." The figure of multiplying "like fish" is a parallel to the earlier figures of "like the stars of the heavens" (15:5; 22:17; 26:4), "like the dust of the earth" (13:16), or "like the sand of the seashore" (22:17).

There are differences of opinion about the term "called by my name," etc. Some hold that this implied only that they would be on a level with Jacob's sons; thus, that they would be adopted as Jacob's sons. But this blessing certainly included more than that. Others refer to this as a matter of being honored by this name (see 12:2). Still others hold that it says that the names of Jacob, Isaac, and Abraham would be carried forward by these young men. The most obvious interpretation is that this is a usage similar to Ruth 4:14, which has been translated "become famous." Thus Jacob implied that these young men would make his name famous or great. In this way it would conform to the promise to Abraham in Genesis 12:2.

48:17–20 *When Joseph saw his father placing his right hand on Ephraim's head he was displeased; so he took hold of his father's hand to move it from Ephraim's head to Manasseh's head. Joseph said to him, "No, my father, this one is the firstborn; put your right hand on his head."*

But his father refused and said, "I know, my son, I know. He too will become a people, and he too will become great. Nevertheless, his younger brother will be greater than he, and his descendants will become a group of nations." He blessed them that day and said, "In your name will Israel pronounce this blessing: 'May God make you like Ephraim and Manasseh.'" So he put Ephraim ahead of Manasseh.

As Joseph observed his father's rather strange position of having his arms crossed, he began to wonder whether the elderly man was confused as to which of the two young men was the older. So Joseph tenderly interrupted his father and tried to correct the position of his hands so that his right hand would rest on Manasseh, the older son. But Jacob insisted that he knew very well what he was doing. By prophetic inspiration he had learned that the younger son would be greater than his older brother and that it was from the younger son, Ephraim, that a group of nations would spring.

As the history of the children of Israel unfolded this greater position of Ephraim was not always evident. In Numbers 2 the tribe of Ephraim included 40,500 fighting men (v. 19) while the tribe of Manasseh numbered 32,200 men (v. 21). However, in Numbers 26 this was reversed and Ephraim numbered 32,500 men (v. 37) while Manasseh had 52,700 men

(v. 34). Later, however, the superiority of Ephraim became clearly evident. When the kingdom was divided, it was the tribe of Ephraim that became the leading force in the northern kingdom of the ten tribes. So strong was this dominance of Ephraim that the northern kingdom was actually called "Ephraim" (see 2 Chron. 25:7; Isa. 7:5ff; 11:13; 28:3ff.; Jer. 31:9, 20; Ezek. 37:19; Hos. 4:17; 5:9ff.; 6:4, 10; 7:8, 11; 8:9, 11; 9:3, 8, 13; 10:6, 11; 11:3, 8; 12:1ff.; 13:1; 14:8; Zech. 9:10; 10:7).

Thereupon Jacob continued his blessing of Joseph's two sons. The prosperity of Ephraim and Manasseh would become proverbial. The name "Israel" is here again used as designating the nation of Israel, in anticipation of what would later occur. Jacob declared that when anyone would pronounce a blessing on Israel it would be pronounced on Ephraim or on Manasseh. In this blessing the two sons were put on an equal level. Even so, Ephraim was given the higher position by being mentioned first.

48:21, 22 *Then Israel said to Joseph, "I am about to die, but God will be with you and take you back to the land of your fathers. And to you, as one who is over your brothers, I give the ridge of land I took from the Amorites with my sword and my bow."*

Finally, Jacob had a personal word for Joseph. He realized that his death was near and that he would not return to Canaan before he died. But God would bless his descendants and would eventually bring them back to the land of promise. In anticipation of that return to Canaan Jacob now gave Joseph a strip of land, as a special inheritance, above that of his brothers. The striking fact about this particular strip, or ridge, of land is that Jacob said that he captured it from the Amorites with his sword and bow.

This is the only place where we read of Jacob waging war. For this reason some interpreters have tried to give this a different reading. Some think that it refers to a later conquest by Jacob's descendants. Others hold that it designates a piece of land that he purchased from the sons of Hamor (33:19). But the text implies that Jacob was referring to a literal, historical military conquest. This need not surprise us. We also read of Abraham that he ventured forth on a military conquest (ch. 14). It is true that there is no record of Jacob's military venture against the Amorites but this does not prove that it did not happen.

Some have suggested that Jacob referred to the conquest of Shechem that is described in chapter 34. They even argue that there is a similarity between the Hebrew word for "ridge" used here and the word "Shechem," but tying this statement of Jacob to the ignominious plunder of Shechem by his sons is unthinkable.

There is some reason to believe that this may have been the piece of land that Jacob purchased from the sons of Hamor (33:19). It should be noted that when Israel left Egypt they took Joseph's bones along for burial in Canaan (50:25; Exod. 13:19). It would be logical to assume that Joseph's remains would be buried on his own inherited piece of land. In Joshua 24:32 we read of the burial of Joseph's bones and there we are told that this burial was in the tract of land that Jacob bought from the sons of Hamor. It is striking that the same words are used in both passages, Genesis 33:19 and Joshua 24:32. Therefore, the only conclusion we can reach is that this piece of land had later been taken from Jacob by the Amorites and then he, in turn, recaptured it with his sword and his bow.

53. *Jacob, on His Deathbed, Blesses His Sons* (49:1–28)

These pronouncements regarding Jacob's sons are similar to the "blessings" (v. 28) given by Noah in Genesis 9:25–27, by Isaac in 27:27–29, and by Jacob with respect to the sons of Joseph in 48:15–20. Those who divide the sources have a difficult time with this material. It is generally accepted that we are dealing with some of the oldest records that were incorporated into the "J" source. Some even ascribe this to the so-called "fourth source."

The precise age of these records is allegedly determined by what scholars call "historical background." Their theory is that these pronouncements are to be dated according to the various events and conditions that are mentioned relative to these tribes when they became historical realities. This theory, of course, rejects the possibility of predictions of future events and conditions. And it is possible to deny the predictive prophetic quality of these blessings and call them *vativinia ex eventu,* that is, pronouncements that were made only after the events that are described had actually happened. As such, they must be classed only as apparent predictions, but this is a seriously prejudiced judgment. The pronouncements of the dying patriarch, Jacob, are given precisely as predictions and promises for the future life of his sons and their respective tribes (v. 1). The denial of predictive prophecy, even by divine inspiration, is a position that calls into question the authenticity of large sections of the Holy Scriptures. We who believe in the reality of divine revelation, not only accept the authenticity of predictive prophecy in the Bible as a whole, but also believe that the aged Jacob was given a revelation of what would take place in the lives of his descendants in the future.

One problem that results from applying this theory of "historical background" to these pronouncements, is that not all of them can be placed in the same time frame. In different declarations the circumstances, relationships, and events reflect entirely different historical periods. It cannot be denied, however, that this entire collection of pronouncements displays an obvious stamp of unity and coherence. But the critics have avoided this by alleging that such pronouncements follow a certain fixed pattern. Others have charged that a later redactor gathered all of these pronouncements from various historical periods and then poured them into a mold that would give them the appearance of unity. If we, on the other hand, accept these statements as being genuinely inspired predictions of the future, the fact that they find their fulfillment in different historical periods causes no problems and requires no such ingenious explanations. In fact, it would be strange indeed if all the revelations that came to Jacob regarding the future of his sons and their tribes would be fulfilled at one and the same time in history. It stands to reason that when the future is seen from the perspective of predictive prophecy, the most significant events on the horizon of time would be emphasized. To assume that all of these events in the history of all of these tribes would be chronologically identical is historically ridiculous.

The details of these predictions will be treated in our commentary following.

A strange interpretation has been attempted by a few scholars who hold that the manner in which the twelve tribes are described here is clothed in symbols that are taken from animal life. On this basis they conclude that this is no more than an allusion to the signs of the Zodiac. This is pure fantasy, however, and finds no basis in the biblical text.

Those who divide the sources remove the first part of verse 1, "Then Jacob called for his sons," and the last part of verse 28, "he blessed them, giving each the blessing appropriate to him," from the actual pronouncements of blessing. These two snatches are then ascribed to another source, "P." It is difficult to understand why the redactor of the Pentateuch, who certainly would want to use an introductory statement for these "blessings," would seek out such statements from an altogether different source from the material he had before him. This would also apply to the conclusion that is used here, in verse 28. That these words are not part of the actual "blessing" is obvious, but can there be any reason why the editor of this section should have taken these words from a completely different source and rather arbitrarily inserted them here?

There is good reason for believing that this rather extensive statement of blessing was put into writing at a very early date. It would be difficult to assume that such detailed information could be preserved merely by oral tradition until the time of Moses or even later, and then be put into writing for the first time. Assuming that we are dealing with a written record, we would then also have to look on verse 1a as the introduction with which this ancient record began. Verse 28, however, can be considered in its entirety as a concluding comment added by the hand that actually placed this material in the Pentateuch.

Some have objected to describing this entire statement as a ''blessing.'' Some of the statements, such as those addressed to Reuben, Simeon, and Levi, include little that is favorable and almost have the nature of being a curse rather than a blessing. This is a matter of semantics, however. We find the same usage in connection with Noah's pronouncements to his sons. There the so-called ''curse of Canaan'' is included. So also with Isaac's pronouncement with respect to Esau. One Jewish commentator has suggested that the ''blessing'' mentioned in the last half of verse 28 actually does not refer to the material in verses 3 to 27. He claims that these statements are no more than a prediction of the future and that the actual blessings that the patriarch bestowed on his sons followed but are not recorded here. This would require a different translation of verse 28 that, of course, would be possible. Even so, this position does present some other difficulties when we consider the passage as a whole. The pronouncements regarding Joseph (vv. 22–26) certainly are a blessing, especially the close of verse 26. It should also be noted that in the statement regarding Simeon and Levi we have the striking use of the first person, as though it was actually God speaking and announcing what He would do. Although the statement was actually a curse rather than a blessing, the fact remains that it was a divinely effective curse. Also, it is more natural to make the verb ''blessing'' in verse 28 refer back to the words of Jacob that immediately preceded, than to words he may have spoken later but are not recorded.

Another noteworthy factor of this chapter is the order in which Jacob's sons are listed. The six natural sons of Leah are mentioned first. This could be expected. But what is striking is that the last two are not mentioned in the order of their birth. Zebulun, the younger, is listed before his older brother, Issachar. After these the four sons of the two slave women, whom Jacob took as wives, are listed, and that in a very strange order. First is the oldest son of Rachel's servant Bilhah, Dan. Then come the two sons of Leah's hand-maid, Zilpah, Gad and Asher in the order of their age. After these we have Bilhah's second son, Naphtali. Finally we are given Rachel's two natural sons, Joseph and Benjamin. There is no apparent reason for this unusual order, and this does confirm that the usual listing of Jacob's sons is not chronological according to age (see under our introduction to ch. 29). This does not imply that this list here in chapter 49 is chronologically arranged, which is certainly not the case. It does indicate, however, that there are other standards used for the order in which Jacob's sons are listed and also the twelve tribes that stemmed from them.

49:1, 2 *Then Jacob called for his sons and said: "Gather around so I can tell you what will happen to you in days to come. Assemble and listen, sons of Jacob; listen to your father Israel.*

Shortly after Joseph's visit to his father's sickbed, as described in chapter 48, the old patriarch, realizing that the end was near, called all his sons to him to take his leave from them. By divine revelation he saw the future of the twelve tribes that would come forth from his sons. The term used in Hebrew for "predict the future" literally means "in the last days." This certainly does not refer to the end of this dispensation but simply indicates the future. How far this future extends must be determined in each individual situation described. Jacob's sons were instructed to gather about their father's bed and listen attentively to his prophetic words.

REUBEN

49:3, 4 *"Reuben, you are my firstborn, my might, the first sign of my strength, excelling in honor, excelling in power. Turbulent as the waters, you will no longer excel, for you went up onto your father's bed, onto my couch and defiled it.*

Our attention is called to the fact that Jacob addressed his son in this case. This is not true in the case of all his sons. Besides Reuben, we note the same approach in the case of Judah in verse 8 and Joseph in verses 25 and 26. In most cases, however, the third person is used. We cannot attach any great significance to this change of approach on Jacob's part; it just happens to be the way the words came out.

Reuben was Jacob's firstborn. As such he should have been an example of honor and power, but alas, he was to demonstrate a less favorable characteristic. Reuben was to be "turbulent as the waters." The word that our translators have rendered "turbulent" has also been translated "full of presumption." The word presents some real difficulty because it appears nowhere else in the Old Testament. There is a verb using the same root in Zephaniah 3:4, which our translators have rendered "arrogant." The same root is also found in a word in Jeremiah 23:32 where it has been translated "reckless." In the context in which Jacob used it the meaning obviously lies in the direction of "insolence" or "shamelessness." This noun form is used to describe a characteristic of Reuben, but this leaves the question about the use of "as the waters," in connection with this characteristic. This probably indicated that Reuben was easily aroused. This would then also lead to the translation our translators have suggested in their use of the word "turbulent."

Because of this characteristic in Reuben, even though he was the firstborn and excelled in other qualities, he would not have the first place among Jacob's sons. The Hebrew has a play on words here. He who "excelled" in honor and power would not "excel" among his brothers.

Finally, Jacob mentioned the specific incident in which Reuben's "presumption," "arrogance," or "turbulence" came into expression. This was the shameful act Reuben had performed with Bilhah, recorded in Genesis 35:22. Jacob had never fully recovered from the shame his oldest son had brought on him by his conduct at that time. Even on his deathbed he cried out, "You defiled my bed."

Little need be said about the fulfillment of this prophecy. It is a known fact that the tribe of Reuben never took a leading position among the people of Israel. It has been observed that this tribe produced no one of any great importance in Israel—no judge, no king, and no prophet. Some have argued that what we have here is the loss of the birthright that should have been Reuben's as the firstborn, but there is no mention of that here. Others insist that the incident of Reuben with Bilhah really never took place but was only a fantasy to try to explain why Reuben did not receive the birthright blessing. These and several other theories that question the historicity of the account of Reuben's affair with Bilhah find no basis in the biblical text but rest purely on conjecture.

SIMEON AND LEVI

49:5–7 *"Simeon and Levi are brothers—their swords are weapons of violence. Let me not enter their council, let me not join their assembly, for they have killed men in their anger and hamstrung oxen as they pleased. Cursed be their anger, so fierce, and their fury, so cruel! I will scatter them in Jacob and disperse them in Israel.*

Regarding Simeon and Levi we are told first of all that they were brothers. This does not refer to their family relationship because that would not be worth mentioning, but refers, rather, to the similarity of their natures. The term "brother" is commonly used in this metaphorical sense in Hebrew. Other examples of this usage are found in Job 30:29, "a brother of jackals," and in Proverbs 18:9, "brother to one who destroys." There is no reason why the term brothers as it is used here must be used in its natural sense. Some scholars have insisted on this, however, and have then argued that Simeon and Levi were the only full brothers of Dinah. This would then explain, according to these scholars, their actions recorded in 34:25.

The word our translators have rendered ''weapons'' appears nowhere else in the Old Testament. Others have rendered it ''axes,'' but the exact meaning of the term is not known. Some claim that it seems to refer to a tool that was used for peaceful work but which could also be used, by an aroused person, as a lethal weapon. Simeon and Levi are here pictured as impetuous characters, who could readily be stirred up to fight. At the slightest pretense they would be apt to take a tool that they were using for their regular work and turn it into a vicious weapon against another person. It cannot be objected that Genesis 34:25 states that they used ''the sword'' against Shechem, since Jacob does not refer to that incident at this point. This comes later. Here we have only a description of the nature of these two men. They were the type of people who were quickly aroused from comparative peacefulness to acts of extreme violence.

Jacob had strong words of judgment for this quality in these two sons. He wanted nothing to do with such activities, and he disclaims all association with such attitudes and inclinations. It is striking the way Jacob speaks about himself in this connection. What he literally says, in Hebrew, is, ''Let not my soul enter into their council, and let my honor not join their assembly.'' The use of the word ''soul'' must not be understood as we generally use it. This usage of the word ''soul'' with the personal pronoun such as ''my soul'' or ''your soul,'' is no more than an emphatic way of saying ''I personally'' or ''you personally.'' And this is the way it is also used here.

In poetic expressions the words ''my honor'' can also be used as simply designating ''my person.'' An example of this usage is found in Psalm 16:9, where there is a similar use of ''heart'' and ''honor,'' side by side. It is correct to translate both of these expressions with the simple pronoun ''me.''

It is only following this that the specific incident that brought this volatile quality in these two brothers to light is mentioned. This was their attack on Shechem, recorded in 34:25–29. In this connection it has been charged that there is a conflict between Jacob's description of that incident, as it is given here, and the original narrative in Genesis 34. Here mention is made of ''hamstringing'' oxen, while in the earlier narrative we are told that the cattle were all taken as booty. Some have suggested that the term ''to hamstring oxen'' was a poetic description of the cruel way the people of Shechem were killed, but it is not necessary to conclude that there is a conflict between these two records. Although chapter 34 does not mention this ''hamstringing of oxen,'' is is altogether possible that some of this went on as Simeon and Levi moved through Shechem in their blood bath of revenge. Even though we can accept that this was part of their bloody conquest, this does not mean that they butchered all of the oxen of Shechem. After their initial terrorist attack, they could have decided that it would be better to save the rest of the cattle and take them as plunder for their own use.

Thereupon, Jacob pronounced his curse on this outburst of violence. He spelled out the judgment that would fall on Simeon and Levi and their descendants. We observed in our introduction to this chapter that the term, "I will scatter," indicates that the spokesman would also be the one who would carry out this curse. Thus it is actually God who was speaking through Jacob. The use of "in Jacob" and "in Israel" are not anachronisms, as some have charged since the old patriarch was fully aware of the fact that a great nation would spring from him.

The specific nature of the curse was that these two tribes would not acquire a portion of the Promised Land as their own but would be scattered throughout the land. This, of course, immediately raises the question of how this was fulfilled.

In the case of Levi the fulfillment of this curse is completely obvious. The tribe of Levi did not receive its own, independent territory among the twelve tribes of Israel. This fact, however, raises the question whether this peculiar position of Levi among the people of Israel can rightly be considered a curse. The reason for their not receiving their own inheritance in Canaan was that they were entrusted with the service of the sanctuary. It is argued that this task should be seen as a distinction rather than a punishment. It should be noted, however, that this special task, assigned to the Levites, is not mentioned until much later (in Exod. 38:21). In that passage we have a discussion about the amount of equipment and material needed for the service of the tabernacle. It was in that connection that Moses commanded Ithamar, the son of Aaron the priest, to employ the service of the Levites for this responsibility. This would imply that the Levites were assigned, in essence, a servant's position, to serve the priests in the work and care of the tabernacle and its equipment.

A second passage in which there is special mention of the Levites is Leviticus 25:32–33. There we have a special directive with respect to their inheritance. We need not discuss all the details of this directive because this would lead us on a tangent with respect to other difficulties in that passage. At this point, it is sufficient to say that this passage indicates that the Levites were given a special position among the Israelites. However, the exact nature of that position is not fully described until still later, in Numbers 1:49–53. In this latter passage we are told that their assignment was to take care of the equipment and provisions involved in the tabernacle and the tabernacle worship, and to carry all of this equipment when they moved from place to place. This, then, must have been the "position" referred to in the earlier passage as well. From this it becomes evident that this special task of the Levites was an honorable role. Some authorities are convinced that this honorable position was assigned to the Levites as a reward for their conduct during the incident with the golden calf (Exod. 32:26–29). In Deuteronomy 10:8 Moses specifically states that it was "at that time" that the Levites were set apart for their special task of caring for the tabernacle and carrying the ark. Thus it can be understood that the scattering of which Jacob spoke was a condition to which the Levites were subjected prior to that time. It is striking that when Moses blessed the people (Deut. 33:8ff.) he spoke of the Levites only with honor. Because of their attitude at the scene of the golden calf, their curse was removed and turned into a blessing.

This brings us to a consideration of the application of this curse to the tribe of Simeon. Let us begin by observing that when the people of Israel were counted, two years after the Exodus at Mt. Sinai (Num. 1 and 2), the tribe of Simeon took its place among the other tribes in a very normal way. In the four groups of three tribes each, into which Israel was divided, Simeon had its place in the second group, along with Reuben and Gad. At that time it was numerically one of the larger tribes, surpassed only by Judah and Dan. At that time, then, there was no evidence of the curse that Jacob pronounced on Simeon and his descendants.

But as we move on in the history of Israel, we see that the situation began to change. A second census was taken after the 40 years of wandering in the wilderness. This was when Israel was camped in the Plain of Moab, at the Jordan, across the river from the location of Jericho (Num. 26:2ff.), and at that point we can observe that a striking change had taken place in the tribe of Simeon. It can be expected that the number of people in each tribe would vary from time to time. For various reasons some would increase and others would decrease, but the change that took place in the tribe of Simeon during this period was so striking that it calls for special attention. At the first census the tribe numbered 59,300 fighting men; but by the time of the second census this number had been reduced to 22,200. Thus the tribe had been reduced by more than one half and Simeon had now become the smallest tribe, with nearly 10,000 fighting men less than the next larger tribe. It is obvious that such a radical change cannot be explained by normal factors. Although the factor involved is not specifically mentioned, something had caused the decline of this tribe at an abnormal rate. This then would be the first evidence of the fulfillment of Jacob's curse on Simeon.

At this point, however, Simeon still held a place among the tribes of

Israel. Even in Deuteronomy 27:11–13 it was still numbered among the tribes. This doesn't mean too much, however, because Levi is also mentioned there and Levi did not receive an inheritance in Canaan. But then comes the striking omission of Simeon from the tribes of Israel when Moses pronounced his blessing on Israel in Deuteronomy 33.

After the land of Canaan was conquered and the country divided among the tribes of Israel, each receiving a portion with definite boundaries, we come upon the amazing discovery that the one tribe, besides Levi, which did not receive a specifically demarked portion of the Promised Land was the tribe of Simeon. According to Joshua 19:1–8, the tribe of Simeon was allotted only a number of cities that were situated within the boundaries of the area assigned to the tribe of Judah. Thus Simeon did not receive a separately designated area of the Promised Land.

Carrying this still further, we read in 1 Chronicles 4:24–31, where the descendants of Simeon are listed, that "their entire clan did not become as numerous as the people of Judah" (v. 27). This would indicate that the limited growth of the tribe of Simeon was a recognized fact within Israel. Then, when we are given the list of cities that were allotted to Simeon, the same that are mentioned in Joshua 19:2–7, we find the further qualifying statement (v. 31), "These were their towns until the reign of David." This seems to imply that at that time there was a change in the rights of the Simeonites to these cities. Some early Jewish scholars hold that when David became king over all Israel, Judah drove the Simeonites out of the cities they had occupied within Judah's borders. This forced the tribe of Simeon to search for other places to live.

From a still later time, during the reign of Hezekiah, there is mention of a settlement of Simeonites (1 Chron. 4:34–41). Some of them had settled in "Gerar." The Hebrew text has "Gedar," but this is probably an error. The Septuagint probably is correct in rendering this "Gerar." In verses 42 and 43 of this passage in 1 Chronicles 4, there is another reference, obviously from a still later time, which sees the Simeonites moving to the mountains of Seir. Thus the scattering of the tribe of Simeon, which Jacob predicted became an ongoing reality.

JUDAH

49:8 *"Judah, your brothers will praise you; your hand will be on the neck of your enemies; your father's sons will bow down to you.*

When the patriarch came to his fourth son, Judah, his tone changed completely. Here there are no curses or rebukes. Judah's brothers would praise him. The personal pronoun, "you," is placed in a position of emphasis in the Hebrew line by placing it directly after Judah's name and then repeating it with the verb. This emphasis places Judah apart from the three brothers already mentioned. Although this is not stated in so many words, this implies that Judah received the rights of the firstborn. It should be noted that Reuben had forfeited this right by his shameful conduct while Simeon and Levi were cursed for their bloodthirsty attitude. This, then, also means that the covenant blessing, which God gave to Abraham, Isaac, and Jacob, would now be carried forward by Judah.

There is an interesting play on words here in the Hebrew, in the use of the word "praise." There is an etymological connection between the name "Judah" and the verb "to praise," *yādāh*. Thus the son whose name meant "praise" would be "praised" by his brothers.

Two things are mentioned about Judah, one pertaining to his relationship to his enemies and one dealing with his brothers. Regarding the first, there is some difference of opinion among scholars as to the exact meaning. Some hold that the statement should read, "your hand will be on the neck of your enemies," as our translators have also rendered it. This would imply that their enemies would be subject to them. Other scholars use a stronger expression and read, "your hand will seize your enemies by the throat." A comparison with Job 16:12 suggests that this stronger reading is probably more correct. This would point to decisive victory in actual combat.

Regarding Judah's relationship to his brothers, we are told that they would bow down to him. This implies that they would acknowledge his superiority. The term "your father's sons" indicates that Judah would be acknowledged as superior, not only by his full brothers, the other sons of Leah, but by all the sons of Jacob by all his wives.

49:9 *You are a lion's cub, O Judah; you return from the prey, my son. Like a lion he crouches and lies down, like a lioness—who dares to rouse him?*

Then we have a description of Judah's glory by means of imagery. He is compared to a lion. It should be noted that there is an interchange between the second person and the third person in this passage. The symbol of the lion as a picture of strength, especially military prowess, is a favorite one in Scripture. In Moses' blessing it is used of both Gad (Deut. 33:20) and Dan (Deut. 33:22). In the proverbs of Balaam (Num. 23:24; 24:9) it is used of Israel as a whole. In Jeremiah 4:7; 5:6; 25:38, it is used to describe the Chaldeans coming down from the north. (See also Jer. 49:19 and 50:44.) In Nahum 2:11–12, it refers to Nineveh. It is certainly a very descriptive analogy, and the figure of the lion is still commonly used in our day in describing great and awesome strength in a person.

There has been considerable discussion about the use of identically the same term, in the same words, by Balaam in Numbers 24:9. Some have claimed that this indicates that Balaam was acquainted with this blessing of Jacob and borrowed it to try to impress Balak with the abiding certainty of this blessing. We believe that this is assuming too much. It should be noted that Balaam applied it to all Israel, while here it is applied only to the tribe of Judah. The use of an identical expression in two different contexts, especially when such an expression has the nature of a handy proverb, does not in itself establish a connection between the incidents in which it is used. Certain proverbial statements are common to many different peoples. This figure of the lion as it is used here is so universal that no conclusions can be drawn from its use in different contexts.

Another question that has been raised involves the statement that our translators have rendered "return from the prey." Literally this reads "climb up from the prey." On the basis of the Septuagint and the Peshitta, some have read this "grow up," as applied to a lion's cub. The figure would then be that a lion's cub grows up as a result of eating the prey. Reference is made to Ezekiel 19:3, which some have translated, "She brought up one of her cubs." However, since that translation is also open to question, it can carry no weight in our present consideration. The most natural reading of the expression would seem to be that after killing and feeding on her prey, the lioness "goes up" into the hills to her lair where she can rest and where no one dares to disturb her.

49:10 *The scepter will not depart from Judah, nor the ruler's staff from between his feet, until he comes to whom it belongs and the obedience of the nations is his.*

We now come to one of the best known verses of the Old Testament, frequently included in a familiar list of Messianic prophecies. The verse has, however, caused some difficulties in interpretation. There is not too much difficulty with the first part of the verse, "The scepter will not depart from Judah, nor the ruler's staff from between his feet." The staff probably refers to the long staff that was usually held so that the lower end rested between the feet.

The question that must be raised, however, is whether "scepter" and "ruler's staff" must be considered as emblems of royal honor and position. If we examine the use of the term "scepter" we observe that it usually is a figure of kingly honor (see Num. 24:17; Ps. 45:7; Amos 1:5, 8). In Judges 5:14, however, this term clearly indicates a position of lower rank, such as one who kept the records. Thus, the word as it is used in our text does not necessarily imply kingly honor and position.

This is also true of the other term, which has been translated ''ruler's staff.'' This term is used in various ways in other Old Testament references, none of which establishes with any conclusiveness that it refers to kingly authority. In the light of our study of these two terms, ''scepter'' and ''ruler's staff,'' as used in the Old Testament as a whole, we cannot establish that the prediction regarding Judah necessarily involved kingly honor and position. Verse 8 does indicate that Judah would have superiority over his brethren and also over his enemies, and this is further developed in the image of the lion in verse 9. The first part of verse 10 obviously refers to this same general superiority on Judah's part. As such, there is no specific reference in these verses to the kingship of the Davidic dynasty that was to rise out of Judah. Although we can interpret the rise of David's kingship as growing out of the general superiority that is here ascribed to Judah, there is no specific reference to it in this passage.

It is in the second half of this verse that the real difficulties seem to surface. Here we have a clause that sets the time and fixes a termination point. Formerly some scholars held that this could be read, ''as long as,'' but the word definitely means ''until.'' The superiority that is predicted for Judah, in the first part of the verse, would continue ''until Shiloh comes.'' The real difficulty comes in translating the word ''Shiloh.'' There are so many different interpretations of this word that we cannot begin to list them all, much less discuss them in detail. We will therefore limit our consideration to a few general comments about the interpretation of this difficult word.

The first matter that we should consider is the context in which the word ''Shiloh'' appears. Then we must ask ourselves what will characterize this coming of ''Shiloh'' by which the conditions previously described would be terminated. It is obvious that the coming of ''Shiloh'' would not be a diminishing of the glory of Judah's superiority. On the contrary, the coming of ''Shiloh'' would be far more glorious than the honor that Judah would attain. What could this then be? We must remember what we said above about Judah receiving the right of the firstborn. This blessing of the firstborn in the patriarchal families was of great importance. This was the blessing promised to Jacob when Isaac was on his deathbed. It was the blessing concerning which Jacob contended with Esau. It was the blessing Abraham bestowed on Isaac. It was the blessing God promised to Abraham in Genesis 12:1–3. This blessing, in its true essence, culminated in the promise of ''the seed of the woman'' who was to come. This, then, was also the heart of the blessing promised to Judah as his portion above that of all his brothers. This blessing would continue until an even greater glory would appear and this can be none other than the promised Messiah. The term "until Shiloh comes," thus predicts the coming of the Messiah.

What, then, does the word "Shiloh" indicate regarding the Messiah who was to come? In earlier times there was another reading of this word when it was seen as *šellô* which means "from whom it is." This has been refined by more recent studies to read "to whom it belongs," as our translators have also rendered it. The thought is that the scepter, or the rulership, would continue until He came to whom it rightfully belonged.

This commentator is convinced that although the term "Shiloh" does refer to the promised Messiah, it does so only as a name. To give this word the meaning that He who was to come would have a right to the rulership of the first part of the text, is to read something into the text that actually is not there. This concept of "having a right to" (to whom it belonged), is found in Ezekiel 21:27, but is not present in Genesis 49:10.

What, then, does this name "Shiloh" mean? This cannot be determined with certainty. It could come from a verb form which means "to be at rest" or "to be content." Then the name would mean "one who brings peace." This led Luther to translate it "hero." It has also been traced to a Hittite word that means "ruler." It is likely that the word "shiloh," as it was originally used, was not actually a proper noun, but it acquired that function through usage, just as the word "seed" did. So it has been translated "the Shiloh" similar to "the Seed of the woman." The use of words taken from other languages to designate the promised Messiah was not unusual (note Ps. 2:12, "kiss the son," where the word for "son" is not a Hebrew word but Aramaic).

At the close of the verse we read, "and the obedience of the nations is his." This is a further qualification of the Messiah that is certainly fitting. He would be one to whom all nations would be subjected. It is clear, then, that in this verse the emphasis falls on the announcement of the coming Messiah. The purpose of this verse is not to point again to Judah's supremacy. That was presented in verses 8 and 9. Here we are concerned with the coming of the Messiah in whom this supremacy would reach its highest and fullest expression. Although it is not specifically stated that the Messiah would stem from Judah, this is obviously implied in this reference to "the coming one" in the context of Judah's supremacy.

49:11, 12 *He will tether his donkey to a vine, his colt to the choicest branch; he will wash his garments in wine, his robes in the blood of grapes. His eyes will be darker than wine, his teeth whiter than milk.*

The symbolic description given in these two verses seems to refer to the "coming one," the Messiah. His donkey would be tied to a vine, even to the most noble branch. We have a reference to a donkey as a mount for the Messiah in Zechariah 9:9. The figure used here seems to indicate that in His day grapevines, the primary agricultural plants of Palestine, would be so abundant that they could be used for other purposes. Even the choicest vines could be used as hitching posts. Thus, the figure denoted a time of exceptional fruitfulness.

This concept is confirmed by another figure, that of washing His garments in the fruit of the vine, that is, wine. What a graphic picture of abundance and even excess!

A description of the outward appearance of His person is also added. His eyes would be "darker than wine, his teeth whiter than milk." Many interpreters have clung to another reading for this line. When the reading of the Septuagint and the Vulgate are taken into account, however, the reading of our translators must be given preference. Both linguistically and as far as meaning is concerned, this translation is more fitting. Thus these figurative descriptions of dark eyes and white teeth so highly valued among people of Eastern countries, picture great outward beauty for the coming Messiah.

It is obvious that we are dealing with language that abounds in symbols and figures of speech. Such figures as tying a donkey to the choice vine and washing clothes in wine can, of course, be descriptive only of natural abundance and fruitfulness. But when we see these figures in the context of the prophecy about Shiloh coming, and when this is, in turn, related to Genesis 3:15 and the covenant promises, we get a picture of the incalculable spiritual abundance and fruitfulness that would be ushered in by the coming Messiah. The curse of Paradise certainly included a devastation in the realms of nature, thorns and thistles, laboring and sweating to bring forth crops, etc. But this was by no means the only nor the primary consequence of man's sin. The essential element in the Paradise curse was humanity's separation from God. Therefore, the gospel, in its deepest essence, promised the overcoming of this estrangement and separation and the restoration of abundance of peace. The "seed of the woman" would crush the spiritual force that stood behind the serpent and its destructive campaign against mankind. The Messiah would bring, first of all, spiritual blessings. The figures used here in this text certainly indicate that those spiritual blessings would be abundant and overflowing, and this would be the true glory of the victory of the Messiah. When Genesis 49:10–12 is related properly to Genesis 3:15, the true glory of the promised Messiah is described with graphic clarity.

Finally, we want to say a word about the fulfillment of these prophecies. As far as the coming of Shiloh is concerned, this can readily be seen since the Messiah was born of the tribe of Judah. Thus, the obedience of the nations and the personal glory that are described here are fully realized in the coming Messiah, Jesus Christ.

But how were these prophecies fulfilled in the tribe of Judah as such? We have already observed, in the first part of verse 10, that Judah's superiority over the other tribes was not necessarily to be kingly, royal superiority. Thus the argument that the kingly "scepter" did not actually continue in the tribe of Judah until the coming of the Messiah carries no weight. The reference is, rather, to a general superiority of Judah and no more than that. This, of course, can be readily established. In the census, taken two years after the Exodus (Num. 2:4), and also in the census at the close of the wilderness wanderings (Num. 26:22), Judah was the largest of the tribes. Judah had the largest number of fighting men according to Numbers 2:9. Throughout the wilderness journeys, Judah was the predominant tribe (Num. 2:3; 10:14). When the tabernacle was dedicated (Num. 7:12), Judah was given the first position again. When Canaan was divided after the conquest of the Promised Land, Judah was the first to be assigned an inheritance (Josh. 15:1). Although this predominance of Judah was less obvious during the period of the Judges, it was still present. Judah was the first to attack the Canaanites (Judg. 1:1–2). Judah was the first to launch the punitive expedition against Benjamin (Judg. 20:18). The tribe of Judah really came into prominence during the Davidic kingdom. Then, when the kingdom was divided, Jerusalem, the capital of Judah, remained the center or religious life for the entire nation, and the southern kingdom was known as the kingdom of Judah. After the destruction of the Ten Tribes of Israel, Judah alone continued and those who returned from exile were primarily of the tribe of Judah. Although there were some traces of descendants from other tribes, the continuing history of Israel up to the time when Christ came actually became the history of Judah, and the people of Israel became known as Judeans.

ZEBULUN

49:13 *"Zebulun will live by the seashore and become a haven for ships; his border will extend toward Sidon.*

The aged patriarch predicted that Zebulun's descendants would live along the sea coast, obviously referring to the coast of the Mediterranean Sea. The reference to "a haven for ships" suggests that the section of the coast that they would occupy would not be the barren, rocky area, but an area where ships could safely dock. Zebulun's area was further described as extending toward Sidon. Although Jacob spoke of Zebulun as a tribe, he pictured the tribe as a person who faced in one direction, that is toward the other tribes, while his back would be toward Sidon. This was to the north of Israel, the area that later became Phoenicia. The fact that there is no mention of Tyre here, even though Tyre was closer to the borders of Israel, can be readily explained. Tyre did not develop into a prominent city until much later, in the 9th and 10th centuries B.C. In Jacob's day, only Sidon was the predominant city of that area.

In considering the fulfillment of this pronouncement, it should be noted that when Canaan was divided among the tribes, Zebulun was not actually assigned a coastal area (Josh. 19:10–16). Zebulun was located in the northern part of Palestine, but not on the shores of the Mediterranean Sea. The inheritance of Asher lay between Zebulun and the coast. It is possible, of course, that later shifts in the population of that area did place Zebulun on the coast, but the Scripture gives us no record of this.

It is noteworthy that there is another prediction regarding Zebulun, in the blessing of Moses in Deuteronomy 33:18–19, which describes this tribe and Issachar as feasting "on the abundance of the seas, on the treasures hidden in the sand." This does not imply necessarily that Zebulun would be located on the seacoast, but could mean that the benefits of the sea, via trade and commerce, would be enjoyed, even though their location was somewhat inland. But the most natural interpretation would be that Zebulun was to have direct access to the sea. Even though there is no biblical evidence to confirm that this actually happened, there is no evidence to the contrary either. Therefore, most scholars are agreed that at one time or another the tribe of Zebulun lived on the Mediterranean coast and thus the prophecy was fulfilled.

ISSACHAR

49:14, 15 *"Issachar is a rawboned donkey lying down between two saddlebags. When he sees how good is his resting place and how pleasant is his land, he will bend his shoulder to the burden and submit to forced labor.*

A rawboned donkey is a strong, powerfully built donkey. When Issachar is compared to such a beast of burden, this is not a derogatory description. Donkeys were held in higher esteem in the ancient East than they are in the Western world today.

The term our translators have rendered "saddlebags," probably refers to open, protected areas such as we describe today in mountainous areas as a "saddle." Such an area, between two elevations, offered a shelter for cattle in time of bad weather. The figure seems to picture a powerful people who lived a relatively sheltered, relaxed life. Thus, it is said that they enjoyed a "resting place" on their land. Even so, they were a people who were able and willing to carry the burdens of others.

As far as the fulfillment of this prophecy is concerned, we may well ask whether this description must be seen as a general characteristic of the people of Issachar, or whether it must be seen as a prediction of conditions during a particular historical event or period. Some interpreters hold that this implies that the tribe of Issachar would be enslaved by their Canaanite neighbors. There is no biblical evidence for this, however. In fact, Judges 5:15 tells us that Issachar joined with Deborah in defeating the Canaanites on the field of battle.

A more acceptable interpretation would be that Issachar settled in the valley of Jezreel. One of the great trade routes passed through this valley, so it is possible that the people of Issachar became involved in supplying both labor and provisions for the traffic that passed through this valley. This could have been what Jacob's prophecy referred to, but the description was primarily a general characterization of these stalwart descendants of Issachar, even though later history gives us no information about them.

DAN

49:16, 17 *"Dan will provide justice for his people as one of the tribes of Israel. Dan will be a serpent by the roadside, a viper along the path, that bites the horse's heels so that its rider tumbles backward.*

In the statement, "Dan will provide justice for his people," we should observe a play on words, similar to "Judah, your brothers will praise you." There happens to be a striking similarity of sound between the Hebrew word translated "provide justice" and the name "Dan." There is some question, however, about the meaning of this characterization. Some scholars hold that the term "his people" would refer only to those who belonged to the tribe of Dan. Others hold that this refers to the entire people of Israel. In favor of the former position is the next statement, "as one of the tribes of Israel." Certainly the responsibility to provide justice was one that rested upon all of the tribes of Israel. What we have here, then, is that Dan would in no way fall behind the other tribes in the matter of providing justice.

The fact that this is emphasized here would suggest that there might be definite reasons for the tribe of Dan not to do this. This is confirmed by the next statement, in which Jacob uses the figure of Dan being like the small serpent along the wayside, which effectively attacks a large horse by biting at its heels and thus causing the rider to be thrown off. This would imply that this tribe, though small, would face powerful antagonists that would place them under great pressure.

When we turn to the fulfillment of this prediction, we can observe, first of all, that the tribe of Dan was divided into two sections. Part of the tribe remained in the southern part of Canaan, near the Mediterranean Sea, where they had the Philistines as their neighbors. The other half of the tribe moved to the far northern part of the country and established themselves near the city of Laish, which later was renamed "Dan" (Judg. 18). That this put considerable strain on their provision of justice should be obvious. Our attention should primarily be given to their close proximity to the powerful Philistines. That part of the tribe was under constant threat from these wily neighbors, as for instance, during the time of Samson. We can then see Jacob's prediction fulfilled in Samson's victories over the Philistines. Here was a clear-cut case of a small people overcoming a strong opposing force—like the small serpent and the big horse.

49:18 *"I look for your deliverance, O Lord.*

After this pronouncement regarding Dan, Jacob cried out, "I look for your deliverance, O Lord." The term deliverance certainly does not apply only to spiritual deliverance. It includes prospering in all areas of life. For instance, it would certainly include Israel's deliverance from Egypt (Exod. 14:13). Our conclusion regarding the intent of Jacob's statement must be based on the context in which it appears. There must be some reason why he made this outcry at this point in his "blessing" of his sons. We can probably find this in Jacob's inspired expectation that God would sustain the tribe of Dan in the difficulties they would face in the future. But there is more than deliverance for Dan involved. Jacob's cry, "I look for your deliverance, O Lord," must have a far wider application. Throughout his many difficulties, Jacob constantly trusted God for deliverance. Now he looked to the future and considered the welfare of his descendants, especially the family of Dan, for whom he foresaw such great difficulties. And so he reaffirms his trust in God's unfailing deliverance.

GAD

49:19 *"Gad will be attacked by a band of raiders, but he will attack them at their heels.*

Regarding Gad, Jacob predicted that his territory would be attacked by a band of raiders, but the tribe would be enabled to rout the enemy and drive them out of their domain.

The fulfillment of this prophecy cannot be pinpointed with specific historical events. Gad's territory was so situated, however, that it was open to this kind of attack. This tribe settled in Transjordan, between the tribe of Manasseh and the tribe of Reuben. Their territory was exposed to raiding parties coming from the desert to the East. One example of this would be the attack by the Ammonites, recorded in Judges 10:7ff. The deliverer in that case was Jephthah (Judg. 11:1), who was of the tribe of Gad. The difficult situation in which the Transjordanic tribes lived is also described in 1 Chronicles 5:18–22, where we are told about their vigorous counterattacks against these enemy raids.

ASHER

49:20 *"Asher's food will be rich; he will provide delicacies fit for a king.*

The blessing bestowed on the tribe of Asher predicted that they would occupy a territory that would produce delicacies in food, food "fit for a king," in fact.

This prediction was fulfilled in the section of Canaan occupied by this tribe after Israel entered the land of Canaan. They settled in the fertile coastal plain that stretched from Mt. Carmel to the borders of Phoenicia. To this day this is one of the more fertile areas of Palestine, and it exports significant supplies of olive oil.

NAPHTALI

49:21 *"Naphtali is a doe set free that bears beautiful fawns.*

The figure used to describe Naphtali is that of a deer. This would imply swiftness and great skill in self-defense. (Cf. Ps. 18:33; 2 Sam. 22:34; Hab. 3:19.) What follows in this statement presents some real difficulties. Literally we read, "he utters beautiful words." But a deer doesn't bring forth words, so the figure of the deer is promptly changed. Just what is meant by "utters beautiful words"? Some have attempted to read this as though Naphtali produced skilled orators and poets; their songs were supposed to be very lyrical and poetic. But there is no evidence to support this.

Others, as our translators, hold that the word in the text has been altered and that it should actually read, "bears beautiful fawns." This gives us little help because we still face the difficulty of applying this in a meaningful way to the tribe of Naphtali. Others have tried to make this a reference to the bearing of beautiful trees, but this also does violence to the original text.

The only conclusion we can reach is that we have no plausible interpretation of the latter part of this statement. There is a strong possibility that there is a corruption in the original text here, but what the original reading was is purely a matter of conjecture. It is possible that some day a satisfying answer to this enigma will present itself.

The fulfillment of the first part of the statement was evidenced in Naphtali's skill in warfare. Judges 4:6 and 5:18 make mention of their expertise in this as they fought against the Canaanites under Barak and Deborah. With respect to the latter part of the statement we must simply admit that we do not know because we do not have a meaningful original text.

JOSEPH

49:22 *"Joseph is a fruitful vine, a fruitful vine near a spring, whose branches climb over a wall.*

Joseph is described as a fruitful vine or fruit tree. To emphasize its fruitfulness, we are told that it was near a spring (see Ps. 1:3). The fruit tree grew so abundantly that its branches extended above the wall that protected it. The nature of the tree is not specified, but many think it was a grapevine. Others have altered the text to make it refer to a young steer, but this can be done only by tampering with the biblical text.

49:23, 24 *With bitterness archers attacked him; they shot at him with hostility. But his bow remained steady, his strong arms stayed limber, because of the hand of the Mighty One of Jacob, because of the Shepherd, the Rock of Israel,*

In these two verses we are told what Joseph had endured in the past. This description refers to Joseph personally and not to the tribe that sprang from him. We have this same factor in the cases of some of the other sons. In speaking of what happened in the past, the reference is to them as persons, but when the future is described the application is to the tribes that stemmed from them.

The statement regarding the fruit tree is an exception to the above in our present statement. It would be difficult to establish the fact that Joseph, personally, had been attacked by archers. We are dealing with figurative statements here. They would then refer to all the hostility to which Joseph was exposed as a young man. Naturally, we think first of how he was treated by his own brothers. Later there were also those in Egypt who tried to "shoot him down."

Since these attacks on Joseph are described by the figure of archery, his defense against these attacks is described by the same figure since "his bow remained steady, and his arms stayed limber." Thus his influence remained powerful. Objection should not be made that Joseph did not actually fight back against his brothers and against Potiphar. We are dealing with a figure, and every detail of that figure should not be stressed. The meaning is obvious. All the opposition Joseph faced did not weaken him as a person, but, in fact, served to make him stronger and more effective. This is emphasized by the following statement which ascribes Joseph's strength to the sustaining hand of God. The names ascribed to God are some of the most descriptive in all of Scripture, and certainly of Scripture up to this point. God is described as "the Mighty One of Jacob," "the Shepherd," and "the Rock of Israel."

49:25, 26 *Because of your father's God, who helps you, because of the Almighty, who blesses you with blessings of the heavens above, blessings of the deep that lies below, blessings of the breast and womb. Your father's blessings are greater than the blessings of the ancient mountains, than the bounty of the age-old hills. Let all these rest on the head of Joseph, on the brow of the prince among his brothers.*

In close connection with the statement that described Joseph's past, the same sentence goes on to speak about his future. God the Almighty, who had turned Joseph's trials into blessings in the past, would continue to favor him abundantly in the future. The blessings that would be bestowed on the house of Joseph are poetically described, and cover a wide range of experiences. "The blessings of the heavens above" could refer to an abundance of dew and rain and sunshine to provide large crops. "Blessings of the deep that lies below," would refer to the lakes and streams that were so vital to those who lived in this desert country. "Blessings of the breast and womb" certainly refer to abundance in the bearing and feeding of children, as well for human children as for the young of livestock. Finally, the blessings that Joseph was to receive are described as "your father's blessings." These blessings are described as greater than the ancient mountains and the "bounty of the age-old hills." One would have to live in a mountainous country, especially where the mountains are in close proximity to the low-lying desert, to appreciate the full power of this statement (see Ps. 121). The figure describes exceptional blessings, abundant beyond understanding. These indescribably rich blessings, Jacob ascribes to Joseph, who is here described as "prince among his brothers" (our translators). I feel that the term "chosen" would be more correct than the word "prince." Joseph's position of honor among his brothers is reflected in the exalted level of the blessings his father pronounced on him.

When we consider the fulfillment of these predictions, it should be observed that the blessings that are specified are of a very general nature. Fruitfulness, in the broadest sense, can certainly be seen in the descendants of Joseph. The fact that two of the twelve tribes of Israel stemmed from Joseph is most significant in this regard. The entire statement makes it obvious that Joseph was still his father's favorite son. Even so, Joseph was not to receive the patriarchal blessing from which the coming Messiah was to come, since this was reserved for Judah. From this we can clearly see that Jacob was not led by his personal preferences in bestowing these blessings, but that his statements were inspired by the Holy Spirit as God's revelation.

BENJAMIN

49:27 *"Benjamin is a ravenous wolf; in the morning he devours the prey, in the evening he divides the plunder."*

Benjamin is compared to a ravenous wolf that is bringing down its prey and devouring it from morning till evening. This undoubtedly refers not to Benjamin as a person, but to the tribe that would stem from him. The Benjamites were to become wild and vigorous warriors.

This prediction regarding the tribe of Benjamin was abundantly fulfilled in later history. Benjamin is lauded in the Song of Deborah in Judges 5:14 as being among the mighty warriors. So too, the tragic events at Gibeah, recorded in Judges 20 and 1 Chronicles 8, feature the warlike character of the Benjamites and their great skill as archers and wielders of sling-shots. (See also 2 Chron. 14:8 and 17:17.)

49:28 *All these are the twelve tribes of Israel, and this is what their father said to them when he blessed them, giving each the blessing appropriate to him.*

This verse is something like a postlude with which the editor of the Pentateuch concludes these statements of blessing by the aged Jacob. He wanted to emphasize the fact that these statements referred not so much to the persons of Jacob's sons as such, but to the tribes that would spring from them. Even so, the actual words were spoken to the sons in person, as they gathered about the deathbed of their father. The entire poetic address was in the form of a "blessing." Each son, and thus each tribe, received a specific blessing that was intended just for him and his descendants.

54. *The Death and Burial of Jacob* (49:29–50:14)

Those who divide the sources ascribe the closing verses of chapter 49 to "P." Their primary reason for doing so is the broadness of the literary style and the painful precision of detail that is evident in this passage. To say the least, this is a very subjective basis for assigning the material before us in this way.

The words "he drew his feet up into the bed," in verse 33 are, however, ascribed to "J." This is based on the use of the word "bed," which is also used in 47:31 and 48:2, passages that are usually ascribed to "J." We need not comment on the credibility of this argument.

The first 14 verses of chapter 50 are generally divided between the three usual sources. Verses 12 and 13 are ascribed to "P" because they point back to 49:29–33. The rest of this section is given to "J," except for a few isolated statements that allegedly came from "E." One basis for identifying an additional source is the use of the name "Israel" in verse 2. We have already discussed this in our introduction to chapter 37. It is also alleged that there is some duplicity evident. In verse 3 there is mention of 40 days, but also of 70 days. But it is obvious that these two figures refer to different activities—embalming and mourning. It is further charged that in verse 8 we are told that Joseph's brothers were present when Jacob's body was carried away, while verse 9 suggests that this was not the case. In response, let it be noted that verse 9 mentions only a military guard that accompanied the procession. Again it is charged that the mourning ceremony is described as taking place at two different locations—according to verse 10, at the threshing floor of Atad, and according to verse 11 at Abel Mizraim. In response it should be seen that verse 11 clearly indicates that these two names designated the same place. When all of these charges are put together they adduce no evidence whatsoever for two or more separate traditions as sources for this narrative.

49:29–32 *Then he gave them these instructions: "I am about to be gathered to my people. Bury me with my fathers in the cave in the field of Ephron the Hittite, the cave in the field of Machpelah, near Mamre in Canaan, which Abraham bought as a burial place from Ephron the Hittite, along with the field. There Abraham and his wife Sarah were buried, there Isaac and his wife Rebekah were buried, and there I buried Leah. The field and the cave in it were bought from the Hittites."*

What is recorded here is closely related to what precedes it. After pronouncing his formal blessing on his sons, Jacob expressed his last desire that he might be buried in his family burial ground in Canaan. Earlier he had made the same request of Joseph, and since Joseph was the one son who had the authority to carry out this request, Jacob had made him promise under oath that he would take care of this (see 47:29–31). Now, shortly before his departure from this life, he made the same request in the presence of all his sons.

Jacob's description of that family burial plot made it clear that he was not satisfied with a grave somewhere in Canaan. It must be the very plot where Abraham and Sarah, Isaac and Rebekah, and his own wife Leah had been laid to rest. (Rachel had been buried elsewhere, according to 35:19, 20.) Although Jacob had been present at the burial of his father, Isaac, he did not mention that in this connection. He did mention that he personally had buried Leah. However, the emphasis falls not on the circumstances of these burials but on the *place* where these members of the patriarchal family had been buried. In verse 29 Jacob spoke of being ''gathered to my people.'' (We discussed this expression under 24:7–10.)

We should comment on the connection between verse 32 and what imemdiately precedes. Some interpreters suggest that the statement ''the field and the cave in it were bought from the Hittites'' forms an independent sentence. This is the way our translators evidently have read it. We prefer that it be seen as a modifying clause, relating to the word ''there,'' which is repeated in verse 31.

Here we should also give some consideration to the difficulty that is presented in Acts 7:16. There Stephen says something different about the burial plot Abraham purchased than what we have in our present passage. Stephen located the burial plot of Abraham at Shechem and added that Abraham bought the plot from the sons of Hamor. We discuss this difficulty at this point because it is in this connection that Stephen said that Jacob and his sons, who had gone to Egypt, were brought back to Shechem after they died and were buried in the plot that Abraham had purchased. This is in conflict with what we are specifically told in Genesis 50:12–13, however.

Further research in the Scriptures indicates that the conflict is not as sharp as it at first appears. When Stephen spoke he did base his remarks on an Old Testament passage, but that passage was not our present reference. It is found rather in Joshua 24:32, where we read that Joseph's bones were brought up from Egypt and were buried at Shechem in the tract of land that Jacob bought for 100 pieces of silver from the sons of Hamor, the father of Shechem.

When Stephen reviewed this history, he offered it in a radically condensed version. In verses 15 and 16 he combined the fortunes of Jacob and Joseph and his brothers into one account. Similarly the incidents involving the burials of Jacob and of Joseph are combined. Stephen took the text from Joshua and presented what actually pertained to Joseph only, and applied it to both Joseph and Jacob. He then added what pertained to Joseph only, and applied it to both Joseph and Jacob. He then added what pertained only to the burial of Jacob, namely that the plot in which he was buried had been purchased by Abraham. The abbreviation of the historical narratives that Stephen attempted actually resulted in a statement that is historically inaccurate. We should then read Stephen's words in the light of what he intended to convey as the narrative of the Old Testament. What he meant to say was that both Jacob and Joseph were buried in Canaan. Jacob, however, was buried in the plot that Abraham purchased from the Hittite, Ephron, at Mamre, while Joseph was buried, years later, near Shechem in a plot that had been purchased from Hamor, the father of Shechem.

49:33 *When Jacob had finished giving instructions to his sons, he drew his feet up into the bed, breathed his last and was gathered to his people.*

After Jacob had made his final request to his sons, he passed away. The old patriarch had planned calmly and carefully for his departure. Now he pulled his feet into the bed and laid back to await his end. Then he breathed his last breath and was gathered to his people. (For this last statement, see v. 29.)

50:1 *Joseph threw himself upon his father and wept over him and kissed him.*

As soon as his father died, Joseph threw himself on the body in uncontrolled weeping and kisses. That only Joseph's reaction is recorded does not imply that the other brothers did not express their sorrow. The biblical narrator focuses on that especially tender relationship between Joseph and his father. Because he was separated for so many years and finally so dramatically reunited in Egypt, his father's death here in Egypt was especially traumatic for Joseph. And so Jacob's favorite son vented his emotions in an unrestrained expression of love for his dead father.

50:2, 3 *Then Joseph directed the physicians in his service to embalm his father Israel. So the physicians embalmed him, taking a full forty days, for that was the time required for embalming. And the Egyptians mourned for him seventy days.*

Soon, however, he collected himself and assumed full charge of the arrangements for having his father's body embalmed by Egyptian physicians. This embalming process, as it was practiced in ancient Egypt, required considerable time. Here we are told that it took 40 days. Other Egyptian sources mention periods as long as 70 days for this highly developed process. The time allotted need not be taken literally but is probably given in round numbers.

Following this period of time set aside for the embalming process, there was a 70-day period of mourning. This period obviously also was determined by Egyptian custom with the length of the mourning time indicating the exalted position of the deceased. Since Jacob was the father of the highest official in Egypt, except for the pharaoh, this period was set accordingly. We are told that the Egyptians also joined in this mourning for Jacob.

50:4–6 *When the days of mourning had passed, Joseph said to Pharaoh's court, "If I have found favor in your eyes, speak to Pharaoh for me. Tell him, 'My father made me swear an oath and said, "I am about to die; bury me in the tomb I dug for myself in the land of Canaan." Now let me go up and bury my father; then I will return.'"*

Pharaoh said, "Go up and bury your father, as he made you swear to do."

After the days of mourning had passed, Joseph addressed the members of Pharaoh's court and asked them to intercede with Pharaoh in his behalf. He told them that he had sworn with an oath to his father that he would bury him in the family tomb in Canaan. Now he requested permission to carry out this mission.

The question has been asked why Joseph did not address his request directly to Pharaoh. This question cannot be answered with certainty. Various answers have been suggested, however. Some have said that there was a policy that a high·official could not address·the pharaoh directly when it involved a personal matter. Others claim that Joseph's request was so out of the ordinary that he hesitated to present it in person. Still others suggest that it was not proper for a grieving person to approach the pharaoh as long as the dead loved one had not yet been interred. This last conjecture may be the most plausible but even so it is no more than an unsubstantiated conjecture. The long delay, of course, was the consequence of the process of embalming practiced in Egypt. At any rate, Pharaoh was wholly consenting to Joseph's request.

50:7–9 *So Joseph went up to bury his father. All Pharaoh's officials accompanied him—the dignitaries of his court and all the dignitaries of Egypt—besides all the members of Joseph's household and his brothers and those belonging to his father's household. Only their children and their flocks and herds were left in Goshen. Chariots and horsemen also went up with him. It was a very large company.*

These verses give us a catalog of all those who made up the funeral procession. Joseph, as the supreme ruler of Egypt, is mentioned first. Then came all the officials of Pharaoh's court and the dignitaries of Egypt. Then all the members of Jacob's family are mentioned. This apparently included the women, although children, as well as their flocks, were left behind in Goshen. There was also a military complement that accompanied the procession, including chariots and horsemen. Altogether it was a very large company. Jacob was brought to his last resting place with great honor.

50:10 *When they reached the threshing floor of Atad, near the Jordan, they lamented loudly and bitterly; and there Joseph observed a seven-day period of mourning for his father.*

The journey ended at a place called "Goren-ha-atad," which was located near the Jordan, most likely on the east side of the river. This seems to imply that the procession did not follow the usual route from Egypt to Canaan but traveled around the Dead Sea and up the east side of the Jordan River. This was the same route the Israelites took later, after their wilderness wanderings. Why this route was chosen at this time is not stated. We can only surmise that there may have been some political complications had this company taken the usual, well-traveled route to Canaan.

The name "Goren-ha-atad" has generally been translated "the threshing floor of Atad." It really means the threshing floor of the thorn bush. The old Dutch *Statenvertaling* rendered it "the plain of the thorn bush." The particular bush indicated was common in that area and was used for hedges or fences with which areas could be enclosed. It is generally thought that the name, then, designated a well-known threshing floor near the Jordan that was identified by the fence that enclosed it, and was made of thorn bushes. It is worthy of note that to this day there are native tribes in Syria who have the custom of carrying their dead, accompanied by all the people of the area, to a threshing floor and there have a seven-day period of mourning. It seems obvious, then, that Joseph first observed the customs of Egypt with a period of mourning there. Then when they came to Canaan they observed a period of mourning that was in keeping with the custom of that area.

50:11 *When the Canaanites who lived there saw the mourning at the threshing floor of Atad, they said, "The Egyptians are holding a solemn ceremony of mourning." That is why that place near the Jordan is called Abel Mizraim.*

This event made a deep impression on the neighboring Canaanitish people. They interpreted it as an especially solemn mourning ceremony on the part of this large company that had come from Egypt. Therefore, they named the place Abel Mizraim. The first part of this name is used in many different names such as Abel Keramim in Judges 11:33, Abel Maim in 2 Chronicles 16:4, and Abel Meholah in Judges 7:22, etc. It originally seems to have referred to a plain or a grassy meadow. Later it was weakened to mean simply "place," usually an open place. Thus the people of the area called it the "place of the Egyptians." It is more than striking that the Hebrew word for "grief" is similar—*'ēbel*.

50:12, 13 *So Jacob's sons did as he had commanded them: They carried him to the land of Canaan and buried him in the cave in the field of Machpelah, near Mamre, which Abraham had bought as a burial place from Ephron the Hittite, along with the field.*

After this period of mourning, Jacob's sons crossed the Jordan to bury the remains of their father in Canaan in the cave of Machpelah, near Mamre, in the field that Abraham had purchased from Ephron the Hittite. The intent of the narrator seems to be to indicate that the large company of Egyptians that had accompanied Joseph and his family did not go along for this final rite. This may have been at Joseph's specific request so that their family privacy could be maintained. It is also possible that there may have been some political involvements as far as the Egyptians were concerned, which made it unwise for them to trespass in the land of Canaan.

50:14 *After burying his father, Joseph returned to Egypt, together with his brothers and all the others who had gone with him to bury his father.*

When the funeral ceremonies were ended they all returned to Egypt. The time had not yet come for Jacob's family to return to Canaan for their place of residence. According to God's instructions, they were still to remain in Egypt for a long time.

55. *Joseph and His Brothers After Jacob's Death* (50:15–26)

Those who divide the sources generally ascribe this section to "E." The basis for this designation is, first of all, that there are certain characteristic expressions that supposedly point to this source. Further, it is argued that this passage related directly to 45:5, 7, and also that the prediction that they would return to Canaan ties in with 48:21, but these arguments offer no firm basis for assigning these verses to a specific source. They indicate only that all the material in this book was put together by the same writer.

A few scholars claim that they find evidence for dividing the material here between "E" and "J." They claim that verse 18 is a parallel to verses

16 and 17, that verse 21 is a repetition of verse 19, that verses 24 and 25 are doublets, and that the references to Joseph's life-span in both verses 22 and 26 indicate that this material comes from two separate sources. Our interpretation of the details of this passage, which follows, will give consideration to all these claims for multiple sources. It will become abundantly clear that there is no genuine basis for such claims regarding this passage.

50:15 *When Joseph's brothers saw that their father was dead, they said, ''What if Joseph holds a grudge against us and pays us back for all the wrongs we did to him?''*

The opening statement of verse 15 offers some difficulty. We read, ''When Joseph's brothers *saw* that their father was dead. . . .'' Now it is obvious that they saw this before the periods of mourning, the trip to Canaan, and the burial of Jacob. The Latin Vulgate reads thus: ''And Joseph's brothers *feared* after their father had died.'' This is possible since the words in Hebrew are very similar. There has understandably been a preference for this reading among Roman Catholic scholars.

Another solution that has been suggested for this difficulty is that it would be possible to conclude that this entire episode recorded in verses 15–21 actually took place before the burial of Jacob in Canaan. This would be in keeping with Hebrew narrative style where events are not always recorded in strict chronological order. We have seen examples of this characteristic in earlier chapters. Terah's death, recorded in 11:32, actually occurred later in the narrative. Isaac and Rebekah sojourned in Gerar (ch. 26) before the birth of their children, which was recorded earlier. The events of chapter 37 took place before the death of Rachel. Thus we could justifiably place the events described in our passage before the trip to Canaan for Jacob's burial. But do we have to resort to this to remove the difficulty at hand? We certainly need not read ''they *saw* that their father had died'' as indicating that now for the first time they saw this. They certainly saw that as soon as their father breathed his last breath. Many scholars have insisted that what we have here is a declaration that now for the first time Joseph's brothers began to realize the full implications of their own situation there in Egypt without the protecting presence of their aged father. It dawned on them that they were now at the mercy of their brother Joseph whom they had wronged so deeply in the past. Feelings of guilt again were aroused within them. Now that their father was out of the picture, what attitude would Joseph assume toward them?

50:16, 17 *So they sent word to Joseph, saying, ''Your father left these instructions before he died: 'This is what you are to say to Joseph: I ask you to forgive your* *brothers the sins and the wrongs they committed in treating you so badly.' Now please forgive the sins of the servants of the God of your father.'' When their message came to him, Joseph wept.*

So the brothers of Joseph conceived a plan to try to dissuade Joseph from any feelings of revenge he might shelter. They realized that their best approach to Joseph was to appeal to his love for his father, so they presented their plea as though it came from the lips of their father. There is no evidence that Jacob actually spoke the words his sons now put into his mouth. The spirit of the statement was, however, in complete accord with Jacob's attitude in such matters.

So fearful were Joseph's brothers that they hesitated to make their request for forgiveness in person but conveyed their message to Joseph via a messenger. They presented their plea as though Jacob, prior to his death, had urged them to ask Joseph for forgiveness for their sins and wrongs. They then added their own plea for forgiveness. In their message to Joseph they described themselves as ''the servants of the God of your father.'' This became the basis for their plea for forgiveness, namely, that they all served the same God, and this was the God whom their father had served and worshiped.

When the messenger conveyed this message to Joseph, he was moved to tears. He accepted the request of his brothers as wholly sincere.

50:18 *His brothers then came and threw themselves down before him. ''We are your slaves,'' they said.*

When the brothers heard what Joseph's reaction had been, they went to him in person and cast themselves in humility before him and offered themselves as his slaves. They had sent him to Egypt to become a slave. Now they were willing to compensate for their deep offense to him by becoming his slaves for life. Their hope, naturally, was that this display of humility and penitence would gain for them Joseph's forgiveness and favor.

50:19–21 *But Joseph said to them, ''Don't be afraid. Am I in the place of God? You intended to harm me, but God intended it for good to accomplish what is now being done, the saving of many lives. So then, don't be afraid. I will provide for you and your children.'' And he reassured them and spoke kindly to them.*

But Joseph looked at all of this from a completely different perspective. He recognized that they had been motivated by evil intentions when they sold him into Egypt, but God was able to turn their evil intentions to good purposes. Joseph pointed to what was now taking place in Egypt in the saving of many lives from the famine. What would have happened in Egypt if he had not been sold into Egypt, there to become the personal advisor to Pharaoh? Therefore, Joseph declared, he had no intention of punishing them and they need have no fear. He did not consider himself to be God and take vengeance for what God had intended for the saving of the lives of many people. Joseph was obviously convinced of the sincerity of their penitence and was willing to leave the events of the past in God's faithful hands.

It is worthy of note that Joseph here described God's purpose differently than he had in 45:7. In the earlier passage he emphasized the fact that he had been sent to Egypt to save a remnant of God's chosen people. Here he seemed to refer to the huge population of Egypt that he had been enabled to keep alive. These two concepts are not in conflict, however. The saving of the population of Egypt served to provide a favorable milieu where the patriarchal family could live in peace and grow into a mighty nation. It was here that God provided the opportunity for His chosen people to develop from a family into a great nation that would then return to Canaan, conquer the land flowing with milk and honey, and occupy it as their homeland in fulfillment of the promise to Abraham, Isaac, and Jacob. This in turn was the opening of the way for the coming of the promised Messiah, the Seed of the woman, who would redeem sin-cursed humanity and in that way "all peoples of the earth would be blessed" through the seed of Abraham.

50:22, 23 *Joseph stayed in Egypt, along with all his father's family. He lived a hundred and ten years and saw the third generation of Ephraim's children. Also the children of Makir son of Manasseh were placed at birth on Joseph's knees.*

The sacred writer stresses again the fact that Joseph and his entire family remained in Egypt. Egypt was to become the "womb" in which the embryo of the nation of Israel was to develop until it was ready for birth as an independent nation. Then, by means of intense birth pains, it was to "come forth" as a nation and take its place among the nations of the earth.

We are further told that Joseph had reached the age of 110 years, and he lived to see his grandchildren. The term used is not altogether clear and may even refer to the following generation. The expression "the third generation of Ephraim's children" does not indicate whether this was the third generation from Joseph or from Ephraim. In the Ten Commandments (Exod. 20:5) we read of "the third and fourth generation." We have a similar usage in Exodus 34:7. Although we cannot speak with certainty regarding this in our present passage, the fact that in Manasseh's case the reference is specifically to grandchildren strongly suggests that the same would be true in Ephraim's case. At any rate, it is clear that Joseph certainly lived to enjoy his grandchildren.

A word should be said about the statement that Manasseh's grandchildren were placed "on Joseph's knees." We encountered a similar statement in 30:3. We would refer our readers to what we presented there. Even so, the statement here is not identically the same as the one used in the earlier reference. It is known that among some present-day Arabian tribes there is a custom of placing a newborn child on the knees of the father of the child. We probably should think of a similar ceremony in connection with Joseph and his grandchildren. Some scholars are convinced that this indicates that Joseph actually adopted these children as his own, but this cannot be determined with certainty.

50:24, 25 *Then Joseph said to his brothers, "I am about to die. But God will surely come to your aid and take you up out of this land to the land he promised on oath to Abraham, Isaac and Jacob." And Joseph made the sons of Israel swear an oath and said, "God will surely come to your aid, and then you must carry my bones up from this place."*

We now read that Joseph, before his death, made the request that his bones be buried in the land of Canaan, in much the same way as Jacob had requested it. In this connection Joseph made a prophetic statement. He did not ask the members of his family to bring his remains to Canaan at the time of his death. He predicted that the people of Israel would eventually return to Canaan, the land promised to Abraham, Isaac, and Jacob. He assured his family that God would surely come to their aid and fulfill this promise. So sure was he of this that he was content to have his remains buried in Egypt with the firm understanding that when the descendants of Israel returned to Canaan, they would take his bones with them. He made the members of his family swear with an oath that they would carry out his wish in this regard when they returned to Canaan.

50:26 *So Joseph died at the age of a hundred and ten. And after they embalmed him, he was placed in a coffin in Egypt.*

The Book of Genesis ends with the account of the death of Joseph. Once again we are told that he was 110 years old when he died. In keeping with his high-ranking position in Egypt his body was properly embalmed according to Egyptian practice. After the proper ceremonies his body was placed in a coffin and entombed in Egypt. There it was to remain until the time of which he had spoken before his death, and that predicted event is recorded in the Book of Exodus.